SECTION ONE
BACKGROUND
Definitions
History
Decision making

SECTION TWO
BASIC MANAGEMENT
FUNCTIONS
Planning
Organizing
Controlling

SECTION THREE
BEHAVIORAL ASPECTS
Motivating
Leadership
Work groups
Conflict
Communication

MANAGEMENT
FOUNDATION

MANAGEMENT
FOUNDATION

SECTION FOUR
EMPHASIS ON
INDIVIDUAL
PERFORMANCE
Encouraging effort
Developing abilities
Defining direction

SECTION FIVE
AN UNDERSTANDING
OF THE PROCESSES
WHICH PRODUCE THE
GOODS OR SERVICES
Basic operations
management concepts
Designing operating systems
Planning and controlling
operations

SUCCESSFUL
MANAGEMENT

SUCCESSFUL
MANAGEMENT

SECTION SIX
AN APPRECIATION OF
CONTEMPORARY ISSUES
AND THE FUTURE
Ethics
Social responsibility
Future of management

RESPONSIBLE
MANAGEMENT

Management
theory and application

The Irwin Series in Management
and
The Behavioral Sciences

L. L. CUMMINGS AND E. KIRBY WARREN   Consulting Editors
JOHN F. MEE, ADVISORY EDITOR

Management

theory and application

LESLIE W. RUE, Ph.D.

and

LLOYD L. BYARS, Ph.D.

Both of the Management Department
School of Business Administration
Georgia State University

1977
RICHARD D. IRWIN, INC. Homewood, Illinois 60430
Irwin-Dorsey Limited Georgetown, Ontario L7G 4B3

4 5 6 7 8 9 0 K 5 4 3 2 1 0 9 8

ISBN 0-256-01885-5
Library of Congress Catalog Card No. 76–25435

Printed in the United States of America

To Penny and Linda

Preface

THIS book was planned and designed around what we believe is an innovative yet logical model for integrating the various facets of the management process into a conceptual whole. Rather than take a "process," "behavioral," or any other labeled approach to the study of management, we have tried to analyze and tie together those things that managers should do or be aware of in the pursuit of good organizational performance. This has resulted in what we believe is a comprehensive and integrated introduction to the process of management.

As suggested by the subtitle, the book was designed to emphasize the application side of management as well as the theory. We hope this has been accomplished by the use of numerous examples scattered throughout the text and by the end of chapter materials. In addition to review questions, each chapter is accompanied by several in-depth discussion questions and two minicases, both of which require application of the theory provided in the chapter.

The book's content is arranged in six major sections: Introduction and Background, Basic Management Functions, Behavioral Aspects, Individual Performance, Operations Management, and Contemporary Management. The first three sections are designed to provide the student with the basic foundation necessary to embark on the practice of management.

Sections Four and Five stress that in order to be successful managers should emphasize individual performance and understand the organizational processes which produce the goods or services.

The final section of the book, Contemporary Management, introduces the ingredients necessary to insure responsible management. This section covers the topics of ethics, social responsibility, and the future of management.

We have attempted to write this book considering the needs of both students and instructors. We have attempted to bring the pieces of the puzzle together in order to provide the student with a comprehensive understanding of the theory and application of management. At the same time, we have attempted to present the material in such a way as to provide a sound framework from which to teach.

As are most authors, we are indebted to our families, friends, colleagues, and students for the assistance we have received. Unfortunately space limits us to naming only a few. Special thanks are due Larry Cummings, John Mee, Kirby Warren, and Bob Dame for their constructive comments and encouragement throughout the project. Linda Byars, Thomas Clark, and Gene Groff all made numerous suggestions which significantly enriched the book. We are grateful to Michael H. Mescon, chairman of the Management Department, and Kenneth Black, Jr., dean of the School of Business Administration, Georgia State University, for providing us with an environment which not only permitted but encouraged this project. Final thanks go to Sandi Mades and Janet Myrick for their assistance in typing the manuscript.

December 1976   LESLIE W. RUE
                                                               LLOYD L. BYARS

Contents

section two   **Basic management functions**   **65**

A cascade approach. Organizational purpose. Long-range and short-range objectives. Policies. Reasons for policies. Types of policies. Origin of policies. How much policy? Formulating and implementing policy. Strategy: How to achieve objectives. Determining organization strategy. Types of organization strategies: *1. Retrenchment strategies. 2. Stability strategies. 3. Growth strategies. 4. Combination strategies.* Integrating objectives, policies, and strategies.

Why plan? A dilemma. Formal planning. Planning horizon: Short-range versus long-range. Tactical versus strategic planning. Origin of organization plans. The organization planning system. Planning in practice: *Self-audit. Survey environment. Set objectives. Forecast. State resource requirements. Develop pro forma statements. Control the plan.*

Division of labor. Departmentation: *Functional departmentation. Product departmentation. Geographic departmentation. Customer departmentation. Other types of departmentation.* Reasons for organizing. Authority, power, and responsibility. Sources of authority. Principles based on authority: *Parity principle. Unity of command. Scalar principle. Span of control. The exception principle.* Centralization versus decentralization. Organization structures: *Line organization. Line and staff organization. Matrix organization. Committee organization.* Organization structure, environment, and technology: *Organization and environment. Organization and technology.* A contingency approach.

Personnel planning: *Job analysis and skills inventory. Personnel forecasting. Personnel transition. A model of the personnel planning process. Special considerations in personnel planning.* Recruitment: *Promotion from within. External sources.* Selection: *Testing. Performance refer-*

Communication barriers. Interpersonal conflict. Strategic conflict. Effects of conflict. Progressive stages of the conflict cycle. Solution of conflict. A model for conflict management: *The conflict interface. Responses of higher-level managers.*

12. Work groups, conformity, and creativity   259

Work groups defined. Importance of work groups. The formation of work groups. Stages of work-group development. Group cohesiveness. Influence of work groups on organizational change. The linking-pin concept. Conformity and work groups: *Group pressures on the individual. Idiosyncrasy credit. Producing conformity.* Creativity in organizations: *The creative process. Aids in creativity.*

13. Communication in organizations   281

Communication — What is it? A model of the communication process: *Information source. Transmitter. Noise source. Receiver. Receiver response. Feedback.* Interpersonal communication: *Semantics. Perception. Listening — An important factor. Individual feedback.* Organizational communication: *Communication patterns. Two early approaches to organizational communication. Downward communication systems. Upward communication systems. Horizontal or lateral communication system. Grapevine.* Information theory. Improving communication within organizations.

---

section four   Individual performance   301

---

14. Recognizing and measuring individual performance   305

Determinants of performance. Environmental factors as performance obstacles. The activity trap: *Causes of the activity trap. Costs of the activity trap.* Measures of performance — Criteria. Subjective criteria. Setting standards. Performance standards: *Average group production as a standard. Standards based on the performance of specially selected individuals. Time study. Experimentally determined times. The use of*

section six   **Contemporary management**   **453**

Centralization or decentralization? The role of middle management. Future organizational structures. Corporate democracy. The public-oriented executive. Management education.

section one

Introduction and background

Section One serves as an orientation for this book. The objectives of Section One are to provide an understanding of the work that a manager does, to develop a historical perspective of how and why management evolved, and to develop an appreciation for the decision-making skills required of a manager.

Chapter 1 discusses the concepts of management and manager. The work of a manager is discussed in terms of the basic functions that a manager performs—planning, organizing, motivating, and controlling. Emphasis is placed on the fact that these functions are performed through people and thus a manager must also have a basic understanding of human behavior.

Chapter 2 presents a chronological development of management as a discipline. The management pioneers are presented in perspective with the events of their day. Emphasis is placed not so much on what and when events happened, but rather on why they happened.

Chapter 3 recognizes that all managers, regardless of their level in the organization, must make decisions. The chapter discusses both theoretical and practical approaches to decision making. The role of values as well as the manager's affinity for risk are discussed. The chapter ends with a discussion of the particular problems associated with making decisions in an organizational context.

Objectives

1 To define management and describe the functions and activities involved in the management process.

2 To show the relationships among management principles, concepts, and theory.

3 To discuss and explain the design philosophy of this book and how it relates to the management process.

GLOSSARY OF TERMS

Behavioral aspects of management Those areas of the behavioral sciences involved in performing the management process. These areas include such topics as motivation, leadership, group activities, and conflict.

Concepts Commonly agreed upon definitions.

Entrepreneur The initiator, innovator, and risk-taker in forming organizations.

Law A statement of an order or relation of phenomena that so far as is known is invariable under the given conditions.

Management A process or form of work that involves the guidance or direction of a group of people toward organizational goals or objectives.

Management functions The activities that a manager performs are called management functions. These are planning, organizing, motivating, and controlling.

Principle A fundamental, primary, or general truth on which other truths depend.

Theory A systematic grouping of concepts and principles.

1

Introduction

The next day Moses sat as usual to hear the people's complaints against each other, from morning to evening.

When Moses' father-in-law saw how much time this was taking, he said, "Why are you trying to do all this alone, with people standing here all day long to get your help?"

"Well, because the people come to me with their disputes, to ask for God's decisions," Moses told him. . . .

"It's not right!" his father-in-law exclaimed. "You're going to wear yourself out—and if you do, what will happen to the people? Moses, this job is too heavy a burden for you to try to handle all by yourself.

"Now listen, and let me give you a word of advice. . . .

"Find some capable, godly, honest men who hate bribes, and appoint them as judges, one judge for each 1,000 people; he in turn will have ten judges under him, each in charge of 100; and under each of them will be two judges, each responsible for the affairs of 50 people; and each of these will have five judges beneath him, each counseling 10 persons. Let these men be responsible to serve the people with justice at all times. Anything that is too important or complicated can be brought to you. But the smaller matters they can take care of themselves. That way it will be easier for you because you will share the burden with them.

*The Living Bible**

MANY WRITERS have used the above example as one of the earliest written descriptions of a manager at work (utilizing, of course, the ever-present management consultant). Prior to the Industrial Revolution, organizational life was dominated by the military, the church, and the state, and thus, the first efforts in management reflected the activities of these organizations. Such an agrarian and craft-oriented society had little need for sophisticated management. However, as

---

* "Book of Exodus," Wheaton, Ill.: Tyndale House, Publishers, p. 64.

the size and complexity of organizations grew, a defined and professional approach to the management process became necessary.
Management, as we know it today, exists in all forms of organizations
—government, religious, and private.

MANAGEMENT DEFINED

Management has been defined in many ways, and even today there
is no universally accepted definition. One frequently used definition
is "getting things done through others." Another popular definition
holds that management is the efficient utilization of resources. For
purposes of this book the following definition of management will
be used:

> Management is a process or form of work that involves the guidance or
> direction of a group of people toward organizational goals or objectives.[1]

MANAGEMENT AND OBJECTIVES

The starting point of the managerial process is the determination
of organizational objectives. Objectives are designed to give an organization and its members direction and purpose. It is very difficult
to have successful management without well-defined objectives.
Managers cannot effectively guide or direct people without well-defined objectives. Precisely what these objectives should be depends
on the particular organization and management philosophy.

Although objectives can range widely from organization to organization, they generally fall into one of three general categories: (1)
profit-oriented, (2) service to customers, and (3) social responsibilities.[2] Profit often serves as a measure of performance for organizations.
Customer service justifies the existence of an organization. Social
responsibilities exist for management as a result of the ethical and
moral codes set forth by the society in which the management operates. Various combinations of goals covering each of these areas are
required for successful management.

MANAGEMENT FUNCTIONS

It is important to note that management is a form of work. The manager is the person that performs this work. In doing this work, a
manager performs certain activities called the "functions of management." These are

---

[1] Throughout this book, the terms *goals* and *objectives* will be used interchangeably.

[2] John F. Mee, "Management Philosophy for Professional Executives," *Business
Horizons*, December 1956, p. 6.

1. Planning—deciding in advance what, when, why, how, and who.
2. Organizing—grouping activities, assigning activities, staffing, and providing the authority to carry out activities.
3. Motivating—directing or channeling human behavior toward goals.
4. Controlling—measuring performance against goals, determining causes of deviations, and taking corrective action where necessary.

Figure 1–1 further details the specific types of activities that are involved in each of the management functions.

FIGURE 1–1
The management functions

Planning	*Organizing*	*Motivating*	*Controlling*
1. Self-audit—Determining the present status of the organization	1. Identify and define work to be performed	1. Communicate and explain objectives to subordinates	1. Monitor results and compare to standards
2. Survey environment	2. Break work down into duties	2. Assign performance standards	2. Determine causes of deviations
3. Set objectives	3. Group duties into positions	3. Coach and guide subordinates to meet performance standards	3. Correct deviations
4. Forecast the future	4. Define position requirements	4. Reward subordinates based on performance	4. Revise and adjust control methods in light of control results and changing conditions
5. Determine resource requirements	5. Group positions into manageable and properly related units	5. Praise and censure fairly	5. Coordinate throughout the control process
6. Develop pro-forma statements	6. Assign work to be performed, accountability, and extent of authority	6. Provide a motivating environment by communicating the changing situation and its requirements	
7. Revise and adjust the plan in light of control results and changing conditions	7. Provide personnel, facilities, and other resources	7. Revise and adjust the work of motivation in light of control results and changing conditions	
8. Coordinate throughout the planning process	8. Revise and adjust the organization in light of control results and changing conditions	8. Coordinate throughout the motivating process	
	9. Coordinate throughout the organizing process		

Every manager, regardless of his level in the organization, performs all of these functions to some degree. However, the management process is an eclectic one composed of a mixture of planning, organizing, motivating, and controlling. Each level of management does not use the same mixture of these functions. A first-line supervisor may use a mixture of 8 percent planning, 8 percent organizing, 50 percent motivation, and 34 percent controlling. A top-level manager, such as corporate president, may use a mixture of 40 percent planning, 30 percent organizing, 15 percent motivating, and 15 percent controlling. Furthermore, different managers occupying similar positions within the organization may use different mixtures of the functions. This may be due to different levels of personal expertise or environmental factors. There is no fixed amount of time required for any one particular function. The allocatioh of time is the manager's own decision. However, a manager who is spending almost all the time doing one particular function with almost no time spent in one or more of the other functions should critically analyze his or her own work performance (see Figure 1–2).

Determining the most important management function is like attempting to determine the most important leg on a chair. All legs are important and must be present in order for the chair to function properly. Just as with the chair, if one of the management functions is weak or missing, the management process does not function properly.

It should be pointed out that all management authors do not agree on what the management functions should be called. Table 1–1 summarizes some of the descriptions by various authors. There is

FIGURE 1–2
Mixture of management functions

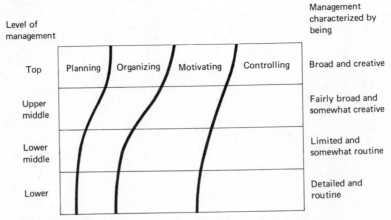

Source: George R. Terry, *Principles of Management*, 6th ed. (Homewood, Ill.: Richard D. Irwin, Inc., 1972), p. 87.

TABLE 1–1
Description of management functions

Name	Planning	Organizing	Controlling	Other
Allen............................	X	X	X	Leading
Dale.............................	X	X	X	Staffing, innovation directing
Davis...........................	X	X	X	—
Drucker..............	Set objective	X	Measurement	Motivate, communicate
Fayol...........................	X	X	X	Command, coordinate
Flippo..........................	X	X	X	Leading
Koontz, O'Donnell..........	X	X	X	Directing, staffing
McFarland.....................	X	X	X	—
Mee.............................	X	X	X	Motivate, innovate
Newman.......................	X	X	X	Assembling resources, directing
Tannenbaum.......	Direction	X	X	—
Terry.................	X	X	X	Actuating

Source: Ervin Williams, "The Management Process from a Functional Perspective," *Atlanta Economic Review*, April 1971, p. 27.

general agreement that planning, organizing, and controlling should be labeled as management functions. The main disagreement involves the name given to the management function dealing with motivation. As shown in Table 1–1, the terms used by different authors vary from *leading* to *commanding*. The term *motivating* will be used in this book.

BEHAVIORAL ASPECTS OF MANAGEMENT

Because the process of management involves guiding or directing people, an understanding of the behavioral sciences and human behavior is necessary. The need for such an understanding is suggested by the motivating function as outlined in Figure 1–1. However, an understanding of other behavioral topics not specifically mentioned in Figure 1–1, such as leadership, group activities, and conflict is also needed.

Many approaches have been suggested to studying the management process. Leading the list are the functional and behavioral approaches. These approaches are usually presented as if they are mutually exclusive. However, a successful manager must understand the work that is to be performed (the management functions) and the people that are to be managed (behavioral sciences). Thus, the functional and behavioral approaches to management should not be viewed as mutually exclusive but rather as necessary and complementary approaches.

MANAGEMENT—ART OR SCIENCE?

The argument over whether management is an art or a science has raged for years. The purpose here is not to enter that battlefield but is merely to make the reader aware of the battle.

The art process has been described as follows:

> . . . art is the imposition of a pattern, a vision of a whole, on many disparate parts so as to create a representation of that vision; art is an imposition of order on chaos. The artist has to have not only the vision that he or she wants to communicate but also skills or craft with which to present the vision. This process entails choosing the correct art form and within that art form, the correct technique. In good art, the result is a blending of vision and craft that involves the viewer, reader, or listener without requiring that he separate the parts in order to appreciate the whole.[3]

In other words, an artist has to have good technical skills and imagination. These technical skills are based on science—whether it be in the field of music composition, engineering, or management. Thus, a good and productive artist uses technical skills that are based on science. Similarly, good management must be based on the principles and concepts that support the art of management.

As pointed out above, art and science are not necessarily mutually exclusive; in fact, they can be complementary. A manager must know and understand not only the concepts and principles of management (the science of management) but also how to use them (the art of management).

PRINCIPLES OF MANAGEMENT

A Frenchman, Henri Fayol, was one of the first writers to introduce the idea of principles of management. Since that time, numerous concepts have been promulgated as principles of management. Fayol was reluctant to use the term "principle" because it implies law and inflexibility. A principle is defined as "a fundamental, primary, or general truth, on which other truths depend."[4] A law is defined as "a statement of an order or relation of phenomena that so far as is

---

[3] Henry M. Boettinger, "Is Management Really an Art?" *Harvard Business Review*, (January–February 1975), pp. 54–55.

[4] *The American Collegiate Dictionary* (New York: Random House, 1957), p. 963.

FIGURE 1-3
Controlled experiment process

known is invariable under the given conditions."[5] Although the above definitions are similar, the difference is that principles have some degree of flexibility while laws are absolutely rigid.

In the physical sciences, laws exist. Examples include the law of gravity, Ohm's Law, and the Law of Action and Reaction. These laws were developed through a careful research process involving controlled experimentation. In this process the researcher sets up an experiment in which he can control many of the input variables. For instance, in a chemical experiment, the researcher may control input variables such as temperature, humidity, and pressure in order to determine the effect of a change in one of these variables on a chemical. By varying one of the input factors and measuring the corresponding change in the other factors, the researcher can establish a relationship between the changes and the chemical. Figure 1-3 illustrates this process.

After the experiment has been repeated many times with identical results, the initial ideas (called hypotheses in scientific terminology) of the researchers are converted into laws. Furthermore, after an hypothesis has been accepted as a law, the law can be used to develop other laws.

Unfortunately one of the major problems in developing principles of management is that it is very difficult to conduct a controlled experiment in a management environment. Cost and the inability to place controls on one of the primary inputs—people—make controlled experimentation difficult. Unable to use the time-tested method of scientific experimentation to develop laws, the remaining logical alternative is to use observation and deduction. This is the method by which most principles of management have been developed. For example, Fayol had more than 40 years of practical business experience to draw upon in the development of his principles.

However, a word of caution is appropriate. Management principles are much more subject to change and interpretation than are the laws

---

[5] *Webster's New Collegiate Dictionary*, 8th ed. (Springfield, Mass.: G.&C. Merriam Company, 1973), p. 651.

of the physical sciences. For instance, the management principle of "unity of command" states that an employee should have one and only one supervisor. However, there are examples of organizational structures that violate this principle and seem to work effectively. Thus management principles must be viewed as guides to action and not laws that must be followed without exception. In summary, management principles should be followed, except where a deviation can be justified on the basis of sound logic.

CONCEPTS AND THEORY OF MANAGEMENT

Concepts have been defined as "abstractions formed by generalizations from particulars."[6] Basically, concepts are commonly agreed upon definitions. Because no progress can be made without a common framework of definitions, concepts are essential for developing principles and theory.

A systematic grouping of concepts and principles creates a theory. In other words, a theory is basically a classification or ordering scheme for principles and concepts. A theory attempts to provide a framework of principles and concepts that can be used to further define and refine the theory. Thus a theory of management involves a systematic synthesis of the concepts and principles of management. The goal of this book is to define the concepts of management as clearly as is possible, to present the principles of management using these concepts, to develop a theory for integrating these concepts and principles, and to encourage the application of these concepts, principles, and theory.

MISCONCEPTIONS ARE COMMON

Management, as a field of study, is greatly misunderstood. Everyone seems to have preconceived notions about management, especially its problems. Usually these notions are based on personal experience and are defended with vigor. Figure 1–4 challenges the reader to test some of his own preconceived notions about human behavior.

The answers to the questions in Figure 1–4 have been empirically verified. However, the natural tendency is to believe our intuition even at the expense of refuting scientific investigation. The same is true in management. Many ideas and fads appear which are nothing more than seat-of-the-pants propositions. These propositions have

---

[6] Fred N. Kerlinger, *Foundations of Behavior Research*, 2d ed. (New York: Holt, Rinehart and Winston, Inc., 1973), p. 28.

FIGURE 1–4
True-false test of human behavior

1. People probably never learn anything while they are deeply asleep. *F*
2. Genius and insanity have little or no relationship to each other. *T*
3. Better college students make less money after graduation than average students. *F*
4. A person who learns rapidly remembers longer than a person who learns slowly. *T*
5. All people in America are born equal in capacity for achievement. *F*
6. Teaching a child to roller-skate very early in life will give him a permanent advantage in this skill. *T*
7. People are definitely either introverted or extroverted. *F*
8. After you learn something you forget more of it in the next few hours than in the next several days. *T*
9. Famous men tend to be born of poor but hard-working parents. *F*
10. Lessons learned just before going to sleep are remembered better than those learned early in the morning. *T*
11. On the average, men of 45 are more intelligent than those of 20. *F*
12. The tendency to imitate is probably learned. *F*
13. There is a law of compensation in nature; for example, blind persons are born with a highly developed sense of touch. *T*
14. An especially favorable environment can probably raise the I.Q. a few points. *T*
15. If a person born blind were to have his sight restored as an adult, he would perceive the world as we see it almost immediately. *F*

Answers: (1) T; (2) T; (3) F; (4) T; (5) F; (6) F; (7) F; (8) T; (9) F; (10) T; (11) F; (12) T; (13) F; (14) T; (15) F.
Source: Gregory A. Kimble and Norman Garmezy, *Principles of General Psychology,* Copyright © 1963,
The Ronald Press Company, New York, p. 4.

some value in that they lead to hypotheses that can be researched. However, the student and practitioner of management must learn to separate management fact from management fiction.

MANAGER AND ENTREPRENEUR

The basic nonlegal distinction between the manager and the entrepreneur is often said to be the higher degree of financial and, perhaps, personal risk borne by the entrepreneur. Traditionally the entrepreneur has been viewed as the initiator, the innovator, and the risk-taker. In these roles, the entrepreneur makes an absolutely essential contribution to the organization and to the economy as well. The manager, however, may have all these characteristics, except that he may not risk his personal fortune to the extent that the entrepreneur does. He can be a risk-taker with the corporation's fortune. He does risk his personal position and reputation. The entrepreneur may fail repeatedly, but if and when he succeeds, he is properly rewarded. In many cases, with today's manager, it's "one strike and you're out." With the growth in size of organizations, a large part of the entrepreneur's role has been transferred to the manager. Both entrepreneurs and managers perform the functions of management. In other words, the entrepreneur is necessarily a manager, but not vice versa.

DESIGN PHILOSOPHY OF BOOK

The preceding discussions represent an attempt to introduce the reader to the basic terms necessary for embarking on the study of management. The following chapters of this book are designed to introduce and study the concepts and principles necessary for developing a theory of management. The book is divided into six basic sections as follows:

Section One – Introduction and Background.

Section Two – Basic Management Functions.

Section Three – Behavioral Aspects.

Section Four – Individual Performance.

Section Five – Operations Management.

Section Six – Contemporary Management.

Section One serves as an orientation to the book. The concepts of management and manager are discussed and the functions of management are briefly introduced. A historical perspective of management is also presented along with a discussion of the manager's role as a decision maker.

Section Two analyzes the basic management functions of planning, organizing, and controlling. Although motivating is recognized as one of the basic management functions it is more appropriately included in Section Three (Behavioral Aspects of Management). In Section Two, the planning function is discussed in two chapters: Chapter 4 on objectives, policies, and strategy; and Chapter 5 on the overall planning process. The organizing function is also presented in two chapters: Chapter 6 dealing with the overall organizing process, and Chapter 7 dealing with staffing. The purpose of Section Two is to provide the reader with the basic concepts and principles relating to the planning, organizing, and controlling functions of management.

Section Three presents a selected set of topics that contribute to the "behavioral" side of the management process. Beginning with motivation, this section includes chapters on leadership, work groups, conflict, and communication. It is difficult, if not impossible, to isolate completely the behavioral topics from other management topics. Therefore, many behavioral topics will appear throughout this book. For example, Chapter 6 in Section Two describes the organizing function and contains many behavioral concepts. Other behavioral concepts are interspersed throughout the text. The purpose of Section Three is to present important behavioral aspects that are not specifically covered elsewhere in this book.

Section Four is designed around the philosophy that the successful manager must have not only knowledge of the functional and behavioral aspects of the management process but also must be able to integrate and apply this knowledge through individuals. This section emphasizes the application and refinement of the management concepts and principles developed in Sections Two and Three in order to attain desired levels of individual performance. Section Four is based on the conviction that individual performance is dependent on three major factors: effort, ability, and task direction.

Section Five discusses the production or operations aspects of the organization. The production of goods and/or services ordinarily involves the largest portion of an organization's financial assets, personnel, and expenditures. The processes which produce the goods or services also usually consume an appreciable amount of time. Thus, the manner in which the operations are managed plays a critical role

FIGURE 1–5
A theory of management

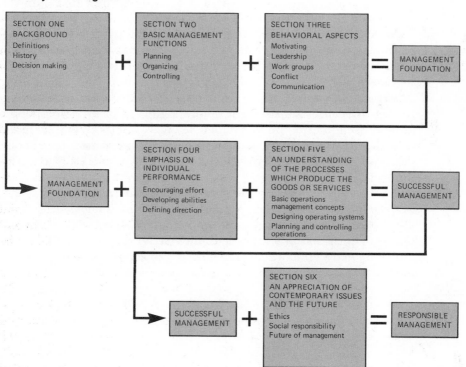

in achieving the organization's goals. Additionally all management personnel will either be a part of or interact with the operations phase of the organization. The design and layout of facilities, scheduling, and inventory control are representative components of operations management.

Section Six looks at the management process from a contemporary viewpoint. The topics of ethics, social responsibility, and the future of management are discussed.

A sequential integration and understanding of the different sections of the book results in a general theory of successful management as summarized in Figure 1–5.

Discussion questions and minicases requiring application of the management concepts and principles discussed in the respective chapters are provided at the end of each chapter. These questions and minicases simulate realistic problem situations that a practicing manager might encounter.

SUMMARY

Management, as we know it today, exists in all forms of organizations—government, religious, and private. As the size and complexity of all types of organizations grew, a defined and professional approach to the management process became a necessity.

Management is a process or form of work that involves the guidance or direction of a group of people toward organizational goals or objectives. In performing this work, the manager uses the functions of management—planning, organizing, motivating, and controlling. This is frequently called the functional approach to the management process. Because management involves guiding or directing people, an understanding of the behavioral sciences is also essential. Therefore, the functional and behavioral approaches to management should not be viewed as mutually exclusive but rather as necessary and complementary.

The argument concerning whether management is an art or a science has raged for years. Art and science are not necessarily mutually exclusive. In fact, they can be complementary. For example, a manager must not only know and understand the concepts and principles of management (the science of management), but he or she must also know how to apply these concepts and principles (the art of management).

Management principles are generally based on observation and deduction and not scientific experimentation. Thus, management principles must be viewed as guides to action rather than inflexible laws.

Concepts are commonly agreed upon definitions within a particular field of study. A theory is a systematic grouping of concepts and principles. The purpose of this book is to use concepts and principles in developing a theory of management.

REVIEW QUESTIONS

1. What is management?

2. What are the three general categories of organizational objectives?

3. Name and describe the basic management functions.

4. Describe the functional and behavioral approaches to the management process. How do these two approaches relate to each other?

5. What is the difference between art and science?

6. What is a principle? How are principles of management developed?

7. What is a law? Does it differ from a principle?

8. What is a concept? What is a theory? How do these terms relate to one another?

9. What is a theory of management?

10. Distinguish between manager and entrepreneur.

DISCUSSION QUESTIONS

1. Management has often been described as a universal process, meaning that the basics of management are transferable and applicable in almost any environment. Comment on this statement.

2. How does one decide who is and who is not a manager in a given organization?

3. Management was defined in the text as a type of work. Comment on this statement.

4. Is the operator of a one person business such as a corner grocery store a manager?

5. Do you think that management can be learned through books and study or only through experience?

SELECTED READINGS

Barnard, Chester I. *The Functions of the Executive.* Cambridge, Mass.: Harvard University Press, 1938.

Boettinger, Henry M. "Is Management Really an Art?" *Harvard Business Review* (January–February 1975), pp. 54–64.

Drucker, Peter. *The Practice of Management*. New York: Harper and Row, 1954.

Koontz, Harold. "The Management Theory Jungle," *Journal of the Academy of Management*, vol. 4, no. 3 (December 1961), pp. 174–88.

Mee, John F. "Management Philosophy for Professional Executives," *Business Horizons*. Bureau of Business Research, School of Business, Indiana University (December 1956), pp. 5–11.

Mintzberg, Henry. *The Nature of Managerial Work*. New York: Harper & Row Publishers, 1973.

Terry, George R. *Principles of Management*. 7th ed. Homewood, Ill.: Richard D. Irwin, 1977.

Tilles, Seymour. "The Manager's Job: A Systems Approach," *Harvard Business Review*, vol. 41 (January–February 1963), pp. 73–81.

Scott, William G. "Organizational Theory: Overview and an Appraisal," *Academy of Management Journal*, vol. 4, no. 1 (April 1961), pp. 7–26.

Woolf, D. A. "The Management Theory Jungle Revisited," *Advanced Management Journal* (October 1965), pp. 6–15.

SELECTED MANAGEMENT AND RELATED PERIODICALS

Selected Periodicals from this list are referenced throughout the text. This list is given here so the reader will have a listing of the more commonly referenced management and related periodicals.

Academy of Management Journal
Academy of Management Review
Administrative Management
Administrative Science Quarterly
Advanced Management Journal
Business Horizons
California Management Review
Decision Sciences
Forbes
Fortune
Harvard Business Review
Industrial and Labor Relations Review
Industrial Management Review
Journal of Applied Behavioral Science
Journal of Applied Psychology
Journal of Business

Journal of Management Studies
Journal of Systems Management
Management Accounting
Management of Personnel Quarterly
Management International Review
Management Review
Management Science
Michigan Business Review
Organizational Behavior and Human Performance
Personnel
Personnel Journal
Personnel Psychology
Public Administration Review
The Wall Street Journal (newspaper)
Training and Development Journal

Case 1–1

The expansion of Blue Streak

Arthur Benton started the Blue Streak Delivery Company five years ago. Blue Streak initially provided commercial delivery services for all packages within the city of Unionville (population 500,000).

Art started with himself, one clerk, and one driver. Within three years Blue Streak had grown to the point of requiring three clerks and 12 drivers. It was then that Art decided to expand and provide state-wide service. He figured that this would initially require the addition of two new offices, one located at Logantown (population 150,000) in the southern part of the state and one at Thomas City (population 250,000) in the northern part of the state. Each office was staffed with a manager, one clerk, and two drivers. Because both Logantown and Thomas City were within 150 miles of Unionville, Art was able to visit each office at least once a week and personally coordinate the operations in addition to providing general management assistance. The statewide delivery system met with immediate success and reported a healthy profit for the first year.

The next year Art decided to expand and include two neighboring states. Art set up two offices in each of the two neighboring states. However, from the start operations never seemed to go smoothly in the neighboring states. Schedules were constantly being fouled up, deliveries were lost, and customer complaints multiplied. After nine months Art changed office managers in all four out-of-state offices. Things still did not improve. Convinced that he was the only one capable of straightening out the out-of-state offices, Art began visiting each office once every two weeks. This schedule required Art to spend at least half of his time on the road traveling between offices. After four months of this activity the entire Blue Streak operation appeared disorganized and profit had declined dramatically.

1. What went wrong with Blue Streak?
2. Do you think Art is a good entrepreneur? A good manager?
3. What would you suggest that Art do at this point?

Case 1–2

Letting go of the business

Franklin Machine Company had come a long way since it was founded in 1949. Starting out in a rented garage with 3 employees, it had rapidly developed into a thriving company of 100 employees with its offices and production facilities occupying the entire three floors of the Franklin Building, which was named after the founder and sole owner of the company, Joe Franklin.

Franklin Machine Company specialized in supplying precision machinery parts to various industries throughout the country. It also had acquired, after 25 years, one of the best reputations in the business. This reputation was a result of the continued excellent quality of the work and the prompt service given customers' orders. Joe Franklin realized this and continuously stressed the importance of quality and service to all employees at the firm.

Joe Franklin had started the company with all his savings plus plenty of hard work and long hours. It was due to his determination that Franklin was where it was today. Although approaching his self-imposed retirement age of 65, he was still very active in the business, doing everything from securing new orders to checking the finished product before delivery to the customer. He was a stickler for detail and had been known, on more than one occasion, to show an employee the right way to cut a particular order.

Joe was generally well-liked and respected by his employees. Many of Joe's employees had been with the company since its early days. He demanded a fair day's work and in return paid a fair day's wage. Franklin had one of the highest pay scales in the industry.

Joe had put 25 hard years into the company and now was looking forward to retirement. As soon as he hired someone to fill the newly created position of Plant Manager, he could begin to enjoy the fruits of his labor.

After countless interviews and with much consideration, Joe hired Tom Johnson to fill the slot. Tom would be perfect. Young, married, ex-military, he was just the man Joe thought he needed.

In order to learn the process at Franklin, Tom worked in the plant for the first couple of months. After he had satisfactorily completed his time there, Joe took over and quickly groomed Tom for the new position. Gradually, Joe began to feel that Tom had control of things and began taking days off here and there. Joe eventually increased his time away from the plant to a week at a time. Whenever he came back from his time off, he saw that everything appeared normal and things were operating smoothly.

It was on Joe's return from a two-month vacation in Europe that he began to notice things around the plant that appeared to need correcting. For one thing, the employees' habits had begun to slide. Coffee breaks stretched on, employees came back from lunch at different times, and material waste had increased.

At their next meeting, Joe pointed out what he saw and was amazed that Tom had also noticed the problems but did not seem too concerned about them. As Tom had indicated, the orders were being processed on time, and no complaints had been received on work already sent out. These were Tom's main areas of concern—not how long employees took on their coffee breaks.

After the meeting Joe mulled over the situation and decided the problems were more serious than Tom realized. Taken individually, none was too serious, but added together and given enough time, they could add up to a sizeable increase in expenses and a resulting decrease in profits. Tom was an excellent manager otherwise, and Joe realized that Tom was just not seeing the problem from Joe's perspective.

1. Do you think that Joe and Tom simply have different management philosophies?
2. Assuming Joe is correct, what might he do in order to "clarify Tom's vision of the problem?"
3. Do you think that owners necessarily make better managers?

Objectives

1. To explore the reasons why management did not emerge as a recognized discipline until the 20th century.
2. To develop an understanding of the events and persons that led to the development of modern management.
3. To provide a historical foundation for later chapters in the text.

GLOSSARY OF TERMS

Bottom-up management A philosophy of management practiced by William B. Given, which encouraged widespread delegation of responsibility and authority in order to solicit the participation of all members of the organization from the bottom to the top.

Captains of industry The name given to a group of men who dominated and built corporate giants during the last 25 years of the 19th century. Captains of Industry included men such as John D. Rockefeller, James B. Duke, Andrew Carnegie, and Cornelius Vanderbilt.

Management theory jungle This term was developed by Harold Koontz and refers to the division of thought that resulted from the multiple approaches to studying the management process.

McCormick multiple-management plan This plan, developed by Charles McCormick, uses participation as a training and motivational tool by selecting several promising young men from various departments within the company to form a junior board of directors.

Process approach to management An approach to the study of management that focuses on the management functions of planning, organizing, motivating, and controlling.

Professional manager A career manager who does not necessarily have a controlling interest in the enterprise for which he works and who realizes that he has a responsibility to the employees, the stockholders, and the public.

Scanlon plan An incentive plan developed in 1938 by Joseph Scanlon which provided the workers with a bonus for tangible savings in labor costs.

Scientific management A philosophy, popularized by Frederick W. Taylor, concerning the relationship between men and work that sought to increase productivity and simultaneously make the work easier by scientifically studying work methods and establishing standards rather than depending on tradition and custom.

Systems approach to management An approach to management which encourages the manager to view the environmental, psychological, physical, and informational facets of the manager's job as linking together to form an integrated whole.

2

The management movement

History is useful to us not because it provides us with final answers about the fate of man, but because it offers us an inexhaustible storehouse of life styles, civilizational modes, and ways of acting that we can draw on as we face the future. History gives us balance, patience, and a deeper understanding of what it means to live and die. History cannot save us in any ultimate sense, but it can deepen our understanding of humanity's potentialities and limitations.

Arthur N. Gilbert[*]

As THE above quote suggests, an understanding of the history of any discipline is necessary if one is to understand where the discipline currently is and where it is going. Management is no exception. Many of today's managerial problems had their genesis in the early management movement. Understanding the historical evolution of these problems better enables the modern manager to cope with them. The challenge to present and future managers is not to memorize historical names and dates but rather to develop a feel for why and how things happened and to apply this knowledge to the practice of management.

Although some need for management existed centuries ago, sophisticated management was needed in very few places prior to the 19th century. Just as traffic lights were not needed, and therefore not invented, before car travel reached a certain level of sophistication, management, as it presently exists, was not needed or even identified before the maturing of the corporate form of organization. The development of management thought and concepts is yet another example

---

[*] *In Search of a Meaningful Past*, New York: Houghton Mifflin Company, 1972, p. 2.

of man responding to the needs of his environment. It is this environment leading up to and surrounding the emergence of management thought that is the subject of this chapter.

U.S. INDUSTRIAL REVOLUTION

Professor Daniel Wren has described the Industrial Revolution in America as having three facets: power, transportation, and communication.[1] The steam engine developed and perfected by James Watt in England in the late 18th century was transplanted to America shortly thereafter. The steam engine provided more efficient and cheaper power, allowed factories to produce more goods at cheaper prices, and increased the markets for goods. An often overlooked contribution of the steam engine was that it allowed factories to be located away from water power. This in itself had a profound effect on the development of this country. Factories could be located near their suppliers, customers, and the most desirable labor markets instead of only near rivers.

The transportation expansion began with the development of canals around 1755. America's first railroad charter was obtained by Colonel John Stevens in 1815. Lacking financial support, Colonel Stevens did not build the first railroad in America until 1830.[2] A railroad boom then followed in the late 1840s. The track mileage increased from just under 6,000 miles in 1848 to over 30,000 miles by 1860.[3] As the railroad network grew so did the size of individual rail companies. By 1855, at least 13 rail companies were operating and maintaining more than 200 miles of track. By the mid-1850s, the railroad industry had clearly established itself as America's first "big business" and as America's first industry with a scope of operations extending beyond the local area.[4] Although textiles represented America's first entry into the industrial age, textiles were basically a local business with much smaller financial requirements than rail companies.[5] Unlike other local industries, railroad networks often spanned hundreds of miles, creating control and communication problems. Facilities could not be inspected in a matter of hours, and decisions had to be made within a relatively rapidly changing frame-

---

[1] Daniel Wren, *The Evolution of Management Thought* (New York: The Ronald Press Company, 1972), p. 81.

[2] Dorothy Gregg, "John Stevens: General Entrepreneur," in *Men in Business*, ed. William Miller (New York: Harper and Row, 1957), pp. 120–52.

[3] Alfred D. Chandler, Jr., "The Railroads: Pioneers in Modern Corporate Management," *Business History Review* vol. 39 (Spring 1965), p. 17.

[4] Wren, *Evolution of Management Thought*, pp. 84–85.

[5] Chandler, "The Railroads," pp. 17–19.

work. Scheduling operations became complicated. Beyond the day-to-day operating decisions, other management decisions became more complex. Long-range decisions had to be made concerning expanding facilities, purchasing new equipment, and financing such operations.

Unlike the textile industry which was transplanted from Europe, few or no precedents were available to guide those charged with managing the country's railroad companies.[6] Thus the rail company executives were the first in this country to need a sophisticated approach to management.

Besides creating the need for sophisticated management techniques, the railroads made another significant contribution to the development of management. Railroads created a national and increasingly urban market. Urban and industrial centers sprang up all along their miles of tracks. Thus, by providing rapid transportation of raw materials and finished goods, railroads made possible the development of a truly national market.

The third facet of the American Industrial Revolution, communication, was primed in 1844 by Samuel F. B. Morse's invention of the telegraph. The telegraph enabled businessmen to coordinate and communicate with speed and efficiency.

By 1860, which is the year generally thought of as the start of the Industrial Revolution in this country, it was evident that the power, transportation, and communication fields had advanced to the point that they served as an inducement to the entrepreneur.

CAPTAINS OF INDUSTRY

During the last 25 years of the 19th century, a significant transformation occurred in American industry. The economy shifted from a primarily agrarian economy to an economy more involved with manufactured goods and industrial markets.[7] This was a direct result of the urbanization brought about by the completion of a nationwide railroad system.

American business during this transition period was dominated and characterized by "Captains of Industry." These Captains of Industry included men like John D. Rockefeller, James B. Duke, Andrew Carnegie, and Cornelius Vanderbilt. Unlike the laissez faire attitudes of previous generations, these men often pursued profit and self-interest above all else. Although their methods have been questioned, they did obtain results. Under the guidance of these men, corporate

---

[6] Ibid., p. 21.

[7] Alfred D. Chandler, Jr., "The Beginnings of 'Big Business' in American Industry," *Business History Review* vol. 33 (Spring 1959), p. 3.

giants grew in industries other than the railroads. Giant companies were formed through mergers in both the consumer and producer goods industries. They created new forms of organizations and introduced new methods of marketing. For the first time nationwide distributing and marketing organizations were brought into existence. The birth of the corporate giant altered the business decision-making environment.

The empire building and methods of the Captains of Industry also had a profound effect on the relationship between government and industry. Government began to legislate business regulations. In 1890 the Sherman Antitrust Act, which sought to check corporate practices "in restraint of trade," was passed.

By 1890, U.S. industry had reached a point where previous management methods were no longer applicable. No longer could the manager make on-the-spot decisions and maintain records in his head. Corporations had developed into large-scale enterprises with national markets. Communication and transportation had expanded and greatly facilitated industrial growth. Technological innovations were contributing to industrial growth. Specifically, the invention of the internal combustion engine and the applications of electricity as a power source greatly accelerated industrial development at the close of the 19th century.

However, contrary to what might appear to have been an ideal climate for prosperity, productivity and wages were low.[8] Production methods were crude and worker training was almost nonexistent. No methods or standards had been developed for measuring work. Work had not been studied to determine the most desirable way to complete a task. The psychological and physical aspects of a job—such as boredom, monotony, and fatigue—had not been studied or even considered in the design of most jobs.

It was at this point in the development of management that the engineering profession made significant contributions. Because engineers designed, built, installed, and made operative the productive system, it was only natural for them to study the methods used in operating these systems.

SCIENTIFIC MANAGEMENT AND F. W. TAYLOR

Departmentalization and specialization had naturally accompanied the rapid industrial growth and the creation of Big Business. One man no longer performed every task but rather specialized in performing only a few functions. This created a need to coordinate, integrate,

---

[8] Harry Kelsey and David Wilkerson, "The Evolution of Management Thought," unpublished paper, Indiana University, 1974, p. 7.

and systematize the work flow. Because of increasing production, the time spent on each operation became more important. One minute saved on each item could be very significant if a company was producing several thousand items. Thus the increased production plus the new need for integration and systematizing caused the engineers of the period to begin to study work flows and job content.

The spark which is generally given credit for igniting the interest of engineers to general business problems was a paper presented in 1886 by Henry Towne, president of Yale and Towne Manufacturing Company, to the American Society of Mechanical Engineers. Towne stressed that the engineer should be concerned with the financial and profit orientation of the business in addition to his traditional technical responsibilities.[9] A young mechanical engineer named Frederick Winslow Taylor was seated in the audience. As we shall see, Taylor later had a profound impact on the development of management.

Although his father was a successful lawyer, Taylor's first job was as an apprentice with the Enterprise Hydraulic Works of Philadelphia.[10] Here Taylor learned pattern making and machining. Upon finishing his apprenticeship in 1878, Taylor joined Midvale Steel Company as a common laborer. In six short years, Taylor rose through eight positions to chief engineer. During his early years at Midvale, Taylor had the opportunity to work with and observe production workers at all levels. It did not take Taylor long to figure out that many workers put forth less than 100 percent effort. Taylor referred to this behavior of restricting output as "soldiering." Because soldiering was in conflict with Taylor's Quaker-Puritan background, it was difficult for him to understand and accept. Taylor, therefore, decided to determine why workers "soldiered."

Taylor quickly perceived that workers had little or no incentive to produce more since most wage systems were based on attendance and position. Piece-rate systems had been tried prior to Taylor's era but generally failed because of poor implementation and weak standards. Taylor believed that a piece-rate system would work if the workers believed that the standard had been fairly set and that management would stick to that standard. Taylor's efforts to scientifically define a full and fair day's standard became the true beginning of scientific management. Taylor wanted to use scientific and empirical methods rather than tradition and custom for establishing standards.

---

[9] Henry R. Towne, "The Engineer as Economist," *Transactions*, ASME, vol. 7 (1886), pp. 428–32.

[10] Frank Barkley Copley, *Frederick W. Taylor: Father of Scientific Management*, vol. 1 (New York: Harper and Row, 1923), pp. 77–79.

Taylor first formally presented his views to the Society of Mechanical Engineers in 1895.[11] His views were expanded in book form in 1903 and in 1911.[12]

Scientific management, as developed by Taylor, was based upon four main principles:

1. The development of the "one best way" of doing a job. This involved the determination of the best method for accomplishing the objectives of a given job. Standards were scientifically established for jobs, and incentive wages were paid for all production above the established standard.

2. The selection and development of workers. Taylor realized the value in matching the job with the worker. Taylor also emphasized the need for properly trained workers. Here his emphasis was on the selection of the best man for the job.

3. The bringing together of methods and men. Taylor believed that workers would exhibit little resistance to a change in methods if they perceived an opportunity for greater earnings for themselves.

4. The close cooperation of managers and workers. Taylor believed that management should continually coordinate with the line workers but not do the line worker's jobs.[13]

Scientific management represented a complete mental revolution on the part of both management and workers.[14] It was a new philosophy and attitude toward the use of human effort. The emphasis was on maximum output with minimum effort through the elimination of waste and inefficiency at the operative level.[15] A methodological approach was used to study job tasks, and standards were established. This approach included research and experimentation methods (scientific methods). The job tasks became the objectives, and standards were set in areas of personnel, working conditions, equipment, output, and procedures. Planning was separated from operative performance. The managers planned the work while the workers performed the work. This resulted in closer cooperation between managers and workers.

The scientific study of work also placed greater emphasis on spe-

---

[11] Frederick W. Taylor, "A Piece-Rate System," *Transactions,* ASME, vol. 16 (1895), pp. 856–83.

[12] Frederick W. Taylor, *Shop Management* (New York: Harper and Row, 1903), and Frederick W. Taylor, *The Principles of Scientific Management* (New York: Harper and Row, 1911).

[13] Alan C. Filley and Robert J. House, *Managerial Process and Organizational Behavior* (Glenview, Ill.: Scott, Foresman and Company, 1969), p. 12.

[14] John F. Mee, *Management Thought in a Dynamic Economy* (New York: New York University Press, 1963), p. 41.

[15] John F. Mee, "Seminar in Business Organization and Operation," unpublished paper, Indiana University, p. 5.

cialization and division of labor. Thus the need for an organizational framework became more and more apparent. The concepts of line and staff were developed. In an effort to motivate workers, wage incentives were developed in most scientific management programs. Once standards were set, managers began to monitor actual performance and compare the outcome with the standards. Thus the managerial function of control came into being.

Scientific management was actually a philosophy concerning the relationship of men and work, not a technique or an efficiency device. Taylor's ideas and scientific management were based on a concern not only for the proper design of the job but also for the worker. This has often been misunderstood. Taylor and scientific management were (and still are) frequently attacked as being inhumane and interested only in output. The key to Taylor's thinking was that he saw his methods as benefiting equally both management and the worker: Management could achieve more work in a given amount of time, and the worker could produce more and hence earn more with little or no additional effort.

OTHER SCIENTIFIC MANAGEMENT PIONEERS

Several disciples and contemporaries of Taylor helped popularize and spread the gospel of scientific management. Carl Barth, who is often called the most orthodox of Taylor's followers, worked with Taylor at Bethlehem Steel and followed him as a consultant when Taylor left Bethlehem. Barth did not alter or add to scientific management in any significant manner but rather spent his efforts popularizing Taylor's ideas.

Morris Cooke was another disciple who worked directly with Taylor on several different occasions. Cooke's major contributions involved the application of scientific management to educational and municipal organizations. Cooke worked hard to bring management and labor together through scientific management. Cooke's rationale was based on the thesis that labor was as responsible for production as management and that increased production would improve the position of both.[16] Thus Cooke broadened the scope of scientific management and helped enlist the support of organized labor.

Henry Lawrence Gantt worked with Taylor at Midvale Steel and at Bethlehem Steel. Gantt is best known for his contribution in the areas of production control. The "Gantt chart" is still in use today. Gantt was also one of the first management pioneers to recognize publicly the social responsibility of management and business. Gantt

---

[16] Wren, *Evolution of Management Thought*, p. 176.

believed that the community would attempt to take over business if the business system neglected its social responsibilities.[17]

Frank and Lillian Gilbreth were a husband and wife team that made significant contributions to the early management movement both as a team and as individuals. Frank Gilbreth's major area of interest was the study of motions and work methods. Lillian Gilbreth's primary field was psychology. Thus, by combining motion study and psychology, the Gilbreths made significant contributions in the areas of fatigue, monotony, micromotion study, and morale.

Harrington Emerson, who coined the term *efficiency engineer*, was one of the first to recognize the importance of good organization. Emerson felt that waste and inefficiency were eroding the American industrial system. He believed that organization and the application of scientific management could eliminate most waste and inefficiency. Emerson also developed organized management consulting at a time when consulting engineers were still mainly concerned with technical rather than managerial problems.

FAYOL'S THEORY OF MANAGEMENT

Henri Fayol, a Frenchman, was first to issue a complete statement on a theory of general management. Born of relatively well-to-do parents, Fayol was graduated as a mining engineer and started in 1860 as a junior executive of a coal mining and iron foundry company. In 1888, when the company was near bankruptcy, Fayol took over as Managing Director and rapidly transformed the company into a financially sound organization. After his retirement in 1918, Fayol spent his remaining years lecturing and popularizing his theory of administration. He became especially interested in the application of administrative theory to government. Although he published earlier papers outlining his general thinking, Fayol's major contribution, *Administration Industrielle et Generale*, was published in 1916.[18] Unfortunately, this work was not translated into English until 1930 and then in only a very limited number of copies. The book was not readily available in English until 1949.

Possibly the most significant of Fayol's work was his discussion of management principles and elements. Fayol stated the following 14

---

[17] Henry L. Gantt, *Organizing for Work* (New York: Harcourt, Brace, Jovanovich, 1919), p. 15.

[18] Henri Fayol, *Administration Industrielle et Generale* (Paris: The Societe de l'Industrie Minerale, 1916). First translated into English by J. A. Coubrough, *Industrial and General Administration* (Geneva: International Management Institute, 1930). Later translated by Constance Storrs, *General and Industrial Management* (London: Sir Isaac Pitman and Sons, 1949).

"principles of management," stressing that managers should be flexible in the application of these principles and that allowances should be made for different and changing circumstances:

1. Division of work.
2. Authority.
3. Discipline.
4. Unity of command.
5. Unity of direction.
6. Subordination of individual interests to the general interest.
7. Remuneration.
8. Centralization.
9. Scalar chain (line of authority).
10. Order.
11. Equity.
12. Stability of tenure personnel.
13. Initiative.
14. Esprit de corps.

Fayol developed his list of principles from those practices which he had used most often in his work. He used them as broad and general guidelines for effective management. The real contribution made by Fayol was not the 14 principles themselves, for many of these were the products of the early factory system, but rather his formal recognition and synthesis of these principles.

In presenting his "elements of management," Fayol was probably the first to outline what today are called the functions of management. Fayol listed planning, organizing, commanding, coordination, and control as elements of management. He placed the greatest emphasis on planning and organizing because he viewed these elements as primary and essential to the other functions.

The works of Taylor and Fayol are essentially complementary. Both believed that proper management of personnel and other resources was the key to industrial success. Both used a scientific approach to management. The major difference in their approaches centered around their orientation. Taylor came up through the ranks and concentrated on the operative level. Fayol spent most of his time in executive positions and had more of a top management perspective.

PERIOD OF SOLIDIFICATION

The 1920s and most of the 1930s represented a period of solidification and popularization of management as a discipline. The recognition of management as a respectable discipline was accomplished through several avenues. Universities and colleges began to acknowledge the subject of management. By 1915, five colleges and schools were offering management classes, and by 1925 most schools of engineering were offering a class or classes in management.[19] Professional societies began to take an interest in management. Much of the earlier work of the management pioneers was presented through the American Society of Mechanical Engineers, but after the turn of the century, many other professional societies began to promote management. In 1912, the Society to Promote the Science of Management was founded. The society was reorganized in 1916 as the Taylor Society and later merged with the Society of Industrial Engineers to form the Society for the Advancement of Management. The American Management Association was founded in 1923.

FIGURE 2–1
Significant events leading to the solidification of management.

First conference on "Scientific Management," October 1911.
First doctoral dissertation on subject of Scientific Management by H. R. Drury at Columbia University, 1915.
Founding of professional management societies: Society to Promote the Science of Management, 1912; Society of Industrial Engineers, 1917; American Management Association, 1923.
First meeting of management teachers, December 1924.

The first meeting of management teachers, sponsored by the Taylor Society, was held in New York in December 1924.[20] At this meeting the participants agreed that the first course in management should be called Industrial Organization and Management (they could not agree on what should be required in a management curriculum). After this meeting professors began writing textbooks in the field of management.

During the 1930s, management teachers and practitioners began to stress organization. *Onward Industry* by Mooney and Reiley appeared in 1931 and generated interest in the historical development of organizations. Several other books which focused on the organizing function were published in this era. By the mid-1930s, management was a truly respectable discipline. The significant events leading to

---

[19] John F. Mee, "Management Teaching in Historical Perspective," *The Southern Journal of Business*, vol. 7, no. 2 (May 1972), p. 21.

[20] Ibid., p. 22.

the solidification of management as a discipline are summarized in Figure 2-1.

THE HUMAN RELATIONS THRUST

After the Great Depression, which saw unemployment in excess of 25 percent, unions sought and gained major advantages for the working class. During this period, known as the Golden Age of Unionism, legislatures and courts actively supported organized labor and the worker.

Because labor and the worker were attracting more attention, emphasis began to be placed on understanding the worker and his needs —hence the birth of the human relations movement. The heretofore absence of proper emphasis on human relations was brought to the forefront by the now famous Hawthorne Studies.[21]

The Hawthorne Studies began in 1924 when the National Research Council of the National Academy of Science undertook a project to determine the relationship between physical illumination and worker efficiency. The Hawthorne Plant of Western Electric in Cicero, Illinois, was the study site. First, the researchers lowered the level of illumination, expecting productivity to decrease. To their astoundment productivity increased. Next they altered such variables as rest periods, workday, noise, etc., and production still increased.

Baffled by the results, a team of psychologists from Harvard University led by Elton Mayo were called in to analyze the problem. After much analysis and review, the researchers concluded that other factors besides the physical environment had effects on worker productivity. They found that workers reacted to the psychological and social conditions at work. These conditions included such things as informal group pressures, individual recognition, and participation in decision making. For the first time, research evidence had indicated the potential impact of the behavioral sciences on management.

Following the Hawthorne Studies, the behavioral sciences were gradually incorporated into management thinking. In 1938, Chester Barnard, who was president of New Jersey Bell Telephone for many years, published a book which combined a thorough knowledge of organization theory and sociology.[22] Barnard viewed the organization as a social structure and stressed the psychosocial aspects of organ-

---

[21] For a detailed description of the Hawthorne studies, see Fritz J. Roethlisberger and William J. Dickson, *Management and Worker* (Cambridge, Mass.: Harvard University Press, 1939).

[22] Chester I. Barnard, *The Functions of the Executive* (Cambridge, Mass.: Harvard University Press, 1938).

izations. Because of his effective integration of traditional management and the behavioral sciences, Barnard's work has had a great
impact on both practicing managers and teachers of management.

THE PROFESSIONAL MANAGER

The career manager or professional manager was nonexistent until
the 1930s. Until this time, managers could be placed into one of three
categories: owner-managers, Captains of Industry, or financial managers. The owner-managers predominated until after the Civil War.
The Captains of Industry controlled organizations from the 1880s
through the turn of the century. The financial managers operated in
much the same way as did the Captains of Industry, except they did
not own the enterprises they controlled and operated. The financial
manager dominated business organizations from around 1905 until
the early 1930s, when public confidence in business organizations
was severely weakened.

It was during this period of weakened public confidence that
people began entering managerial positions to perform the functions
of managing rather than because they owned the business. This
marked the emergence of the professional manager. The professional
manager can be described as a career person who does not necessarily have a controlling interest in the enterprise for which he or she
works. The professional manager realizes that he or she has a responsibility to three groups: the employees, the stockholders, and the
public.

As technology expanded and organizations became more complex,
the professional manager became more and more prevalent.

CHANGING STYLES OF MANAGEMENT

As organizations grew in size and complexity, managers began
emphasizing the importance of the worker and his or her needs. As
managers began to study the worker and develop theories concerning
worker behavior, new styles and methods of managing began to
emerge.

One such innovative style of managing was that of James F. Lincoln. The serious illness of his brother forced Lincoln to assume the
top management position of the Lincoln Electric Company in 1913.[23]
Knowing little about managing a business and having no previous
top management experience, Lincoln, remembering his former foot-

---

[23] Charles W. Brennan, *Wage Administration*, rev. ed. (Homewood, Ill.: Richard D.
Irwin, Inc., 1963), p. 289.

ball days and the cooperation needed on the gridiron, solicited the help of his employees in managing the company. Lincoln realized that effective cooperation would not be achieved without rewards. Therefore he designed a plan which coupled an incentive system with a request for cooperation. Lincoln emphasized the fact that his plan appealed to the basic need of every individual to express himself. Specifically the plan contained the following components:

1. An advisory board of employees.
2. A piece-rate method of compensation wherever possible.
3. A suggestion system.
4. Employee ownership of stock.
5. Year-end bonus.
6. Life insurance for all employees.
7. Two weeks' paid vacation.
8. An annuity pension plan.
9. Promotion policy.

If the success of Lincoln Electric Company can be attributed to its innovative management, then it certainly was successful. Over a 30-year period, Lincoln workers have consistently been among the highest paid in their industry in the world; Lincoln's selling price has consistently been lower than any comparable product; and the company has consistently paid a dividend since 1918.

Another innovative manager, Henry Dennison (1877–1952), felt that the strengths of an organization come from its members, and that the sources of power are the incentives, habits, and traditions that move the men and women of an organization.[24] Dennison believed that an organization's greatest strength is realized if all of its members are strongly impelled, if their acts lose no effectiveness by frictions, conflicts, or unbalance, and if their acts move in a single direction reinforcing each other. He believed that the organization's primary purpose was to provide the conditions under which men work most readily and effectively. Instead of designing the organization structure and tasks first, Dennison advocated finding "like-minded" people, grouping them, and then developing the total organizational structure. In summary, Dennison believed that management attention must focus on causes and effects in the field of human behavior. Dennison successfully practiced his management approach in the 1920s and 1930s at the Dennison Manufacturing Company, which was also one of the early companies to practice the Taylor system of Scientific Management.

---

[24] Henry S. Dennison, *Organization Engineering* (New York: McGraw-Hill Book Company, 1931).

Charles McCormick and William Given, Jr., were two top managers who applied a human relations philosophy to their organizations. Both McCormick's and Given's style of management were based on worker participation in the decision-making process.

Charles McCormick, the manufacturer of spices and extracts, developed and made famous the McCormick multiple-management plan.[25] This plan used participation as a training and motivational tool by selecting 17 promising young men from various departments within the company to form a junior board of directors. The junior board met with the senior board once a month and submitted its suggestions. Aside from the immediate benefits of providing good suggestions, the junior board provided early identification of management talent, opened communication channels, and relieved senior board members of much of the detailed planning and research. The overwhelming success of the junior board led to the creation of a sales board and a factory board which operated in much the same fashion.

Using the term "bottom-up management," William Given, president of American Brake Shoe and Foundry Company, encouraged widespread delegation of responsibility and authority in order to solicit the participation of "all those down from the bottom up. . . ."[26] Given's approach promoted considerable managerial freedom in decision making, free interchange of ideas, and the recognition that managerial growth involves some failure. Given's style was based on his belief that the judgment, initiative, and creativeness of all employees in a business organization provide a better end result than the autocratic administration of any single individual.

In 1938, Joseph Scanlon developed a productivity plan which provided the workers with a bonus for tangible savings in labor costs. The Scanlon plan was unique in at least three respects: (1) joint management and union committees were established to discuss and propose labor saving techniques; (2) group rewards, not individual rewards, were made for suggestions; and (3) the worker shared in reduced costs as opposed to increased profits.[27] Scanlon believed that participation was desirable not merely to create a "feeling" of belonging but rather to recognize explicitly the role of the worker and union representative in suggesting improvements.

While many of the emerging styles of management of the 1930s and 1940s had distinct differences, most had a common thread based on

---

[25] Charles P. McCormick, *Multiple Management* (New York: Harper and Row, 1938).

[26] William B. Given, Jr., *Bottom-Up Management* (New York: Harper and Row, 1949).

[27] Joseph Scanlon, "Enterprise for Everyone," *Fortune*, January 1950, pp. 41, 55–59; and Wren, *Evolution of Management Thought*, p. 330.

the human relations thrust and especially on participation. The emergence of the professional manager and the rapidly rising standard of living contributed to a greater concern for the worker and hence the development of participative forms of management. The professional manager realized that a greater concern for the worker would most likely result in greater productivity and therefore greater profits. The rising standard of living made the worker more mobile, increased the number of employment options open to him, and made him less likely to settle for a strictly authoritarian environment.

MANAGEMENT PROCESS PERIOD

During the late 1940s, management thought began to move toward the idea of a "process for management."[28] This was an attempt to identify and define a process that could be used to attain desired objectives. The "process approach" led management to become primarily concerned with the identification and refinement of the subfunctions or components of the management process.

As we have seen, Henri Fayol was the first management scholar to present explicitly a functional analysis of the management process. Fayol listed planning, organizing, commanding, coordination, and control as subfunctions of management.

Oliver Sheldon, an Englishman, also presented an early breakdown of the components of the management process.[29] In 1923 Sheldon saw management as the determination of business policy, the coordination of the execution of policy, the organization of the business, and the control of the executive.

Ralph C. Davis was the first American to publish a functional breakdown of the management process.[30] Davis subdivided the management process into three functions: planning, organizing, and controlling.

While all of the above management scholars made early reference to a functional approach to management, the concept was not widely accepted until after Constance Storrs' translation of Fayol became readily available in 1949. Thus it is evident that Henri Fayol was truly responsible for fathering the functional approach to the study of management.

During this same time process management was gaining acceptance as a discipline that could be taught. Heretofore, management,

---

[28] Mee, *Management Thought*, p. 53.

[29] Oliver Sheldon, *The Philosophy of Management* (London: Sir Issac Pitman and Sons, Ltd., 1923).

[30] Ralph C. Davis, *The Principles of Business Organization and Operation* (Columbus, Ohio: H. L. Hedrick, 1935), pp. 12–13.

while accepted as a discipline, had been modeled after certain successful individuals. The functional approach offered a new, logical, and concrete method of presenting management.

A second generation of management process thinkers evolved after the 1949 translation of Fayol's work and capitalized on teaching management via the functional approach.

George Terry was the first to publish a basic management text called *Principles of Management*.[31] The first edition of Terry's book was divided into six major sections — three of which discussed planning, organizing, and controlling. The book presented management as a series of functions and principles that could be learned and synthesized in a logical fashion. It should be noted that Terry did not view management principles as laws but rather as management guideposts.

Harold Koontz and Cyril O'Donnell followed Terry with a second *Principles of Management* text based on a functional approach to management.[32] Koontz and O'Donnell, stressing that the management functions are not necessarily practiced in any particular order, listed planning, organizing, staffing, directing, and controlling as the functions of management. They also attempted to further Fayol's idea that management was a universal discipline.

The early to mid-1950s represented an era of almost complete agreement concerning the composition and teaching of management. The management process or functional approach was the accepted methodological approach to the study of management.

THE MANAGEMENT THEORY JUNGLE

The late 1950s ushered in a new era in the study of management. Many scholars were becoming uneasy with the process approach to management and began to adopt new approaches. The former production management and industrial engineering approaches began experimenting with mathematical and modeling approaches in an attempt to quantify management. As a result, a mathematical school of thought and a decision theory school of thought were developed for the study of management. The decision theory school was founded largely on economic theory and the theory of consumer choice. The mathematical school viewed management as a system of mathematical relationships. The behavioral scientists were studying management

---

[31] George R. Terry, *Principles of Management* (Homewood, Ill.: Richard D. Irwin, Inc., 1953).

[32] Harold Koontz and Cyril O'Donnell, *Principles of Management: An Analysis of Managerial Functions* (New York: McGraw-Hill Book Company, 1955).

as small group relations, thus depending heavily on psychology and social psychology. Drawing on the work of Chester Barnard and sociological theory, another group developed a social system school which saw management as a system of cultural interrelationships. An empirical school of thought was developed by those management scholars that used the case approach. The basic premise of this school was that effective management could be learned by studying the successes and failures of other managers.

Harold Koontz was the first management scholar to recognize explicitly this fragmentation movement.[33] Koontz accurately referred to this division of thought as the "Management Theory Jungle." Many conferences and discussions followed Koontz's analysis in an attempt to disentangle the theory jungle and to synthesize the various schools of thought. While some progress was made, a unified theory of management has not been realized.

THE SYSTEMS APPROACH

The fragmentation period of the late 1950s and early 1960s has been followed by an era of attempted integration. Many management theorists sought to use a "systems approach" in order to integrate the various management schools. The systems approach was viewed as "a way of thinking about the job of managing . . . [which] provides a framework for visualizing internal and external environmental factors as an integrated whole."[34] The manager was encouraged to view the human, physical, and informational facets of the manager's job as linking together to form an integrated whole.

One popular thrust was to use a systems approach to integrate the other schools of management into the traditional functional approach. The idea here was to integrate the human relations and mathematical approaches into the appropriate functional areas. Thus while studying planning, a systems approach might discuss applicable mathematical forecasting techniques.

Other versions of the systems approach have been much more grandiose and based on General Systems Theory. These versions have attempted to analyze management in terms of other disciplines and other cultures. Often referred to as "comparative management" this approach evolved as a result of the multinational firms and the need for managing in diverse fields.[35]

---

[33] Harold Koontz, "The Management Theory Jungle," *Academy of Management Journal*, vol. 4, no. 3 (December 1961), pp. 174–88.

[34] Richard A. Johnson, Fremont E. Kast, and James E. Rosenzweig, *The Theory and Management of Systems* (New York: McGraw-Hill Book Company, 1963), p. 3.

[35] Wren, *Evolution of Management Thought*, p. 434.

FIGURE 2–2
Major components and related events of the management movement

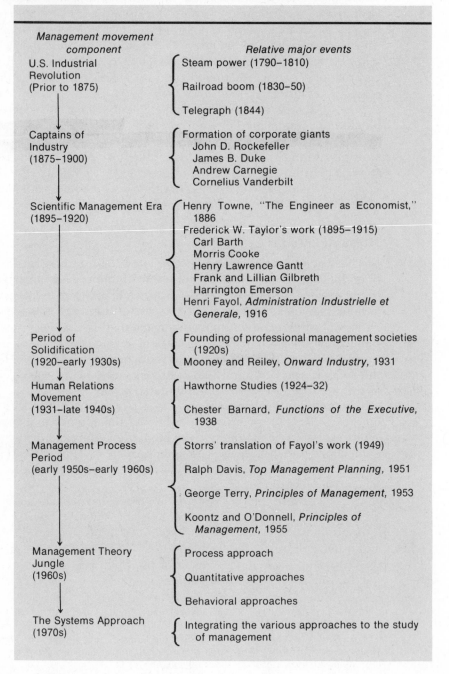

Management movement component	Relative major events
U.S. Industrial Revolution (Prior to 1875)	Steam power (1790–1810) Railroad boom (1830–50) Telegraph (1844)
Captains of Industry (1875–1900)	Formation of corporate giants John D. Rockefeller James B. Duke Andrew Carnegie Cornelius Vanderbilt
Scientific Management Era (1895–1920)	Henry Towne, "The Engineer as Economist," 1886 Frederick W. Taylor's work (1895–1915) Carl Barth Morris Cooke Henry Lawrence Gantt Frank and Lillian Gilbreth Harrington Emerson Henri Fayol, *Administration Industrielle et Generale*, 1916
Period of Solidification (1920–early 1930s)	Founding of professional management societies (1920s) Mooney and Reiley, *Onward Industry*, 1931
Human Relations Movement (1931–late 1940s)	Hawthorne Studies (1924–32) Chester Barnard, *Functions of the Executive*, 1938
Management Process Period (early 1950s–early 1960s)	Storrs' translation of Fayol's work (1949) Ralph Davis, *Top Management Planning*, 1951 George Terry, *Principles of Management*, 1953 Koontz and O'Donnell, *Principles of Management*, 1955
Management Theory Jungle (1960s)	Process approach Quantitative approaches Behavioral approaches
The Systems Approach (1970s)	Integrating the various approaches to the study of management

Figure 2–2 presents a summation in chronological order of the major components and related events which have contributed to the management movement.

SUMMARY

Management, as we know it today, grew out of the American Industrial Revolution. Not until industry reached a certain level of sophistication was management necessary as a distinct discipline.

The railroads represented the first big industry in this country in terms of sophistication and capital requirements. The railroads also acted as a catalyst in the development of other industries. They provided rapid transportation of raw materials and finished goods, thus allowing companies great flexibility. Taking advantage of the situation, men like Rockefeller, Duke, and Carnegie developed giant corporations in other industries by the end of the 19th century. These new corporate giants, along with the railroads, required new methods of management. No longer could business be run out of the home or on an informal basis.

It was at this point that the engineering profession made significant contributions to the development of management thought. Challenging previous methods of managing a business, Frederick Taylor devised and popularized Scientific Management. Although often misunderstood, scientific management, as presented by Taylor, was a philosophy concerning the relationship of men and work. The basis for this relationship was finding the "one best way" for doing a job and finding the proper person for each job.

By the 1930s, the field of management had gained general acceptance as a discipline that could be taught and learned. Professional societies and related organizations were formed and were contributing to the development of the discipline.

Following this period of solidification during the 1920s and early 1930s, the human relations movement made a significant impact on the management discipline. The Hawthorne Studies focused attention on human relations and specifically the psychological and sociological aspects of work.

Although his work was not readily available in English until 1949, Henri Fayol was the first to present a functional approach to the study of management. Fayol was also one of the first to develop "principles of management."

By the mid-1950s, there was general agreement that management should be taught using a process or functional approach similar to that of Fayol. However, this period of general agreement was short-lived and was followed in the early 1960s by a fragmentation era.

During this fragmentation period, several different schools of thought were pursued by management scholars.

In an effort to again unify management thought, a systems approach was developed. This approach is an attempt to tie all of the various schools of thought together within an overall "systems framework."

REVIEW QUESTIONS

1. What were the three facets of the Industrial Revolution in America? Discuss what impact each of these facets had on the development of industry as it is today.

2. What effect did the Captains of Industry have on the relationships between government and industry?

3. What is Scientific Management? Discuss the four main principles of Scientific Management.

4. Discuss the major contribution to scientific management of Morris Cooke, Henry Lawrence Gantt, Frank and Lillian Gilbreth, and Harrington Emerson.

5. What was Henri Fayol's major contribution to the management movement?

6. Discuss the impact of the Hawthorne Studies on management thought.

7. Describe in detail the following approaches to the management process: Lincoln Electric Company, McCormick multiple-management plan, Bottom-up management, and Scanlon plan.

8. What is the process approach to management? Discuss some of the major contributors to this approach.

9. Discuss the factors which led to the Management Theory Jungle.

10. What is the systems approach to the management process?

DISCUSSION QUESTIONS

1. Why did the professional manager not emerge until the 20th century?

2. How were Taylor and Fayol's approaches to the management process different and how were they similar?

3. Why do you think Taylor and scientific management have been misunderstood by many people as being inhumane?

4. Do you think the systems approach to management will result in a unified and widely accepted approach to the management process?

SELECTED READINGS

Barnard, Chester I. *The Functions of the Executive.* Cambridge, Mass.: Harvard University Press, 1938.

Fayol, Henri L. *General and Industrial Management.* London: Sir Isaac Pitman and Sons, 1949.

Gantt, Henry L. *Organizing for Work.* New York: Harcourt, Brace & Jovanovich, 1919.

George, Claude S. *The History of Management Thought.* Englewood Cliffs, N.J.: Prentice-Hall, Inc., 1968.

Given, William B., Jr. *Bottom Up Management.* New York: Harper and Row, 1949.

McCormick, Charles P. *Multiple Management.* New York: Harper and Row, 1938.

Mee, John F. "Management Teaching in Historical Perspective," *The Southern Journal of Business* (May 1972), pp. 20–24.

_____. *Management Thought in a Dynamic Economy.* New York: New York University Press, 1963.

Merrill, C. F., ed. *Classics in Management.* New York: American Management Association, 1960.

Mooney, J. D., and A. C. Reiley. *Onward Industry!* New York: Harper Brothers Publishers, 1931.

Roethlisberger, Fritz J., and William J. Dickson. *Management and Worker.* Cambridge, Mass.: Harvard University Press, 1939.

Scanlon, Joseph. "Enterprise for Everyone," *Fortune* (January 1950), pp. 41–59.

Sheldon, Oliver. *The Philosophy of Management.* London: Sir Isaac Pitman and Sons, Ltd., 1923.

Taylor, Frederick W. *Shop Management.* New York: Harper and Row, 1903.

_____. *The Principles of Scientific Management.* New York: Harper and Row, 1911.

Wren, Daniel. *The Evolution of Management Thought.* New York: The Ronald Press Company, 1972.

Case 2–1

Granddad's company

The J. R. V. Company, which manufactures industrial tools, was founded in 1905 by James R. Vail, Sr. Currently, James R. Vail, Jr., is the president of the company and his son Richard is executive vice president. James Vail, Jr., has run the company the past 30 years in a fashion very similar to that of his dad. The company currently uses a piece-rate incentive program with the standards being set by time and motion studies. All employees receive two weeks' paid vacation and participate in a company insurance plan. Other than these benefits, the J. R. V. employees are generally considered to be the lowest paid in the industry. The present J. R. V. building was built in 1920 but has had minor modifications added, such as florescent lighting and an employees' lunchroom.

Recently James Jr., who is planning on retiring in a few years, and Richard, his planned successor, have had disagreements concerning management style and philosophy. Richard's primary argument is that times have changed, and therefore, J. R. V. needs to modernize and show more concern for its employees. On the other hand, James Jr. argues that J. R. V. has been successful under its present management philosophy for many years and to change would be "foolish."

1. Do you agree with Richard?
2. How might Richard convince his father that things have changed?
3. How does the future look for the J. R. V. Company?

Case 2–2

Return to scientific management

Recently a professor at State University was lecturing in a management development seminar on the topic of motivation. Each of the participants candidly discussed problems that existed in their respective organizations. Problem areas mentioned included absenteeism, turnover, and poor workmanship. The participants managed a variety of workers such as automobile assembly workers, clerical workers, key punch operators, sanitation workers, and even some middle-level managers.

During the discussion, one of the participants made the following statement: "What we need to stop all of these problems is a little scientific management."

1. What do you think the man means?
2. Do you agree? Discuss.
3. Take one of the jobs in the above case and show how you could apply scientific management.

text 1-6 CH ~~Tuesday~~ Tuesday about 45 to an hour.

TonF m.c.

deffinition

Objectives

1. *To demonstrate that decision making pervades all of the management functions and thus all managers are decision makers.*
2. *To present current theories of decision making and to relate these theories to the job of the manager.*
3. *To introduce and discuss the concept of "satisficing."*
4. *To emphasize the role that values play in decision making.*
5. *To develop an appreciation for making decisions within an organizational context.*

GLOSSARY OF TERMS

Level of aspiration The level of performance that a person expects or hopes to attain.

Certainty situation Decision situation in which the decision maker knows the state of nature and can calculate exactly what will happen.

Decision making A process that involves searching the environment for conditions requiring a decision, developing and analyzing possible alternatives, and then selecting a particular alternative.

Optimizing The practice of selecting the best possible alternative.

Risk situation Decision situation in which the decision maker has some information and can calculate probabilistic estimates concerning the outcome of each alternative.

"Satisficing" The practice of selecting the first alternative that meets the decision maker's minimum standard of satisfaction.

Uncertainty situation Decision situation in which the decision maker has no knowledge concerning the relative probability associated with the different possible outcomes.

Value Conception, explicit or implicit, defining what an individual or a group regards as desirable.

3

The manager as a decision maker

"Executive" derives from a Latin word meaning "to do," and the Oxford dictionary defines it in terms of "the action of carrying out or carrying into effect." Neither of these approaches would suggest that the main responsibility and function of the executive is to make decisions. Yet in modern business and industry this is precisely what is expected of him. He is rewarded and evaluated in terms of his success in making decisions.

David W. Miller and Martin K. Starr*

SOME AUTHORS use the term *decision maker* as if it were synonymous with manager. Although managers are decision makers, the converse is not necessarily true. Not all decision makers are managers. For example, a person sorting fruit or vegetables is required to make decisions, but he is not a manager. However, all managers regardless of their position in the organization must make decisions in the pursuit of organizational objectives. In fact, decision making pervades all of the basic management functions: planning, organizing, motivating, and controlling. Although different types of decisions are required in performing the respective management functions, they all require decisions.

Herbert Simon has described the manager's decision process in three stages: (1) intelligence, (2) design, and (3) choice.[1] The intelligence stage involves searching the environment for conditions requiring a decision. The design stage entails inventing, developing, and analyzing possible courses of action. The final stage, choice, re-

---

* *Executive Decisions and Operations Research.* New York: Prentice-Hall, Inc., 1960, p. 10.

[1] Herbert A. Simon, *The New Science of Management Decision* (New York: Harper and Row, 1960), p. 2.

fers to the actual selection of a particular course of action. Analyzing the decision process by stages emphasizes the difference between management and nonmanagement decisions. Nonmanagement decisions are concentrated in the last (choice) stage. The fruit or vegetable sorter has only to make a choice as to the size or quality of the goods. Management decisions place greater emphasis on the intelligence and design stages. If the decision-making process is viewed as being composed only of the choice stage, then managers spend very little time making decisions. If, however, decision making is viewed as encompassing not only the actual choice but also the intelligence and design work necessary for making the choice, then managers spend most of their time making decisions.

THE THEORETICAL APPROACH TO DECISION MAKING

The theoretical approach to decision making is presented diagrammatically in Figure 3–1. Once the need for making the decision has

FIGURE 3–1
The theoretical decision model

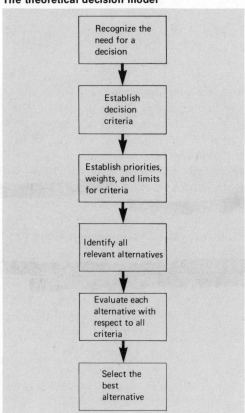

been recognized, criteria must be established in terms of the results that are expected from the decision. These criteria should reflect how the decision will be evaluated. The criteria should then be ranked and weighted according to their relative importance.

Next, all alternatives that meet the stated criteria are identified. After all alternatives have been identified, each is then evaluated with respect to all the criteria. The final selection or choice is then made based on the alternative which best meets the criteria.

AN EXAMPLE

Suppose Mr. Smith is trying to reach a decision concerning the purchase of a new car. He recognized the need to make a decision yesterday when the engine of his present car blew up and he discovered that it would cost more to fix the car than it was worth. After consultation with his wife, they jointly selected the following criteria for the new car: price, appearance, economy of operation, reliability, passenger capacity, driving ease, and comfort. After further study and consultation they established the priorities, weights, and limits for the criteria as shown in Table 3–1.

TABLE 3–1
Priorities, weights, and limits of car buying criteria

Criteria	Priority	Weight (1–5)	Limit, if any
Reliability	1	5	—
Economy	2	4	At least 18 mpg
Price	3	4	Less than $4,000
Passenger capacity	4	2	At least 4 adults
Comfort	5	1	Air conditioning and radio
Driving ease	6	1	—
Appearance	7	1	Two-door model

After reading *Consumer Reports* and doing extensive shopping, they identified the following possible choices within the limits of the criteria: Vega, Nova, Datsun, Pinto, Colt, and Volkswagen.

Next each alternative was evaluated with respect to each criterion. Table 3–2 shows the results of this exercise using a scale of from 1 (low) to 10 (high). The total for each line was found by multiplying each individual criterion evaluation by its respective weight and then summing all of these scores for the respective alternative.

Now that each alternative has been evaluated with regard to the criteria, the Volkswagen should be selected because it received the highest total points.

TABLE 3-2
Evaluation of each alternative

Weight	5	4	4	2	1	1	1	
Criteria Alternative	Relia-bility	Econ-omy	Price	Capac-ity	Com-fort	Driving ease	Appear-ance	Total
Vega	6	7	8	3	3	6	5	110
Nova	7	4	5	8	8	5	7	107
Datsun	8	3	4	8	9	5	8	106
Pinto	4	6	7	3	4	7	5	94
Colt	3	6	6	4	4	7	5	87
Volkswagen	8	7	8	2	2	8	2	116

PROBLEMS WITH THE THEORETICAL DECISION PROCESS

The theoretical approach to decision making is based on the concept of an "economic man." The economic man concept postulates that man behaves rationally and that his behavior is based on the following four major assumptions:

1. People have clearly defined criteria, and the relative weights which they assign to these criteria are stable.
2. People have knowledge of all relevant alternatives.
3. People have the ability to evaluate each alternative with respect to all the criteria and arrive at an overall rating for each alternative.
4. People have the self-discipline to choose the alternative which rates highest (they will not manipulate the system).

In many instances, these assumptions are not very realistic. First, difficulties arise in setting decision objectives because the decision maker may not always know the criteria used in evaluating the decision. Factors that are considered to be important by the decision maker may not be viewed as important by his superiors. In the example of purchasing an automobile Mr. and Mrs. Smith may not have been able to agree on the proper criteria for buying a new car. Even if they could agree on the criteria, they might have disagreed on the priorities, weights, or limits. An additional problem is that most decisions are based on limited knowledge. In the above example, one or several alternatives could have been omitted due to lack of knowledge (for instance, a Chevette or Toyota may not even have been considered). Although most decisions are based on less than perfect information, in many situations a manager has very limited or no control over the information used to make the decision. For example, information might be generated by outside sources or even a competitor. With new products or innovative ideas, information may be nonexistent. In such instances, the ability to evaluate each alternative and to reach the best decision may be hampered by a lack of information. Probably the most difficult step in the decision process is the evaluation or the prediction of outcomes for the various alternatives. Even in the simple car-buying example, it would be hard to evaluate accurately each criteria for each alternative. Since the final selection is based on predicted outcomes, inaccurate predictions may lead to poor decisions. A final problem is the temptation to manipulate the information and choose a "favored," but not necessarily the best, alternative. This temptation may come from within the decision maker or it may come from exterior forces such as the decision-maker's superiors. Again referring to the car purchasing example, Mr. Smith's wife might persuade him to buy the Nova "just because she likes it."

ECONOMIC MAN VERSUS ADMINISTRATIVE MAN

Believing that the assumptions concerning "economic man" are generally unrealistic, Herbert Simon developed the principle of bounded rationality which states:

> The capacity of the human mind for formulating and solving complex problems is very small compared with the size of the problems whose solution is required for objectively rational behavior—or even for a reasonable approximation to such objective rationality.[2]

Thus, the principle of bounded rationality states that there are definite empirical limits to human rationality. As an outgrowth of the principle of bounded rationality, Simon has proposed a decision theory based on what he has labeled "administrative man." The administrative man theory is based on the following assumptions:

1. There are limitations to a person's knowledge of alternatives and criteria.
2. People act on the basis of a simplified, ill-structured, mental abstraction of the real world, and this abstraction is influenced by personal perceptions, biases, and so forth.

_____

[2] Herbert A. Simon, *Model of Man* (New York: John Wiley and Sons, Inc., 1957), p. 198.

3. People do not attempt to optimize but will select the first alternative which satisfies their current level of aspiration.
4. An individual's level of aspiration concerning the decision fluctuates upward and downward depending on the values of the most recently found alternatives.

The first assumption is a synopsis of the principles of bounded rationality. The second assumption follows naturally from the first. If limits do exist to human rationality, then an individual must make decisions based on limited and incomplete knowledge. The third assumption also naturally follows from the first assumption. If the decision-maker's knowledge of alternatives is incomplete, then he or she cannot optimize but only satisfice. Optimizing refers to the practice of selecting the best possible alternative; whereas satisficing refers to the practice of selecting the first alternative that meets the decision-maker's minimum standard of satisfaction. Assumption four is based on the belief that the criteria for a satisfactory alternative is determined by the current aspiration level of the decision maker. Level of aspiration refers to the level of performance that a person expects to attain and is determined by his prior successes and failures.

Figure 3–2 represents a model of administrative man's behavior. If the decision maker is satisfied that the best alternative has been found, that alternative is selected. Otherwise, the decision maker searches for an additional alternative. In the car-buying example, the purchaser would select the first satisfactory car rather than looking at

FIGURE 3–2
Model of administrative man's behavior

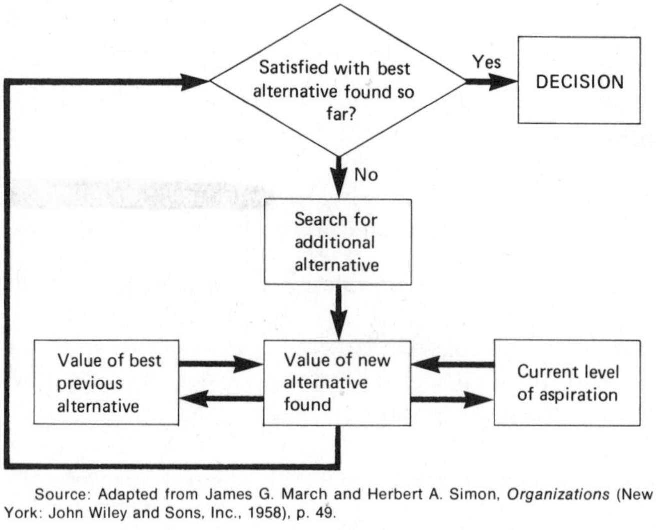

Source: Adapted from James G. March and Herbert A. Simon, *Organizations* (New York: John Wiley and Sons, Inc., 1958), p. 49.

all possibilities. Once an additional alternative is found, its value to the decision maker is evaluated. This evaluation is influenced by the value of the previous best alternative and by the current level of aspiration. The last car the purchaser had looked at and the last car the purchaser had owned would both influence his evaluation of a new car. In Figure 3–2 the double arrows between the value of the best previous alternative and the value of the new alternative indicate a two-way relationship; that is, the value of the new alternative is influenced by the value of the previous best alternative, and the value of the best previous alternative is, in turn, influenced by the value of the new alternative. As indicated by the arrows, a similar two-way relationship exists between the value of the new alternative and the current level of aspiration. The net result of this evaluation determines whether or not the decision maker is satisfied with the alternative. Thus, administrative man selects the first alternative that meets his or her minimum satisfaction criteria and makes no real attempt to optimize.

THE ROLE OF VALUES IN DECISION MAKING

A value is a conception, explicit or implicit, defining what an individual or a group regards as desirable.[3] Values play an important role in the decision-making process. People are not born with values but acquire and develop them early in life. Parents, teachers, relatives, and others influence an individual's values. As a result, every manager and employee brings a certain set of values to the work place. Edward Spranger, a German philosopher, has developed the following generalizations concerning the predominant values of human beings.

1. The *theoretical* man is primarily interested in the discovery of truth, in the systematic ordering of his knowledge. In pursuing this goal he typically takes a "cognitive" approach, looking for identities and differences, with relative disregard for the beauty or utility of objects, seeking only to observe and to reason. His interests are empirical, critical, and rational. He is an intellectual. Scientists or philosophers are often of this type (but they are not the only ones).

2. The *economic* man is primarily oriented toward what is useful. He is interested in the practical affairs of the business world; in the production, marketing, and consumption of goods; in the use of economic resources; and in the accumulation of tangible wealth. He is thoroughly "practical" and fits well the stereotype of the American businessman.

---

[3] William D. Guth and Renato Tagiuri, "Personal Values and Corporate Strategy," *Harvard Business Review*, September–October 1965, pp. 124–25.

3. The *aesthetic* man finds his chief interest in the artistic aspects of life, although he need not be a creative artist. He values form and harmony. He views experience in terms of grace, symmetry, or harmony. Each single event is savored for its own sake.

4. The essential value for the *social* man is love of people — the altruistic or philanthropic aspect of love. The social man values people as ends, and tends to be kind, sympathetic, unselfish. He finds those who have strong theoretical, economic, and aesthetic orientations rather cold. Unlike the political type, the social man regards love as the most important component of human relationships. In its purest form the social orientation is selfless and approaches the religious attitude.

5. The *political* man is characteristically oriented toward power, not necessarily in politics, but in whatever area he functions. Most leaders have a high power orientation. Competition plays a large role in all life, and many writers have regarded power as the most universal motive. For some men, this motive is uppermost, driving them to seek personal power, influence, and recognition.

6. The *religious* man is one "whose mental structure is permanently directed to the creation of the highest and absolutely satisfying value experience." The dominant value for him is unity. He seeks to relate himself to the universe in a meaningful way and has a mystical orientation.[4]

Using a questionnaire based on Spranger's classification of value orientation, Renato Taguiri measured the relative strength of each of the six value orientations of high-level U.S. executives attending the Advanced Management Program at the Harvard Business School. Designing the questionnaire to yield a total of 240 points distributed over the six value dimensions, Taguiri obtained the following average profile for the executives.[5]

Value	Score
Economic	45
Theoretical	44
Political	44
Religious	39
Aesthetic	35
Social	33
	240

The high rankings of the economic and political value orientation are clearly in line with the business executive image. The high rank-

---

[4] Ibid., pp. 125–26.

[5] Ibid., p. 126; and Renato Tagiuri, "Value Orientation and the Relationship of Managers and Scientists," *Administrative Science Quarterly*, June 1965, pp. 39–51.

ing of the theoretical value can be explained by the fact that a manager must have theories and rational approaches in order to satisfy economic and political values.

The value profile given above is based on averages, and any individual's values may differ greatly from this average. The researchers also found that the average value profile for business executives is different from the average value profile of other professions.

A person's values have an impact on the selection of performance measures, alternatives, and choice criteria in the decision process. Differences in values often account for the use of different performance measures. For example, a manager primarily concerned with economic values would probably measure performance differently from a manager primarily concerned with social values. The former manager might measure performance strictly on profit, where the latter might be more concerned with customer complaints. Differences in values might also cause decision makers to generate different alternatives. A viable alternative to one person might be completely unacceptable to another because of differences in values. Because the final choice criteria depend on the performance measures used, they are also affected by values.

EMOTIONAL ATTACHMENTS OF DECISION MAKERS

Decision makers sometimes become so emotionally attached to certain positions that almost nothing will change their minds. Under such circumstances decision makers develop the attitude of "Don't bother me with the facts—my mind is made up." George Odiorne has isolated the following emotional attachments which can adversely affect decision makers:

1. They fasten on the big lie and stick with it.
2. They are attracted to scandalous issues and heighten their significance.
3. They press every fact into a moral pattern.
4. They overlook everything except the immediately useful.
5. They have an affinity for romantic stories and find such information more significant than any other kind, including hard evidence.[6]

Such emotional attachments can be very real and can have serious consequences for the organization. They can lead to poor decisions. Emotional attachments most often affect managers or decision makers who are living in the past and either will not or cannot modernize. An

---

[6] George S. Odiorne, *Management and the Activity Trap* (New York: Harper and Row, 1974), pp. 128–29.

example is the manager who insists on making decisions just as the founder did 50 years ago.

Odiorne offers two suggestions for managers and decision makers engulfed by emotional attachments.[7] The first suggestion is for the decision maker to become aware of biases and to make allowances for them. Undiscovered biases do the most damage. The second suggestion is for the decision maker to seek out independent opinions. It is always good practice to ask the opinion of some person who has no vested interest in the decision.

STATES OF NATURE

When analyzing alternatives the decision maker must project the possible outcomes of the decision under different states of nature. For example, a person who is going outside may elect to take or not to take an umbrella. The more desirable alternative is then determined by the state of nature—whether it rains or not. The state of nature is not controlled by the decision maker. Table 3–3 represents the various combinations of alternatives and states of nature with their respective outcomes for the individual who is going outside and trying to decide whether or not to take an umbrella.

TABLE 3–3
The best alternative is determined by the state of nature

	State of nature	
Alternative	No rain	Rain
Take umbrella	Dry, but inconvenient	Dry
Do not take umbrella	Dry	Wet

Certainty

If the decision maker knows exactly which state of nature will occur, that person is operating under a situation of certainty. Under a situation of certainty the decision maker can often calculate the precise outcome associated with each alternative. Referring to the previous example, if it is raining when the person goes out, the person knows the state of nature and therefore knows the most desirable alternative (take umbrella).

---

[7] Ibid., pp. 142–43.

Risk

Unfortunately, the state of nature is not always known in advance. The decision maker often can obtain, at some cost, information relating to the state of nature. The desirability of obtaining the information is determined by weighing the costs of obtaining the information against the value of the information. A decision maker is operating under a situation of risk if the relative probabilities associated with each state of nature are known. Again referring to the previous umbrella example, the decision maker is operating under a situation of risk if the weatherman has said there is a 40 percent chance of rain.

For most practical problems, the precise probabilities of the various states of nature are not known. However, reasonably accurate probabilities based on historical data and past experiences can often be calculated. When no historical data exists it is difficult to estimate probabilities. One approach taken under such circumstances is to survey individual opinions.

When making decisions under conditions of risk, expected value analysis can be used to assist the decision maker. By using expected value analysis, the expected payoff of an act can be mathematically calculated. One shortcoming of expected value analysis is that it represents the *average* outcome if the event is repeated a large number of times. Such an approach is of little help if the act only takes place once rather than a large number of times. For example, an airplane passenger is not interested in the average fatality rates, but rather what happens on his or her particular flight.

Uncertainty

When the decision maker knows the possible states of nature but has no knowledge of the relative probabilities associated with the respective states of nature, that person is operating under a situation of uncertainty. For example, if one was taking a trip to New York, has never been there before, and has not heard a weather forecast concerning New York, one would have no knowledge about the likelihood of rain and hence whether or not to carry an umbrella.

If the decision maker has little or no knowledge about which state of nature will occur, that person can take one of three basic approaches in making a decision. The first approach is to choose the alternative whose best possible outcome is the best of all possible outcomes for all alternatives. This is an optimistic or gambling approach. Referring to the umbrella example, a decision maker using this approach would not take the umbrella since the best possible outcome is no rain and no umbrella.

A second approach to dealing with uncertainty is to compare the worst possible outcomes of each of the alternatives and select the alternative whose worst possible outcome is least bad. This is a pessimistic approach. Using the umbrella example, the decision maker would compare the worst possible outcome of taking an umbrella to that of not taking an umbrella. The decision maker would then decide to take an umbrella, since it is better to carry an unneeded umbrella than to get wet.

The final approach is to choose the alternative which has the least variation among its possible outcomes. This is a risk-averting approach and makes for more effective planning. If the decision maker chooses not to take an umbrella, the outcomes can vary from staying dry to getting wet. By choosing to take an umbrella, the outcomes can vary from being inconvenienced and dry to dry. Thus the risk-averting decision maker would take an umbrella and be sure of staying dry.

The specific approach used by the decision maker under conditions of uncertainty is contingent on the individual's aversion to risk and the consequences of making a bad decision.

GROUP DECISION MAKING

Everyone is familiar with the old axiom that two heads are better than one. Empirical evidence generally supports this view with a few minor qualifications. It has been found that group performance is frequently better than that of the average group member.[8] It has also been found that groups take longer to solve problems than does the average individual.[9] Thus group decisions are generally advantageous in situations where avoiding mistakes is of greater importance than speed.

Group performance is generally superior to that of the average group member for two basic reasons. First, the sum total of the group's knowledge is greater, and secondly, the group possesses a much wider range of problem-solving approaches.

Group decision making also has other benefits. Participation in the decision-making process increases acceptance of the decision by group members and eliminates the problem of persuading the group to accept the decision. This is especially true when change is being

---

[8] I. Lorge, et al., "A Survey of Studies Contrasting the Quality of Group Performance and Individual Performance, 1930–1957," *Psychological Bulletin*, November 1958, pp. 337–72; and Ross A. Webber, "The Relation of Group Performance to the Age of Members in Homogeneous Groups," *Academy of Management Journal*, September 1974, pp. 570–74.

[9] M. E. Shaw, "A Comparison of Individuals and Small Groups in the Rational Solution of Complex Problems," *American Journal of Psychology*, July 1932, pp. 491–504; and Lorge, "Survey of Studies."

implemented in the organization.[10] A more complete understanding of not only the decision but also the alternatives results from group decision making. This is especially helpful when the individuals who must implement the decision participate in the decision process.

However, some potential drawbacks can drastically limit the effectiveness of group decision making. One individual may dominate or control the group. This situation occurs frequently when the organization president or other "higher-ups" participate in the decision process. Because of their presence many members become inhibited. The social pressures of conformity can also inhibit group members.

FIGURE 3–3
Conditions conducive to group decision making

When the problem has a definite and identifiable solution.

When the initial judgements of the individuals in the group are not homogeneous so that a range of possible solutions is initially available to the group for its consideration.

When the task requires that each member make a judgment about the same matter.

When rewards and punishments are given to the group as a whole rather than to individuals within the group.

When the task can be subdivided.

When the task includes "traps" that single individuals might miss.

Source: Bernard Berelson and G. A. Steiner, *Human Behavior* (New York: Harcourt, Brace, and World, 1964), p. 355.

Competition can develop within the group to such an extent that winning an issue becomes more important than the issue itself. A final hazard results from the dynamics involved in group decision making. Groups can tend to accept the first potentially positive solution and give little attention to other solutions.

One additional interesting characteristic of group decision making concerns the risk that individuals are willing to take as compared with the risk taken by a group composed of the same individuals. Laboratory experiments have shown that decisions taken on a unanimous group basis are consistently more risky than the average of the individual decisions.[11] This is somewhat surprising in view of the fact that group pressures often inhibit the members. One possible ex-

---

[10] For example, see L. Coch and J. R. P. French, Jr., "Overcoming Resistance to Change," *Human Relations*, vol. 1, no. 4 (1948), pp. 512–32.

[11] M. Wallach, N. Kogan, and D. J. Bem, "Group Influence on Individual Risk Taking," *Journal of Abnormal and Social Psychology*, August 1962, pp. 75–86.

planation is that individuals feel less responsible for the outcome of a group decision than when acting alone.

Figure 3–3 lists the general conditions which are most conducive to group decision making.

DECISION MAKING IN AN ORGANIZATIONAL CONTEXT

The particular style used by managers in making decisions varies greatly. For example, some managers prefer to share decision making with their subordinates. In contrast, other managers seldom ask for the opinions of their subordinates. Aside from personality characteristics and personal experiences a decision-maker's style is greatly influenced by his environment. This environment includes the organization itself, groups within the organization, and individuals within the organization.

The freedom which a manager has in making a decision depends to a large extent on the manager's position within the organization and the organizational structure. In general, the higher the manager is in the organization, the more flexibility and discretion in making decisions. The patterns of authority as outlined by the formal organization structure also influence the flexibility afforded the decision maker.

Another important factor which influences decision-making style is the purpose and tradition of the organization. For example, a military organization requires a different style of decision making than does a volunteer organization.

The formal and informal group structures within the organization affect the decision-making styles. These groups may range from labor unions to advisory committees.

A final subset of the environment, individuals, includes all the decision-maker's superiors and subordinates. The personalities, backgrounds, and expectations of these individuals influence the decision-maker's style. Figure 3–4 summarizes the major factors that affect a decision-maker's style in an organization.

Thus, successful managers must develop an appreciation for the different environmental forces that influence them and that are in turn influenced by their decisions. They must develop a multilevel perspective (organizational, group, and individual) toward decision making. To continually view decisions from a single level perspective whether it be from the organization's perspective, a group perspective, or the individual's perspective will not result in optimal decisions. For example, managers who view decisions only from the

FIGURE 3-4
Factors influencing decision making in an organization

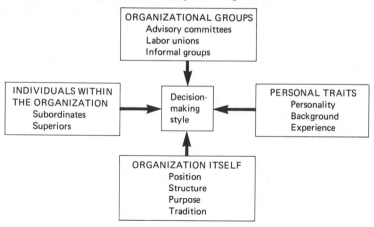

organizational perspective with no appreciation for the groups and individuals making up the organization will eventually experience behavioral problems. "Country club" managers, who are only concerned about their employees and neglect the organization's goals in their decisions, will probably not keep their jobs. The same is true of managers who become overly concerned with organizational groups and neglect either the individual's or the organization's goals. The key to good decision making is a balanced multilevel perspective.

SUMMARY

Decision making pervades all of the management functions, and therefore all managers are decision makers. Decision making is a process that involves searching the environment for conditions requiring a decision, developing and analyzing possible alternatives, and then selecting a particular alternative.

The "administrative man" theory of decision making is based on Herbert Simon's principle of bounded rationality, which states that there are empirical limits to a person's rationality. The basic premise of this theory is that a person does not attempt to optimize in the decision process but rather selects the first alternative that satisfies that person.

Values play an important role in the decision-making process. Because individuals have different values they often make different decisions based on the same information. Edward Spranger has identified six basic values of people: theoretical, economic, aesthetic, social, political, and religious.

Decision makers can become so emotionally attached to a certain position that almost nothing will change their minds. Under such circumstances decision makers are not interested in facts but only in their positions.

The state of nature coupled with the chosen alternative determine the outcome of a decision. Conditions of certainty exist when the state of nature is known. A situation of risk exists when the relative probabilities of the various states of nature are known. Conditions of uncertainty exist when nothing is known concerning the probabilities of the various states of nature.

Groups can be effective decision-making bodies and are especially advantageous in situations where avoiding mistakes is of greater importance than speed.

Successful managers develop a multilevel perspective toward decision making. This multilevel perspective includes the ability to evaluate a decision from an organizational, group, and individual perspective.

REVIEW QUESTIONS

1. What are three stages in the decision-making process?

2. Describe the theoretical approach to decision making.

3. What criticisms can be made concerning the theoretical approach to decision making?

4. Describe the "administrative man" approach to decision making.

5. What is the difference between satisficing and optimizing?

6. What are values?

7. Distinguish between the decision situations of certainty, risk, and uncertainty.

8. Describe some positive and negative aspects of group decision making.

DISCUSSION QUESTIONS

1. Do you subscribe to the belief that many managers only attempt to satisfice rather than optimize when making decisions? Support your answer with examples.

2. Specifically how can managers' values affect their decisions?

3. What factors do you think affect the amount of risk that a manager is willing to take when making a decision?

4. Comment on the following statement: "Groups always make better decisions than individuals acting alone."

5. How does decision making within an organization differ from individual or personal decision making?

SELECTED READINGS

Guth, W. D., and R. Taguiri. "Personal Values and Corporate Strategy," *Harvard Business Review* (September–October 1965), pp. 123–32.

Kepner, Charles H., and Benjamin B. Tregoe. *The Rational Manager.* New York: McGraw-Hill Book Co., 1965.

Odiorne, George S. *Management and the Activity Trap,* New York: Harper and Row, 1974, pp. 127–43.

Simon, H. *The New Science of Management Decision.* New York: Harper and Row, 1960.

———. *Models of Man.* New York: John Wiley and Sons, 1957.

Case 3–1

Moving to the south

The Avery Corporation manufactures industrial supplies and equipment. The company was founded in 1918 and is considered to be "one of the best."

The manufacturing plant and home office are located in New England, although there are sales offices in several major cities throughout the country. During the past several years management has determined that it needs to expand its manufacturing capacity.

During a recent conference, Joe Rankin, the vice president of manufacturing, announced that he had looked at several areas for locating a new factory and was recommending that the company build in a town in South Carolina. "The climate, the people, and the community are just perfect."

Russ Stover, the sales manager, said, "What are you trying to do to the company? You are looking for low-cost labor so that you can keep your production costs down. What about our market? Have you forgotten that our big market is in the West? Only 5 percent of our customers are in the South."

"That is your fault," replied Rankin. "There is more industrial growth in the South than anywhere in the country. You just haven't gone after the business there. I'm saying we go to South Carolina, and that is final. I feel there is a big market potential, and I feel it is a good location."

Stover looked at the company president and said, "This is no way to make a decision. I feel we will always have our market outside the South, and it would be absurd to locate a plant there."

1. Do you think that Stover and Rankin are using the same decision criteria? Discuss.

2. Explain what you think Stover meant when he said, "This is no way to make a decision."

3. What would you do as the company president?

Case 3–2

The city of Yorkville

In a newspaper interview the mayor of Yorkville, Paul Williams, stated that he planned to extend sewer and water services to the north of the city to serve the ever-increasing suburban population.

Upon release of the statement by the press, Bob Franklin, the city planner, was overwhelmed with phone calls. People wanted to know when and where service was to be provided. Bob handled these calls as politely as possible and called for a meeting with the mayor.

In the meeting with the mayor, Franklin said, "You know good and well that we have no plans to go north with sewage service. The terrain and soil characteristics make it economically prohibitive to implement such plans. Besides, the main growth of the city is to the east, not the north."

The mayor said, "I know, Bob, but election time is coming up and I need support on the north side of town. The people out there want to annex the Pine Hills community. We need to provide service to them if annexation is to be a reality."

Franklin said, "I am sure that you would like to get political support, but is this the way to get it? Think of the people on the south and east sides who may swing support elsewhere if this action gets bad publicity. We have committed ourselves to improving our service to city residents on the east side. There is no way to justify spending funds to please people outside the city in anticipation that they will vote for annexation. Mr. Mayor, I will not allow this."

"Just a minute, Bob, who runs the city, the mayor or the planner?"

"I have no political aspirations," said Franklin, "but I do want a good city. I work here because I feel I am making a contribution. If you insist on making statements which are not in the best interest of the city, I shall be forced to go to the newspaper."

1. Is this the way decisions are normally made?
2. What decision criteria is the mayor using?
3. Can the situation be changed?

section two

Basic management functions

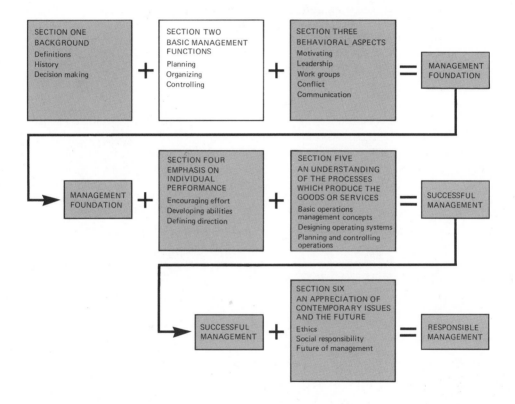

4 Objectives, policy, and strategy
5 Planning: The fundamental function
6 Organizing: The ordering function
7 Staffing
8 Controlling: The containment function

Section One discussed the work that a manager does. Section Two deals specifically with the basic functions of planning, organizing, and controlling that a manager must engage in while doing this work. Although motivating is recognized as a basic management function, it is more appropriately included in Section Three, which deals specifically with the behavioral aspects of management. As indicated by the management model on the preceding page, developing an understanding of the planning, organizing, and controlling functions is a necessary requirement for developing a management foundation.

Chapter 4 is the first of two chapters related to the planning function. Chapter 4 introduces and discusses the planning-related concepts of objectives, policies, and strategies. The primary intent is to define the concepts and clarify the relationship between each of these concepts as preparatory work before discussing the overall planning process in Chapter 5.

Chapter 5 discusses the various dimensions of the planning process as well as a step-by-step discussion of how to plan. Chapters 4 and 5 both emphasize that today's manager must be future-oriented.

Chapter 6 introduces the organizing function through a discussion of division of labor. Authority is presented as the concept most central to the organizing function. Specific methods of organizing and types of organizational structures are illustrated.

Chapter 7, which is an extension of Chapter 6, stresses the staffing aspects of the organizing function. Human resource planning, recruitment, selection, and other personnel-related activities are discussed.

Chapter 8 is concerned with the controlling function. The reasons for management control are discussed along with the requirements of a control system. Several management control methods and techniques are discussed and illustrated.

Objectives

1. To define and discuss the importance of organizational objectives and to illustrate various types of objectives.
2. To explain the reasons for and the use of organizational policies.
3. To define and illustrate the concept of strategy.
4. To clarify the relationships among organizational objectives, policies, and strategies.

GLOSSARY OF TERMS

Goal A statement (used interchangeably with objective) designed to give an organization and its members direction and purpose.

Long-range objectives Objectives that extend beyond the current fiscal year of the organization.

Objective A statement (used interchangeably with goal) designed to give an organization and its members direction and purpose.

Organizational purpose Term that refers to identifying an organization's current and future business. It can be viewed as the primary objective of the organization.

Policies Broad, general guides to action which relate to goal attainment.

Procedures A series of related steps or tasks expressed in chronological order to achieve a specific purpose.

Rules Guidelines that require that specific and definite actions be taken or not be taken with respect to a given situation.

Short-range objectives Objectives that are generally tied to a specific time period of a year or less and are derived from an in-depth evaluation of long-range objectives.

Strategy A mix of goals and major policies which results in a specific action and usually requires the deployment of resources.

4

Objectives, policy, and strategy

Of course, objectives are not a railroad timetable. They can be compared to the compass bearing by which a ship navigates. The compass bearing itself is firm, pointing in a straight line toward the desired port. But in actual navigation the ship will veer off its course for many miles to avoid a storm. She will slow down to a walk in a fog and heave to altogether in a hurricane. She may even change destination in mid-ocean and set a new compass bearing toward a new port—perhaps because war has broken out, perhaps only because her cargo has been sold in mid-passage. Still, four fifths of all voyages end in the intended port at the originally scheduled time. And without a compass bearing, the ship would neither be able to find the port nor be able to estimate the time it will take to get there.

Peter F. Drucker*

IF YOU don't know where you're going, how will you know when you get there? Objectives or goals are designed to give an organization and its members direction and purpose. Few managers question the importance of objectives. The debate arises in deciding what the objectives should be.

Management is a process or form of work that involves the guidance or direction of a group of people toward organizational goals or objectives. Thus, the management process centers around organizational objectives. Management cannot be properly practiced without pursuing specific objectives.

Too many managers become so involved in the day-to-day routine of the job that they forget the major reasons for performing their work.

---

* *The Practice of Management* New York: Harper & Brothers, 1954, pp. 60–61.

Having the proper physical and human resources are prerequisites for successful performance; however, these resources must be properly channeled and directed toward defined objectives. Managers of today and perhaps even more in the future must concentrate on where they and their organizations are headed.

A CASCADE APPROACH

A suggested approach to setting objectives is to have the objectives "cascade" down through the organizational hierarchy:

1. The objective-setting process begins at the top with a clear, concise statement of the central purpose of the enterprise.
2. Long-range organizational goals are formulated from this statement.
3. The long-range goals lead to the establishment of more short-range performance objectives for the organization. When tied to a specific time period, such as a year, these performance objectives become the basis for and an integral part of the objectives of the chief executive and the top management team.
4. Derivative objectives are then developed for each major division or department.
5. Objectives are then established for the various subunits in each major division or department.
6. The process continues on down through the organizational hierarchy.[1]

The cascade approach to goal setting, as outlined above and as depicted in Figure 4–1, does not imply autocratic or "top down" management. It merely ensures that the objectives of individual units within the organization will be in phase with the major goals of the firm and that the entire objective-setting process will be coordinated.

ORGANIZATIONAL PURPOSE

Defining the organizational purpose is crucial. It is also more difficult than one might initially think. Peter Drucker emphasizes the point that an organization's purpose should be examined and defined not only at the inception or during difficult times but also during successful periods.[2] If the railroad companies of the early 1900s had defined their organizational purpose as developing a firm position in the transportation business rather than limiting themselves strictly

---

[1] Anthony Raia, *Managing by Objectives* (Glenview, Ill.: Scott, Foresman and Company, 1974), p. 30.

[2] Peter F. Drucker, *The Practice of Management* (New York: Harper and Brothers, Publishers, 1954), p. 51.

FIGURE 4–1
Cascade approach to objective setting

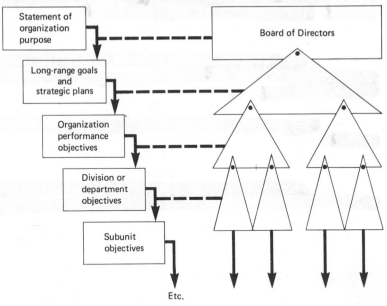

Etc.

Source: Anthony Raia, *Managing by Objectives* (Glenview, Ill.: Scott, Foresman and Company, 1974), p. 30.

to the rail business, they might today hold the same economic position that they did at the turn of the century.

Drucker argues that an organization's business is not determined by the producer but by the consumer.[3] The satisfaction the customer gains from buying an organization's product or service defines the business more than does the organization name, statutes, or articles of incorporation.

In identifying the present business, Drucker outlines three questions that need to be answered. First, management must identify the customer—where the customer is, how the customer buys, and how the customer can be reached. For example, is the customer a retail or a wholesale customer? Second, management must determine what the customer buys. For instance, does the Rolls Royce owner buy transportation or prestige? Finally, management must determine what the customer is looking for in the product. For example, does the homeowner buy an appliance from Sears Roebuck because of price, quality, or service?

In addition to defining the current business, management must

---

[3] Ibid., pp. 50–57.

also identify what the future business will be and what it should be. Drucker presents four areas to be investigated in identifying future business. The first is market potential and trend. Assuming no major changes in market structure, how large is the potential market, and what does the long-term trend look like?

Second, what changes in market structure might occur as a result of economic developments, changes in styles or fashions, or moves by the competition? For example, how has the energy crisis affected the automobile market structure?

Third, what possible innovations will alter the customers' buying habits? What new ideas or products might create new customer demands or eliminate old demands? Consider, for example, the impact of the minicalculator on the marketability of slide rules.

Finally, what needs does the customer presently have that are not being adequately served by available products and services. The success of the Xerox Corporation is a well-known example of identifying and filling a current customer need.

LONG-RANGE AND SHORT-RANGE OBJECTIVES

Long-range objectives generally extend beyond the current fiscal year of the organization. Long-range objectives must support and not be in conflict with the stated organizational purpose. However, long-range objectives may be quite different from the organizational purpose and still support it. For instance, the organizational purpose of a fast food restaurant might be to provide rapid hot food service to a certain area of the city. One long-range objective might be to increase sales to a specific level within the next four years. Obviously, this long-range objective is quite different from the organizational purpose but still supportive of the purpose.

Short-range objectives are properly derived from an in-depth evaluation of long-range objectives. Such an evaluation should result in a listing of priorities of the long-range objectives. Once the priorities have been established, short-range objectives can be set to help achieve the long-range objectives.

Departmental, sectional, and even individual goals should be derived from the long-range and short-range objectives of the organization. The methods for deriving and implementing small unit and individual goals will be covered in detail in Chapter 17. However, the important point in deriving organizational objectives at any level is that they be coordinated with and subordinate to the objectives of the next higher level. Such a system ensures that all objectives are synchronized and not working against each other.

Specifically, objectives should be clear, concise, and quantified whenever possible. They should be detailed enough so that the affected personnel clearly understand what is expected. Objectives should span all significant areas of the organization and not just a single area. The problem with one overriding objective is that it is often achieved at the expense of other desirable objectives. While objectives in different areas may serve as checks on each other, they should be reasonably consistent with each other. Objectives should be dynamic in that they should be reevaluated as the environment and opportunities change. Finally, objectives should represent a mix of business skills and personal management values. This is especially true with today's increasing concern for the environment and other social concerns. Professor John Mee has classified modern organizational objectives into three general categories:[4] (1) profit as the motivating force for managers; (2) service to the customers as justifying the existence of the business; and (3) social responsibilities for managers in accordance with ethical and moral codes established by society. It should be noted that even "non-profit" organizations must be concerned with profit in the sense that they generally must operate within a budget. The following items represent potential areas for establishing objectives in most organizations.[5]

1. *Profitability* can be expressed in terms of profits, return on investment, earnings per share, or profit-to-sales ratios, among others. Objectives in this area may be expressed in such concrete and specific terms as "to increase return on investment to 15 percent after taxes within five years" or "to increase profits to $6 million next year."

2. *Markets* may also be described in a number of different ways, including share of the market, dollar or unit volume of sales, and niche in the industry. To illustrate, marketing objectives might be "to increase share of market to 28 percent within three years," or "to sell 200,000 units next year," or "to increase commercial sales to 85 percent and reduce military sales to 15 percent over the next two years."

3. *Productivity* objectives may be expressed in terms of ratio of input to output (for example, "To increase number of units to X amount per worker per eight-hour day"). The objectives may also be expressed in terms of cost per unit of production.

4. *Product* objectives, aside from sales and profitability by product or product line, may be stated as, for example, "to introduce a product in the middle range of our product line within two years" or "to phase out the rubber products by the end of next year."

5. *Financial resource* objectives may be expressed in many different ways, depending upon the company, such as capital structure, new issues of

---

[4] John F. Mee, "Management Philosophy for Professional Executives," *Business Horizons* (supplement to *Indiana Business Review*), December 1956, pp. 5–11.

[5] Raia, *Managing by Objectives*, p. 38.

common stock, cash flow, working capital, dividend payments, and collection periods. Some illustrations include "to decrease the collection period to 26 days by the end of the year," "to increase working capital to $5 million within three years" and "to reduce long-term debt to $8 million within five years."

6. *Physical facilities* may be described in terms of square feet, fixed cost, units of production, and many other measurements. Objectives might be "to increase production capacity to 8 million units per month within two years" or "to increase storage capacity to 15 million barrels next year."

7. *Research and innovation* objectives may be expressed in dollars as well as in other terms: "to develop an engine in the (specify) price range, with an emission rate of less than 10 percent, within two years at a cost not to exceed $150,000."

8. *Organization* changes in structure or activities are also included, and may be expressed in any number of ways, such as "to design and implement a matrix organizational structure within two years" or "to establish a regional office in the South by the end of next year."

9. *Human resource* objectives may be quantitatively expressed in terms of absenteeism, tardiness, number of grievances, and training, such as "to reduce absenteeism to less than 4 percent by the end of next year" or "to conduct a 20-hour in-house management training program for 120 front-line supervisors by the end of 1978 at a cost not to exceed $200 per participant."

10. *Customer service* objectives may be expressed in explicit terms such as "reduce the number of customer complaints by 30 percent by the end of the year" or "reduce delivery time from three to two weeks by the end of this quarter."

11. *Social responsibility* objectives may be expressed in terms of types of activities, number of days of service, or financial contributions. An example might be "to hire 120 hard-core unemployables within the next two years."

POLICIES

Policies are broad, general guides to action which relate to goal attainment. Policies give guidance as to how management should order its affairs and its attitude toward major issues; they indicate the intentions of those who guide the organization. Policies define the universe from which future decisions are made.

Alan Filley and Robert House have outlined four major characteristics describing policies:

1. Policies are guides to action, which direct organization activities toward prescribed goals.

2. Policies often limit behavior by prescribing *methods* of goal accomplishment and therefore can be a device for controlling behavior.

3. Policies aid in decision making by establishing rules judging the acceptability or unacceptability of alternative courses of action.

4. Policies help insure stable, consistent, uniform, and viable behavior, which is desirable for the organization.[6]

REASONS FOR POLICIES

Policies aid in preventing deviation from the desired course of action by providing definite guides to follow. Policies provide communication channels between the organizational units, thus facilitating the delegation process. Policies ensure that the different elements within the organization are all operating under the same ground rules and within the same boundaries. Policies promote closer coordination and cooperation among the organizational elements. Easier delegation and closer coordination permit a greater degree of decentralization within the organization. Policies foster individual initiative and eliminate the need to reanalyze important decisions each time they arise. Personnel are more likely to take action and voluntarily assume greater responsibility when they are aware of organizational policies. If personnel are confident that their actions are consistent with organizational policy, they are more likely to take action than to do nothing.

TYPES OF POLICIES

George A. Steiner has developed a pyramid which demonstrates the relationship among the various types of business policies (Figure 4–2).[7]

According to Steiner's pyramid, major policies are formulated at the top of the organization and relate to the company's purpose. They provide guidelines pertaining to such things as the lines of business and the ethical conduct of the organization.

Secondary policies, often called corporate policies, are broad, general policies formulated at the upper levels of the organization. Secondary policies apply to the entire organization and deal with business facets such as the selection of major products and the selection of marketing areas. Much of the information generated in the

---

[6] Alan Filley and Robert House, *Managerial Process and Organizational Behavior* (Glenview, Ill.: Scott, Foresman, and Company, 1969), p. 160.

[7] George Steiner, *Top Management Planning* (New York: Macmillan, 1969), p. 270.

FIGURE 4–2
Steiner's pyramid of business policies

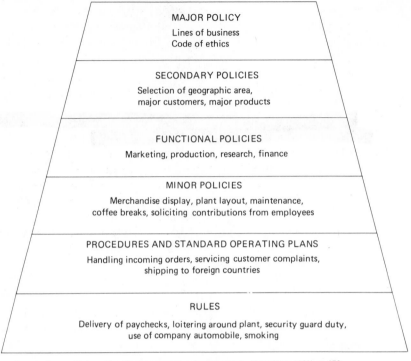

MAJOR POLICY
Lines of business
Code of ethics

SECONDARY POLICIES
Selection of geographic area,
major customers, major products

FUNCTIONAL POLICIES
Marketing, production, research, finance

MINOR POLICIES
Merchandise display, plant layout, maintenance,
coffee breaks, soliciting contributions from employees

PROCEDURES AND STANDARD OPERATING PLANS
Handling incoming orders, servicing customer complaints,
shipping to foreign countries

RULES
Delivery of paychecks, loitering around plant, security guard duty,
use of company automobile, smoking

Source: George Steiner, *Top Management Planning* (New York: Macmillan, 1969), p. 270.

proper formulation of major policies can be used in determining secondary policies. Secondary policies are more specific than major policies. "The XYZ Company will limit its marketing effort to the five New England states" is an example of a secondary policy.

Functional policies deal with a specific functional area of the organization. They include policies that specifically relate to marketing, production, finance, and other functional areas. "The XYZ Company will accept customer exchanges made within one month after purchase" is an example of a functional policy relating to marketing.

Minor policies are subordinate to functional policies and define such details as coffee breaks, maintenance scheduling, and plant layout.

A procedure is a series of related steps or tasks expressed in chronological order to achieve a specific purpose. Procedures define in step-by-step fashion the methods by and through which policies are achieved. They outline precisely the manner in which an activity must be accomplished. Procedures generally allow for little flexibility and deviation. A company's policy may be to accept all customer returns submitted within one month of purchase; company procedures would outline exactly how a return should be processed by the salespeople. Well-established and formalized procedures are often known as standard operating procedures (SOP). For example, standard operating procedures may be established for handling customer complaints.

Rules require that specific and definite actions be taken or not taken with respect to a given situation. Rules leave little doubt concerning what is to be done. They permit almost no flexibility and deviation. Unlike procedures, rules do not specify sequence. For example, "no smoking in the conference room" is a rule.

As can be gleaned from the above discussion, procedures and rules are subsets of policies. All provide guidance in solving a particular problem. The differences lie in the ranges of applicability and the degree of flexibility. For instance, a no smoking rule is much less flexible than a procedure for handling customer complaints, which is likewise less flexible than a hiring policy.

ORIGIN OF POLICIES

Policies can also be classified into one of three categories depending on how the policy evolved.[8] The first category includes policies formed by tradition. Traditional policies emerge from history, tradition, and earlier events. In the worst case, traditional policies may be static and inflexible. In other cases, traditional policies may be very desirable. Usually, traditional policies evolve for some justifiable reason. However, the reason for the policy, along with the surrounding circumstances, often disappears, and yet the policy remains in effect. In modern organizations, outdated, traditional policies may be of little consequence and affect the organization only in minor ways. On the other hand, they can inhibit organizational performance.

The second type of policy by origin includes those policies that are arbitrarily announced by an individual or group of individuals. These are referred to as policies by fiat. Policies by fiat emerge from situations lacking precedence, historical background, or obvious rationale. In the absence of precedence or clear-cut rationale, it may be necessary for an individual to improvise policies so as to insure some degree of order. However, in most instances rule by fiat has undesirable effects. The potential problem is twofold. First, policy by fiat binds the subordinate to the policy maker. Such a situation makes it difficult for the subordinate to "be his own person" as opposed to a "yes per-

---

[8] Filley and House, *Managerial Process*, p. 161.

son" for the policy maker. Second, because the policy maker can re-
define and/or change the policy at any time, the subordinate never
knows what to expect next. Policy by fiat is potentially very satisfying
for the policy maker but very frustrating for those subject to the policy.

The final category of policy by origin includes what are called
rational policies. Rational policies are initiated by the board of directors or a policy committee in most organizations. Unlike traditional
policies and policies by fiat, rational policies may be altered depending upon conditions and the situation. Rational policies provide
general guides to action and general guides for avoiding undesirable
behavior. One danger is that a rational policy, through time and
neglect, may turn into a traditional policy. One effective guard against
such deterioration is to record the assumptions, conditions, and
reasons used in the original formulation of the policy and to reevaluate policies periodically.

HOW MUCH POLICY?

It has already been pointed out that policies can have positive
effects on the organization. However, the degree of structuralization

FIGURE 4–3
Relationship between productivity and control

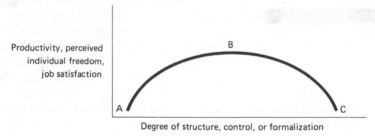

Degree of structure, control, or formalization

and formalization imposed by policies can be overdone. While individuals desire and need a certain amount of structure in the environment, too much can have equally bad effects. Ralph Stogdill has
proposed a curvilinear relationship between the degree of structure,
control, or formalization in a situation and productivity, individual
freedom, and job satisfaction (see Figure 4–3).[9]

Stogdill's model can be easily explained in terms of our earlier

---

[9] Ralph Stogdill, *Individual Behavior and Group Achievement* (New York: Oxford
University Press, 1959), pp. 284–85.

discussion. At Point A, one has no guidelines and is unsure of what one's behavior should be. Therefore, one flounders around or does nothing. At Point B, one has a firm idea of what is expected of oneself and others.. Having a good understanding of these expectations, the individual takes the initiative and thus feels greater satisfaction and freedom. At Point C, the individual once again feels restricted and tends to withdraw or fight the system.

One point should be made clear. The proper blend of policy and structure is a necessary but not sufficient condition for organizational performance. Without policies, the organization will almost certainly not function properly and efficiently, but having policies does not, in itself, ensure desired performance.

FORMULATING AND IMPLEMENTING POLICY

When formulating policies, the policy maker must analyze several factors. First and foremost, the policy maker must appraise the organizational objectives in order to have a complete understanding of where the organization is going before setting the guides to action. In order to avoid conflict, the policy maker must consider both the long-term and short-term objectives.

Because the organization must be concerned with its public image, formulators of policy must be cognizant of the social and ethical responsibilities of the organization. Today's emphasis on social responsibility has focused increased attention on the image of the corporation. Because the policies of the organization directly reflect the ethical philosophy of the company, they often dictate how employees, customers, competitors, the government, and others view the organization. For example, a company policy to actively support the United Way Campaign might contribute positively to the public's view of the corporation.

The organizational structure affects policy formulation. A multi-location or a multinational company may have different policies for each location because of environmental differences. The policies of a U.S. plant regarding working hours, employee selection, and so on, may not be appropriate for a Brazilian plant.

The policies of the competition may have a great impact on an organization's policies. This is particularly true with personnel policies, such as employee benefits and reward structure, management development, and working conditions.

The final factor affecting policy formulation involves the analysis of the general organizational environment. This includes the identification and consideration of such factors as economic trends, social and political trends, the competitive environment, technological breakthroughs, and so forth. The establishment of policies without first considering such factors could be disasterous.

During the policy formulation process, the Principle of Participation should be practiced. The Principle of Participation means that the people to be affected by a policy have the right to a voice in making the policy. This principle does not intend that the affected individuals should have the right to dictate the policy, but rather they have a right to be heard.

Proper use of the Principle of Participation greatly aids in the implementation of a policy. If the affected individuals feel that they at least have some input into the formulation of the policy they are much more likely to accept the policy.

STRATEGY: HOW TO ACHIEVE OBJECTIVES

The word strategy originally came from the Greeks around 400 B.C. and pertained to the art and science of directing military forces.[10] Only in recent times has the word found its way into organizational circles.

A strategy defines the mode or plan of action for allocating scarce resources to gain a competitive advantage and achieve an objective or objectives at an acceptable level of risk.[11] In other words, strategy is a mix of goals and major policies which results in a specific action and usually requires the deployment of resources. Strategies outline the basic approach to be followed in reaching certain goals.

DETERMINING ORGANIZATION STRATEGY

The process of determining an organization's strategy, although very complex, can be broken down into four major stages. First, those charged with strategy formulation must identify the opportunities and threats. This involves analyzing the organizational environment. The organizational environment involves everything from organizational policies to the competition.

After the opportunities and threats have been identified, the strategist must estimate the risk associated with the various possible opportunities and threats. Essentially this involves estimating the probability that an event will occur and assessing the consequence of that occurrence. An event estimated to have a high probability of occurrence but a small effect on the organization would result in a

---

[10] Steiner, *Top Management Planning*, p. 237.

[11] David C. D. Rogers, *Corporate Strategy and Long Range Planning* (Ann Arbor, Mich.: The Landis Press, 1973), p. 10.

FIGURE 4–4
The strategy formulation process

Source: Adapted from Frank T. Paine and William Naumes, *Strategy and Policy Formation: An Integrative Approach* (Philadelphia: W. B. Saunders Co., 1974), p. 13.

small risk to the organization. On the other hand, an event with a medium probability of occurrence but a major impact on the organization would represent a major risk.

Thirdly, the strategy formulators must appraise the organization's strengths and weaknesses based on current organizational resources. What are the organization's primary strengths in sales and marketing, production, personnel, and so forth? A good strategy will build on the organization's strengths and minimize the impact of its weaknesses.

Matching opportunities and capabilities in the pursuit of organizational objectives and at an acceptable level of risk is the final step in the strategy formulation process. This matching process is actually an integration of each of the previous three steps. There is no defined or set manner for deciding what is an acceptable level of risk. An acceptable level of risk depends on management values and philosophy and might vary with the specific opportunity. The end result is an outline of the general approach to be followed in attaining certain goals by appropriately mixing opportunities and capabilities.

The very nature of the strategy formulation process makes it a dynamic and iterative process. For example, the results of a current strategy could change the environment to such an extent that the values of management would change and lead to a revised strategy. Figure 4–4 summarizes the strategy formulation process.

TYPES OF ORGANIZATION STRATEGIES

Professor William Glueck has outlined four basic types of strategies of which three are fundamental, and the fourth is a combination of the other three.[12]

---

[12] William F. Glueck, *Business Policy: Strategy Formation and Executive Action* (New York: McGraw-Hill Book Company, 1972), p. 186.

1. Retrenchment strategies

Retrenchment strategies can be one of three types: to reduce the level of operation of the organization; to become a captive of another organization; or to sell or dissolve the organization. Retrenchment strategies usually are chosen by default when no better alternative exists.

Retrenchment to reduce the level of operation is most common in recessionary or difficult times. The general intention is to eliminate the "excess fat" and operate more efficiently. Retrenchment strategies of this type may include cutting staff personnel, replacing higher paid employees with lower paid employees, eliminating marginal or unprofitable products, reducing expense accounts, and even cutting back marketing efforts. The overall idea is to retain the present level of service or production and operate more efficiently. Little emphasis is given to growth because of the initial expenses involved. Retrenchment to reduce the level of operation is generally a short-range strategy.

Retrenchment to become a captive of another organization has more permanent ramifications than a cutback strategy. This is the situation whereby an independently owned organization allows another organization's management to make certain decisions for it in return for a "guarantee" that the managing organization will buy a certain amount of the captive organization's product. Generally such arrangements are made between a small to medium-size manufacturer or supplier and a larger retailer. The captive organization may give up decisions in the areas of sales, marketing, product design, and even personnel. Retrenchment to become a captive can take place unconsciously as well as consciously. A small manufacturer can slowly do more and more business with one large supplier until it no longer has a choice about becoming a captive. Although retrenchment to become a captive can work out well for both parties, it usually occurs either by default or because of a long and gradual increase in dependence of one organization on another organization.

The final retrenchment strategy is to sell out or dissolve the organization. The decision to sell or dissolve may come by choice or by force. Many times the owners of an organization decide to sell out because they are tired of the business or because they are near retirement. The chance to "get rich quick" has lured many owners of small, closely held organizations into selling. In other situations the owners may have a negative view of the organization's future potential and, therefore, desire to sell while they can still get a good price. If an organization is forced to sell out, the decision usually occurs because of a deteriorated financial condition. Obviously, such circumstances leave the seller in a weak bargaining position. Certain organizations may be dissolved because the products or services they offer are no longer needed.

2. Stability strategies

Stability strategies are followed when the organization is satisfied with its present course of action. Management may make efforts to eliminate minor weaknesses, but generally its actions will be such as to maintain the status quo. As long as the organization is doing well, many managers are very reluctant to change anything. This strategy does work for many organizations in both the short and long run. However, problems can arise if a stability strategy is followed too closely and management becomes complacent. In good economic times it is easy to make money — even with poor management practices. However, when economic conditions deteriorate, organizations guided by weak management are the first to flounder. Organizations conditioned to a stability strategy have difficulty reacting to sudden or radical changes.

Stability strategies are most likely to be successful in unchanging or very slowly changing environments. Organizations employing a stability strategy are usually staffed by executives who feel comfortable with a slow-going, stable operation.

3. Growth strategies

Growth strategies are followed when the organization makes a conscious effort to grow or expand as measured by sales, product line, number of employees, or other similar measures. Growth strategies have dominated the philosophy of many American organizations since World War II. It has been a widely held opinion that an organization must grow to survive. This opinion is most often based on the belief that a smaller organization cannot be competitive and will eventually be gobbled up by larger organizations. Thus, many organizations have followed growth strategies because they were afraid not to grow. Furthermore, growth strategies have been socially very acceptable, especially in the post-war era.

Another reason for pursuing growth strategies may be the personality and personal goals of the chief executive. There is some inherent pleasure in seeing an organization grow and become larger. The thought of providing new direction and growth to the organization is very satisfying to many executives.

Finally, growth strategies may be chosen out of necessity. This usually occurs in rapidly changing environments where the product or service life cycle is relatively short. If the organization does not engage in a growth strategy its product line may be obsolete within a few years.

A growth strategy can be pursued either internally or externally and can be either vertical or horizontal. Internal growth is realized through expansion of present products or services. External growth is usually accomplished through mergers and/or acquisitions. Vertical growth is attained by adding to or expanding the current operations and functions relating to the present products or services. A manufacturer of radios might expand vertically by making more of the component parts itself or by opening its own stores for marketing the radios. Horizontal growth is accomplished by expanding the products or services offered. The manufacturer of radios could expand horizontally by making stereos and television sets.

Organizations following strict growth strategies are often headed by "fast movers" or aggressive executives who like a challenge. With the shortages of raw materials that are becoming more and more common, growth strategies may become less and less popular.

4. Combination strategies

Combination strategies are followed when the organization uses any combination of the aforementioned strategies. For example, it is certainly feasible for an organization to follow a retrenchment strategy for a short period of time due to general economic conditions and then pursue a growth strategy once the economy strengthens. The obvious combination strategies include (a) retrench, then stability; (b) retrench, then growth; (c) stability, then retrench; (d) stability, then growth; (e) growth, then retrench; and (f) growth, then stability.

It can be argued that some of the combination strategies would never be conscientiously selected by management [such as (e) above] but could occur by default. The same argument might be made regarding the selection of any strategy. Although most organizations do adhere to one of the general strategies outlined above, many never formally acknowledge that such a strategy exists.

INTEGRATING OBJECTIVES, POLICIES, AND STRATEGIES

Organizational objectives, policies, and strategies are not mutually exclusive components of the management process. Rather they are highly interdependent and inseparable. One cannot talk about attaining objectives without knowing the policy guidelines that must be followed. Similarly, a strategy cannot be determined without first knowing the objectives to be pursued and the policies to be followed. David Rogers provided the basis for the following analogy which

FIGURE 4–5
Conceptual analogy for integrating objectives, policies, and strategies

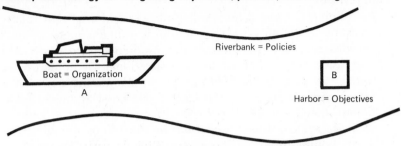

Source: Adapted from David C. D. Rogers, *Corporate Strategy and Long Range Planning* (Ann Arbor, Mich.: The Landis Press, 1973), p. 18.

demonstrates the interdependencies among objectives, policies, and strategies.[13]

Consider the situation of a boat going up a river. The organizational purpose represents the surrounding terrain; it influences the general flow and direction of the river. The primary objective is a harbor or stopping point some distance up the river to be reached by a certain time (Point B in Figure 4–5). Organizational performance objectives and other subordinate goals can be represented by other milestones between the boat's present position and the harbor. Policies are the river banks which help guide the boat toward the harbor. Like the river banks, policies remain in effect after the primary objective is reached. They are independent of time and must be reviewed as to applicability and consistency whenever new objectives are set. Strategy defines a major pattern of action for getting to the harbor (Point B) from where the boat currently is (Point A). This would involve stipulating such things as what kind of boat to use, what route to follow, and so on. Obviously the strategy selected depends on the specific harbor (objective) to be reached and the flow of the river (purpose and policies) between the boat and the harbor.

SUMMARY

The management process centers around predetermined organizational objectives. The objective setting process should begin at the top with a clear statement of the organization's purpose and should cascade down through the organizational hierarchy. In order to ensure continuity, short-range, departmental, sectional, and other objectives

---

[13] Rogers, *Corporate Strategy*, p. 13.

should be derived only after an in-depth evaluation of the long-range objectives.

Policies are broad, general guides to action which relate to goal attainment. Policies furnish communication channels, promote closer coordination among organizational elements, foster individual initiative, and ensure that all the organizational elements are operating under the same ground rules. When formulating policy, the policy maker must analyze several factors. He must appraise the organizational objectives; he must be cognizant of the social and ethical responsibilities of the organization; he must know the general policies of the competition; and he must identify current economic trends in the environment.

Strategy is a mix of goals and major policies which results in a specific action and usually requires the deployment of resources. The process of determining an organization's strategy, although very complex, can be broken down into four major stages: (1) identifying the opportunities and threats of the organization, (2) estimating the risk associated with the various possible opportunities and threats, (3) appraising the organization's strengths and weaknesses, and (4) matching the opportunities and capabilities at an acceptable level of risk.

REVIEW QUESTIONS

1. What is the purpose of organizational objectives or goals?

2. Describe the cascade approach to setting objectives.

3. What questions must be answered in identifying an organization's present business? What areas must be investigated in identifying an organization's future business?

4. List several areas for which objectives might be set by the organization.

5. What are policies? Describe in detail the pyramid of business policies.

6. Define the following types of policies: traditional policies, policies by fiat, and rational policies.

7. What factors must be analyzed in formulating policies?

8. What is strategy? Describe the strategy formulation process.

9. Describe four basic types of corporate strategies.

DISCUSSION QUESTIONS

1. What percentage of managers do you think have a clear understanding of what they are supposed to do? How might this percentage be improved?

2. Is it acceptable to have conflicting organizational objectives? Support your answer with examples.

3. "Policy should always be made at the top" is the belief of many managers. What do you think?

4. What is the relationship between organizational objectives, policies, and strategies?

5. "How can we develop long-term objectives and strategies when we do not know what we are going to do tomorrow?" is a question often posed by managers. How would you answer this question?

SELECTED READINGS

Carroll, Stephen J., and Henry L. Tosi, Jr. *Management by Objectives.* New York: The Macmillan Company, 1973.

Drucker, Peter F. *The Practice of Management.* New York: Harper and Brothers Publishers, 1954.

Etzioni, Amitai. "The Organizational Goal: Master or Servant," *Modern Organizations.* Englewood Cliffs, N.J.: Prentice-Hall, Inc., 1964.

Glueck, William F. *Business Policy: Strategy Formation and Executive Actions.* New York: McGraw-Hill Book Company, 1972.

Higginson, M. Valliant. *Management Policies I: Their Development as Corporate Guides.* New York: American Management Association, 1966.

———. *Management Policies II: Sourcebook of Statement.* New York: American Management Association, 1966.

Hughes, Charles L. *Goal Setting, Key to Individual and Organizational Effectiveness.* New York: American Management Association, 1965.

Humble, J. W. *Management by Objectives.* London: Industrial Education and Research Foundation, 1967.

Odiorne, George. *Management by Objectives.* New York: Pitman, 1964.

Raia, Anthony. *Managing by Objectives.* Glenview, Ill.: Scott, Foresman and Company, 1974.

Rogers, David C. D. *Corporate Strategy and Long Range Planning.* Ann Arbor, Mich.: The Landis Press, 1973.

Simon, Herbert A. "On the Concept of Organization Goal," *Administrative Science Quarterly*, vol. 9, no. 1 (June 1964), pp. 1–22.

Case 4–1

The Hudson Shoe Company

Mr. John Hudson, president of the Hudson Shoe Company, and his wife spent the month of February in Santo Oro in Central America on a long vacation. After two weeks, Mr. Hudson became restless and started thinking about an idea he had considered for several years but had been too busy to pursue—entering the foreign market.

Mr. Hudson's company, located in a midwestern city, was started some 50 years ago by his father, now deceased. It has remained a family enterprise, with his brother David in charge of production, his brother Sam the comptroller, and his brother-in-law Bill Owens taking care of product development. Bill and David share responsibility for quality control, and Bill often works with Sam on administrative matters and advertising campaigns. Many competent subordinates are also employed. The company has one of the finest reputations in the shoe industry. Their integrity of product and behavior is to be envied and is a source of great pride to the company.

During John's stay in Santo Oro, he decided to visit some importers of shoes. He spoke to several and was most impressed with Señor Lopez of Bueno Compania. After checking Señor Lopez's bank and personal references, his impression was confirmed. Señor Lopez said he would place a small initial order if the samples proved satisfactory. John immediately phoned his office and requested that they rush samples of their best numbers to Señor Lopez. These arrived a few days before John left for home. Shortly after arriving home, John was pleased to receive an order for 1,000 pairs of shoes from Señor Lopez.

John stayed in touch with Lopez by telephone and within two months after the initial order Hudson Shoe received an order for 5,000 additional pairs of shoes per month. Business continued at this level for about two years until Señor Lopez visited the plant. He was impressed and increased his monthly order from 5,000 to 10,000 pairs of shoes.

This precipitated a crisis at Hudson Shoe Company, and the family held a meeting. They had to decide whether to increase their capacity with a sizeable capital investment or drop some of their customers. They did not like the idea of eliminating loyal customers but did not want to make a major investment. David suggested that they run a second shift which solved the problem nicely.

A year later Lopez again visited and left orders for 15,000 pairs per month. He also informed them that more effort and expense was now required on his part for a wide distribution of the shoes. In addition to his regular five percent commission, he asked John for an additional commission of $1 per pair of shoes. When John hesitated, Lopez assured him that Hudson could raise their selling price by $1 and nothing would be lost. John felt uneasy but went along because the business was easy, steady, and most profitable. A few of Hudson's smaller customers had to be dropped.

By the end of the next year, Lopez was placing orders for 20,000 pairs per month and asked that Hudson bid on supplying boots for the entire police force of the capital city of Santo Oro. Hudson received the contract and within a year was also supplying the army and navy of Santo Oro and three other Central American countries with their needs.

Again, several old Hudson customers could not get their orders filled. Other Hudson customers were starting to complain of late deliveries. Also, Hudson seemed to be less willing to accept returns at the end of the season or to offer markdown allowances or advertising money. None of this was necessary with their export business. However, Hudson Shoe did decide to cling to their largest domestic customer—the largest mail order chain in the United States.

In June of the following year Lopez made a trip to Hudson Shoe. He informed John that in addition to his $1 per pair, it would also be necessary to give the Minister of Revenue $1 per pair if he was to continue granting import licenses. Moreover, the defense ministers, who approved the army and navy orders in each country where they did business, also wanted $1 per pair. Again, selling prices could be increased accordingly. Lopez informed John that shoe manufacturers in the United States and two other countries were most anxious to have this business at any terms. John asked for ten days to discuss this with his partners. Lopez agreed and returned home to await their decision. The morning of the meeting of the Board of Directors of the Hudson Shoe Company a wire was received from the large domestic chain stating that they would not be buying from Hudson next season. John Hudson called the meeting to order.

1. What were the objectives of Hudson Shoe?
2. What policies existed?
3. Do you agree with Hudson's strategy?
4. What would you do if you were John Hudson?

Case 4–2

Flexible rules

Joe Storrs works as a mechanic for the Vacation Rent-A-Car Company. He has been employed for six months and has been tardy about five times each month. His boss, Craig Terrell, called Joe in to discuss his tardiness. The following discussion occurred:

Craig: Joe, you have been tardy too much. I have no complaints about your work. You are doing an excellent job, but you must start getting here on time.

Joe: Well Craig, I didn't realize it was so important.

Craig: You know the rules.

Joe: Yes, I know the rules, but it seems that the rules are different for different people.

Craig: What do you mean?

Joe: Well, the rumor is that you and Susan James are dating and that you have clocked her in on several occasions when she was late.

Craig: We are not talking about Susan. We are talking about your tardiness. You are violating the rules and this must stop.

Joe: OK, but rules are for everyone. I intend to see my union steward to insure that Susan does not get special treatment.

1. Rules are for everyone. Do you agree?
2. What do you think will happen when the union steward enters the picture?

Objectives

1. To emphasize the importance of planning in the management process.
2. To discuss and illustrate different types and levels of plans.
3. To compare and contrast formal and informal planning as well as strategic and tactical planning.
4. To outline the role and responsibilities of an organization planner or a planning department.
5. To suggest a systematic approach to planning.

GLOSSARY OF TERMS

Budget A statement of expected results or requirements expressed in financial or numerical terms.

Forecasting The fourth step in the planning process; it involves making predictions about the future.

Formal plan A written, documented plan developed through an identifiable process.

Functional plans Plans that originate from the functional areas of an organization such as production, marketing, finance, and personnel.

Group plans Plans that originate from groups of units or subsidiary organizations which are regarded as separate profit centers.

Long-range plans Plans that generally pertain to a period which starts at the end of the current year and extends forward into the future.

Organization plans Plans that affect the organization as a whole and not just its parts.

Planning A process of deciding what objectives to pursue during a future time period and what to do in order to achieve those objectives.

Pro forma statements Statements which make certain financial projections concerning a specified future time period.

Regional plans Plans that originate from the various regional offices and plants of a multiregional organization.

Self-audit The first step in the planning process; it answers the question "Where are we now?"

Short-range plans Plans that can generally be defined as covering up to one year.

Strategic planning Planning that is concerned with the formulation of goals and the selection of the means by which the goals are attained.

Survey environment The second step in the planning process; it involves surveying factors which may influence the operation and success of the organization but are not under the control of the organization.

Tactical planning Planning that presupposes a set of goals handed down by a higher level in the organization and describes ways of attaining them.

Unit plans Plans that originate from operating units which have an identifiable business activity.

Planning: The fundamental function

Once upon a time there were two pigs (a third one had gone to market and disappeared) who were faced with the problem of protecting themselves from a wolf.

One pig was an old-timer in this wolf-fending business, and he saw the problem right away—just build a house strong enough to resist the huffing and puffing he had experienced before. So, the first pig built his wolf-resistant house right away out of genuine, reliable lath and plaster.

The second pig was green at this wolf business, but he was thoughtful. He decided that he would analyze the wolf problem a bit. He sat down and drew up a matrix (which, of course, is pig latin for a big blank sheet of paper) and listed the problem, analyzed the problem into components and possibilities of wolf strategies, listed the design objectives of his wolf-proof house, determined the functions that his fortress should perform, designed and built his house, and waited to see how well it worked.

All this time, the old-timer pig was laughing at the planner pig and vehemently declined to enter into this kind of folly. He had built wolf-proof houses before, and he had lived and prospered, hadn't he? He said to the planner pig, "If you know what you are doing, you don't have to go through all of that jazz." And with this, he went fishing, or rooting, or whatever it is that pigs do in their idle hours.

The second pig worked his system anyway, and designed for predicted contingencies.

One day the mean old wolf passed by the two houses (they both looked the same—after all, a house is just a house). He thought that a pig dinner was just what he wanted. He walked up to the first pig's house and uttered a warning to the old-timer, which was roundly rejected, as usual. With this, the wolf, instead of huffing and puffing, pulled out a sledge hammer, knocked the door down, and ate the old-timer for dinner.

Still not satisfied, the wolf walked to the planner pig's house

*and repeated his act. Suddenly, a trap door in front of the
house opened and the wolf dropped neatly into a deep, dark pit,
never to be heard from again.*

Morals: 1. *They are not making wolves like they used to.*
           2. *It's hard to teach old pigs new tricks.*
           3. *If you want to keep the wolf away from your door,
               you'd better plan ahead.*

Roger A. Kaufman*

PLANNING is the process of deciding what objectives to pursue during
a future time period and what to do in order to achieve those objectives. Thus, the process is composed of two major segments—(1) setting objectives and (2) determining the course of action to be used in
achieving those objectives. Planning is the management function that
produces and integrates objectives, policies, and strategies. Planning
answers three basic questions:

1. Where are we now?
2. Where do we want to be?
3. How can we get there from here?

The first question calls for an assessment of the present situation.
The second question involves determining the desired objectives.
The final question requires an outline of actions and an analysis of the
financial impact of those actions. It should be stressed that planning
is concerned with *future implications of current decisions,* not with
decisions to be made in the future.[1] The planner should examine how
current decisions will limit the scope of future actions.

Many authors separate the objective setting process from the
planning process. In such cases, planning is viewed in the more narrow sense of determining a course of action toward some predetermined goal or objective. At the upper levels of management, the
planning process usually does involve the setting of objectives. However, it is not uncommon for top management to dictate the objectives
for a division or department and then ask the respective manager to
develop a plan for attaining those objectives. The latter and more
narrow definition is sometimes referred to as action planning. Whether
or not the objective setting process is viewed as an integral part of the
planning process or as a precedent of the planning process, objectives
must be set before the planning process can be completed. Obviously,

---

* "Why System Engineering? A Fable" (original source unknown).

[1] David C. D. Rogers, *Corporate Strategy and Long Range Planning* (Ann Arbor,
Mich.: The Landis Press, 1973), p. 12.

it is not possible to outline a course of action for reaching some objective if one does not know what the objective is.

WHY PLAN?

The fable at the beginning of the chapter provided some insights into the reasons for planning. Planning is the primary management function and is inherent in everything a manager does. It is futile for a manager to attempt to perform the other management functions without having a plan. Managers who attempt to organize without a plan will find themselves reorganizing on a regular basis. The manager who attempts to staff without a plan will be constantly hiring and firing employees. Motivation is almost impossible in an organization characterized by continuous reorganization and excessive employee turnover.

Planning enables a manager or organization to affect rather than accept the future. By setting objectives and charting a course of action, the organization commits itself to "making it happen." Such a commitment allows the organization to affect the future. Without a planned course of action, the organization is much more likely to sit back and "let things happen" and then react to these happenings in a crisis mode.

Planning provides a means for actively involving personnel from all areas of the organization in the management of the organization. Involvement produces a multitude of benefits. First, soliciting inputs from throughout the organization improves the quality of the plans. Good suggestions concerning the future of the organization can come from any level in the organization. Involvement in the planning process also enhances the overall understanding of the organization's direction. Understanding the big picture can minimize friction between departments, sections, and individuals. Planning enables the sales department to understand and appreciate the goals of the production department and their relationship to organizational goals. Involvement in the planning process fosters a greater personal commitment to the plan because it develops an attitude toward the plan as "our plan" rather than "their plan." Positive attitudes created by involvement also improve the overall company morale and loyalty.

A final reason for planning is that it positively affects managerial effectiveness. Laboratory studies have demonstrated that employees who stressed planning earn very high performance ratings from supervisors.[2] Field studies have also shown that planning has a positive

---

[2] J. J. Hemphill, "Personal Variables and Administrative Styles," in *Behavioral Science and Educational Administration* (National Society for the Study of Education, 1964), chap. 8.

impact on the quality of work produced.[3] Another study showed that organizations using formal plans significantly outperformed organizations using informal plans with respect to several economic measures, such as return on investment and earnings.[4] Furthermore, this same study showed that the organizations using formal planning bettered the records they had achieved before formal planning was adopted. Not only does the evidence support a positive relationship between planning and performance, but the relationship appears to hold at all levels: the individual manager, decision-making groups, and the company as a whole.[5] The difference between formal and informal planning is discussed later in this chapter.

A DILEMMA

Planning is easiest where environmental change is least. Planning is most useful where environmental change is greatest. The environmental change since the Industrial Revolution has been unparalleled in man's history. Jean Predseil has uniquely presented a verbal picture of the incredible speed with which economic change has occurred.

Let us suppose that we can reduce to one year of 12 months the total duration of the known period of the history of man: some 30,000 years. In these 12 months which represent the life of all our ancestors from the Age of Stone until our days, it is toward the 18th of October that the Iron Age starts. It is the 8th of December that the Christian era begins.

It is on the 29th of December when Louis XVI ascends the throne of France. What mechanical power does mankind possess at that epoch?

Exactly the same as that which the caveman had possessed plus whatever he was able to derive from draft animals after the invention of the yoke.

By the 30th of December, in the first 18 minutes of the morning, Watt invents the steam engine. On the same day, the 30th of December, at 4 P.M. the first railway begins to operate.

And thus we reach the last day of the year. The 31st of December. At 5:31 A.M. Edison invents the first incandescent lamp. By afternoon, at 2:12 P.M. Bleriot crossed the Channel. And not until 4:14 P.M.

---

[3] A. L. Comrey, W. High, and R. C. Wilson, "Factors Influencing Organization Effectiveness: A Survey of Aircraft Workers," *Personnel Psychology*, vol. 8 (1955), pp. 79–99.

[4] S. Thune, "An Investigation into the Effect of Long-Range Planning in Selected Industries," unpublished M.B.A. thesis, Bernard M. Baruch College, School of Business, City University of New York, 1967; also S. Thune and R. J. House, "Where Long-Range Planning Pays Off," *Business Horizons*, August 1970, pp. 81–87.

[5] Alan C. Filley and R. J. House, *Managerial Process and Organizational Behavior* (Glenview, Ill.: Scott, Foresman and Company, 1969), p. 206.

does World War I begin. At this date Western man disposes of 8/10 of a horsepower: This is a notable and brutal progress because:

During the whole year he has lived with only 1/10 of a horsepower. In one day he has multiplied it by 8, but only five hours suffice to bring this figure to 80.

It is a fact that on the 31st of December at the 11th stroke of midnight Frenchmen dispose of 8 horsepower each. And at the same time, the Americans have 60 each while the inhabitants of New York 270 each. At precisely midnight there is the explosion of the first atomic bomb.[6]

Since this was written, man has been to the moon several times. There is no doubt that the rate of change of technology and the economy has been increasing at a staggering pace. This rapid rate of change has made planning much more difficult but also much more necessary. John Argenti, a British planning consultant, has described the present phenomenon as creating a vicious cycle which results in an ever-lengthening planning horizon accompanied by increased risks:

All types of planning, including strategic, have lately entered this vicious circle. Decisions are becoming more difficult; so it is necessary to spend longer on planning. If one spends longer on planning one must plan further ahead. If one plans further ahead it means making forecasts further into the future. The further ahead one forecasts the greater will be the level of uncertainty. The greater the uncertainty the more difficult the decision—and so back to the start of the vicious circle of spending longer on the planning, planning still further ahead with still more errors in the forecast and so on.[7]

Any good plan has built in contingencies and alternatives. One real payoff in planning comes from the search and identification of contingencies. The search process causes the planners to consider events and evaluate their potential impact on the organization. If and when such events occur, the organization is in a much better position to take the proper actions. The fable presented at the beginning of this chapter very clearly exemplifies the need for contingency planning.

---

[6] Reprinted by permission of the publisher from R. Nordling, "Social Responsibilities of Today's Industrial Leader," quoting Jean Predseil, S.A.M. *Advanced Management Journal*, April 1957, © 1957 by Society for Advancement of Management, pp. 19–20. All rights reserved.

[7] John Argenti, *Systematic Corporate Planning* (New York: Halsted Press, 1974), p. 23.

FORMAL PLANNING

All managers plan. The difference lies in the methods employed and the extent to which they plan. Most planning is carried out on an informal or casual basis. This occurs when the planner does not record his thoughts but rather carries them around in his head. A formal plan can be defined as a written, documented plan developed through an identifiable process. Figure 5–1 highlights the strengths of formal planning as compared to informal planning.

FIGURE 5–1
General characteristics of formal planning versus informal planning

Formal planning	Informal planning
Rational	Emotional
Systematic	Disorganized
Regular intervals	Sporadic episodes
Future improvement	Past evaluation
Hard document	Memory

The absence of a formal planning system often results in continuous fire fighting behavior by managers. Unless a formal system has been established with objectives and schedules, daily problems generally receive precedence over planning.

Additionally, formal planning enhances the integration of managerial activity in organizations. A formal planning process forces collaboration between organizational subunits, such as the functional areas of marketing, production, finance, and accounting.

Of course the sophistication of formal planning processes can vary greatly. One organization might have a 2-page formal plan while another has a 200-page document. The appropriate degree of sophistication depends on the needs of the individual organization. The environment, size, and type of business are factors which typically affect the planning needs of an organization.

PLANNING HORIZON: SHORT-RANGE VERSUS LONG-RANGE

Short-range plans can generally be defined as those plans covering up to one year. Long-range planning pertains to a period which starts at the end of the current year and extends forward into the future.

FIGURE 5–2
Short-range versus long-range planning

	Short range (1 year)	*Long range (over 1 year)*
	(quantified—included in quarterly budgets and action programs)	*(broadly quantified as long-range plans in corporate development)*
Basic objectives, guidelines, and policy	Profits and sales Costs Finance	Growth Reduction Finance
Capital expenditures	Minor items, expendables, and short-life equipment	Basic equipment, buildings, infrastructures, and land
Sales	By salesman, products, customers and markets, home sales and promotions	By markets and industries Exports
Personnel	Operating and clerical classes	Supervisory, middle and top management
R&D, design	Fashion goods, short-life items, etc.	Basic research, especially associated with human, animal, and plant health, and items of high capital cost
Broad classes from the gross domestic product	Few, if any	Agriculture, forestry, and fishing Construction Gas, electricity, and water, transport and communications Distributive trades, insurance, banking etc., public administration, defense, health, and education
Examples of manufactured goods	Short life-cycle products, fashion goods, toiletries, household products, items for decoration, retail articles, etc.	Longer life-cycle products, motor cars, chemicals, textiles, food, consumer durables, basic commodities, etc. Houses, biological chemicals, basic commodities, high technology content products, etc.

Source: Adapted from Harry Jones, *Preparing Company Plans* (New York: Halsted Press, 1974), p. 39.

The question of "How long should a long-range plan be?" cannot be answered specifically. Circumstances vary from organization to organization, and therefore, the appropriate time frame varies with the nature of the specific environment and activity. What may be long-range for an organization operating in a rapidly changing environment may be short-range for an organization operating in a relatively static environment. In practice, most long-range plans span three to five years into the future (see Figure 5–2).[8]

Formal long-range planning did not become popular until after World War II. A 1939 survey conducted by Stanford University found that about half of the 31 companies interviewed made plans in some detail up to a year in advance.[9] However, only 2 of the 31 firms established plans for as long as five years. A 1956 survey by the National Industrial Conference Board found that 142 out of 189 responding organizations employed planning programs further than one year ahead.[10] A 1973 survey by one of the authors revealed that 328 out of 398 organizations did prepare some form of documented long-range plan covering at least three years.[11]

Several developments have contributed to the increased attention given to long-range planning. First, the rate of technological change has increased continually since World War II. Expenditures for research and development have increased almost exponentially during the past 30 years. The post-war era has also resulted in continuous expansion in size and complexity of firms. Such rapid growth in size and complexity requires extensive forward planning. More recently, the development and refinement of digital computers and sophisticated mathematical models have added to the potential and precision of long-range planning. Finally, the post-war economy has succeeded in avoiding the radical fluctuations experienced in the earlier decades of the 20th century. This phenomenon has made longer term planning more realistic.

TACTICAL VERSUS STRATEGIC PLANNING

Management writers have also categorized planning as either tactical or strategic. Russell Achoff has identified three differences

---

[8] Leslie W. Rue, "The How and Who of Long-Range Planning," *Business Horizons*, December 1973, p. 29.

[9] Paul E. Holden, Lounsbury S. Fish, and Hubert L. Smith, *Top-Management Organization and Control* (New York: McGraw-Hill Book Company, 1941), p. 405.

[10] Arthur D. Baker, Jr. and G. Clark Thompson, "Long-Range Planning Pays Off," *Conference Board Business Record*, October 1956, pp. 435–43.

[11] Leslie W. Rue, "Tools and Techniques of Long-Range Planners," *Long Range Planning*, October 1974, p. 1.

between strategic and tactical planning.[12] The first is concerned with their respective ranges in time. Generally, very short-range plans are considered to be tactical. Production schedules and day-to-day action plans are normally regarded as tactical. The question then becomes "How long must the range of planning be in order to be strategic?" As with long-range planning, there is no one answer. The second distinction involves the number of organizational functions affected by the plan. The more functions affected, the more strategic the plan. Strategic plans are broad in scope while tactical plans are narrow. A corporate level plan is likely to be more strategic than a production plan. The third and final distinction deals with the emphasis on the establishment of goals. Strategic planning is concerned with the formulation of goals and the selection of the means by which the goals are to be attained. Tactical planning presupposes a set of goals handed down by a higher level in the organization and describes ways of attaining them.

Thus strategic planning is long-range organization planning that is goal oriented. Organizational strategy results from strategic planning. Tactical planning is concerned with a short-time span and emphasizes the actions necessary to attain a given set of goals. It should be noted that the distinctions made between tactical and strategic planning are relative and not absolute. A plan may be more strategic than tactical. In practice, the terms strategic planning and long-range planning are often used interchangeably. This is not in conflict with our definition of a long-range plan because long-range planning usually affects most of the organization and is goal oriented. In other words, a long-range plan usually meets the additional requirements of a strategic plan.

ORIGIN OF ORGANIZATION PLANS

The origin of a plan depends on several organizational factors. Some of these factors include the size of the organization, the complexity of the organization, the structure of the organization, and the operating environment of the organization. Depending on these factors, five basic types of plans can be described:[13]

1. Unit or divisional plans
2. Functional plans
3. Regional (geographic) plans

---

[12] Russell Ackoff, "A Concept of Corporate Planning," *Long Range Planning*, September 1970, p. 3.

[13] Harry Jones, *Preparing Company Plans* (New York: Halsted Press, 1974), p. 31.

4. Group plans (groups of units or subsidiary organizations)
5. Organization plans

Unit or divisional plans originate from operating units that have an identifiable activity. For example, a manufacturer of electric motors may have a retail and a wholesale division, each of which prepares its own plan. Likewise, service or governmental organizations may have subunits that have separate, identifiable activities with each unit preparing its own plan.

Functional plans originate from the functional areas of a organization such as production, marketing, finance, and personnel. Functional plans are necessary when the functional units are treated as separate cost centers.

Regional or geographic plans originate from either various regional offices or plants of a multiregional organization. The regions are generally defined on a geographic basis.

Group plans originate from groups of units or subsidiary organizations which are regarded as separate profit centers. A profit center is any subunit of an overall organization which is responsible for its own individual profits. The Buick division of General Motors is an example of a profit center. Buick is responsible as a unit for its profits (as opposed to including Buick's profits in with the other divisions and arriving at one profit figure for General Motors).

Organization plans, called corporate plans in a business environment, refer to those plans that affect the organization as a whole and not just parts of it. Organization plans may exist for each unit making up a conglomerate or multicompany organization. Figure 5–3 demonstrates the kinds of plans that might exist in a simple, divisional business organization. Figure 5–4 shows the various types of plans and how they might fit together in a large multidivisional, multifunctional organization.

While unit or divisional plans are the lowest level of plan outlined above, planning can take place at the departmental, sectional,

FIGURE 5–3
Plans in a basic type organization

Source: Harry Jones, *Preparing Company Plans* (New York: Halsted Press, 1974), p. 32.

FIGURE 5–4
Plans in a multidivisional, multifunctional organization

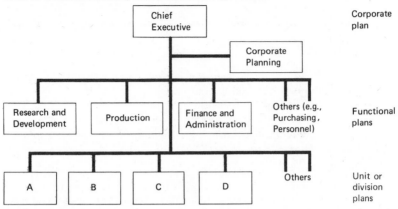

Source: Harry Jones, *Preparing Company Plans* (New York: Halsted Press, 1974), p. 32.

and individual levels. The procedures and methods necessary to prepare a plan do not differ significantly at the various planning levels; what does differ are the content and the level of the information used in developing the plan.

THE ORGANIZATION PLANNING SYSTEM

This chapter has examined planning as it relates to the needs of various levels of the organization. The organization planning system is the framework that ties the various plans and levels together. The organization planning system ensures that short-range plans are in accord with long-range plans and that the various level plans mesh together in an effort to accomplish the goals of the organization as a whole, not just parts of it.

Generally, an organization planner or planning department is used for the purpose of directing the organization planning system. In very small organizations, a part-time advisor or visiting consultant might fill the role. Many think it is a mistake to have a full-time employee function as an organization planner in addition to other duties and responsibilities. The reasoning is that the day-to-day problems often seem more urgent than the longer term problems and thus take precedence. The end result often is that the part-time organization planner spends all the time with daily problems and rarely plans for the long term. Figure 5–5 outlines the functions and related activities of the organization planner.

Although the organization planner and planning department have wide-ranging duties and responsibilities as outlined in Figure 5–5,

FIGURE 5–5
Functions and activities of the organization planner

Basic function
To ensure that plans are made at all levels.

Organizational relationships
1. Reports to: chief executive.
2. Supervises: staff assistants.
3. Other contacts: corporate executives, heads of business divisions and functions, and through them the appropriate members of their staffs.

Activities and responsibilities
Methodology
1. Prepare an agreed planning system, appropriate to the organization and the interests of the firm, in which the participation of the heads of key departments is specified.
2. Ensure that the planning system and the roles of the participants are known and understood through their presentation in a corporate planning manual which embraces detailed formats, instructions, and timetables for the annual cycles of planning, and for the monitoring and control of activities.
3. Continuously revise and update the manual so that it always reflects the planning needs of the company and developments in planning techniques.

Formal activities
As a staff executive, act on behalf of the chief executive at all the key stages of planning, and assist:
1. In the preparation of planning documents.
2. In the coordination and integration of unit plans.
3. In the preparation of the corporate plan.
4. In the control procedures for reporting on progress toward goals.

Functional activities
1. Participate in the determination of basic corporate objectives, guidelines, and policy.
2. Propose basic economic and general assumptions.
3. Propose specific business objectives, primarily at corporate level but also for business divisions and functions.
4. Assist the chief executive and others in the identification and selection of strategies to achieve the objectives.
5. Participate in the challenge of unit plans and ensure that they are consistent with the overall objectives of the company.
6. Through liaison between executives, ensure coordination between the plans of different units.
7. Integrate unit plans in the preparation of the corporate plan.

FIGURE 5–5 (Continued)

8. Assist and advise all executives in the preparation and presentation of their plans.
9. Organize and participate in periodic reviews and reporting of progress toward objectives.

Specific functional activities
1. Prepare the information base for the company as a whole, particularly concerning political, economic, sociological, legal, fiscal, and monetary matters; also in respect of general trends in business, industry, and markets.
2. Identify corporate opportunities for the growth of profitability in the context of external trends, especially in technology, competition developments, and diversification expansion goals. Recognize internal improvement opportunities in the light of strengths, weaknesses, and resources.
3. Propose objectives and strategies to exploit the growth opportunities in the preceding activity.
4. Keep abreast of developments in management techniques which are of assistance in planning.

Source: Adapted from Harry Jones, *Preparing Company Plans* (New York: Halsted Press, 1974), p. 44.

their overriding objective is to systematize and coordinate all the planning efforts of the organization. Therefore, their activities require constant interaction with the other elements of the organization.

PLANNING IN PRACTICE

Although the practice of planning may vary from industry to industry, firm to firm, and even within the different components of the same organization, certain steps must be followed in developing and implementing all plans, regardless of the level of the organizational unit preparing the plan. The relative attention devoted to each step may vary but not the value of their presence. The following steps for a successful plan should not be treated as mutually exclusive events but rather should be viewed as overlapping and interacting components of the planning system.

Self-audit

The first step in the planning process is a self-audit. A self-audit answers the question "Where are we now?" Before an organizational unit can set realistic objectives it must know where it stands. In practice, a checklist of factors should be used in auditing the organization on a periodic basis. A typical checklist might include the following factors:

1. Financial position.
2. Condition of facilities and equipment.
3. Quantity and quality of personnel.
4. Appropriateness of organizational structure.
5. Major policies and strategies.
6. Competitive position.
7. Profitability of various product lines.

Survey environment

The second step in the planning process is a survey of the environmental and external factors of the organizational unit preparing the plan. Generally this includes factors which may influence the operation and success of the organizational unit but are not under the control of that unit. For top levels in the organization the environmental factors include those factors external to and not under the control of the organization. For a department, the environment might include other departments within the organization in addition to factors outside the organization. Ignoring environmental factors is similar to an ostrich burying its head in the sand. By developing an awareness of the external environment, the organization can better respond to change. Some general areas which might be surveyed are:

1. Population growth and movement.
2. Economic conditions and their effect on product or service demand.
3. Government regulation (taxes, wage and price controls, OSHA, pollution control, equal opportunity).
4. Labor supply.
5. Competitors.
6. Suppliers.
7. Financial community.
8. Social attitudes.

Set objectives

Once the self-audit and environmental survey have been completed, management can set objectives. The actual process of selecting objectives involves the application of the decision-making concepts of Chapter 3. Many different objectives are considered in the process of selecting the combination that best reflects the aims of the entire organization. Chapter 4 discussed in detail the process of setting objectives.

Forecast

Planning is incomplete unless predictions are made about the future. Although the level of sophistication may vary greatly, most managers engage in some type of forecasting.

The most common method of forecasting is to use a jury of opinion. This method is practiced whenever forecasts are based on the opinions of experts and/or top management. Such a method has the advantage of being simple but the disadvantage of not necessarily being based on facts.

A second common method of forecasting is to use a sales force composite. A sales force composite is obtained by combining the views of salesmen and sales managers as to expected sales. This method is based on the belief that those actually doing the selling should have the best knowledge of the market. However, a potential problem is that salesmen may tend to be overly optimistic or pessimistic. If a salesman is working under a quota system, he may be overly conservative; if he wants more liberal expenses, he may tend to be overly optimistic. In other words, the forecast may be biased due to external, nonfactual factors.

A third general method of forecasting is to survey major customers as to their expected purchases. The user's expectation method obviously works best in situations where a small number of customers account for a large portion of the organization's business. Such a system can tap information not normally available. However, to be successful, a feeling of mutual trust must exist between the parties. The customer's intentions must not be interpreted as commitments. There is also the danger of large estimates by the customer to ensure availability.

Statistics and mathematical methods represent the most sophisticated and reliable approach to forecasting. The advent and growth of the electronic computer has made statistical and mathematical forecasting not only possible, but feasible. Such methods include time series analyses, regression and correlation analyses, and simulation experiments. A major drawback to the use of statistical and mathematical methods is the cost of gathering and analyzing data. Another drawback is that most statistical and mathematical analyses are based on historical data which may not be representative of the future.

State resource requirements

After the forecasts and objectives have been developed, they must be converted into actual resource requirements. Anticipated demands must be translated into labor, material, floor space, and equipment requirements. Schedules for arriving at the resource levels required should be developed. Naturally, the more reliable the forecasts, the easier it is to develop accurate resource requirements.

A major part of stating the resource requirements in many organizations is the budgeting process. A budget is a statement of expected results or requirements expressed in financial or numerical terms. Because budgets are also used extensively in the control process, they will be discussed at length in Chapter 8.

Develop pro forma statements

Once objectives have been set, forecasts made, and resource requirements determined, pro forma financial statements should be developed to evaluate the feasibility of the plans. Basically pro forma statements forecast the future financial impact of a particular course of action (plan). Cash flow statements, balance sheets, and income statements are the most frequently used pro forma statements.

Control the plan

All too often a plan is developed and placed in a bottom file drawer never to be looked at again. Periodically the plan should be reviewed and compared with actual events to determine any major deviations between the plan and reality. If major deviations have occurred, they should be analyzed and then the proper adjustments should be made in the organization or to the plan. It may be that certain environmental factors beyond the control of the organization have changed and thus the plan needs updating. On the other hand, it may be that certain problems have arisen within the organization that need to be corrected. The frequency with which a plan is formally reviewed varies with the application, but a good rule of thumb is to review it at least quarterly.

Figure 5–6 outlines the sequence of events included in the planning process.

SUMMARY

Planning is the process of deciding what objectives to pursue during a future time period and what to do in order to achieve those ob-

FIGURE 5–6
The planning process

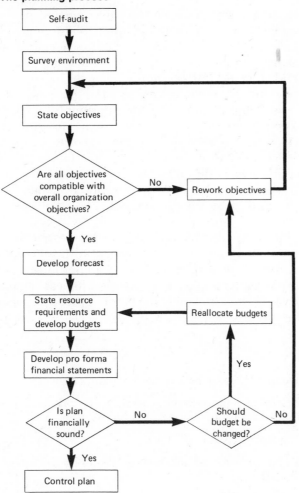

jectives. Planning is concerned with future implications of current decisions and how the current decisions might limit the scope of future actions.

When properly practiced, planning has many positive effects on an organization. It allows management to affect rather than accept the future, it provides a means for actively involving personnel from all areas of the organization, and it can positively affect individual and organizational performance. Implementation of planning presents a serious dilemma for the planner. It is easiest where environmental change is least, yet it is most useful where environmental change is greatest.

Formal planning results in a written, documented plan and has several advantages over informal planning. Short-range plans are generally defined as those plans covering up to one year. Long-range planning pertains to a period which starts at the end of the current year and extends forward into the future.

Strategic planning is long-range organization planning and is concerned with the determination and identification of goals. Tactical planning is concerned with a short time span and emphasizes the means and actions necessary to attain a given set of goals.

Plans may be generated at almost any level or functional area of an organization. The five basic types of plans are unit, functional, regional, group, and organization. An organization planning system is the framework used to tie the various plans together within an organization.

Although the practice of planning may vary from organization to organization, certain steps must be followed in developing and implementing a plan. These steps consist of performing a self-audit, surveying the environment, setting objectives, forecasting the future, stating the resource requirements, developing pro forma statements, and controlling the plan.

REVIEW QUESTIONS

1. What is planning? What questions does planning answer?

2. Discuss the relationship between objectives and planning. Give an example of this relationship.

3. Why is it necessary to plan?

4. Distinguish between formal and informal planning. How is most planning conducted?

5. Explain the difference between tactical and strategic planning.

6. Describe the five basic types of plans.

7. Discuss the steps in the planning process.

DISCUSSION QUESTIONS

1. Can you resolve the dilemma that planning is easiest where environmental change is least but more useful where environmental change is greatest?

2. If you were serving as a planning consultant how might you answer the question "How can I plan for next year when I don't even know what I'm going to do tomorrow?"

3. With the rapid pace of change in today's world, why should management try to plan ahead?

4. What are some of the problems that an organization planner might experience in attempting to coordinate the plans of various subunits?

5. Discuss the following statement: "Planning is something a manager should do when he has nothing else to do."

SELECTED READINGS

Ackoff, Russell. "A Concept of Corporate Planning," *Long Range Planning* (September 1970), pp. 2–8.

Argenti, John. *Systematic Corporate Planning*. New York: Halsted Press, 1974.

Chambers, J. C., S. K. Mullick, and D. A. Goodman. "Catalytic Agent for Effective Planning," *Harvard Business Review* (January–February 1971), pp. 110–19.

Golightly, H. O. "What Makes a Company Successful?" *Business Horizons* (June 1971).

Jones, Harry. *Preparing Company Plans*. New York: Halsted Press, 1974.

LeBreton, P., and D. A. Henning. *Planning Theory*. Englewood Cliffs, N.J.: Prentice-Hall, Inc., 1961.

Litschert, Robert J. "Some Characteristics of Organization for Long-Range Planning," *Academy of Management Journal*, vol. 10, no. 3 (September 1967), pp. 247–56.

————. "Some Characteristics of Long-Range Planning: An Industry Study," *Academy of Management Journal*, vol. 11, no. 3 (September 1968), pp. 315–28.

Mason, R. H. "Developing a Planning Organization," *Business Horizons* (August 1969), pp. 61–69.

Most, K. S. "Wanted: A Planning Model for the Firm," *Managerial Planning* (July–August 1973), pp. 1–6.

Rue, Leslie W. "Tools and Techniques of Long-Range Planners," *Long Range Planning* (October 1974), pp. 61–65.

————. "The How and Who of Long-Range Planning," *Business Horizons* (December 1973), pp. 23–30.

Steiner, G. A. *Top Management Planning*. New York: The Macmillan Company, 1969.

————. "Rise of the Corporate Planner," *Harvard Business Review* (September–October 1970), pp. 133–39.

Wheelwright, S. S. "Strategic Planning in the Small Business," *Business Horizons* (August 1971), pp. 51–58.

Case 5-1

What's the plan?

Write Way Pen Company was founded in 1925 to make mechanical pencils. With the advent of the ball-point pen in 1940, they added this to their product line. In 1950, the marketing manager discovered a Vu-Lighter, which was being marketed by a small obscure company and purchased it to round out the product line.

During this period, profits were high because selling prices were set by competition and had no relation to cost. Materials were abundant with dealers carrying stock available for instant delivery. Due to material costs being a minor part of total cost, no material control or forecasting procedures were utilized, and parts or raw stock were ordered as needed.

In the late 1960s, two simultaneous changes occurred which affected this situation. Material, once plentiful, began to become more scarce. Lead times lengthened and prices quadrupled. In addition, competition suddenly became tougher due to the entrance of Gillette and Bic into the market.

With the new competition, prices were reduced for the product while costs soared. But Gillete and Bic, through large volume purchasing and automated production lines, made money, while the previous leaders lost money and sales.

The following personnel are employed by Write Way Pen:

Jim Jones is a dynamic young accountant now executive vice president.

John Smith is marketing manager and sales forecaster. John hopes to recoup the market share of Write Way Pen.

Milford Bachtel is the controller and material control manager. His goal is reducing inventory, increasing the inventory turnover, and maintaining production levels.

Jack Armstrong is an ambitious purchasing manager trying to meet all the inventory goals simultaneously.

At a meeting in which all the above are in attendance the following transpires:

Jim Jones: We're going to operate this company efficiently. I want you to meet all your goals, and in addition we must ship all our customer orders within seven days.

Milford Bachtel: Will I be able to build a finished goods inventory based on our average semiannual production requirements?

Jim Jones: No, we'll manufacture a month ahead or to customer orders. We'll live by the forecast, right John?

John Smith: That's right; it's a good forecast, and we'll be revising it as necessary.

Jack Armstrong: Can I order for six months into the future with scheduled deliveries?

Milford Bachtel: No, we want to turn the inventory six times a year, and we'll only be manufacturing a month in advance. So only order three months out with split deliveries.

Jack Armstrong: You know that lead times for most materials are now six to eight weeks?

Milford Bachtel: Just use the forecast and review it frequently.

Two months later there's a sudden crisis. A number of critical materials have run out and additional deliveries are four weeks away. The production lines are shut down and customers are cancelling orders.

Jim Jones: What's wrong with you people? I thought we told you how to manage this program.

Milford Bachtel: Jack, I thought we told you to watch the forecast and the actual orders and respond accordingly. You've let us run out! What happened?

Jack Armstrong: Well, in two months' time we've used up enough material for the first four months of the forecast. I ordered the way you said, and that didn't account for such an unexpected high volume of sales.

John Smith: Just because I forecast month by month doesn't mean it'll happen on exactly that date. You should be more flexible.

Jim Jones: Milford, you and Jack get together and figure this out so it doesn't happen again. Remember inventory must be kept low if we're going to make a profit.

1. What went wrong?
2. What suggestions would you make to Write Way Pen?

Case 5–2

Planning by a student

Susan Good is a senior majoring in management at the local university. She has been an excellent student with a 3.4 out of a 4.0 grade point average. However, she really hasn't decided on what she wants to do. Her interviews for jobs through the university placement office have confused her even more. Each interviewer has asked her what she wanted to do, and she really had no adequate answer. Because of her dilemma, Susan went by to see Professor Chapman, one of her management professors, and discussed the problem with him. His reply was:

> Your problem is not all that unusual. Many students feel the same way. Why don't you use some of the planning concepts you have learned in management and develop a personal career plan?

1. Can general planning concepts be used for personal career planning?
2. Develop a five-year career plan for your own career.

Objectives

1. *To introduce the organizing function and to show how organization is achieved through division of labor.*
2. *To discuss the role of authority and related concepts and principles.*
3. *To present several types of organization structures and to explore the relationships between organization structure, environment, and technology.*
4. *To develop an appreciation for the contingency approach to organization theory.*

GLOSSARY OF TERMS

Authority The right to command and expend resources.

Centralized organization A type of organization in which little authority is delegated to lower levels of management.

Decentralized organization A type of organization in which a great deal of authority is delegated to lower levels of management.

Departmentation A form of division of labor that involves grouping activities into related work units.

Exception principle States that a manager should concentrate his efforts on matters which deviate significantly from normal and let his subordinates handle routine matters.

Informal organization The aggregate of the personal contacts and interactions and the associated groupings of people working within the formal organization.

Job depth Refers to the freedom of the worker to plan and organize his own work, to work at his own pace, and to move around and communicate as desired.

Job scope Refers to the number of different types of operations performed.

Line and staff organization A type of organization that results when staff specialists are added to a line organization.

Line functions Those functions and activities of the organization that are directly involved in producing the organization's goods or services.

Line organization An organization whose structure is characterized by direct vertical links between the different levels of the organization.

Matrix organization A hybrid type of organization formed by individuals assigned from different functional areas to work on a specific project or task.

Organization A group of people working together in some type of concerted or coordinated effort to attain objectives.

Organization structure The framework which defines the boundaries of the formal organization and within which the organization operates.

Organizing The grouping of activities necessary to attain common objectives and the assignment of each grouping to a manager who has the authority necessary to supervise the people performing the activities.

Parity principle States that authority and responsibility must coincide.

Power The ability to command or apply force and is not necessarily accompanied by authority.

Responsibility Accountability for the attainment of objectives, the use of resources, and the adherence to organizational policy.

Scalar principle States that authority in the organization flows, one link at a time, through the chain of managers ranging from the highest to lowest ranks.

Span of control Refers to the number of subordinates a manager can effectively manage.

Staff functions Functions that are advisory and supportive in nature and are designed to contribute to the efficiency and maintenance of the organization.

Unity of command States that an employee should have one and only one immediate boss.

6

Organizing: The ordering function

If the employer fails to apportion the work among his assistants, it is likely that they will duplicate one another's work. If he neglects to distinguish between the kinds of work as promptly as the amount of endeavor permits, he will lose the advantages of specialization. If he delays too long in appointing supervisors, with the result that the task of oversight exceeds his capacity, the work will not be as well done as it might. Any of these errors reduces, if it does not prevent, the success of the enterprise. In each case, organization has been neglected; it has not performed its mission as a means to more effective concerted endeavor.

Alvin Brown*

MOST WORK today is accomplished by organizations. An organization is a group of people working together in some type of concerted or coordinated effort to attain objectives. As such, an organization provides a vehicle for accomplishing objectives that could not be achieved by individuals working separately. The process of organizing is the grouping of activities necessary to attain common objectives and the assignment of each grouping to a manager who has the authority necessary to supervise the people performing the activities.[1] Thus, organizing is basically a process of division of labor accompanied by appropriate delegation of authority. As illustrated in the above introductory quote, proper organizing results in the better use of resources. The framework which defines the boundaries of the formal organiza-

---

* *Organization of Industry,* Prentice-Hall, 1947, p. 15.

[1] Harold Koontz and Cyril O'Donnell, *Principles of Management: An Analysis of Managerial Functions,* 4th ed. (New York: McGraw-Hill Book Company, 1968), p. 231.

117

tion and within which the organization operates is the organization structure. A second and equally important element of an organization is the informal organization. The informal organization refers to the aggregate of the personal contacts and interactions and the associated groupings of people working within the formal organization.[2] The informal organization has a structure but it is not formally and consciously designed.

DIVISION OF LABOR

Organizing is basically a process of division of labor. The merits of dividing labor have been known for centuries. Taking the very simple task of manufacturing a pin, Adam Smith in 1776 demonstrated how much more efficiently the task could be performed through division of labor.[3]

Labor can be divided either vertically or horizontally. Vertical division of labor is based on the establishment of lines of authority and defines the levels that make up the vertical organizational structure. In addition to establishing authority, vertical division of labor facilitates the flow of communication within the organization.

Horizontal division of labor is based on specialization of work. The basic assumption underlying horizontal division of labor is that by making each worker's task specialized, more work can be produced with the same effort through increased efficiency and quality. Specifically, horizontal division of labor can result in the following advantages:

1. Fewer skills required per person.
2. Easier to specify the skills required for selection or training purposes.
3. Repetition or practice of the same job develops proficiency.
4. Efficient use of skills by primarily utilizing each worker's best skills.
5. The ability to have concurrent operations.
6. More conformity in the final product if each piece is always produced by the same person.

The major problem with horizontal division of labor is that it can result in job boredom and even degradation of the worker. An extreme example of horizontal division of labor is the automobile assembly line. It is not hard to imagine the behavioral problems associated with

---

[2] Chester Barnard, *Functions of the Executive* (Cambridge, Mass.: Harvard University Press, 1938), pp. 114–15.

[3] Adam Smith, *The Wealth of Nations* (New York: Modern Library, Inc., 1917); originally published in 1776.

such an assembly line. Before discussing the problems associated with horizontal division of labor, it is necessary to identify two dimensions of the job: scope and depth.[4]

Job scope refers to the number of different types of operations performed. In performing a job with narrow scope, the worker would perform few operations and repeat the cycle frequently. The negative effects of jobs lacking in scope vary with the person performing the job but can result in more errors and lower quality.

Job depth refers to the freedom of the worker to plan and organize his own work, to work at his own pace, and to move around and communicate as desired. A lack of job depth can result in job dissatisfaction and work avoidance which can in turn lead to absenteeism, tardiness, and even sabotage.

Divison of labor is not more efficient or even desirable in all situations. At least two basic requirements must exist for the use of division of labor. The first requirement is a relatively large volume of work. Enough volume must be produced to allow for specialization and also to keep each worker busy. A second basic requirement is stability in the volume of work, worker attendance, quality of raw materials, product design, and production technology.

DEPARTMENTATION

Departmentation is the most frequently used method for implementing division of labor. Departmentation involves grouping activities into related work units. The work units may be related on the basis of work functions, product, customer, geography, technique, or time.

Functional departmentation

Functional departmentation occurs when organization units are defined by the nature of the work. Although different terminology may be used, most organizations have three basic functions—production, sales, and finance. Production refers to the actual creation of something of value, either goods or services or both. The distribution of the goods or services created is usually referred to as sales or marketing. Finally any organization, whether manufacturing or service, must provide the financial structure necessary for carrying out its activities.

Each of the above basic functions may be further subdivided as

---

[4] Alan Filley and Robert House, *Managerial Process and Organizational Behavior* (Glenview, Ill.: Scott, Foresman and Company, 1969), p. 214.

necessary. For instance, the production department may be departmentalized into maintenance, quality control, engineering, manufacturing, and so on. The marketing department may be grouped into advertising, sales, and research. Figure 6–1 illustrates a typical organization with functional departmentalization.

The primary advantage of functional departmentation is that it allows for specialization within functions. It also provides for efficient use of equipment and resources. Functional departmentation, however, can be accompanied by some negative effects. Members of a functional group may develop more loyalty to the functional group's goals than to the organization's goals. If the group's goals and the

FIGURE 6–1
Functional departmentation

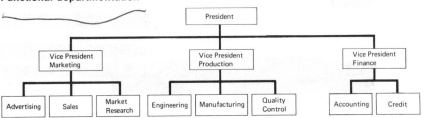

organization's goals are divergent, such activity can lead to suboptimization. Conflict may also develop between different departments striving for different goals. This type of conflict is discussed in greater depth in Chapter 11.

Product departmentation

Under departmentation by product or service, all the activities necessary to produce and market a product or service are usually under a single manager. Product departmentation allows individuals to identify with a particular product and thus develop esprit de corps. It also facilitates managing each product as a different profit center. Product departmentation provides opportunities for training executive personnel by allowing them to experience a broad range of functional activities. Problems can arise under product departmentation if departments become overly competitive to the detriment of the overall organization. A second potential shortcoming of product departmentation is that duplication of facilities and equipment may be necessary. Product departmentation is most adaptable to large, multi-product organizations (see Figure 6–2).

FIGURE 6–2
Product departmentation

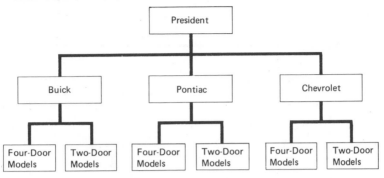

Geographic departmentation

Departmentation by territories is most likely to occur in organizations which maintain physically dispersed and autonomous operations or offices. Geographic departmentation permits the use of local workers and/or salespeople. This can create customer goodwill and an awareness of local feelings and desires. Geographic departmentation can also provide a high level of service.

Customer departmentation

Another type of departmentation is based on division by customers served. A common example is an organization which has one department to handle retail customers and one to handle wholesale or industrial customers.

Other types of departmentation

In addition to the above most popular types of departmentation, several other types are possible. Departmentation by simple numbers is practiced when the most important ingredient to success is number of workers. Organizing for a local Community Chest drive might be an example. Departmentation by process or equipment is another possibility. Not totally different from functional departmentation, activities can be grouped according to the equipment or process used. A final type of departmentation is by time or shift. Organizations that work around the clock may departmentalize according to shift.

Departmentation is practiced not only to implement division of labor but also to improve control and communications. Because of

FIGURE 6-3
Possible departmentation mixes for a sales organization

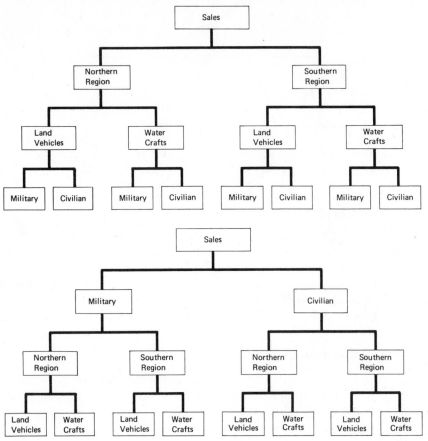

the advantages and disadvantages associated with the various types of departmentation, most organizations do not use the same type of departmentation at all levels of the organization. Figure 6–3 presents two different departmentation mixes that are possible for a sales organization.

REASONS FOR ORGANIZING

One of the primary reasons for organizing is to establish lines of authority. Establishing lines of authority creates order within the group. The absence of authority almost always leads to chaotic situations in which everyone is telling everyone else what to do.

Secondly, organizing improves the efficiency and quality of work through synergism. Synergism occurs when individual or separate units work together to produce a whole greater than the sum of the parts. Synergism results when three men working together produce more than four men working separately. Synergism can result from division of labor or from increased coordination both of which are products of good organization.

A final reason for organizing is to increase communication. A good organization structure clearly defines channels of communication among the members of the organization. Such a system also ensures more efficient communications. The role of communication in the management process will be discussed in Chapter 13.

AUTHORITY, POWER, AND RESPONSIBILITY

Authority is the right to command and expend resources. Lines of authority serve to link the various organizational components together. Unclear delegation of authority is a major source of confusion and conflict within an organization.

Many people confuse power with authority. Power is the ability to command or apply force and is not necessarily accompanied by authority. Power is derived from the control of resources. A man with a pistol may have the power to shoot another, but he does not have the right to do so. Similarly, a manager may have the power to make frivolous expenditures, but he does not have the right to do so.

Responsibility is accountability for the attainment of objectives, the use of resources, and the adherence to organizational policy. Once responsibility is accepted it becomes an obligation to perform assigned work.

SOURCES OF AUTHORITY

Traditionally authority has been viewed as a function of position, flowing from top to bottom through the formal organization. According to this view, people hold authority because they occupy a certain position; once removed from the position they lose their authority. Taking this theory one step further, one can say that the American people, through the Constitution and laws, represent the ultimate source of authority in this country. The Constitution and laws guarantee the right of free enterprise. The owners of a free enterprise organization have the right to elect the board and top management. Top management selects the general and department managers. This process continues down to the lowest person in the organization. This traditional view of authority is also called the formal theory of authority.

A second theory of authority was first proposed by Chester I. Barnard in 1938 and is called the acceptance theory of authority.[5] Barnard maintained that the source of authority lies with the subordinate because he or she has the power to either accept or reject a superior's command. Presumedly, if the subordinate does not accept the authority of the superior, it does not exist. Barnard viewed disobedience of a communication from a superior as a denial of authority by the subordinate.

PRINCIPLES BASED ON AUTHORITY

Because authority is a key element in management and organizations, numerous related principles have been developed. Before proceeding, recall from Chapter 1 that management principles are not ironclad laws but rather suggested guides.

Parity principle

The parity principle states that authority and responsibility must coincide. Management must delegate sufficient authority so the subordinate can do his job. At the same time the subordinate can be expected to accept responsibility only for those areas within his authority. Some people believe that authority but not responsibility can be delegated. Both can be delegated, but delegation does not alter the degree of authority or responsibility retained by the superior. Both authority and responsibility must be accepted by the subordinate before the delegation process has been completed. Management sometimes expects employees to seek and assume responsibility that they have not been asked to assume and then to bid for the necessary authority. Such a system leads to guessing games which do nothing but create frustration and waste energies. Resisting the delegation of authority is natural. The following quote from Robert Townsend illustrates this point:

> Many give lip service, but few delegate authority in important matters. And that means all they delegate is dog-work. A real leader does as much dog-work for his people as he can: He can do it, or see a way to do without it, ten times as fast. And he delegates as many important matters as he can because that creates a climate in which people grow.[6]

William H. Newman has listed three components of the delegation process: (1) the assignment of duties by a manager to his immediate subordinates; (2) the granting of permission (authority) to make commitments, use resources, and take all actions which are necessary to

[5] Barnard, *Functions of the Executive*, p. 163.

[6] Robert Townsend, *Up the Organization* (New York: Alfred A. Knopf, 1970), p. 46.

perform the duties; and (3) the creation of an obligation (responsibility) on the part of each subordinate to the delegating executive to perform the duties satisfactorily.[7]

In order to best assign duties to subordinates, the manager must be well-acquainted with the skills of his immediate subordinates. The manager must also be able to determine the functions and duties that can be delegated and those that cannot.

The second and third components of Newman's delegation process stress the parity principle. The still unanswered question is "How much authority should be delegated?" As mentioned previously, management must delegate sufficient authority to allow the subordinate to perform his job. Precisely what can and what cannot be delegated depends on the commitments of the manager and the number and quality of his subordinates.

Unity of command

The principle of unity of command states that an employee should have one and only one immediate superior. The difficulty of serving more than one superior has been recognized for thousands of years. Recall the Sermon on the Mount when Jesus said, "No man can serve two Masters."[8] Experts have speculated that violation of this one concept accounts for as many as 30 percent of the human relations problems in American industry.[9] In its simplest form, this problem arises when two managers tell the same subordinate to do different jobs at the same time. The subordinate is thus placed in a no-win situation. Regardless of which manager he or she obeys, the other will be dissatisfied. Violation of the principle of unity of command generally is caused by unclear lines of authority.

Scalar principle

The scalar principle states that authority in the organization flows, one link at a time, through the chain of superiors ranging from the highest to lowest ranks. Commonly referred to as the chain of command, the scalar principle is based on the need for communication and the principle of unity of command.

A common misconception is that every action must painfully progress through every link in the chain, whether its course is upward or downward. Colonel Lyndell Urwick has refuted this point:

---

[7] William H. Newman, *Administrative Action*, 2d ed. (Englewood Cliffs, N.J.: Prentice-Hall, 1963), pp. 185–86.

[8] *The Holy Bible,* Revised Standard Version.

[9] E. T. Eggers, "Authority and Responsibility," *Atlanta Economic Review,* February 1970, p. 32.

Provided there is proper confidence and loyalty between superiors and subordinates, and both parties take the trouble to keep the other informed in matters in which they should have a concern, the "scalar process" does not imply that there should be no shortcuts. It is concerned with authority and provided the authority is recognized and no attempt is made to evade or to supercede it, there is ample room for avoiding in matters of action the childish practices of going upstairs one step at a time or running up one ladder and down another when there is nothing to prevent a direct approach on level ground.[10]

As Fayol stated, years before Urwick, "it is an error to depart needlessly from the line of authority, but it is an even greater one to keep to it when detriment to the business ensues."[11] Both men are simply saying that in certain instances one can and should shortcut the scalar chain if it is not done in a secretive or deceitful manner.

Span of control

The span of control refers to the number of subordinates a manager can effectively manage. Although the concept was discussed by Fayol, Sir Ian Hamilton, the World War I British general, is usually given credit for developing the first popular version of the concept of a limited span of control. Sir Ian argued that a narrow span of control (with no more than six subordinates reporting to a superior) would enable the executive to get his job accomplished in the course of a normal working day.[12]

In 1933, V. A. Graicunas published a classical paper which analyzed subordinate-superior relationships in terms of a mathematical formula.[13] This formula was based on the theory that the complexities of managing increase geometrically as the number of subordinates increases arithmetically.

Graicunas' reasoning was that not only did the number of direct single relationships increase but so did the number of direct group relationships and cross relationships:

Thus, if Tom supervises two persons, Dick and Harry, he can speak to each of them individually or he can speak to them as a pair. The be-

---

[10] L. F. Urwick, *The Elements of Administration* (New York: Harper and Brothers, Publishers, 1943), p. 46.

[11] Henri Fayol, *General and Industrial Management* (London: Sir Isaac Pitman and Sons, Ltd., 1949), p. 36.

[12] Sir Ian Hamilton, *The Soul and Body of an Army* (London: Edward Arnold and Company, 1921), p. 229.

[13] V. A. Graicunas, "Relationship in Organization," *Bulletin of the International Management Institute* (Geneva: International Labour Office, 1933), reprinted in L. Gulick and L. F. Urwick eds., *Papers on the Science of Administration* (New York: Institute of Public Administration, 1937), pp. 181–87.

FIGURE 6–4

Illustrations of Graicunas' direct, cross, and group relationships

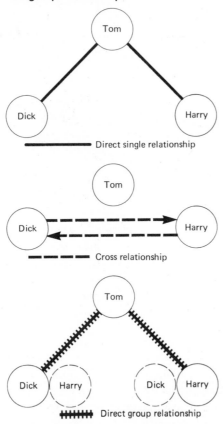

Direct single relationship

Cross relationship

Direct group relationship

Source: V. A. Graicunas, "Relationship in Organization," *Bulletin of the International Management Institute* (Geneva: International Labour Office, 1933), reprinted in L. Gulick and L. F. Urwick, eds., *Papers on the Science of Administration* (New York: Institute of Public Administration, 1937), p. 184.

havior of Dick in the presence of Harry or of Harry in the presence of Dick will vary from this behavior when with Tom alone. Further, what Dick thinks of Harry and what Harry thinks of Dick constitutes two cross relationships which Tom must keep in mind in arranging any work over which they must collaborate in his absence.[14]

Figure 6–4 graphically illustrates the various possible relationships envisioned by Graicunas. Observing the numbers in Table 6–1, it is easy to see why Graicunas advocated a limited span of control.

---

[14] Ibid., p. 187.

TABLE 6-1
Graicunas' direct, cross, and group relationships

Number of subordinates	Number of direct single relationships	Number of cross relationships	Number of direct group relationships	Number of total relationships
1	1	0	0	1
2	2	2	2	6
3	3	6	9	18
4	4	12	28	44
5	5	20	75	100
6	6	30	186	222
7	7	42	441	490
8	8	56	1016	1080

Based on personal experiences and the works of Sir Ian Hamilton and Graicunas, Lyndall Urwick first stated the concept of span of control as a management principle in 1938: "No superior can supervise directly the work of more than five or, at the most, six subordinates whose work interlocks."[15]

Since the publication of Graicunas' and Urwick's works, the upper limit of five or six subordinates has been continuously criticized as being too restrictive. Many practitioners and scholars contend that there are situations in which more than five or six subordinates can be effectively supervised. Their beliefs have been substantiated by considerable empirical evidence showing that the limit of five or six subordinates has been successfully exceeded in many situations.[16] Urwick has suggested that these exceptions can be explained by the fact that senior workers often function as unofficial managers or leaders.[17]

In view of the recent evidence relating to the span of control, it has been revised to state that the number of people who should report directly to any one person should be based upon the complexity of the jobs, the proximity of the jobs, the variety of the jobs, and the quality of the people filling the jobs. Thus, in situations where workers are engaged in simple, repetitive operations, the span of control could

---

[15] L. F. Urwick, "Scientific Principles and Organization," *Institute of Management Series no. 19*, American Management Association, 1938, p. 8.

[16] For a brief discussion of some such situations see Leslie W. Rue, "Supervisory Control in Modern Management," *Atlanta Economic Review*, January–February 1975, pp. 43–44.

[17] L. F. Urwick, "V. A. Graicunas and the Span of Control," *Academy of Management Journal*, June 1974, p. 352.

be very large. In other situations involving highly diversified and technical work, the span of control might be as low as three or four.

The exception principle

The exception principle (also known as management by exception) states that a manager should concentrate his efforts on matters which deviate significantly from normal and let his subordinates handle routine matters. The idea here is that the manager should concentrate on those matters that require his abilities and not become bogged down with insignificant and routine matters. The exception principle can be abused by incompetent and insecure subordinates who refer everything to their superiors because they are afraid to make a decision. On the other hand, the superior should refrain from making everyday decisions which have been delegated to a subordinate.

CENTRALIZATION VERSUS DECENTRALIZATION

There are limitations to the authority of any position. These limitations may be external in the form of laws, politics, or social attitudes, or they may be internal as delineated by the job description or the organization's objectives. The tapered concept of authority states that the breadth and scope of authority become more limited as one descends the scalar chain (see Figure 6–5).

The top levels of management establish the shape of the funnels in Figures 6–5 and 6–6. The more authority that top management chooses to delegate, the less conical the funnel becomes. The less conical the funnel, the more decentralized is the organization. Centralization or decentralization refers to the degree of authority delegated by upper management. This is usually reflected by the numbers and kinds of decisions made by the lower levels of management. As the number and importance of lower level decisions increase, the degree of de-

FIGURE 6–5
Tapered concept of authority

Scope of authority

◄— Board of Directors

◄— President

◄— Vice President

◄— General Manager

◄— Superintendent

◄— Employee

FIGURE 6–6
Centralized versus decentralized authority

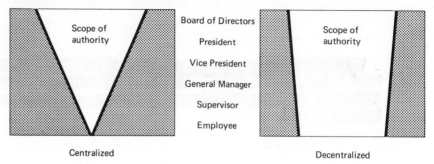

Centralized   Decentralized

centralization also increases. Thus, an organization is never totally centralized or totally decentralized. Rather, it falls along a continuum ranging from highly centralized to highly decentralized.

The question concerning how much an organization should decentralize cannot be answered for the general case. The answer depends on the specific situation and organization. Decentralization allows for more flexibility and quicker action. It also relieves executives from time-consuming detail work. Often, decentralization results in higher morale by allowing lower levels of management to be actively involved in the decision-making process. The major disadvantage of decentralization is the potential loss of control. Duplication of effort can also accompany decentralization.

Because no magic formula exists for determining the appropriate degree of decentralization, top management periodically must evaluate their particular situation in light of the advantages and disadvantages of greater decentralization.

ORGANIZATION STRUCTURES

Some people believe that a good employee should be able to perform satisfactorily regardless of the organization structure. Others believe that given the right organization structure, anyone should be able to perform in an acceptable fashion. The truth lies somewhere between the above propositions. An appropriate organization structure is a prerequisite to good employee performance. Clear and appropriate lines of authority coupled with proper departmentation form the basis for the organization structure. The organization structure forms the framework within which the organization operates. While thousands of different organization structures exist, all are variations or combinations of three basic types: the line organization; the line and staff organization; and the matrix organizations.

Line organization

The line organization is the simplest organization structure. It is characterized by direct vertical links between the different levels of the organization. Because no staff exists, all members of the organization receive instructions through the scalar chain. The most important aspect of the line organization is that the work of a group or department represents an end in itself; its purpose is not to aid another department. One advantage of the line organization is the clear authority structure. Such a structure promotes rapid decision making and prevents the practice of "passing the buck" or blaming someone else. A disadvantage of the line organization is that it may overextend the manager by forcing him to perform a broad range of duties. The line organization structure may also cause the organization to become overly dependent on one or two key individuals who are capable of performing many duties.

Line and staff organization

The addition of staff specialists to a line organization creates a line and staff organization. As a line organization grows in size, staff assistance often becomes necessary. Staff functions are advisory and supportive in nature and are designed to contribute to the efficiency and maintenance of the organization; whereas line functions are directly involved in producing the organization's goods or services. Staff functions include research and development, public relations, personnel management and training. The line and staff organization allows for much more specialization and flexibility than the line organization; however, it sometimes creates conflict. Some staff specialists resent the fact that they may be acting only as advisors to line personnel and have no real authority. In such a situation they may overstep their bounds of authority and create a line-staff conflict. On the other hand, many line managers do not like the idea of staff specialists telling them what to do. By being unreceptive, the line manager may create a line-staff conflict. An additional factor contributing to line-staff conflict is the fact that line and staff personnel may be different in personal characteristics and behavior. One study conducted in three industrial plants found that staff personnel were generally younger and came from different social backgrounds than the line personnel.[18] The potential problem of a line-staff conflict should not be taken lightly. A study conducted by the American Management Association found that 41 out of 100 companies reported some form of a line-staff conflict.[19] As will be explored in Chapter 11, not all conflict is undesirable. However, some types of line-staff conflict can be very costly to the organization.

Matrix organization

The matrix form of organization has recently evolved as a way of forming project teams within the traditional line-staff organization. A project is "a combination of human and non-human resources pulled together in a temporary organization to achieve a specified purpose."[20] The marketing of a new product and the construction of a new building are examples of projects. Because projects have a temporary life, a method of managing and organizing them was sought so that the existing organization structure would not be totally disrupted and would still maintain a degree of efficiency.

Under the matrix structure, individuals working on a project are officially assigned to the project *and* to their original or base department. A manager is given the authority and responsibility for meeting the project objectives in terms of cost, quality, quantity, and time of completion. The project manager is then assigned the necessary personnel from the functional departments of the parent organization. Thus, a line organization develops for the project and leaves the parent line functions in a support relationship to the project organization.[21] Under such a system, the functional personnel are assigned and evaluated by the project manager while they work on the project. Upon completion of the project or completion of their contribution to the project, the functional personnel return to their functional departments. Figure 6–7 illustrates a matrix organization.

A major advantage of matrix organization is that the combination of people and resources which are used on the project can readily be changed to correspond to changing project needs. One serious potential disadvantage is that matrix organization can result in a violation of the principle of unity of command. A role conflict can develop if

---

[18] M. Dalton, "Conflicts between Staff and Line Managerial Officers," *American Sociological Review*, June 1950, pp. 342–51.

[19] Ernest Dale, *Organization* (New York: American Management Association, 1967), p. 67.

[20] David Cleland and William King, *Systems Analysis and Project Management*, 2d ed. (New York: McGraw-Hill Book Company, 1975), p. 184.

[21] John F. Mee, "Matrix Management," *Business Horizons*, June 1969, p. 60.

FIGURE 6–7
Illustrative matrix organization

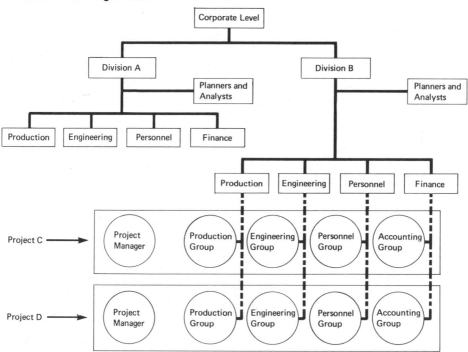

Source: David Cleland and William King, *Systems Analysis and Project Management*, 2d ed. (New York: McGraw-Hill Book Company, 1975), p. 184.

the authority of the project manager is not clearly delineated from that of the functional managers. In such a case the personnel assigned to the project might receive conflicting assignments from their project manager and their functional manager. A second problem occurs when the personnel assigned to a project are still evaluated by their functional manager who has little opportunity to observe their work on the project.

Committee organization

Actually, committees are a form of matrix organization in that they are superimposed on the existing line or line and staff structure. Committees can be permanent (standing) or temporary and are usually in charge of or supplementary to the line and staff functions. Committees enjoy many of the same strengths of the matrix organization and are subject to the same criticisms.

ORGANIZATION STRUCTURE, ENVIRONMENT, AND TECHNOLOGY

Figure 6–8 depicts the different stages of an organization as it grows and matures. The craft stage is characterized by the absence of formal policies, objectives, and structure.[22] Generally the operations of the organization at this stage center around one individual and one functional area. During the entrepreneurial stage the organization grows first at an increasing and then decreasing rate. An atmosphere of optimism pervades the entire organization as sales and profits rise rapidly. By the third stage of growth, the entrepreneur has been re-

FIGURE 6–8
Organization growth and change

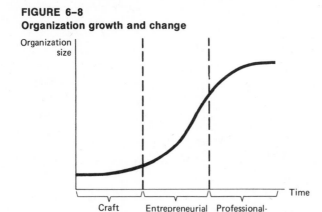

placed by or evolved into a manager who performs the processes of planning, organizing, motivating, and controlling.[23] Profits are realized more from internal efficiency and less from external exploitation of the market. At this stage the organization becomes characterized by written policies, procedures, and plans.

As the organization moves through the craft stage and into the entrepreneural stage, an organization structure must be developed. This is a critical stage for the organization. If an appropriate structure is not established and utilized, the entrepreneur may lose control and cause the entire organization to collapse. An organization structure must be developed which allows the organization to adapt to change in its environment.

---

[22] Filley and House *Managerial Process*, pp. 443–55.
[23] Ibid.

Organization and environment

A landmark study relating organization to environment was conducted by Tom Burns and G. M. Salker in the United Kingdom.[24] By examining some 20 industrial firms, both in a dynamic, changing industry and in a more stable, established industry, Burns and Stalker focused on how a firm's pattern of organization was related to certain characteristics of the external environment. The researchers identified two distinct organizational systems. One, labeled "mechanistic systems," is characterized by a rigid delineation of functional duties, precise job descriptions, fixed authority and responsibility, and a well-developed organizational hierarchy through which information filters up and instructions flow down. "Organic systems" are characterized by less formal job definitions, greater emphasis on adaptability, more participation, and less fixed authority. Burns and Stalker found that successful firms in stable and established industries tended to be "mechanistic" in structure. Successful firms in dynamic and changing industries tended to be "organic" in structure.

Paul Lawrence and Jay Lorsch conducted a later study dealing with organizational structure and its environment.[25] Their original study included ten firms in three distinct industrial environments. Reaching conclusions similar to Burns and Stalker, Lawrence and Lorsch found that in order to be successful firms operating in a dynamic environment needed a relatively flexible structure, firms operating in a stable environment needed a more rigid structure, and firms operating in an intermediate environment needed a structure somewhere between the two extremes.[26]

Numerous other studies have been conducted in the past few years investigating the relationship between organization structure and environment. In general, they have all concluded that the most appropriate organization structure for a given organization is contingent to some degree on the conditions of its environment.

Organization and technology

In recent years numerous studies have been conducted investigating potential relationships between technology and organizational

[24] Tom Burns and G. Stalker, *The Management of Innovation* (London: Tavistock Institute, 1962).

[25] Paul Lawrence and Jay Lorsch, "Differentiation and Integration in Complex organizations," *Administrative Science Quarterly,* June 1967, pp. 1–47; and Paul Lawrence and Jay Lorsch, *Organization and Environment* (Homewood, Ill.: Richard D. Irwin, Inc., 1969). Originally published in 1967 by Division of Research, Graduate School of Business Administration, Harvard University.

[26] Ibid.

structure. One of the most significant of these studies was conducted by Joan Woodward in the 1950s.[27] Her study was based on an analysis of 100 manufacturing firms in the South East Essex area of England. The general approach taken by Woodward was to classify firms along a scale of "technical complexity" with particular emphasis on three modes of production: (1) unit or small batch production e.g., custom made machines; (2) large batch or mass production e.g., an automotive assembly plant; and (3) continuous flow or process production e.g., a chemical plant. The unit or small batch production mode represents the lower end of the technical complexity scale while the continuous flow mode represents the upper end.

After classifying each firm into one of the above categories, Woodward investigated a number of organizational variables. Some of her findings are presented below:

1. The number of levels in an organization increased as technical complexity increased.
2. The ratio of managers and supervisors to total personnel increased as technical complexity increased.
3. Using Burns and Stalker's definition of organic and mechanistic systems, organic management systems tended to predominate in firms at both ends of the scale of technical complexity, while mechanistic systems predominated in firms falling in the middle ranges.
4. No significant relationship existed between technical complexity and organizational size.

A similar study was undertaken a few years later by Edward Harvey.[28] Rather than use Woodward's "technical complexity" scale, Harvey grouped his firms along a continuum from technical diffuseness to technical specificity. Technically diffused firms have a wider range of products, produce products that vary from year to year, and produce more "made to order" products. Harvey's findings were similar to Woodward's in that he found significant relationships between technology and several organizational characteristics.

The general conclusion reached in the Woodward and the Harvey studies was that they both clearly reflected the presence of a relationship between organizational technology and a number of aspects of organizational structure.

---

[27] Joan Woodward, *Industrial Organization: Theory and Practice* (London: Oxford University Press, 1965).

[28] Edward Harvey, "Technology and the Structure of Organizations," *American Sociological Review*, April 1968, pp. 247–59.

A CONTINGENCY APPROACH

The studies discussed above support what practicing managers have been saying for years—there is no organization structure applicable to all situations. The most appropriate organization structure depends on the particular technology employed, the rate of change in the environment, and many other dynamic forces.

Recognition by management practioners and scholars that there is no universal best way to organize but that the design is conditional has led to the evolvement of a contingency or situational approach

FIGURE 6–9
Variables affecting appropriate organization structure

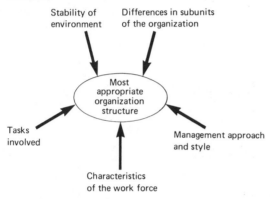

to organizing. Paul Lawrence and Jay Lorsch concluded in their study dealing with organization structure and environment (which was discussed in the Organization and Environment section of this chapter) that different organizations in different environments require different kinds of organization structures at different stages in their growth.[29] Figure 6–9 depicts many of the potential variables that can have an impact on determining the most appropriate organization structure.

Once management adopts a contingency view, it will begin to thoroughly analyze the relevant variables and then identify the appropriate pattern of structure. The result is essentially a matching process. Because each of the interacting forces is dynamic, top management should periodically analyze and appraise their organization structure in light of any relevant changes. Fremont Kast and James

---

[29] Lawrence and Lorsch, "Differentiation and Integration."

Rosenzweig have offered the following clarification of the contingency approach:

> The general tenor of the contingency view is somewhere between the simplistic, specific principles and complex, vague notions. It is a mid-range concept which recognizes the complexity involved in managing a modern organization but uses patterns of relationships and/or configurations of subsystems in order to facilitate improved practice.[30]

SUMMARY

An organization is a group of people working together in some type of concerted or coordinated effort to attain common objectives. As such, an organization provides a vehicle for accomplishing objectives that could not be achieved by individuals working separately. Specific reasons for organizing include the need to establish lines of authority, improve efficiency and quality of work through synergism, and increase communication.

Horizontal and vertical division of labor are the means by which organization is accomplished. Departmentation is the most frequently used method for implementing division of labor. Departmentation refers to the grouping of activities into related work units. The work units may be related on the basis of work function, product, customer, geography, techniques, or time.

Authority is the right to command and expend resources. Power is the ability to command or apply force. Responsibility is accountability for the attainment of objectives, the use of resources, and the adherence to organizational policy.

Many management principles are based on the concept of authority. These include the parity principle (authority and responsibility must coincide); unity of command (an employee should have one and only one immediate supervisor); the scalar principle (authority in the organization flows, one link at a time, through the chain of superiors ranging from highest to lowest ranks); span of control (the number of people who directly report to any one person should be based on the complexity of the jobs, the proximity of the jobs, the variety of the jobs, and the quality of the people filling the jobs); and the exception principle (a manager should concentrate on matters which deviate significantly from normal and let his subordinates attend to the routine). While all managers should be familiar with the basic management and organization principles, they should be used as guides for action and not as laws.

---

[30] Fremont Kast and James Rosenzweig, "General Systems Theory: Applications for Organization and Management," *Academy of Management Journal*, December 1972, p. 463.

Appropriate organization structure is a necessary but not a sufficient condition for outstanding performance. Many different organization structures exist; however, all are variations or combinations
of three basic types: the line organization, the line and staff organization, and the matrix organization.

Many studies have been conducted to support what practicing
managers have been saying for years—there is no organization
structure applicable to all situations. The most appropriate organization structure depends on the particular technology employed, the
environment, and numerous other factors. The recognition that there
is no universal, best way to organize has led to the evolution of the
contingency approach to organizing. The contingency view requires
a thorough analysis of the relevant variables followed by the identification of the most appropriate pattern of structure. The end result is
an organization structure which is best suited to the needs and
environment of the organization.

REVIEW QUESTIONS

1. What is an organization? Define the management function of organizing.
   Define organizational structure. What is the informal organization?

2. What is the difference between horizontal and vertical division of
   labor? What is the difference between job scope and job depth?

3. Explain:
   a. Functional departmentation.
   b. Product departmentation.
   c. Geographic departmentation.
   d. Customer departmentation.

4. Discuss the reasons for organizing.

5. Define authority, power, and responsibility.

6. Discuss two approaches to viewing the sources of authority.

7. What is the parity principle?

8. Describe three components of the delegation process.

9. What is the unity of command principle?

10. What is the scalar principle?

11. What is the span of control?

12. What is the exception principle?

13. What is the difference between a highly centralized and highly de-
    centralized organization?

14. What are line functions? What are staff functions?

15. Explain:
    a. Line organization.
    b. Line and staff organization.
    c. Matrix organization.
    d. Committee organization.

16. What are the stages of organizational growth?

17. What is the contingency approach to organizing?

DISCUSSION QUESTIONS

1. Do you think that division of labor has been emphasized too much in our highly mechanized and efficient society of today?

2. Comment on the following statement which is attributed to Robert Heinlein:

   A human being should be able to change a diaper, plan an invasion, butcher a hog, conn a ship, design a building, write a sonnet, balance accounts, build a wall, set a bone, comfort the dying, take orders, give orders, cooperate, act alone, solve equations, analyze a new problem, pitch manure, program a computer, cook a tasty meal, fight efficiently, die gallantly. Specialization is for insects.

3. The Que Company has 712 employees and annual sales of $11.2 million. The entire company is located in one office building on Main Street. Based on this information, what can you say about the degree of centralization of authority in this organization?

4. How could you ever justify the use of a matrix organization structure since it clearly violates the unity of command principle?

5. Do you think that the contingency approach to organizing is a useful concept that can be implemented or is it really a "cop out?"

SELECTED READINGS

Albanese, Robert. "Substitutional and Essential Authority," *Academy of Management Journal*, vol. 9, no. 2 (June 1966), pp. 136–44.

Barnard, Chester. *Functions of the Executive*. Cambridge, Mass.: Harvard University Press, 1938.

Dale, Earnest. *Organization*. New York: American Management Association, 1967.

Davis, Ralph C. *The Fundamentals of Top Management*. New York: Harper & Brothers, 1951.

Eggers, E. T. "Authority and Responsibility," *Atlanta Economic Review* (February 1970), pp. 31–32.

Filley, Alan C., and Robert J. House. *Managerial Process and Organizational Behavior.* Glenview, Ill.: Scott, Foresman and Company, 1969.

Lawrence, Paul, and Jay Lorsch. *Organization and Environment.* Homewood, Ill.: Richard D. Irwin, 1969.

Litterer, Joseph A. *The Analysis of Organizations.* New York: John Wiley & Sons, Inc., 1965.

Newman, William H. *Administrative Action.* 2d ed. Englewood Cliffs, N.J.: Prentice-Hall, 1963.

Scott, William G. *Organization Theory.* Homewood, Ill.: Richard D. Irwin, Inc., 1967.

Suojanen, Waino. "The Span of Control — Fact or Fable?" *Advanced Management,* vol. 20 (November 1955), pp. 5–13.

Urwick, Lyndell F. "The Manager's Span of Control," *Harvard Business Review,* vol. 35 (May–June 1956), pp. 39–47.

Woodward, Joan. *Industrial Organization: Theory and Practice.* London: Oxford University Press, 1965.

Case 6-1

Who's the boss?

Bob Davis began working for Sim's Furniture in October of 1970. Sim's Furniture was a retail furniture company with six branch stores in a large southern city. In six months, Bob was made store manager of the downtown branch. Six months later, Bob was offered the job of general manager by Tom Sims, president and owner of Sim's Furniture. Considering the relatively short time he had worked for Sim's Furniture, Bob was flattered at being chosen. The general manager's responsibility covered all of the operations of the branch stores.

Initially, Bob spent a great deal of time working with the other store managers. His purpose was both to gain insight into problems as they saw them as well as to gain their confidence. This daily routine became increasingly difficult due to a general slump in the economic environment. Many days were spent with the advertising agency attempting to coordinate advertising with dwindling inventory levels. To further complicate matters, the condition of receivables was deteriorating rapidly as a result of the economy. During the first few months in the position, Bob had managed to spend lengthy amounts of time with each store manager carefully explaining how he, generally after conferring with Mr. Sims, had arrived at his decisions. He now had to make such decisions in less time, and while he never failed to explain his reasons, he frequently did not enter into a lengthy discussion as to each of the inputs determining it. As the weeks passed he began to sense an air of doubt when dealing with many of the managers.

During the month of December, Bob visited Mr. Sims to discuss a few of the problems plaguing him. Unfortunately, Mr. Sim's answers to those questions were rather vague. Bob left confused. He recalled how, just last month, he was reprimanded for overstepping his bounds, and again for not exercising sufficient authority.

When Bob arrived for work the morning of January 14, the office secretary advised him that Jim Wagner, a store manager, had called in and was having an emergency operation that would cause him to be out of work for one month. With the tight budget, Bob knew he would have to select one of the assistants from one of the other branches to run Jim's store. There was little doubt as to who it would be. Since the recent closing of the Memorial Drive store, John Wallace had been working at the Ben Hill Branch assisting the manager there. John had worked as a store manager for years, and Bob felt he would welcome a chance to "be in charge" again. Bob called John and explained the situation, indicating that the change should not extend for more than a month. Following this conversation, as Bob was leaving his office, his phone rang. Bob recognized John's voice, "Bob, have you discussed this move with Mr. Sims?" "No," Bob answered, "It's simply a matter of putting the most qualified man in the position, and we need you there now." Later in the day Bob learned that John had phoned Mr. Sims to discuss the matter prior to assuming control of the store.

As closing time approached, Mr. Sims visited Bob and commented, "You know, lately it seems I've had to spend more and more time with the store managers resolving minor problems. Don't forget your primary responsibilities and be sure you don't fall into bad habits and force the store managers to come to me with every minor problem."

1. What principles of good organization have been violated?
2. What would you do in Bob's position to correct the problem?

Case 6–2

The vacation request

Tom Blair has a week's vacation coming and really wants to take it the third week in May, which is the height of the bass fishing season. The only problem is that two of the other five members of his department have already requested and received approval from their boss, Luther Jones, to take off that same week. Afraid that Luther would not approve his request, Tom decided to forward his request directly to Harry Jensen, who is Luther's boss and who is rather friendly to Tom (Tom has taken Harry fishing on several occasions). Not realizing that Luther has not seen the request, Harry approves it. Several weeks pass before Luther finds out, by accident, that Tom has been approved to go on vacation the third week of May.

The thing that really "bugs" Luther is that this is only one of many instances in which Luther's subordinates have gone directly to Harry and gotten permission to do something. In fact, just last week he overheard a conversation in the washroom to the effect that "if you want anything approved, don't waste time with Luther, go directly to Harry."

1. What should Harry have done?
2. Who is at fault, Harry or the subordinates?
3. Suppose you confront Harry with the problem and he simply brushes it off by saying that he is really only helping?

Objectives

1. *To develop an appreciation for the importance of staffing.*
2. *To describe and illustrate the personnel planning process.*
3. *To discuss some significant government legislation related to staffing.*
4. *To explore the processes of recruitment, selection, employee development, transfers, promotions, and separations.*

GLOSSARY OF TERMS

Age Discrimination in Employment Act of 1967 An act which went into effect on June 12, 1968, and was designed to protect individuals from 40 to 65 years of age from discrimination in hiring, retention, compensation, and other conditions of employment.

Civil Rights Act of 1964 Title VII of this act was designed to eliminate discrimination in employment related to race, color, religion, sex, or national origin in organizations that conduct interstate commerce.

Criterion A measure of job success or performance.

Employee development A process concerned with the improvement and growth of the capabilities of individuals and groups within the organization.

Equal Pay Act of 1963 Law which became effective in June 1964, and prohibits wage discrimination on the basis of sex.

Job analysis Process of determining, through observation and study, the pertinent information relating to the nature of a specific job.

Job description A written description of a job and its requirements.

Personnel forecasting An attempt to determine the future personnel needs of an organization.

Personnel planning The process by which the organization ensures that it has the right number of people and the right kind of people, at the right places, at the right time, doing things for which they are economically most useful.

Peter Principle An idea popularized by Lawrence Peter which states that managers tend to be promoted to their level of incompetence.

Promotion The act of moving an employee to a job involving higher pay, status, and thus higher performance requirements.

Recruitment The process of seeking and attracting a supply of people from which qualified candidates for job vacancies can be selected.

Separation Either voluntary or involuntary termination of an employee.

Staffing Part of the organizing function that involves securing and developing personnel for the jobs which were created by earlier phases of the organizing function.

Tests Instruments used in the selection process which provide a sample of behavior that is used to draw inferences about the future behavior or performance of an individual.

Test reliability The consistency or reproducibility of the results of a test.

Test validity The extent to which a test measures what it purports to measure; generally this refers to the extent that a test predicts future job success or performance.

Transfer The act of moving an employee to another job at approximately the same level in the organization with basically the same pay, performance requirements, and status.

Staffing

All the activities of any enterprise are initiated and determined by the persons who make up that institution. Plants, offices, computers, automated equipment, and all else that a modern firm uses are unproductive except for human effort and direction. Human beings design or order the equipment; they decide where and how to use computers; they modernize or fail to modernize the technology employed; they secure the capital needed and decide on the accounting and fiscal procedures to be used. Every aspect of a firm's activities is determined by the competence, motivation, and general effectiveness of its human organization.

Rensis Likert[*]

STAFFING is part of the organizing function and involves securing and developing personnel for the jobs which were created by earlier phases of the organizing function. The objective of staffing is to obtain the best available people for the organization and to develop the skills and abilities of these people. Obtaining the best available people for the organization generally involves forecasting personnel requirements and recruiting and selecting new employees. Developing the skills and abilities of an organization's employees involves the general area of employee development as well as the proper use of promotions, transfers, and separations. In recent years, the staffing function has become much more complex due to increased government regulation in the areas of equal employment opportunity.

Traditionally many of the staffing activities have been conducted by personnel or human resource departments and have been considered relatively unimportant by line managers. However, obtaining and developing qualified personnel should be a major concern of all managers.

---

[*] *The Human Organization*, New York: McGraw-Hill Book Company, 1967, p. 1.

PERSONNEL PLANNING

Personnel planning has been defined as "the process by which an organization ensures that it has the right number of people and the right kind of people, at the right places, at the right time, doing things for which they are economically most useful."[1] Basically, personnel planning involves the application of the planning concepts discussed in Chapter 5 to the personnel, or human resources, of the organization.

The first basic question (Where are we now?) addressed by the planning process is frequently answered in personnel planning by using job analyses and a skills inventory.

Job analysis and skills inventory

Job analysis is the process of determining, through observation and study, the pertinent information relating to the nature of a specific job. The end product of a job analysis is a job description which identifies and describes the job and specifies the requirements of the job. Frequently, job analyses are conducted by specialists from the personnel department. However, managers should provide input for developing the final job descriptions for the jobs they are managing.

A skills inventory includes basic types of information on all of the employees of an organization. Names such as Manpower Information System, Personnel Register, Personnel Inventory, and others have been used to describe the skills inventory. Thomas H. Patten has outlined seven broad categories of information that should be included in a skills inventory:

1. Personal data history—age, sex, marital status, and so on.
2. Skills—education, job experience, training, and so on.
3. Special qualifications—memberships in professional groups, special achievements, and so on.
4. Salary and job history—present salary, past salary, dates of raises, and various jobs held, and so on.
5. Company data—benefit plan data, retirement information, seniority, and so on.
6. Capacity of individual—test scores on psychological and other tests, health information, and so on.
7. Special preferences of individual—location or job preferences, and so on.[2]

---

[1] Thomas H. Patten, Jr., *Manpower Planning and the Development of Human Resources* (New York: John Wiley & Sons, 1972), p. 14.

[2] Ibid., p. 243.

As can be seen, the skills inventory gives a comprehensive picture of the individual. Its purpose is to consolidate information on the organization's human resources to aid in personnel planning.

In recent years, steps have been taken to computerize skills inventories. Many large organizations such as Ford, General Electric, Xerox, RCA, and branches of the federal government have or are currently establishing computerized skills inventories.

The real value of a skills inventory is that it provides a current listing of the talents on hand within the organization. Combining a skills inventory with job analyses enables the organization to evaluate its present position with regard to human resources.

Personnel forecasting

The second basic question addressed by the planning process is "Where does the organization want to be?" Personnel forecasting is used to answer this question. Personnel forecasting is an attempt to determine the future personnel needs of an organization. Some of the many variables considered in a forecast are future sales projections, potential new business ventures, skills required in potential new business ventures, composition of present work force, technological changes, and others. All levels of management should participate in developing the forecast.

Personnel forecasting is presently conducted on a largely intuitional basis. The experience and judgment of the manager is used to determine future personnel needs. Of course, this assumes that all managers in the organization are aware of future plans of the total organization. Unfortunately, this is not true in many cases. For instance, a decision to increase the number of sales representatives in an organization could very likely have personnel implications for all departments of the organization. Ideally, an increase in the number of sales representatives would generate more sales which would then require increased production and increased invoicing to customers. Thus, the production and accounting departments would need to increase their personnel.

Various mathematical and statistical techniques are also used to project future personnel needs. A simple example of such a method is the use of sales forecasts to determine personnel needs.

Personnel transition

The final phase of personnel planning is to determine how the organization can proceed from where it presently is to where it wants to be. Included in this phase are such activities as recruitment, selection, and employee development. Other factors that must be considered in answering this question include organizational policies on promotion, transfer, and separation. Generally, the activities of recruitment, selection, and much of employee development are delegated to a personnel or human resources department.

A model of the personnel planning process

The personnel planning process can be diagrammed as shown in Figure 7–1. Although the model implies a sequencial process, most of the activities are conducted on a continuous basis.

FIGURE 7–1
Personnel planning process

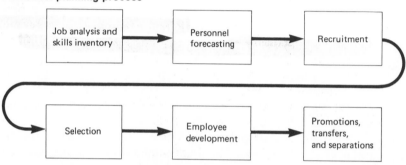

Personnel planning must be coordinated with other organizational plans and with the overall corporate plan. It cannot be successfully conducted in isolation by the personnel department.

Special considerations in personnel planning

Government legislation now plays a vital role in personnel planning. Alleged discriminatory personnel practices by many organizations led to this legislation. Three significant government bills in this area are the Equal Pay Act of 1963, the Civil Rights Act of 1964, and the Age Discrimination in Employment Act of 1967.

The Equal Pay Act of 1963 which became effective in June 1964, prohibits wage discrimination on the basis of sex. The law states: "No employer . . . shall discriminate . . . between employees on the basis of sex by paying wages . . . at a rate less than the rate at which he pays wages to employees of the opposite sex . . . for equal work on jobs the performance of which requires equal skill, effort, and responsibility and which are performed under similar working conditions. . . ."[3]

Title VII of the Civil Rights Act of 1964 is designed to eliminate discrimination in employment related to race, color, religion, sex, or national origin in organizations that conduct interstate commerce. Due to the importance of this bill its two most significant sections are shown in Figure 7–2.

The Age Discrimination in Employment Act was passed by Congress in 1967 and went into effect on June 12, 1968. It was designed to protect individuals from 40 to 65 years of age from discrimination in hiring, retention, compensation, and other conditions of employment.

Other factors affecting personnel planning are the changing attitudes toward female employment and new attitudes concerning handicapped workers. Union contracts also influence personnel planning when they contain clauses regulating transfers, promotions, and so on.

RECRUITMENT

Recruitment involves the activities of seeking and attracting a supply of people from which qualified candidates for job vacancies can be selected. The amount of recruiting that must be done by an organization is determined by the difference between the forecasted personnel needs and the talent available within the organization as outlined by the skills inventory.

After the decision to recruit has been made, the sources of supply must be explored.

Promotion from within

If an organization has been doing an effective job of selecting employees, one of the best sources of supply for job openings is its own employees. Promotion from within is a policy that many organizations follow. Obviously, this policy is only applicable for jobs above the entry level.

Promotion from within has several advantages. First, an organization should have a good idea about the strengths and weaknesses of its own employees. Employee morale and motivation are positively affected by internal promotions assuming such promotions are perceived as being equitably related to performance. Finally, most

---

[3] "Equal Pay for Equal Work under the Fair Labor Standards Act," U.S. Department of Labor, *Interpractices Bulletin*, Title 29, pt. 800, 1967.

FIGURE 7–2
Title VII of the Civil Rights Act of 1964

Section 703

(a) It shall be an unlawful employment practice for an employer—

    (1) to fail or refuse to hire or to discharge any individual, or otherwise to discriminate against any individual with respect to his compensation, terms, conditions, or privileges of employment, because of such individual's race, color, religion, sex, or national origin; or

    (2) to limit, segregate, or classify his employees in any way which would deprive or tend to deprive any individual of employment opportunities or otherwise adversely affect his status as an employee, because of such individual's race, color, religion, sex, or national origin.

(b) It shall be an unlawful employment practice for an employment agency to fail or refuse to refer for employment, or otherwise to discriminate against, any individual because of his race, color, religion, sex, or national origin, or to classify or refer for employment any individual on the basis of his race, color, religion, sex, or national origin.

(c) It shall be an unlawful employment practice for a labor organization—

    (1) to exclude or to expel from its membership, or otherwise to discriminate against any individual because of his race, color, religion, sex, or national origin;

    (2) to limit, segregate or classify its membership, or to classify or fail or refuse to refer for employment any individual in any way which would deprive or tend to deprive any individual of employment opportunities, or would limit such employment opportunities or otherwise adversely affect his status as an employee or as an applicant for employment, because of such individual's race, color, religion, sex, or national origin or

    (3) to cause or attempt to cause an employer to discriminate against an individual in violation of this section.

(d) It shall be an unlawful employment practice for any employer, labor organization, or joint labor-management committee controlling apprenticeship or other training or retraining, including on-the-job training programs to discriminate against any individual because of his race, color, religion, sex, or national origin in admission to, or employment in, any program established to provide apprenticeship or other training.

Section 704

(b) It shall be an unlawful employment practice for an employer, labor organization, or employment agency to print or publish or cause to be printed or published any notice or advertisement relating to employment by such an employment agency, indicating any preference, limitation, specification, or discrimination, based on race, color, religion, sex, or national origin. . . .

Source: Title VII, Equal Employment Opportunity, Civil Rights Act of 1964.

organizations have a sizable investment in employees, and using the employees' abilities to the fullest extent improves the organization's return on its investment.

However, certain potential dangers must be realized before adopting a policy of promotion from within. One danger has been popularized by Lawrence Peter and states that managers tend to be promoted to their level of incompetence.[4] According to the Peter Principle, successful managers are continually promoted until they finally reach a level at which they are unable to perform.

The Peter Principle can and does occur in organizations. Knowing the manager's present skills (skills inventory) and knowing the skills required by a new job (job analysis) minimizes the occurrence of the Peter Principle.

A second danger involves the inbreeding of ideas. When all vacancies are filled from within, caution must be taken to insure that new ideas and innovations are not stifled by attitudes such as "We've never done it before," or "We did all right without it."

External sources

Organizations have a wide range of external sources available for obtaining personnel. Probably the most widely used method for obtaining external staff is the Help Wanted advertisement. Recruitment on college and university campuses is also used by many organizations. Other sources for obtaining personnel include employment agencies (public and private), management consulting firms, employee referrals, and labor unions.

The primary requisite for effective recruitment is that the organization know the requirements for the particular jobs that it is attempting to fill. Only then can it seek qualified candidates.

SELECTION

The purpose of selection is to choose individuals that are most likely to succeed from those that are available. The process is entirely dependent on proper personnel planning and recruitment. Furthermore, only when an adequate pool of qualified candidates is available can the selection process function effectively.

Figure 7–3 is a suggested procedure for selecting employees. The procedure starts with several candidates for a particular job. At each stage in the process individuals are rejected for various reasons.

The preliminary screening and preliminary interview eliminate

---

[4] L. J. Peter and R. Hall, *The Peter Principle* (New York: Bantam Books, Inc., 1969).

FIGURE 7–3
The selection process

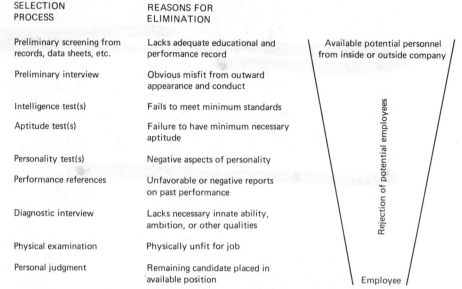

STAGES OF THE
SELECTION   REASONS FOR
PROCESS   ELIMINATION

Stages of the Selection Process	Reasons for Elimination	
Preliminary screening from records, data sheets, etc.	Lacks adequate educational and performance record	Available potential personnel from inside or outside company
Preliminary interview	Obvious misfit from outward appearance and conduct	
Intelligence test(s)	Fails to meet minimum standards	
Aptitude test(s)	Failure to have minimum necessary aptitude	
Personality test(s)	Negative aspects of personality	
Performance references	Unfavorable or negative reports on past performance	
Diagnostic interview	Lacks necessary innate ability, ambition, or other qualities	
Physical examination	Physically unfit for job	
Personal judgment	Remaining candidate placed in available position	Employee

Source: L. C. Megginson, *Providing Management Talent for Small Business* (Baton Rouge: Division of Research, College of Business Administration, Louisiana State University, 1961), p. 108.

candidates who are obviously not qualified for the job. In preliminary screening, application blanks, personnel data sheets, school records, work records, and similar sources are reviewed to determine characteristics, abilities, and past performance of the individual. The preliminary interview is then used to screen out unsuitable and uninterested applicants who passed the preliminary screening phase. If caution is not exercised by the organization during the preliminary interview, some qualified applicants may be eliminated. The danger of this happening can be minimized by using structured interviews with specific screening criteria.

Testing

One of the most controversial areas of staffing is employment testing. Generally tests provide a sample of behavior that is used to draw inferences about the future behavior or performance of an individual. Tests used by organizations can be grouped into five general categories: personality, interest, aptitude (potential ability), achievement (knowledge), and mental ability (general intelligence).[5] The popu-

---

[5] A large number of tests are described in detail in O. K. Buros, *The Sixth Mental Measurements Yearbook* (Highland Park, N.J.: Gryphon Press, 1964).

TABLE 7–1
Selection tests used by firms

Percent of firms using tests	Type of test
77	Mechanical
73	Intelligence
93	Clerical ability
39	Personality
31	Interest

larity of testing in the selection process was reflected in a study of 384 firms conducted by the National Industrial Conference Board.[6] All of the firms employed 250 or more people and 77 percent had testing programs of some description. Table 7–1 summarizes the types of tests used by those firms having testing programs. The study also revealed that larger firms were more likely to use tests.

Employment testing is legally subject to the requirements of validity and reliability. Test validity refers to the extent to which a test predicts a specific criterion. For organizations, the criterion generally used is performance on the job. Thus test validity generally refers to the extent to which a test predicts future job success or performance. The selection of criteria to define job success or performance is a most difficult problem, and its importance cannot be understated. Obviously, test validity cannot be measured unless satisfactory criteria exist.

Test reliability refers to the consistency or reproducibility of the results of the test. Three methods are commonly used to determine the reliability of a test. The first method, called test-retest, involves testing a group of people and then retesting them at a later date. The degree of similarity between the sets of scores determines the reliability of the test. The second method, called parallel forms, entails giving two separate but similar forms of the test. The degree to which the sets of scores coincide determines the reliability of the test. The third method, called split-halves, divides the test into two halves to determine if performance is similar on both halves. Again, the degree of similarity determines the reliability. All of these methods require statistical calculations for determining the degree of reliability of the test.

In the past, organizations have frequently used tests without establishing their validity or reliability. As a result of such practices, test-

---

[6] National Industrial Conference Board, "Personnel Practices in Factory and Office: Manufacturing," *Studies in Personnel Policy*, no. 194 (1964), pp. 14–15.

ing has recently come under a great deal of attack. The previously discussed Civil Rights Act of 1964 includes a section specifically related to the use of tests:

> . . . nor shall it be an unlawful employment practice for an employer to give and to act upon the results of any professionally developed ability test provided that such a test, its administration or action upon the results is not designed, intended, or used to discriminate because of race, color, religion, sex, or national origin. . . .[7]

The primary concern normally raised in discrimination questions about tests concerns the validity of the test. Robert M. Guion describes the situation as follows: "Unfair discrimination exists when persons with equal probabilities of success on the job have unequal probabilities of being hired for the job."[8] In other words, the test does not measure success on the job. Usually this results from a poor selection of criteria. For example, a test used to measure mathematical ability would probably not be valid for an assembly line worker.

Two recent Supreme Court decisions have had a profound impact on the use of testing by organizations. First, in the case of *Griggs* vs *Duke Power Company*, the court ruled that any test which has an adverse effect on women or minority group applicants must be validated as job related, regardless of whether the employers intended to discriminate.[9] In *Albemarle Paper Company* v. *Moody*, the Supreme Court ruled that a specified methodology must be used in validating tests.[10] The methodology designated by the Supreme Court was developed by the Equal Employment Opportunity Commission (EEOC).

In summary, many technical, ethical, and administrative problems exist in the use of tests. Generally tests should be used in conjunction with other data about the applicant. Tests should be used as an aid in the selection process and not as the sole deciding factor.

Performance references

Performance references or reference checks are often used to obtain additional information about a potential employee. Generally this involves verifying by mail or by telephone information given by the applicant. The assumption made by organizations using per-

---

[7] Title VII, Section 703(h).

[8] Robert M. Guion, *Personnel Testing* (New York: McGraw-Hill Book Company, 1965), p. 492.

[9] *Griggs* v. *Duke Power*, U.S. Supreme Court (1971).

[10] *Albemarle Paper Company* v. *Moody*, U.S. Supreme Court (1975).

formance references is that past performance is a good predictor of future performance. One survey indicated that 99 percent of the reporting firms communicated with the previous employers of their applicants.[11]

Diagnostic interview

The interview has been called a "conversation with a purpose."[12] The diagnostic interview focuses all of the information obtained in the previous stages of the selection process toward the ultimate objective of hiring the best individual for the job.

Interviews can either be structured or unstructured. In the structured interview, the interviewer knows in advance the questions that are to be asked and generally merely proceeds down the list of questions recording the interviewee's responses. Some advantages to using structured interviews are that it gives a common body of knowledge on all interviewees, it allows for a systematic coverage of all information deemed necessary by the organization, and it provides a means of minimizing personal biases and prejudices of the interviewer.

Unstructured interviews have no definite checklist or preplanned strategy for the interview. The interviewee largely determines the path of the interview. Questions such as "Tell me about your previous job" are asked and generally require a greater participation on the part of the interviewee than in the case of a structured interview.

Three other types of interviewing techniques have been used by organizations to a more limited extent. The stress interview places the interviewee on the defensive and attempts to confuse him as to his progress. The purpose of this type of interview is to detect the highly emotional individual. Panel or board interviews have also been used. Here a group of people question the interviewee using either a structured or unstructured technique. Finally, group interviews have been used where a group of job candidates are observed in group discussions.

It is highly unlikely that any one type of interview is appropriate for all situations.[13] The most appropriate type of interview depends on the type of information that the organization wants to obtain from the interviewee and the nature of the job to be filled.

---

[11] National Industrial Conference Board, "Personal Practices," p. 12.

[12] Walter Van Dyke Bigham and Bruce V. Moore, *How to Interview*, 3d rev. ed. (New York: Harper & Brothers, 1941), p. 1.

[13] J. M. Frazer, T. M. Higham, and J. Chapman, "The Ultimate Interview," *Personnel and Training Management*, vol. 12 (1967), pp. 22–26.

Interviews, like tests, have the same basic problems of validity and reliability. Research has shown that interviewers often report extreme differences when evaluating the same individual.[14] Milton M. Mandell of the U.S. Civil Service Commission has described the interviewing process as follows:

> The basic difficulty of (the) interview, as usually conducted, is that it involves making extensive inferences from limited data obtained in artificial situations by unqualified observers.[15]

However, regardless of the criticism, interviewing is still a widely used technique in the selection process. Crossvalidation of the interview with other data obtained in the selection process is one method of attempting to solve the validity and reliability problems. Presently the structured interview has the most promise for high validity.[16]

Several suggestions have also been offered concerning improving the interviewing process. Most of these are not based on scientific evidence, and thus interviewing is still more of an art than a science. The most frequently discussed guidelines for the interviewing process are:

1. Advance planning of the interview.
2. Establish and maintain rapport with the interviewee.
3. Maintain the primary goal in mind and move the interview toward that goal. The goal is to determine information that will aid in the employment decision.
4. Record results. The results of the interview should always be recorded to ensure that facts and information are not forgotten.

One of the best ways to determine the success of an organization's interviewing program is to compare performance ratings of individuals hired against their appraisal based on the interviewing process. This crossvalidation can prove quite beneficial not only to the interviewer but to the total organization.

Physical examination

After the potential employee has cleared the preceding hurdles, most organizations require a physical examination. The physical examination is given not only to determine his eligibility for group life, health, and disability insurance but also to determine if the in-

---

[14] Daniel Sydiaha, "Bales' Interaction Process Analysis of Personnel Selection Interviews," *Journal of Applied Psychology*, vol. 45, no. 6 (December 1961), pp. 393–401.

[15] Milton M. Mandell, "The Group Oral Performance Test," *Personnel Administration*, vol. 15, no. 6 (November 1952), p. 2.

[16] Wendell French, *The Personnel Management Process*, 2d ed. (Boston: Houghton Mifflin Company, 1970), p. 231.

dividual is physically capable of performing the job. As with most of the steps in the selection process, changes are also occurring in this area. New definitions and policies are emerging for hiring handicapped people. Many jobs are also being reexamined to determine the exact physical requirements of the job.

Personal judgment

The final step in the selection process is the personal judgment that is required in selecting one individual for the job. Of course, the assumption made at this point is that there will be more than one individual qualified for the job. If this is true, a value judgment using all of the data obtained in the previous steps of the selection process must be made in selecting the best individual for the job. If the previous steps have been performed successfully, the chances of success in this personal judgment are dramatically improved.

The individual making the personal judgment should also recognize that in some cases none of the applicants are satisfactory. If this occurs, the job should be redesigned, more money should be offered to attract more qualified candidates, or other actions should be taken. Caution should be taken against accepting the best individual that has been seen if the individual is not what is needed to do the job.

EMPLOYEE DEVELOPMENT

Employee development is a process that is concerned with the improvement and growth of the capabilities of individuals and groups within the organization. The goal of employee development is to facilitate the achievement of organizational goals. Included in this process are such activities as determining employee development needs, training and development programs, performance reviews, and employee counseling.

The importance of employee development cannot be understated. Frequently employee development is viewed by management as a nicety that is encouraged in good economic times but is quickly reduced or eliminated in bad economic times. Such a short-term position often causes the organization to suffer in the long run.

Chapter 16, which focuses on developing individual abilities and traits, discusses specific methods and techniques of employee development.

TRANSFERS, PROMOTIONS, AND SEPARATIONS

Recalling Figure 7–1, the final step in the personnel planning process involves promotions, transfers, and separations. Each of these types of changes obviously influences the total personnel situation. Transferring an employee merely involves moving an employee to another job at approximately the same level in the organization with basically the same pay, performance requirements, and status. Planned transfers can serve as an excellent development technique. Transfers can also be helpful in balancing varying departmental work load requirements. The most common problem relating to transfers occurs when a "problem employee" is unloaded on an unsuspecting manager. Training, counseling, or corrective punishment of the delinquent employee may eliminate the need for such transfers. If the employee cannot be rehabilitated, discharge is preferable to transfer.

A promotion involves moving an employee to a job involving higher pay, status, and thus higher performance requirements. The two basic criteria used by most organizations in promotions are merit and seniority. Union contracts often require that seniority be considered in promotions. Many organizations prefer to base promotions on merit as a way of rewarding and encouraging performance. Obviously, this assumes that the organization has a method for evaluating performance and determining merit. An organization must also consider the requirements of the job for which an individual is being considered and not just performance in previous jobs. Potential and past performance must be considered. Success in one job does not automatically insure success in another job. Furthermore, evaluating potential in addition to past performance lessens the probability of the occurrence of the Peter Principle.

A separation involves either voluntary or involuntary termination of an employee. In voluntary terminations, many organizations attempt to determine why the employee is leaving by using exit interviews. This type of interview provides insights into problem areas in the organization that need to be corrected. Involuntary separations should be made only as a last resort. When a company has hired an employee and invested resources in the employee, termination results in a low return on the organization's investment. Training and counseling often are tried before firing an individual. However, when rehabilitation fails, the best course of action is usually termination because of the negative impact a disgruntled and misfit employee can have on others in the organization.

SUMMARY

Staffing is part of the organizing function and involves securing and developing personnel to fill the jobs that have been created by earlier phases of the organizing function.

Personnel planning is the process by which an organization ensures that it has the right number of people and the right kind of people, at the right places, at the right time, doing things for which they are economically most useful. The personnel planning process involves job analyses, skills inventories, personnel forecasting, recruitment, selection, employee development, promotions, transfers, and separations.

Job analysis is a process of determining, through observation and study, the pertinent information relating to the nature of a specific job. A skills inventory provides basic information on all the employees of an organization. Combining the skills inventory with the job analyses enables the organization to determine its present position with regard to its human resources.

Personnel forecasting is an attempt to determine the future personnel needs of the organization. Recruitment involves the activities of seeking and attracting a supply of people from which qualified candidates for job vacancies can be selected.

The purpose of the selection process is to choose the individuals that are most likely to succeed from those that have been recruited. Steps involved in the selection process are preliminary screening and interviewing, testing, performance reference checks, diagnostic interviews, physical examinations, and a personal judgment.

Employee development is a process that is concerned with the improvement and growth of the capabilities of individuals and groups within the organization. The goal of employee development is to facilitate the achievement of organizational goals.

Promotions, transfers, and separations are the final steps that influence the personnel planning process. Transferring an employee involves moving the employee to another job at approximately the same level in the organization with basically the same pay, performance requirements, and status. A promotion involves moving an employee to a job involving higher pay, status, and thus higher performance requirements. A separation involves either voluntary or involuntary termination of an employee.

REVIEW QUESTIONS

1. How does staffing relate to the organizing function?

2. What is personnel planning?

3. What is a job analysis? A job description? A skills inventory?

4. What is personnel forecasting?

5. Describe a model of the personnel planning process.

6. Describe the purpose of the three following government bills:
   a. Equal Pay Act of 1963.
   b. Civil Rights Act of 1964.
   c. Age Discrimination in Employment Act of 1967.

7. What is recruitment? Describe some sources of recruitment.

8. What is selection? Describe the steps in the selection process.

9. What is test reliability? What methods are commonly used to determine test reliability?

10. What is test validity?

11. What is employee development? Cite some of the activities involved in employee development.

12. What is a transfer? A promotion? A separation?

DISCUSSION QUESTIONS

1. Discuss the following statement: "If an individual owns a business, he should be able to hire anyone and shouldn't have to worry about the government."

2. Defend your position on the following statement: "Tests do not reflect an individual's ability."

3. Many managers believe that line managers should not have to worry about personnel needs and that this should be handled by the personnel department. What do you think?

4. One common method of handling problem employees is to transfer them to another department of the organization. Discuss your feelings on this practice.

5. Joe Holland has been a senior engineer with the Nu-Way Company for 18 years. A management position related to engineering has just become vacant. Should Joe be promoted to this job?

SELECTED READINGS

Alfred, Theodore M. "Checkers or Choice in Manpower Management," *Harvard Business Review*, vol. 45, no. 1 (January–February 1967), pp. 157–69.

American Society for Training and Development. *Training and Development Handbook*, Robert L. Craig and Lester R. Bittel, eds. New York: McGraw-Hill Book Co., 1967.

Black, James M. *How to Get Results from Interviewing*. New York: McGraw-Hill Book Company, 1970.

Buros, O. K., ed., *Sixth Mental Measurements Yearbook.* Highland Park, N.J.: Gryphon Press, 1965.

French, Wendell. *The Personnel Management Process.* 2d ed. Boston, Mass.: Houghton Mifflin Company, 1970.

Guion, Robert M. *Personnel Testing.* New York: McGraw-Hill Book Company, 1965.

Hamner, W. Clay, and Frank L. Schmidt. *Contemporary Problems in Personnel.* Chicago, Ill.: St. Clair Press, 1974.

Megginson, Leon C. *Personnel: A Behavioral Approach to Administration.* rev. ed. Homewood, Ill.: Richard D. Irwin, Inc., 1972.

Patten, Thomas H., Jr. *Manpower Planning and the Development of Human Resources.* New York: John Wiley and Sons, 1972.

Walker, James W. "Trends in Manpower Management Research," *Business Horizons,* vol. 11, no. 4 (August 1968), pp. 37–46.

Case 7–1

Problems in city government

The city of Windsor, like most city governments, has a centralized personnel operation. The Personnel Department does the recruiting and testing and works with all operating departments in selecting new employees. They, like other governmental agencies, employ the merit system for job selection and promotion.

Until recently, the Windsor Personnel Department used the following process when a job was to be filled by hiring from outside the organization:

1. A job description was prepared and advertised. This description was very general and included all the tasks which the person might perform.
2. Minimum or desirable requirements were established. These requirements were based on what operating departments wanted and what the Civil Service Board thought was reasonable. It was not based on any demonstrable criteria.
3. Tests were given to those who met minimum requirements. Those who passed the tests were interviewed.
4. A register was established ranking the qualified applicants on a scale from 70 to 100.
5. Departments then chose one of the top three applicants on the register.

Two years ago, based on pressure from EEOC and on various court decisions, Windsor's Personnel Department realized that their personnel selection process had to be changed. Federal regulations were requiring them to prove that certain job requirements were necessary to perform certain jobs.

The Personnel Department made a number of adjustments. In the past, if 100 people applied for a job and 75 met the minimum requirements but 15 looked like good applicants, only the 15 people would be sent letters saying they would be interviewed and further tested.

Today, if 100 people apply for a job and 75 meet the minimum requirements, then all 75 people receive letters saying they will be interviewed and further tested. After the interviews and tests, these 75 people are then placed in three groups – qualified, well-qualified, and very well-qualified – and the names are sent to the department where the job opening occurs. Previously, only the names of the top three people would be sent to the departments, and the departments could select one name from this list. Now they can select any name from any of the three groups as long as the applicant is qualified.

The present situation has created problems for departments that are trying to fill a position. A department, under the old process, would have been involved in the 15 interviews, but when a selection was made, they had to choose one person from the top three. Now a department is involved in interviewing all qualified people (in the above case, 75 people), and when a list is sent to them the department has three groupings and can still select anyone from any of the three groups.

As a result of the present selection process, a great deal of animosity has developed between the Personnel Department and other departments. Other departments question why the Personnel Department exists at all. The departments are spending much more time interviewing applicants. After the interviews, the Personnel Department still sends all the names to the departments and the departments select from the list.

1. Do you agree with the other departments?
2. What can be done to resolve this situation?
3. Do you agree with the system that is used? How could it be improved?

Case 7–2

The new employee

Jerry Taylor is a supervisor in a textile production plant. He has 15 years service with the company. The last ten have been as a supervisor. His unit is usually among the leaders in production, and he gets along well with the local union. Ralph Jones, who is a college graduate with five years of work experience, is Jerry's supervisor. Ralph has been in this current job less than six months. Luther Pippen is a new employee with the textile firm. He is just out of high school and has no other work experience. His new employee probationary period is due to end in two more months. Charlie Phillips is the area union representative and has been the elected representative of the local union for the past eight years. He is respected by the members of the union and by the members of management.

Ralph Jones is finishing up his paperwork on Friday afternoon and preparing to leave for the weekend when Jerry Taylor comes in to see him.

Taylor: Ralph I'd like to talk with you for a few minutes. I've got something that I would like you to think over this weekend. I have a new man, Luther Pippen, whose probationary period is going to expire in a couple of months. I've been working with this man very closely ever since he first arrived at the plant, and I'm convinced that he should be terminated before the end of his probationary period.

Jones: If he still has two months to go on his probation, that means he's only been with us four months. What makes you so sure that this man is unsuitable?

Taylor: Ralph, I seriously doubt if this man has the mental capacity to work safely around the equipment in our department. I went over to Personnel and checked his entrance tests and they were all minimum. I think the man was given this job as a borderline case, and he's demonstrated to me that he just can't cut it.

Jones: Let me see your folder on this man. I hope you've got pretty good documentation to back up your assertions. Even though we have a probationary period for evaluating new employees, I can't ever recall an employee being terminated during the probationary period.

Taylor: I'll admit it's unusual, but I really think we've got a case here.

Jones reviewed the employee's file, which contained a record of all the counseling sessions that Taylor had given Pippen. The folder documented that Taylor had briefed Pippen on all the company plans, policies, and safety procedures during his first week on the job. After that time, Pippen was given the normal rotation of menial jobs in order to familiarize him with the operation of the plant. Throughout this orientation period Taylor had documentation of repeated reinstruction that was given to Pippen in order to clarify minor procedural points and safety problems. Taylor had also recorded several safety infractions which had been noted by the plant safety inspector on tours through the area. After each one of the infractions, Taylor had taken Pippen off the job, sat down, and reinstructed him on the correct method for doing the work. Subsequent records showed that Pippen recommitted each one of the safety infractions at a later date.

As the trend of repeated safety infractions and poor adherence to procedures began to develop, the records show that Taylor had brought the union representative, Charlie Phillips, into the picture. Many sessions regarding repeat safety and procedural infractions were conducted with the union representative present.

Jones: Well, Jerry, you seem to have a pretty complete book on this man. Tell me, what was Pippen's reactions to all of your comments and re-instructural sessions?

Taylor: Ralph, the guy just sat there smiled and said he'd try and do a better job. The guy really puzzles me. He really seems like he wants to do a good job, but he just cannot seem to grasp even the simplest operations.

Jones: What is Charlie's reaction to terminating this employee?

Taylor: Charlie hasn't really committed to me one way or another. I have mentioned it to him on several occasions, but he just backs off, "Now Jerry, he's a new man, and we've got to work with him." I think that his reaction is just to make sure that nobody can accuse him of not backing the man.

Jones: Okay, Jerry, I'll think about it over the weekend. One thing I do want you to do for me: Have Charlie Phillips come in and see me on Monday morning.

1. What should Jones do?
2. If a person tries, should he be penalized merely because he can't do the job?
3. Do you think that Taylor has done all he can do?

Objectives

1. To define management control and discuss the major elements of the managerial control process.
2. To develop an appreciation for the economic and behavioral aspects of a management control system.
3. To introduce and describe several specific management control methods and techniques.

GLOSSARY OF TERMS

Audit A method of control that is normally involved with financial matters but also can include other areas of the organization.

Break-even chart Charts used to depict graphically the relationship of volume of operations to profits.

Budgets A statement of expected results or requirements expressed in financial or numerical terms.

Control A process of ensuring that organizational activities are going according to plan. Control is accomplished by comparing actual performance to predetermined standards or objectives and then taking action to correct for any deviations.

CPM (Critical Path Method) A planning and control technique that graphically depicts the relationships between the various activities that compose a project. CPM is used when time durations of activities in the project are accurately known and have little variance.

Flexible budget A special type of budget which allows certain expenses to vary with the level of sales or output.

Gantt chart A control device that graphically shows work planned and work accomplished in their relation to each other and in relation to time.

Management audit An attempt to evaluate the overall management practices and policies of the organization.

Management by objectives (MBO) A management system in which the superior and subordinate jointly define the objectives and responsibilities of the subordinate's job and then use these as criteria in evaluating the subordinate's performance.

PERT (Performance Evaluation and Review Technique) A planning and control technique that graphically depicts the relationships between the various activities that compose a project. PERT is used when the durations of the project activities are not accurately known.

Standard A value used as a point of reference for comparing other values.

8

Controlling: The containment function

> In many circumstances the more managers attempt to obtain
> and exercise control over the behavior of others in the organiza-
> tion, the less control they have. Furthermore, often the less
> control they have, the more pressure they feel to exert greater
> control, which in turn often decreases the amount of control they
> have, etc., etc.
>
> Gene Dalton and Paul Lawrence*

THE BASIC premise of organizations is that all activities will function smoothly; however, the possibility of this being false gives rise to the need for control. Control simply means knowing what is actually happening in comparison to predetermined standards or objectives. Management control is a process of ensuring that organizational activities are going according to plan. Control is accomplished by comparing actual performance to predetermined standards or objectives and then taking action to correct any deviations from the standard. However, as the quote above implies, control is a sensitive and complex component of the management process.

Controlling is similar to planning in that it addresses the basic questions of: Where are we now? Where do we want to be? How can we get there from here? The difference is that controlling takes place after the planning has been completed and after the organizational activities have begun. Comparatively speaking, controlling is after the fact, whereas planning is before the fact. This does not mean that control is practiced only after problems occur. Control can be preventive. Control decisions can also affect future planning decisions.

---

* *Motivation and Control in Organizations*, Richard D. Irwin, Inc., 1971, p. 5.

167

TWO CONCERNS OF CONTROL

When practicing control the manager must simultaneously balance two major concerns: stability and objective realization. In order to maintain stability the manager must be sure that the organization is operating within its established boundaries of constraint. The boundaries of constraint are determined by policies, budgets, ethics, laws, and so on. The second concern of control, objective realization, requires continual monitoring to ensure that adequate progress is being made toward the accomplishment of established objectives.

One danger is that a manager will become overly worried about one of the above concerns at the expense of the other. The most common example of this behavior occurs when the manager becomes preoccupied with the stability of the operation and neglects the goal. Such behavior can lead to excessive activity but very little output. The manager who is obsessed with the manner or style with which a job is accomplished exemplifies this behavior. On the other hand, the manager may lose sight of stability and experience glamorous but short-lived success. The manager who sets production records by eliminating safety checks is an example of this behavior.

THE MANAGEMENT CONTROL PROCESS

Figure 8–1 is a simple model of the management control process. Activities and outputs from the activity are monitored by some type of sensor and compared to preselected standards (normally set during the planning process). The manager acts as the regulator and takes corrective action when the outputs do not conform to the standards.

The manager's actions may be directed at the inputs to the activity or the activity itself. Such a system where outputs from the system affect future inputs or future activities of the system is called a feedback or closed system. In other words, a feedback system is a system influenced by its own past behaviors.[1] The heating system of a house is a common example of a mechanical feedback system. The thermostat compares the temperature resulting from heat previously generated by the system to some predetermined standard (the desired temperature setting) and responds accordingly. Another common household example of a feedback system is the flush toilet which shuts off the flow of water automatically when it senses that the tank is full.

Feedback is a necessary component of the control process. Although precautionary, before-the-fact steps can often be taken to aid

---

[1] Jay W. Forrester, *Principles of Systems* (Cambridge, Mass.: Wright-Allen Press, Inc., 1968), pp. 1–5.

FIGURE 8–1
The control process

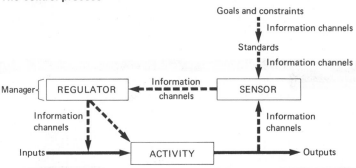

the control process, total control cannot be practiced without feedback. Managers may receive and act on information concerning the inputs or the activity itself; however, they ultimately must know what is happening in the organization and feedback provides them with this information.

THREE REQUIREMENTS FOR CONTROL

The process of control has three basic requirements: (1) establish standards; (2) monitor results and compare to standards; and (3) correct deviations. The first requirement (setting standards) is part of the planning process while the latter two (monitoring and correcting) are unique to the control process. All three requirements are essential to maintaining effective control.

Setting standards

A standard is a value used as a point of reference for comparing other values. As such, a standard outlines what is expected of the job and/or individual. An objective can be a standard. Because much of the manager's work deals with people and varying personalities, it may be unwise for the manager to always compare an individual with a group average.[2] Different criteria may have to be set for each individual. Ideally, standards are easily measured and definable. Such standards may deal with production output per hour as determined by time and motion studies, quality control as demanded by customer satisfaction, or production schedules prepared in accordance with

---

[2] E. T. Eggers, "The Need for Definite Standards and Criteria," *Atlanta Economic Review*, June 1971, p. 38.

established procedures.[3] The process of setting standards is discussed in depth in Chapter 14.

Monitoring performance

The overriding purpose of monitoring performance is to isolate problem areas. Once actual performance has been determined and compared to the standard or plan, the proper corrective action can be determined. The nature and type of standard being used often dictates the type of checks to be made. Obviously the entire control system is no better than the information on which it operates, and much of this information is gathered from the monitoring process.

The major problems of monitoring performance are deciding when, where, and how often to inspect or check. Checks must be made often enough to provide adequate information. However, if overdone, the monitoring process can become expensive and can also result in adverse reactions when people are being monitored. It is not uncommon for a manager to become obsessed with the checking process. Timing is equally important in the monitoring of performance. The manager must recognize a deviation in time to correct it. For example, inventory control personnel must consider the reorder time and not wait until the stocks have been depleted to reorder.

Correcting for deviations

All too often managers set standards and monitor results but do not follow up with appropriate actions. The first two steps are of little value if corrective action is not taken. It is entirely possible that the corrective action may be to continue the status quo. Action of this type would be contingent upon standards being met in a satisfactory manner. If standards are not being satisfactorily met, the manager must

FIGURE 8–2
Potential causes of performance deviations

Faulty planning
Lack of communication within the organization
Personal ineptness or negligence
Need for training
Lack of motivation
Outside forces

---

[3] Ibid., p. 39.

find the cause of the deviation and correct it. It is not enough simply to eliminate the deviation itself or treat only the symptoms. This action is analogous to replacing a car battery when the real problem is a faulty generator. In a short period of time, the battery will go dead again. It is also possible that a careful analysis of the deviation will require a readjustment of the standard. The standard may have been improperly set initially or changed conditions may require a readjustment. Figure 8–2 lists some potential causes of deviations between desired and actual performance.

CONTROL TOLERANCES

Actual performance rarely conforms exactly to standards or plans. A certain amount of variation will normally occur as a result of chance. Therefore, the manager must set limits concerning the acceptable degree of deviation from standard. In other words, how much variation from standard is tolerable? The manner in which the manager sets control tolerances depends on the particular goal or standard being used for comparison. Frequently the manager must make subjective judgments as to when the system or factor being monitored is "out of control." If the activity being monitored lends itself to numerical measurement, statistical control techniques can be used. In any case, one element influencing how much deviation is acceptable is the risk of being "out of control" and not realizing it. In general, the lower the risk, the wider the tolerances. Figure 8–3 illustrates the idea of control tolerances. It should be noted that the tolerance levels may be formalized, or they may merely exist in the mind of the manager. The important point is that the manager must develop some

FIGURE 8–3
Control tolerance limits

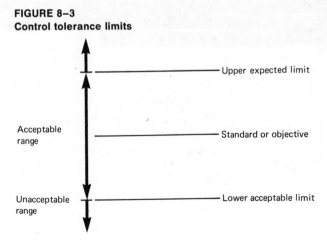

guidelines as to what is acceptable (in control) and what is not acceptable (out of control).

HOW MUCH CONTROL?

When deciding how much control should be exercised in an organization, two major factors must be appraised: (1) economic considerations and (2) behavioral considerations.

Economic considerations

To install and operate control mechanisms costs money. For instance, a good quality control system requires additional labor if nothing else. The equipment costs of sophisticated electronic and mechanical control systems can be very high. Ideally, control systems should be installed as long as they save more than they cost. The costs of implementing a control system can usually be estimated or calculated much more accurately than can the benefits. It is, at best, difficult to quantify and measure the true benefits of a quality control system. Supposedly the quality control system increases goodwill, but how does one measure this attribute? The decision is obviously much easier in situations where the costs of not maintaining control are either very high or very low. Despite the problems associated with measuring the economic benefits of a system of controls, management should periodically undertake such a study to insure that gross misapplications do not occur.

Behavioral considerations

Negative behavioral reactions often are the most frequently encountered problems related to the control function. The major problem is deciding how much control is necessary. Very few people like to work in an environment where there is no control. An absense of control creates an uncertain environment in which people do not know what is expected of them. On the other hand, most people do not like to work in an overly controlled environment.

Figure 8–4 shows a simplified version of a model developed by Alvin Gouldner which illustrates a dilemma related to control. This dilemma often occurs when management has little or no feel for the appropriate degree of control.

Gouldner's model begins with top management's demand for control over operations. This is attempted through the use and enforcement of general and impersonal rules regulating work procedures. These rigid rules provide intentional guides for the behavior of the

FIGURE 8–4
Simplified Gouldner model of organization control

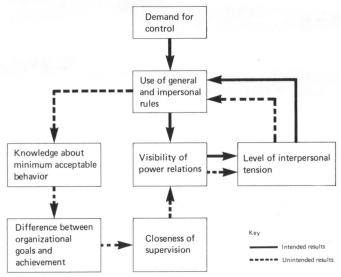

Source: James G. March and Herbert A. Simon, *Organizations* (New York: John Wiley & Sons, Inc., 1958), p. 45.

organizational members, but they also have the unintentional effect of indicating minimum acceptable behavior. In organizations where there is not a high level of congruence between individual and organizational goals or there is not a high acceptance of organizational goals, the effect is a reduction of performance to the minimally acceptable level (people not highly committed to organizational goals will perform at the minimally acceptable level). Management views such behavior as the result of inadequate control and therefore responds with closer supervision. This closer supervision increases the visibility of power which in turn raises the level of interpersonal tension in the organization. A raising of the tension level elicits even closer enforcement of the general and impersonal formal rules and hence the cycle repeats itself. Thus the overall effect is increased control, increased interpersonal tension, and a lowering of performance.

One difficulty in determining the appropriate degree of control is that different individuals react differently to similar controls. Research has suggested that individual reactions to patterns of organizational control differ according to personality and prior experiences.[4]

---

[4] For a discussion of some such studies see Arnold S. Tannenbaum, "Control in Organizations: Individual Adjustment in Organization Performance," *Administrative Science Quarterly*, September 1962, pp. 241–46.

Problems can occur from anticipated reactions to control because of both compliance and resistance.[5] Problems from compliance arise when individuals adhere to the behavior prescribed by controls even when such behavior is inappropriate. The salesperson who will not vary from prescribed procedures in order to satisfy a customer complaint is a common example of over-compliance. Problems resulting from resistance to controls arise when individuals attempt to preempt, circumvent, or sabotage the controls. Distorting a report or padding the budget is a form of control resistance. Many of the behavioral problems associated with controls result from a lack of understanding of the nature and purpose of the controls. It is a natural reaction for humans to resist anything new that they do not understand. Therefore the manager who is responsible for installing new controls should make sure that the purpose and nature of the controls are fully communicated to all affected employees.

A contingency approach

For years management and behavioral scholars maintained that control in organizations was a fixed commodity and that control should only rest in the hands of top management. Arnold Tannenbaum has formulated a theory which states that the total amount of control in an organization may increase or decrease.[6] Tannenbaum's theory postulates that increased control when exercised by both managers and subordinates can lead to more effective organizational performance. Building on Tannenbaum's work, Timothy McMahon and G. W. Perritt have formulated a contingency theory of control.[7] They state ". . . that organizational effectiveness will be enhanced to the extent that there is a high amount of control exerted within the management system, and that this control is distributed in a power equalized fashion and that there is agreement among managerial echelons as to the amount and distribution of control within the system."[8] Essentially McMahon and Perritt are saying that the more control, the better, provided the control is shared by individuals close to the work and that there are no disagreements concerning the distribution of the controls. Sharing the controls with individuals close to the work can be accomplished by placing the controls as far down in the organiza-

---

[5] Gene W. Dalton and Paul R. Lawrence, *Motivation and Control in Organizations* (Homewood, Ill.: Richard D. Irwin, Inc., 1971), p. 8.

[6] Arnold S. Tannenbaum, *Control in Organizations* (New York: McGraw-Hill Book Co., 1968), pp. 12–25.

[7] J. Timothy McMahon and G. W. Perritt, "Toward a Contingency Theory of Organizational Control," *Academy of Management Journal*, December 1973, pp. 624–35.

[8] Ibid., p. 634.

tional structure as possible. Involving the lower echelons in the control process minimizes communication problems and also elicits support. The second contingency of McMahon and Perritt concerning the distributions of the controls is necessary to avoid conflicts as to who has the control. Such conflicts can adversely affect the processes of communicating, organizing, and motivating.

CONTROL METHODS AND SYSTEMS

One of the most common mistakes made by management is to assume that a new method or system of control will in itself solve problems. Methods and systems in themselves do not control! Control methods and systems in conjunction with good administration and intelligent interpretation provide control. The most appropriate control system is almost worthless if not properly administered. Likewise, an appropriate control system which is suitably administered can only produce information which requires intelligent interpretation. Thus the methods and systems presented in this section should not be viewed as solutions to control problems but rather as potential aids in the control process.

Before or after the fact?

In general, methods of exercising control can be described as either before-the-fact or after-the-fact. Before-the-fact methods of control are anticipatory in nature and attempt to prevent a problem from occurring. Requiring prior approval for purchases of all items over a certain dollar value is a before-the-fact method of control. After-the-fact methods of control are designed to detect a potential problem or an existing one before it gets out of hand. Most written or periodic reports represent after-the-fact control methods.

Budgets

Budgets are probably the most widely used control devices. A budget is a statement of expected results or requirements expressed in financial or numerical terms. Budgets express plans, objectives, and programs of the organization in numerical terms. While preparation of the budget is primarily a planning function, its administration is a controlling function.

Many different types of budgets are in use. Figure 8–5 outlines some of the most common types of budgets. Although the dollar is usually the common denominator, budgets may be expressed in other

FIGURE 8–5
Types and purposes of budgets

Type of Budget	Brief Description or Purpose
Revenue and expense budget	Provides details for revenue and expense plans
Cash budget	Forecasts cash receipts and disbursements
Capital expenditure budget	Outlines specific expenditures for plant, equipment, machinery, inventories, and other capital items
Production, material, or time budget	Expresses physical requirements of production, or material, or the time requirements for the budget period
Balance sheet budgets	Forecasts the status of assets, liabilities, and net worth at the end of the budget period

terms. Equipment budgets may be expressed in numbers of machines. Material budgets may be expressed in pounds, pieces, gallons, and so on. Budgets not expressed in dollars can usually be translated into dollars for incorporation into an overall budget.

While budgets are useful for planning and control they are not without their dangers. Perhaps the greatest potential danger is inflexibility. Inflexibility is a special threat to organizations operating in an industry characterized by rapid change and high competition. Rigidity in the budget can also lead to a subordination of organizational goals to budgetary goals. The financial manager who won't spend $5 over the budget in order to make $500 is a classic example. Budgets can hide inefficiencies. The fact that a certain expenditure was made in the past often becomes justification for continuing the expenditure, when in fact the situation has changed considerably. Budgets can also become inflationary and inaccurate. This happens when a manager pads his budget because he knows it will be cut by his superiors. Since he is never sure of how severe the cut will be, the result is often an inaccurate if not unrealistic budget.

Flexible budgets

In order to overcome many of the shortcomings resulting from inflexibility in budgets, flexible or variable budgets are designed to vary with volume of sales or some other measure of output. Because

TABLE 8–1
Simplified flexible budget

Unit sales..........................	$ 5,000	$ 6,000	$ 7,000	$ 8,000	$ 9,000
Product cost	10,000	12,000	14,000	16,000	18,000
Advertising......................	5,000	5,000	5,000	5,000	5,000
Shipping costs	5,000	5,500	6,000	6,500	7,000
Sales commissions	2,500	3,000	3,500	4,000	4,500
Budgeted expenses	$27,500	$31,500	$35,500	$39,500	$43,500

of their nature, flexible budgets are generally limited in application to expense budgets. The basic idea is to allow material, labor, advertising, and other related expenses to vary with the volume of output. Because the actual level of sales or output is not known in advance, flexible budgets are more useful for evaluating what the expenses should have been under the circumstances but have limited value for providing planning information to the overall budgeting program. Table 8–1 illustrates a simplified flexible budget.

Direct observation

A plant manager's daily tour of the plant, a president's annual visit to all installations, and a methods study by a staff industrial engineer are all examples of control by direct observation. Although it is time-consuming, personal observation is sometimes the only way to get an accurate picture of what is really happening. A hazzard of personal observation is the possibility that the subordinates may misinterpret a superior's visit and consider such action as meddling or eavesdropping. A potential inaccuracy associated with personal observation is that behaviors change when they are being watched or monitored. When the boss or methods engineer walks into the room, behaviors may change. Another potential inaccuracy lies in the interpretation of the observation. The observer must be careful not to "read into the picture" events that did not actually occur. Visits and direct observation can also have very positive effects when viewed by the workers as a display of the superior's interest.

Written reports

Written reports can be prepared on a periodic or "as necessary" basis. There are two basic types of written reports: (1) analytical and

(2) informational. Analytical reports interpret the facts they present, whereas informational reports only present the facts. Preparing a report is a four or five step process depending on whether it is informational or analytical. The steps are (1) planning the attack on the problem; (2) collecting the facts; (3) organizing the facts; (4) interpreting the facts (this step is omitted with informational reports); and (5) preparing the report.[9] When preparing a report it should be kept in mind that most reports are primarily written for the benefit of the reader and not the writer. The reader wants useful information that he does not already have. The need for a report should be carefully evaluated. Periodic reports have a way of continuing long past their usefulness. Such unnecessary reports can represent a substantial waste of organizational resources.

Audits ρ

Audits can be conducted either by internal or external personnel. An external audit is normally conducted by outside accounting personnel and is limited to financial matters. Such an audit is generally performed to certify the accounting methods used as to fairness, consistency, and conformity with existing rules. Most audits performed by outside accounting firms do not delve into nonfinancial matters such as management practices. The internal audit is normally similar to the external audit except it is performed by the organization's own personnel.

When the auditing procedure evaluates areas other than finances and accounting it is known as a management audit. Management audits attempt to evaluate the overall management practices and policies of the organization. Management audits can be conducted by outside consultants or inside staff; however, an audit conducted by inside staff can easily result in a biased report.

Break-even charts $\mathcal{f}$

Break-even charts are used to depict graphically the relationship of volume of operations to profits. Specifically, the break-even point is the point at which sales revenues exactly equal expenses. Total sales below the breakeven point (BEP) result in a loss, and total sales above the BEP result in a profit.

---

[9] J. H. Menning and C. W. Wilkinson, *Communicating through Letters and Reports,* 5th ed. (Homewood, Ill.: Richard D. Irwin, Inc., 1972), p. 493.

Figure 8–6 illustrates a typical break-even chart. The horizontal axis represents output; the vertical axis represents expenses and revenues. Although not a requirement, most break-even charts assume that there are linear relationships and that all costs are either fixed or variable. Fixed costs are those that do not vary with output, at least in the short run. Examples include rent, insurance, and administrative salaries. Variable costs are those that vary with output. Typical variable costs include direct labor and materials. The purpose of the chart is to show the exact break-even point and the effects of changes in output.

FIGURE 8–6
Break-even chart

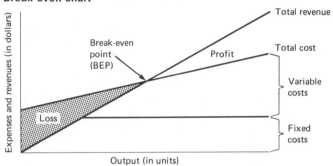

The appendix at the end of this text contains a more detailed discussion of break-even analysis.

Time related charts and techniques⫽⌐

"Plan your work and work your plan" has long been a byword for many organizations. Several useful graphical and analytical techniques have been developed to aid in the planning and controlling processes. The overriding purpose of such techniques is to permit the manager to see how the various segments of the operation interrelate and to evaluate the overall progress being made.

The Gantt chart is the oldest and simplest method of graphically showing both the anticipated and completed production. Developed by Henry L. Gantt in the early 1900s, the distinguishing feature of the Gantt chart is that work planned and work accomplished are shown in their relation to each other and in relation to time. Figure 8–7 presents a typical Gantt chart.

FIGURE 8–7
Gantt chart with heavy lines indicating work completed

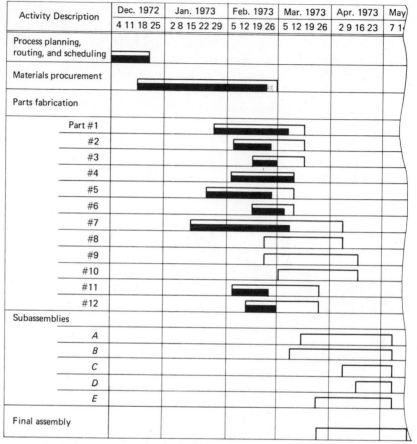

Adapted from Elwood S. Buffa, *Modern Production Management,* 4th ed. (New York: John Wiley & Sons, 1973), p. 576.

Gantt charts emphasize the element of time by readily pointing out any actual or potential slippages. One criticism of the Gantt chart is that it can require considerable time to incorporate any scheduling changes such as rush orders. To accommodate such scheduling changes rapidly, mechanical boards using movable pegs or cards have been developed.

The Gantt chart concept of identifying work to be done and graphing it against time formed the foundation for network analysis.[10] The

---

[10] There is evidence that there were other forerunners to CPM and PERT. See Edward R. Marsh, "The Harmonogram of Karol Adamiecki," *Academy of Management Journal,* June 1975, pp. 358–64.

most popular network analysis approaches are CPM (Critical Path Method) and PERT (Program Evaluation and Review Technique). These two techniques were developed almost simultaneously in the late 1950s. CPM grew out of a joint study undertaken by DuPont and Remington Rand Univac to determine how to best reduce the time required to perform routine plant overhaul, maintenance, and construction work.[11] PERT was developed by the Navy in conjunction with representatives of Lockheed Aircraft Corporation and the consulting firm of Booz, Allen, and Hamilton to coordinate the development and production of the Polaris weapons system.

CPM and PERT are both techniques which result in a graphical network representation of a project. The graphical network is composed of activities and events. An activity is the work necessary to complete a particular event, and it usually consumes time. Events denote a point in time and their occurrence signifies the completion of all activities leading into the event. All activities originate and terminate at events. Activities are normally represented by arrows in a network while events are represented by a circle. The dashed arrows in a project network, called dummies, show dependencies or precedence relationships. Dummy activities require no time or resources to perform. They simply denote that the starting of an activity or set of activities depends on the completion of an activity.

Figure 8–8 shows a simple project represented by a Gantt chart and a project network. The project network has two distinct advantages over the Gantt chart: (1) the dependencies of the activities on each other are noted explicitly, and (2) the activities are shown in greater detail.

The path through the network which has the longest duration (based on a summation of estimated individual activity times) is referred to as the critical path. If any activity on the critical path lengthens, then the entire project duration lengthens.

The major difference between CPM and PERT centers around the activity time estimates. CPM is used for projects whose activity durations are accurately known and whose variance in the performance time is negligible. On the other hand, PERT is used when the activity durations are more uncertain and variable. CPM is based on a single estimate for an activity duration where PERT is based on three time estimates for each activity: an optimistic (minimum) time, a most likely (modal) time, and a pessimistic (maximum) time.

Project network analysis can provide much information beyond simple project planning and control. By knowing the critical activities,

---

[11] Joseph J. Moder and Cecil R. Phillips, *Project Management with CPM and PERT* (New York: Van Nostrand Reinhold Company, 1970), by Litton Educational Publishing, Inc., p. 6.

FIGURE 8–8
Project represented by Gantt chart and a project network

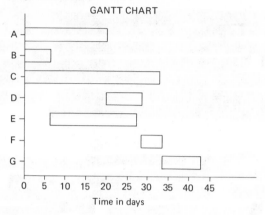

GANTT CHART

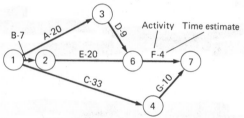

PROJECT NETWORK

the project manager can best allocate limited resources and make more accurate time-cost trade-offs. The appendix at the end of this text contains a more detailed discussion of CPM and PERT.

Management by objectives

Management by objectives (MBO) is another method which can be used for control purposes. Emerging in the early 1950s, MBO has been described in the following manner:

> A process whereby the superior and subordinate managers of an organization jointly identify its common goals, define each individual's major areas of responsibility in terms of the results expected of him, and use these measures as guides for operating the unit and assessing the contribution of each of its members.[12]

---

[12] From the book, *Management by Objectives* by George Odiorne. Copyright © 1965 by Pitman Publishing Corp. Reprinted by permission of Pitman Publishing Corp.

MBO is the control process applied on an individual basis. Standards (objectives) are set, performance is monitored, and corrective action taken where necessary. MBO requires that the subordinate and superior *jointly* set the objectives by which the subordinate will be evaluated. MBO is discussed in more depth in Chapter 17.

SUMMARY

Management control is a process of ensuring that organizational activities are going according to plan. The process of control has three basic requirements: (1) establish standards or objectives; (2) monitor results and compare to standards; and (3) correct for deviations. All three requirements are essential to maintaining effective control.

Because actual performance rarely conforms exactly to standards or plans, the manager must set limits as to which deviations from standard are acceptable and which are not. Such deviations are referred to as control tolerances.

Two major factors must be appraised when deciding the degree of control that should be exercised in an organization: (1) economic (cost) considerations and (2) behavioral considerations. Although the benefits from a particular system are often hard to calculate precisely, management should periodically attempt to measure the cost benefit of a system of controls. Such an investigation ensures that gross misapplications do not occur. In order to lessen negative behavioral reactions to control, the manager should make sure that the purpose and nature of the controls are fully understood by all affected employees. A contingency theory of control states that the amount of control exerted within an organization is contingent on the degree to which the control is shared by individuals close to the work and the degree of agreement concerning the distribution of the controls.

Several control methods and systems were discussed. These included budgets, personal observation, written reports, audits, break-even charts, time related charts, and management by objectives.

REVIEW QUESTIONS

1. What is management control? What are the two major concerns in management control?

2. Describe a model of the management control process.

3. Outline the three basic requirements of control.

4. How much control should be exercised in an organization?

5. Describe the following control methods and systems.
   a. Budgets.
   b. Direct observation.
   c. Written reports.
   d. Audits.
   e. Break-even charts.
   f. Time related charts and techniques.
   g. Management by objectives.

DISCUSSION QUESTIONS

1. What factors should you consider before installing tighter controls, and how might you evaluate these factors?

2. If you were implementing a new control system designed to check more closely the expenses of your salespeople, what actions might you take in order to minimize negative reactions?

3. Why are many managers reluctant to take the actions necessary to correct for deviations?

4. How should you deal with managers who are "so married" to their departmental budget that they will not let you spend one dollar in order to make ten dollars?

SELECTED READINGS

Burton, J. C. "Management Auditing," *The Journal of Accounting* (May 1968), pp. 41–46.

Emery, J. C. *Organizational Planning and Control Systems: Theory and Technology.* New York: MacMillan Company, 1969.

Goetz, Billy E. *Management Planning and Control.* New York: McGraw-Hill Book Company, 1949.

Johnson, Richard A., Fremont E. Kast, and James E. Rosenweig. *The Theory and Management of Systems.* 3d ed. New York: McGraw-Hill Book Company, 1973.

Mantz, R. K., and F. L. Neumann. "The Effective Corporate Audit Committee," *Harvard Business Review* (November–December 1970), pp. 57–65.

Mockler, R. J. "The Corporate Control Job: Breaking the Mold," *Business Horizons* (December 1970), pp. 73–77.

Moder, Joseph J., and Cecil R. Phillips. *Project Management with CPM and PERT.* New York: Van Nostrand Reinhold Company, 1970.

Odiorne, George. *Management by Objectives.* New York: Pittman Publishing Company, 1965.

Schonberger, R. J. "Custom-Tailored PERT/CPM Systems," *Business Horizons* (December 1972), pp. 64–66.

Strong, Earl P., and Robert D. Smith. *Management Control Models*. New York: Holt, Rinehart, and Winston, Inc., 1968.

Tannenbaum, A. S. *Control in Organizations*. New York: McGraw-Hill Book Company, 1968.

Case 8–1

"Bird dogging" the employee

Ace Radio, Inc., is a small company located in Centerville. The company is owned and operated by Al Abrams. Mr. Abrams, a highly experienced electronics man, founded the company in 1962.

Ace Radio's basic product is a walkie-talkie which is sold primarily to the U.S. military. The walkie-talkie units are relatively simple to produce; Ace merely purchases the parts—cables, wires, transistors, and so on—and assembles them with hand tools. Because of this moderate level of complexity, Ace employs semiskilled workers at low wage rates.

Although Ace has made a profit each year since it started production in 1962, Al Abrams was becoming increasingly concerned. Over the past six years he has noticed a general decline in employee morale, concomitantly he has observed a decline in his employee's productivity and his company's profit margin.

As a result of his concern, Mr. Abrams asked his supervisors to keep a closer watch on the hour-to-hour activities of the workers. In the first week they discovered two workers in the restroom reading magazines. This "bird dogging" technique, as it was called by management, or "slave-driving," as it was called by the workers, failed to increase production or productivity.

Mr. Abrams recognized that the lack of performance on the part of some of the workers affected the production of everyone. This phenomenon was caused by the balanced assembly line under which the walkie-talkies were assembled. If an employee next to a normally productive employee did not work fast enough, walkie-talkies would back up on the line. Instead of a back-up occurring, however, what usually occurred was a readjustment of the assembly line to the production rate of the slower workers.

In addition, another situation developed to lower productivity and increase unit costs. Ace was required by the government to meet monthly production and delivery schedules. If they failed, there was a very substantial financial penalty. In recent years the production and delivery schedule had become more difficult to meet. As a matter of fact, for the last eight months Al Abrams had scheduled overtime in order to meet the production and delivery schedule and thus avoid the financial penalty. This overtime not only increased unit production costs but as a result of this consistent use of overtime many employees began to realize that if they worked slower at the beginning of the month, they could receive more overtime at the end of the month.

This slowing down to increase overtime wages was practiced by even the senior employees. Abrams was very reluctant to fire employees, especially senior employees. Even if he was inclined to do so, it was difficult to "catch" employees slowing down or to provide any reasonable evidence for such a rash action.

Mr. Abrams was frustrated and perplexed.

1. Describe in detail the control dilemma that exists.
2. Are Mr. Abrams and the workers getting the same feedback?
3. What should Mr. Abrams do?

Case 8–2

Mickey Mouse controls

"Hey, John, I could sure use some help. We regional supervisors are caught in the middle. What do you do about all this red tape we're having to put up with? The Accounting Department is all bothered about the way people are padding their expenses and, of all things, taking someone to lunch and long-distance calls. You know — their answer is nothing but more red tape."

"Well, Bill, I don't know, but I'm feeling the heat too. Upper management wants us to maintain our contacts with our brokers and try to get the money out in loans. So we push the district supervisors to see our best contacts or at least call them frequently. Yet, lately I've been having a heck of a time getting my men reimbursed for their expenses. Now the Accounting Department is kicking because we spend a few bucks taking someone to lunch or making a few long-distance calls."

"I really don't know what to do, John. I'll admit that some of my people tend to charge the company for expenses that are for their personal entertainment. But how can I tell whether they're buttering up a broker or just living it up on the company? The Accounting Department must have some receipts and records to support expenses. Yet I think that getting a receipt from a parking lot attendant is carrying this control stuff too far. As a matter of fact, the other day,

I caught a taxi at the airport and failed to get a receipt—I'll bet I have a hard time getting that money from the company even if I sign a notarized affidavit."

"Well, the way I handle those things is to charge the company more for tips than I actually give—and you know they don't require receipts for tips. I just don't know how to decide whether those reimbursement requests that I sign for my boys are legitimate. If I call a guy up and ask him about some items on a reimbursement request, he acts as though I'm charging him with grand larceny. So far, I've decided to sign whatever requests they turn in and leave it to the Accounting Department to scream if they want to. The trouble is that I don't have any guidelines as to what is reasonable."

"Yeah, but I don't want to ask questions about that because it would just result in more doggone controls," Bill added. "It isn't up to me to be a policeman for the company. The Accounting Department sits back looking at all those figures—they should watch expenses. I ran into one of them the other day on what he called an internal audit trip, and he told me that they aren't in a position to say whether a $25 lunch at a restaurant is necessary to sell a loan. He said that the charge was made by one of my men and that I should check it out! Gosh, am I a regional production man or am I an accountant? I've got enough to do meeting my regional quota with my five district men. I can't go snooping around to find out whether my men are taking advantage of the company. My men may get the idea that I don't trust them, and I've always heard that good business depends on trust. Besides our department makes the company more money than any other one. Why shouldn't we be allowed to spend a little of it?"

"Well, I must say that the brass is getting hot about a relatively small problem. A little fudging on an expense account isn't going to break the company. I learned the other day that the Accounting Department doesn't require any receipts from the Securities Department people. They just give them a per diem for travel and let them spend it however they want to, just so long as they don't go over the allotted amount for the days that they're on trips."

"Now that sounds like a good idea. Why can't we do that?" Bill replied. "It sure would make my life easier. I don't want to get a guilt complex about signing reimbursement requests that may look a little out of line. Why should I call a district man on the carpet for some small expense he swears really was the reason that he got the deal? Production is our job, so why can't the company leave us alone? They should let us decide what it takes to make a deal. Then if we don't produce the loans, we should catch the dickens about something that's important—not about these trifling details."

"Bill, I've got to run now, but honestly if I were you, I wouldn't worry about these Mickey Mouse controls. I'm just going to do my job and fill in the cotton pickin' forms in a way to stay out of trouble on the details. It's not worth getting upset about."

1. Has the company imposed overly restrictive controls?
2. Do you think the company has a good conception of control tolerances?
3. What should Bill do?

section three

Behavioral aspects

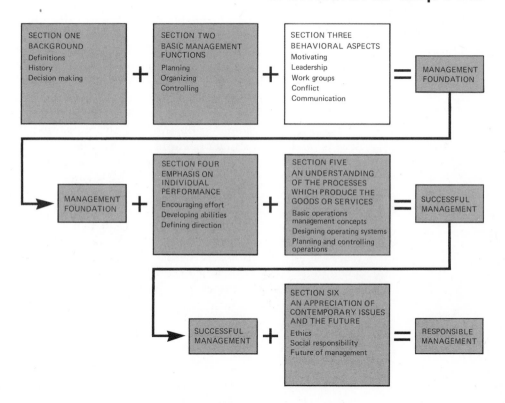

Management is a process or form of work that involves the guidance or direction of a group of people toward organizational goals or objectives. Everything that managers do is related to their behavior or the behavior of others. All of the basic management functions discussed in Section Two are implemented through people and depend on people for their success. Therefore an understanding of human behavior in organizations is another requirement for building a sound management foundation.

It is difficult if not impossible to isolate completely the behavioral aspects from other management topics. For example, appropriate managerial controls and organization can only be determined in light of certain behavioral considerations. Therefore many behavioral concepts are interspersed throughout all sections of the text. However, the purpose of this section is to isolate and emphasize the major aspects of human behavior in organizations.

Chapter 9 introduces the topic of motivation by presenting current theories. Human needs are shown to be the common thread running through the different theories.

Building on the previous chapter, Chapter 10 discusses the topic of leadership. Different styles of leadership are discussed and evaluated. Several contemporary leadership theories are also presented. A strong argument is made for a situational approach to leadership.

Chapter 11 focuses on organizational conflict. Conflict is presented as a normal and natural organizational activity which can produce positive results if properly managed. Conflict is analyzed as both internal and external to the individual.

Because both formal and informal work groups exist in most organizations, Chapter 12 is devoted to discussing work groups and their impact on the organization. As with conflict, informal work groups are shown to be assets of the organization if properly managed. The topics of conformity and creativity are also introduced.

Chapter 13, the final chapter in this section, deals with the topic of communication, which is relevant to all managers and employees.

Objectives

1. *To develop an overall understanding of the motivation process.*
2. *To present current theories of motivation.*
3. *To outline the relationships among current theories of motivation.*
4. *To develop an appreciation for the difficulties involved in applying different theories of motivation.*

GLOSSARY OF TERMS

Incongruity model A motivation model that contends that there is a lack of congruity between the needs of healthy individuals and the demands of the organization.

Job enlargement Involves making a job structurally larger by giving a worker more similar operations or tasks to perform.

Job enrichment Upgrading a job with factors such as more meaningful work, more recognition, more responsibility, and more opportunities for advancement.

Motivation A causative sequence, illustrated by the following diagram, which elicits increased effort.

Needs --------➤Drives --------➤Achievement
         or   of
     motives   goals

Motivation-maintenance theory A theory of motivation which states that all work related factors can be grouped into one of two categories: maintenance factors which will not produce motivation but can prevent motivation and motivators which can encourage motivation.

Need hierarchy Refers to the five different levels of individual needs (physiological, safety, social, esteem or ego, and self-actualization) which were identified by Abraham H. Maslow.

Reinforcement theory An approach to motivation based on the idea that behavior which is reinforced will be repeated, and behavior that is not reinforced will not be repeated.

Theory X A set of assumptions about human behavior which assumes that people are basically lazy and will not work or accept responsibility unless they are coerced, controlled, or threatened.

Theory Y A set of assumptions about human behavior which assumes that people are not basically lazy and that they will work and seek responsibility on their own accord.

Motivation:
The moving function

The early bird catches the worm. That fact
Has been into every young cranium packed
It's really absurd the talk that is heard
Of the wonderful thrift of that wonderful bird
And not the least mention is made of the worm
That equally early set out on a squirm
Except that within that most provident bird
The poor little fellow was thus early interred
Now it seems there's a word on both sides to be said
For had he but snugly remained in his bed
Or curled up for a nap
In mother earth's lap
The poor little chap
Would doubtless have lived to Methuselah's age
And another tale figured in history's page.

Moral: maxims and rules
That are taught in the schools
Are excellent truly for governing fools
But you of your actions get up early of course
But if you're a worm don't be so absurd
As to get up at dawn to be caught by a bird.*

"OUR EMPLOYEES are just not motivated." "The way to get more productivity is to motivate people." "How do I motivate my employees?" Statements and questions such as these are often expressed by managers. Motivation is one of the most frequently discussed topics among managers.

The problem of motivation is not a recent development. Research

---

° *The Early Bird,* source unknown.

FIGURE 9–1
Potential influence of motivation on performance

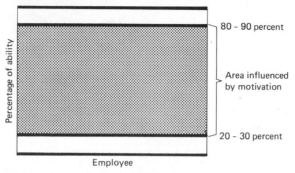

Source: Paul Hersey and Kenneth H. Blanchard, *Management of Organizational Behavior: Utilizing Human Resources*, 2d ed., © 1972, p. 5. Reprinted by permission of Prentice-Hall, Inc., Englewood Cliffs, N.J.

conducted by William James in the late 1800s indicated the importance of motivation.[1] James found that hourly employees could keep their jobs by using approximately 20 to 30 percent of their ability. James also found that when employees are highly motivated they will work at approximately 80 to 90 percent of their ability. Figure 9–1 illustrates the potential influence of motivation on performance. As can be seen, high motivation of employees can bring substantial increases in performance, and this is critically important for effective management.

THE MEANING OF MOTIVATION

Numerous definitions are given for the word motivation. Usually included in these definitions are such words as aim, desire, end, impulse, intention, objective, and purpose. The word motivation comes from the Latin word "movere," which means to move. Two formal definitions of motivation are as follows:

> . . . all those inner striving conditions described as wishes, desires, drives, etc. . . . It is an inner state that activates or moves.[2]

> . . . the combination of forces which initially direct, and sustain behavior toward a goal.[3]

---

[1] Paul Hersey and Kenneth H. Blanchard, *Management of Organizational Behavior: Utilizing Human Resources*, 2d ed., © 1972, p. 5. Reprinted by permission of Prentice-Hall, Inc., Englewood Cliffs, N.J.

[2] Bernard Berelson and Gary A. Steiner, *Human Behavior* (New York: Harcourt, Brace & World, Inc., 1964), p. 240.

[3] Donald B. Lindsley, "Psychophysiology and Motivation," *Nebraska Symposium on Motivation*, ed. Marshall R. Jones (1957), p. 48.

FIGURE 9–2
The motivation sequence

Needs ⟶ Drives or Motives ⟶ Achievement of Goals

The process of motivation can best be understood through the causative sequence shown in Figure 9–2.

In the motivation process, needs produce motives which lead to the accomplishment of goals. Needs are caused by deficiences. These deficiencies can be either physical or psychological. For instance, a physical need exists when an individual goes without sleep for 48 hours. A psychological need exists when an individual has no friends or companions. Man's basic needs will be explored in much greater depth in a later section of this chapter.

A motive is a stimulus which leads to an action that satisfies the need. In other words, motives produce action. Lack of sleep (the need) activates the physical changes of fatigue (the motive) which produces sleep (the action or, in this example, inaction).

Achievement of the goal in the motivation process satisfies the need and reduces the motive. When the goal is reached, balance is restored. However, other needs arise which are then satisfied by the same sequence of events. Understanding the motivation sequence, in itself, offers the manager little help in determining what motivates people. The following theories of motivation will be described to help provide a broader understanding of what motivates people: traditional theory, need hierarchy theory, motivation-maintenance theory, preference-expectancy theory, and the reinforcement theory.

TRADITIONAL THEORY

The traditional theory of motivation evolved from the work of Frederick W. Taylor and the scientific management movement which was discussed in Chapter 2. Taylor's ideas were based on the belief that existing reward systems were not designed to reward a person for high production. Taylor felt that when a highly productive person found out that the compensation was the same as that for someone producing less, the productive person's output would decrease. Taylor's solution was simple. He designed a system whereby the worker was compensated according to productivity.

One of Taylor's problems was determining a reasonable standard of performance. Taylor solved the problem by breaking jobs down into components and measuring the time necessary to accomplish each component. In this way, Taylor was able "scientifically" to establish standards of performance.

Taylor's plan was unique in that he had one rate of pay for units produced up to the standard. Once the standard was reached, a significantly higher rate was paid not only for the units above the standard, but for all units produced during the day. Thus, under Taylor's system workers could, in many cases, significantly increase their pay with above-standard production.

The traditional theory of motivation is based on the assumption that money is the primary motivator. Under this assumption, financial rewards are directly related to performance in the belief that if the reward is great enough workers will produce more.

NEED HIERARCHY THEORY

The need hierarchy theory is based on the assumption that workers are motivated to satisfy a number of needs and money can satisfy directly or indirectly only some of these needs. The need hierarchy theory is largely based on the work of Abraham Maslow.[4]

Maslow's need hierarchy

Maslow felt that several different levels of needs exist within individuals and these needs relate to each other in the form of a hierarchy. Maslow's hierarchy of needs consists of five levels which are shown in Figure 9–3. In Figure 9–3 the physiological needs are shown as having the highest strength; they tend to dominate all other needs until they are substantially satisfied. Once the physiological needs have been satisfied, the safety needs become dominant in the need structure. This process continues with different needs emerging as each respective level of need is satisfied. Figure 9–4 shows a situation in which safety has become the dominant need.

The physiological needs are basically the needs of the human body that must be satisfied to maintain homeostasis. There are also various physiological needs that are not necessarily associated with homeostasis — sexual desire, sleepiness, activity, and so on. Safety needs are concerned with protection against danger, threat, or deprivation. Since all employees have, to some degree, a dependent relationship with the organization, safety needs can be critically important. Favoritism, discrimination, and arbitrary administration of organizational policies are all actions which arouse uncertainty and therefore affect the safety needs.

It is important to note that in our society the physiological and

---

[4] Abraham H. Maslow, *Motivation and Personality* (New York: Harper and Row, Publishers, 1954).

FIGURE 9–3
Maslow's need hierarchy

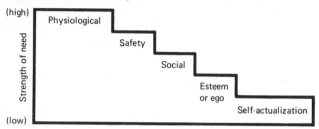

safety needs are more easily and therefore more generally satisfied than the other needs. In fact, Maslow estimated the percentage of satisfaction as follows: physiological – 85 percent; safety – 70 percent; social – 50 percent; ego – 40 percent; and self-actualization – 10 percent.

The third level of needs are the social needs. Generally categorized under the social needs are the needs for love, affection, belonging – all of which are concerned with establishing one's position relative to others. This does not necessarily mean sex, which, of course, is categorized with the basic physiological needs, but rather love as exemplified by the development of meaningful personal relations and acceptance into meaningful groups of individuals.

The fourth level of needs are the esteem needs. This includes both self-esteem and the esteem of others. Maslow contends that all people have a need for a stable, firmly based, high evaluation of themselves, that is, for self-respect, self-esteem, and for the esteem of others. This need is concerned with the development of various kinds of relationships based on adequacy, independence, and the giving and receiving of indications of self-esteem and acceptance.

The highest level in Maslow's need hierarchy is concerned with the need for self-actualization or self-fulfillment, that is, the need of a person to reach his full potential in terms of the application of his

FIGURE 9–4
Dominant safety need

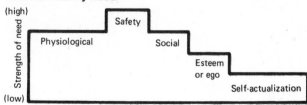

own abilities and interests in functioning in his environment. This need is concerned with the will to operate at the optimum and thus receive the rewards that are the result of that attainment. The rewards may be not only in terms of economic and social remuneration, but also in terms of psychological remuneration. As Maslow terms it, "What a man can be, he must be."[5] The need for self-actualization or self-fulfillment is never completely satisfied; one can always reach one step higher. Figure 9–5 lists several examples of each need level.

FIGURE 9–5
Examples of needs

Physiological Needs
1. Food and thirst
2. Sleep
3. Health
4. Body needs
5. Exercise and rest
6. Sex

Safety Needs
1. Security and safety
2. Protection
3. Comfort and peace
4. No threats or danger
5. Orderly and neat surroundings
6. Assurance of long-term economic well-being

Social Needs
1. Acceptance
2. Feeling of belonging
3. Membership in group
4. Love and affection
5. Group participation

Esteem (or Ego) Needs
1. Recognition and prestige
2. Confidence and leadership
3. Competance and success
4. Strength and intelligence

Self-Actualization Needs
1. Self-fulfillment of potential
2. Doing things for the challenge of accomplishment
3. Intellectual curiosity
4. Creativity and aesthetic appreciation
5. Acceptance of reality

---

[5] Ibid., p. 91.

FIGURE 9-6
Need hierarchy dominated by two needs

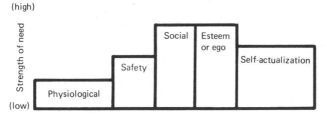

Although the needs of the majority of people are arranged in the sequence shown in Figure 9–3, differences in the sequence can occur depending on the individual's learning experience, culture, social upbringing, and numerous other aspects of the individual personality.

It is important to note that the strength or potency of these needs may shift back and forth under different situations. For instance, during bad economical times the physiological and safety needs might tend to dominate an individual's behavior; whereas, in good economic times higher order needs might dominate an individual's behavior.

Another major assumption of the need theory—that as one need is satisfied then and only then does another need emerge—is not always correct. Some needs may be partially but not completely met. Such instances can result in an opportunity for another need to present itself. For instance, it is possible to be motivated by the social and esteem needs at the same time. Figure 9–6 illustrates such a situation.

The unconscious character of the various needs should be recognized. In addition, there is a certain degree of cultural specificity of needs. In other words, the ways by which the various needs can be met tend to be controlled by cultural and societal factors. For example, the particular culture may dictate one's eating habits, social life, and numerous other facets of life.

Finally, different methods can be used by different individuals to satisfy a particular need. Two individuals may be deficient in relation to the same physiological needs, but the way in which each individual chooses to satisfy that need may vary considerably.

As far as the motivation process is concerned, the thrust of the need hierarchy theory is that a satisfied need is not a motivator. Consider the basic physiological need for oxygen. Only when an individual is deprived of oxygen can it have a motivating effect on his or her behavior. Many of today's organizations are applying the logic of the need hierarchy. For instance, wage and salary systems and fringe benefit programs are generally designed to satisfy lower order

FIGURE 9–7
Assumptions about people

Theory X

1. The average human being has an inherent dislike of work and will avoid it if he can.
2. Because of this human characteristic of dislike of work, most people must be coerced, controlled, directed, threatened with punishment to get them to put forth adequate effort toward the achievement of organizational objectives.
3. The average human being prefers to be directed, wishes to avoid responsibility, has relatively little ambition, wants security above all.

Theory Y

1. The expenditure of physical and mental effort in work is as natural as play or rest.
2. External control and the threat of punishment are not the only means for bringing about effort toward organizational objectives. Man will exercise self-direction and self-control in the service of objectives to which he is committed.
3. Commitment to objectives is a function of the rewards associated with their achievement.
4. The average human being learns, under proper conditions, not only to accept but seek responsibility.
5. The capacity to exercise a relatively high degree of imagination, ingenuity, and creativity in the solution of organizational problems is widely, not narrowly, distributed in the population.
6. Under the conditions of modern industrial life, the intellectual potentialities of the average human being are only partially utilized.

Source: From *The Human Side of Enterprise* by Douglas McGregor, copyright © by McGraw-Hill, Inc. Used with permission of McGraw-Hill Book Co., 1960, pp. 33–34 and 47–48.

needs—physiological and safety. On the other hand, interesting work and opportunities for advancement are designed to appeal to higher order needs. Thus the job of a manager is to determine the need level that any individual employee is attempting to attain and then provide the means by which the employee can satisfy that need. Obviously determining the need level of one particular individual is a difficult process because all people are not operating at the same level on the need hierarchy and all people do not react similarly to the same situation. In addition, it must be pointed out that little research has been conducted to test the validity of the need hierarchy theory. Its primary value seems to be that it provides a structure for analyzing needs and, as will be seen later in this chapter, is used to build other theories of motivation.

Theory X and Theory Y

Another important consideration in motivation theory was presented by Douglas McGregor in his assumptions about people. McGregor termed these assumptions Theory X and Theory Y. Theory X and Theory Y are summarized in Figure 9–7.

These two divergent attitudes concerning the basic nature of people have been in existence for thousands of years. Figure 9–8 presents some divergent views on human nature that have been categorized as representing either a Theory X or Theory Y viewpoint.

FIGURE 9–8
Statements about people

Theory X

We all know how little boys love fighting. They get their heads punched. But they have the satisfaction of having punched the other fellow's head.

Henri Bergson

And therefore if any two men desire the same thing, which nevertheless they cannot both enjoy, they become enemies.

Niccolo Machiavelli

It is not from the benevolence of the butcher, the brewer, or the baker that we expect our dinner, but from their regard of their own self-interest. We address ourselves not to their humanity, but to their self-love, and never talk to them of our own necessities, but of their advantage.

Adam Smith

Psychoanalysis has concluded . . . that the primitive, savage, and evil impulses of mankind have not vanished in any individual, but continue their existence, although in repressed state . . . and . . . they wait for opportunities to display their activity.

Sigmund Freud

Man is a predator with an instinct to kill and a genetic cultural affinity for the weapon.

Robert Ardrey

Figure 9–8 — (continued)

Theory Y

The state of nature has a law of nature to govern it, which obliges everyone; and reason, which is that law, teaches all mankind who will but consult it that, being all equal and independent, no one ought to harm another in his life, health, liberty, or possessions.

John Locke

The concealed assumption of the doctrine of original sin invalidates the psychoanalytic findings. The theory that life is a strenuous fight to subdue perversion, that the human mind is by nature "pathogenic" (i. e., predisposed to the pathological) is not a starting point for biological observation.

Elton Mayo

All of man's natural inclinations are toward the development of goodness, toward the continuance of states of goodness and the discontinuance of unpleasant states.

Ashley Montagu

All through the animal kingdom from amoeba to insects, or to man — animals show automatic unconscious proto-cooperation or even true cooperation. There is much evidence that the drift toward natural cooperation is somewhat stronger than the opposing tendency toward disoperation (among crowded animals).

W. C. Allee

The most beautiful as well as the most ugly inclinations of man are not part of a fixed and biologically given human nature but result from the social process.

Erich Fromm

Source: Adapted from Henry P. Knowles and Borje O. Saxberg, "Human Relations and the Nature of Man." *Harvard Business Review* (March–April 1967), p. 224.

From a motivational viewpoint, Theory X and Theory Y relate directly to the need hierarchy theory. Theory X assumes that lower order needs are dominant in motivating people. Theory Y assumes that higher order needs are dominant in motivating people.

Assuming that in our society the lower order needs have been largely satisfied, then Theory Y assumptions would be more effective in the motivational process. However, it is important to remember that the level of need may vary among individuals. Thus, either Theory X or Theory Y assumptions might be appropriate in a particular situation.

Furthermore, Theory X and Theory Y are concerned with *assumptions* that people make about the behavior of other people and do not *necessarily* reflect the *actions* that an individual takes. For instance, a police officer is not necessarily acting under Theory X assumptions if you get a ticket when you have violated a law. Likewise, managers are not necessarily acting under Theory Y assumptions merely because they are soft and smooth in their relations with employees.

Incongruity model

A further extension of the need hierarchy theory is the incongruity model proposed by Chris Argyris. Basically, Argyris is concerned with the fifth level in the need hierarchy—self-actualization. He contends that self-actualization is the process of striving to achieve one's objectives, maintaining one's self internally, and adapting to one's internal environment. He further contends that as individuals grow and mature they strive toward self-actualization. The characteristics that change from infancy to adulthood are summarized in Figure 9–9.

Argyris contends that most individuals who are employed by organizations will want to express adult characteristics; however, the basic principles of organization create an environment requiring infancy characteristics. Such an environment assumes that concentrating effort on a limited field of endeavor increases quality and quantity of output. The basic principles most frequently criticized by Argyris are task specialization, chain of command, unity of direction, and span of control. If these principles are followed as defined, Argyris contends that individuals will be passive, dependent, short time oriented, and will exhibit characteristics of children.

Thus Argyris postulates that there is a lack of congruity between the needs of healthy individuals and the demands of the organization. His approach to motivation involves creating an environment in which an individual can satisfy the self-actualization needs.

FIGURE 9–9
Development characteristics

Infancy Characteristics	Adult Characteristics
Passivity	Increased activity
Complete dependence on others	Relative independence
Erratic, casual, shallow interest	Longer, deeper, more consistent interests
Short time perspective	Long time perspective
Subordinate position in family	Equal or superordinate position in family
Lack of awareness of self	Awareness of self

/ATION-MAINTENANCE THEORY

Frederick Herzberg has developed a theory of work motivation which has had a wide acceptance in management circles. His theory is referred to by several names: motivation-maintenance theory; dual factor theory; or the motivation-hygiene theory.

The initial stages in the development of the theory involved extensive interviews with approximately 200 engineers and accountants from 11 industries in the Pittsburgh area. Herzberg's initial purpose was stated as follows:

> To industry, the payoff for a study of job attitudes would be increased productivity, decreased absenteeism, and smoother working relations. To the individual, an understanding of the forces that lead to improved morale would bring greater happiness and greater self-realization.[6]

In conducting the interviews Herzberg and his colleagues, Bernard Mausner and Barbara Snyderman, used what is called the critical incident method. This method involved interviewing subjects and asking them to recall work situations in which they had experienced periods of high and low morale. They were asked to recount specific details about the situation, and the effect of the experience over time.

It was found through analysis of the interviewees' statements that different factors were associated with good and bad feelings. The findings fell into two major categories. Those factors that were most frequently mentioned in association with a favorably viewed incident had to do with the type of work itself. These factors were achievement, recognition, responsibility, advancement, and the characteristics of the job. But when subjects felt negatively oriented toward a critical work incident, they were more likely to mention factors associated with status, interpersonal relations with supervisors, peers, and subordinates, technical aspects of supervision, company policy and administration, job security, working conditions, salary, and aspects of personal life that were affected by the work situation. Herzberg referred to the latter set of factors as "hygiene" or "maintenance" factors. These terms were used because these factors are preventative in nature. In other words, they will not produce motivation but can prevent motivation from occurring. Proper attention to hygiene factors is a necessary but not sufficient condition for motivation.

The first set of factors were called "motivators." These factors are largely related to the work that is being performed. Herzberg contends that these factors must be present in order for motivation to occur. Herzberg does not imply that the hygiene factors can be ig-

---

[6] Frederick Herzberg, Bernard Mausner, and Barbara Snyderman, *The Motivation to Work* (New York: John Wiley & Sons, Inc., 1959), p. ix.

FIGURE 9–10
Hygiene — motivator factors

Hygiene factors (environmental)	Motivator factors (job itself)
Policies and administration	Achievement
Supervision	Recognition
Working conditions	Challenging work
Interpersonal relations	Increased responsibility
Personal life	Advancement
Money, status, security	Personal growth

nored. Rather, he contends that the hygiene factors must be provided or efforts to enrich the job with motivator factors will most certainly fail.

In summary, Herzberg contends that motivation comes from the individual not from the manager. At best, proper attention to the hygiene factors will keep an individual from being unsatisfied but will not make that individual satisfied. Both hygiene and motivator factors must be present in order for the motivation process to occur.

As a solution to motivation problems, Herzberg developed an approach called "job enrichment." Unlike "job enlargement," which merely involves giving a worker more of a similar type operations to perform, job enrichment involves an upgrading of the job by adding motivator factors. Designing jobs that provide for meaningful work, achievement, recognition, responsibility, advancement, and growth is the key to job enrichment.

As can be seen from Figure 9–11, Herzberg's motivation-maintenance theory is very closely related to the need hierarchy theory of motivation and, thus, is subject to the same criticisms.

In terms of application, there have been a large number of studies concerning the motivation-maintenance theory. These studies have produced mixed, positive, and negative outcomes. The majority of the studies have shown that when the subjects were very similar to Herzberg's initial subjects, accountants and engineers, the results were supporting.[7] In terms of lower management, blue-collar workers,

---

[7] M. Myers, "Who Are the Motivated Workers?" *Harvard Business Review*, vol. 42 (1964), pp. 73–88; M. M. Swartz, E. Janusaits, and H. Stark, "Motivational Factors among Supervisors in the Utility Industry," *Personnel Psychology*, vol. 16 (1963), pp. 45–53; F. Friedlanger and E. Walton, "Positive and Negative Motivations toward Work," *Administrative Science Quarterly*, vol. 9 (1964), pp. 194–207; T. M. Lodahl, "Patterns of Job Attitudes in Two Assembly Technologies," *Administrative Science Quarterly*, vol. 8, pp. 482–519.

FIGURE 9–11
**A comparison of Maslow's need hierarchy theory with
Herzberg's motivation-maintenance theory**

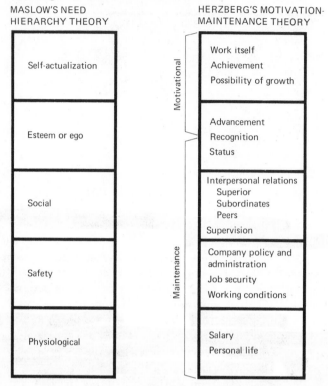

women, and low-level routine white-collar workers, the results have
been confounding and nonconfirming.[8]

PREFERENCE-EXPECTANCY THEORY

An additional theory of motivation was developed by Victor H.
Vroom.[9] Called the preference-expectancy theory, Vroom's theory can
be analyzed with the aid of Figure 9–12. Theoretically, a probability

[8] M. D. Dunnett, "Factor Structures of Unusually Satisfying and Unusually Dis-
satisfying Job Situations for Six Occupational Groups," paper presented at Midwestern
Psychological Association meeting, Chicago, 1965; R. B. Ewen, "Some Determinants
of Job Satisfaction: A Study of the Generality of Herzberg's Theory," *Journal of Applied Psychology*, vol. 47 (1963), pp. 246–50; A. W. Kornhauser, *Mental Health of the
Industrial Worker* (New York: John Wiley & Sons, 1965); P. F. Wernicht, "Intrinsic
and Extrinsic Factors in Job Satisfaction," doctoral thesis, University of Minnesota,
Minneapolis, 1964.

[9] Victor H. Vroom, *Work and Motivation* (New York: John Wiley & Sons, Inc., 1967).

FIGURE 9–12
Model of expectancy

```
              E-P                       P-O
          Expectancy                Expectancy
   Effort ──────────→ Performance ──────────→ Outcomes
```

or likelihood can be placed on the expectancy that effort will lead to performance (E-P Expectancy). For example, there is some probability that increasing the number of sales calls (effort) by a sales person will increase total sales (performance). In addition, each individual has beliefs or expectations that performance will lead to certain outcomes (P-O Expectancy). For instance, a noncommissioned salesperson may feel that there is a high probability (high expectancy) of receiving a pay raise if sales increase. On the other hand, the person might feel that increased sales would not result in a pay raise (low expectancy). The expectancy of increased effort leading to increased performance (E-P) multiplied times the expectancy of increased performance leading to a particular outcome (P-O) yields a measure of the individual's total expectation.

The preference component (Vroom calls it valence) is the value that an individual places on a particular outcome. This could range from a +1.0 to a −1.0. Thus, a person may place a high value or preference on a promotion and assign a high positive value to the outcome; on the other hand the same person may not be interested in a promotion and assign a negative value to the outcome.

Under the preference-expectancy model, an individual's motivation is determined by multiplying the individual's total expectations by his preferences:

$$\text{Motivation} = (\text{E-P Expectancy}) \times (\text{P-O Expectancy}) \times \text{Preference}$$
$$(0 - 1) \qquad\qquad (0 - 1) \qquad\qquad (+1 \text{ to } -1)$$

Thus if an individual has high expectation that effort will lead to a desirable outcome, level of motivation will be high. If either the expectation of obtaining the outcome or the value of the outcome is low, then the level of motivation will be low. Vroom's theory is based on the belief that individual expectations and preferences do exist even though they may be unconscious.

The following example is intended to illustrate the preference-expectancy theory. Assume that John Doe, an employee, comes to work late on a regular basis. His effort (or in this case lack of effort) is producing a performance record (tardiness). His E-P expectancy is high. In other words, the probability of his tardiness producing a record of tardiness is 1.0. Past experience has shown that management does not enforce a tardiness policy. Therefore, the likelihood of his performance (tardiness record) producing an outcome (disciplinary action) is relatively low and his P-O expectancy is likely to be close to 0. Finally, even if John wishes to avoid disciplinary action and places a high value or preference on the avoidance of disciplinary action, he still will not be motivated to be at work on time because of his low P-O expectancy.

REINFORCEMENT THEORY

The final theory of motivation to be explored in this chapter is reinforcement theory, which is closely related to the preference-expectancy theory. Reinforcement theory is based primarily on the work of B. F. Skinner. The general idea behind the theory is that reinforced behavior will be repeated, and behavior that is not reinforced will not be repeated. For instance, if an employee is given a pay increase when performance is high, then the employee is likely to continue to strive for high performance. Reinforcement theory assumes that the consequences of an individual's behavior determine his or her level of motivation. Thus an individual's motives are considered to be relatively minor in this approach.

Reinforcers are not necessarily rewards and do not necessarily have to be positive in nature. For instance, in the example of tardiness given in the discussion of the preference-expectancy theory, the desire of the employee to avoid disciplinary action would be an avoidance reinforcer. Similarly, decreasing a salesperson's salary when their sales fall illustrates a negative reinforcer. The word negative reinforcer is used because in order for the individual to stop the action that is being taken (decreasing salary), his or her behavior must change (increase sales).

The emphasis in current management practices on the use of reinforcement revolves around positive reinforcement. Little applied research has been conducted on reinforcement theory, and therefore organizations should be cautious with its application.

IMPLICATIONS FOR MANAGEMENT

In summarizing all of the theories presented—traditional, need hierarchy, motivation-maintenance, preference-expectancy and reinforcement—the common thread of thought in motivation theory is that motivation is a goal-directed behavior. The simple model in Figure 9–2 which depicts motivation as a goal-directed behavior serves as a basis for motivation theory. Numerous research studies have been conducted on the motivation theories discussed in this chapter. The results have been mixed. Research can be cited to both support and refute most of the theories. Alan C. Filley and Robert J. House summarize the situation as follows:

> Perhaps the major conclusion to be drawn from the review of theory and research presented . . . is that human motivation is so complex that it can only be discussed in simple proportions and dealt with in an abstract and general manner, as in Vroom's, preference-expectation theory.[10]

Managers must keep in mind that the motivation of subordinates is not a simple process. Several different approaches to the process have yielded successful results. Most of these approaches are not in conflict with one another but rather look at a different segment of the overall motivational process or look at the same segment from a different perspective. Knowing the models and applying them in the proper situation is one of the keys to effective management.

Chapter 15 will discuss the application of these concepts and theories to encouraging individual effort in organizations.

SUMMARY

The motivation process begins with needs which cause motives which lead to the accomplishment of goals. Needs are caused by deficiencies. Motives are stimuli that cause an action to be taken to satisfy the need. Achievement of the goal in the motivation process satisfies the need and reduces the motive. When the goal is reached, balance is restored and, of course, other needs arise. These new needs must also be satisfied by the motivation process.

The five basic theories of motivation are the traditional theory, need hierarchy theory, motivation-maintenance theory, preference-expectancy theory, and reinforcement theory. Traditional theory is based on the assumption that money is a primary motivator.

The need hierarchy theory is based on the assumption that workers are motivated to satisfy a variety of needs, only some of which can be satisfied by money. The needs of an individual exist in a hierarchy and range from low to high as follows: physiological, safety, social, esteem, and self-actualization. Once a need has been sufficiently satisfied, it can no longer be used to motivate an individual.

Theory X and Theory Y are assumptions made about the basic

---

[10] Alan C. Filley and Robert J. House, *Managerial Process and Organizational Behavior* (Glenview, Ill.: Scott, Foresman and Company, 1969), p. 386.

nature of people. Theory X assumptions are based on the belief that people can best be motivated by appealing to their lower order needs. Theory Y assumes that people can best be motivated by appealing to their higher order needs.

The incongruity model deals primarily with the need of self-actualization. This model assumes that a basic incongruity exists between the needs of the individual and the organization. Resolving this incongruity can lead to greater motivation of employees.

The motivation-maintenance theory states that there are two categories of factors which relate to motivation. The first category, called hygiene or maintenance factors, includes characteristics of every job. These factors relate to the work environment and include status, interpersonal relations, supervision, company policy and administration, job security, working conditions, salary, and personal life. The hygiene factors are important and must be present in the job or it is impossible to provide motivation. However, providing the hygiene factors does not satisfy the employee but rather keeps the employee from being dissatisfied. The second category of factors, called motivators, relate to the work itself. These factors include such things as recognition, advancement, achievement, growth potential, and responsibility. Only if both the hygiene and motivator factors are properly provided will motivation occur.

The preference-expectancy theory of motivation implies that motivation depends on the preferences and expectations of the individual. The preference-expectancy theory is more an explanation of the motivation process than a prescription for management behavior.

The reinforcement theory of motivation is based on the idea that reinforced behavior will be repeated, and behavior that is not reinforced will not be repeated. The theory assumes that the consequences of an individual's behavior determine his or her level of motivation.

No one motivation theory or model applies to all situations. However, practicing managers must be aware of the basic theories in order to begin to understand employee behavior. Choosing the most appropriate model and applying it to the proper situation is part of the challenge of the management process. The potential payoff of increased motivation is unbounded.

REVIEW QUESTIONS

1. Explain the motivation sequence.

2. Describe the following theories of motivation:
   a. Traditional theory.
   b. Need hierarchy theory.

c. Motivation-maintenance theory.

d. Preference-expectancy theory.

e. Reinforcement theory.

3. What are the concepts of Theory X and Theory Y? How do they relate to motivation?

4. Explain the incongruity model and its relationship to motivation.

DISCUSSION QUESTIONS

1. "Most people can be motivated with money." Discuss your views on this statement.

2. Discuss the following statement: "A manager should not try to motivate other people. It is impossible."

3. How would you attempt to motivate a class of college students?

4. Discuss the similarities between the five motivation theories discussed in this chapter. In other words, how do the different theories relate to each other?

SELECTED READINGS

Annas, J. W. "Profiles of Motivation," *Personnel Journal* (March 1973), pp. 205–8.

Argyris, Chris. *Integrating the Individual and the Organization.* New York: John Wiley and Sons, Inc., 1964.

Bockman, V. M. "The Herzberg Controversy," *Personnel Psychology* (Summer 1971), pp. 155–89.

Davis, Keith. *Human Behavior at Work.* 4th ed. New York: McGraw-Hill Book Company, 1972.

Eckerman, A. C. "A New Look at Need Theory," *Training and Development Journal* (November 1968), pp. 18–22.

Fein, Mitchell. *Motivation for Work,* New York: American Institute of Industrial Engineers, Inc., 1971.

Gellerman, Saul W. *Motivation and Productivity.* New York: American Management Association, Inc., 1963.

Herzberg, Frederick. *Work and the Nature of Man.* Cleveland, Ohio: World Publishing Company, 1966.

Herzberg, Frederick, Bernard Mausner, and Barbara Snyderman. *The Motivation to Work.* New York: John Wiley and Sons, Inc., 1959.

Maslow, Abraham H. *Motivation and Personality.* New York: Harper and Row, Publishers, 1954.

McGregor, Douglas. *The Human Side of Enterprise.* New York: McGraw-Hill Book Company, 1960.

Myers, M. Scott. "Who Are Your Motivated Workers?" *Harvard Business Review* (January–February 1964), pp. 73–88.

Wenrich, W. W. *A Primer of Behavior Modification.* Belmont, Calif.: Brooks/ Cole Publishing Company, 1970.

Vroom, Victor H. *Work and Motivation.* New York: John Wiley and Sons, Inc., 1967.

Whyte, William F. *Money and Motivation.* New York: Harper and Row, 1955.

Case 9–1

Our engineers are just not motivated

Situation: You are a consultant to the manager of mechanical engineering for a large company (8,000 employees, $200 million annual sales) that manufactures industrial equipment. The manager has been in this position for six months, having moved from a similar position in a much smaller company.

Manager: I just can't seem to get these guys to perform. They are all extremely competent, but they just don't seem to be willing to exert the kind of effort that we need and expect to have if this company is going to remain successful.

Consultant: What types of work do they do?

Manager: Primarily designing minor modifications to existing equipment lines to keep up with our competition and to satisfy special customer requirements.

Consultant: How do you evaluate their performance?

Manager: Mainly on whether they meet project deadlines. It's hard to evaluate the quality of their work, since most of it is fairly routine, and the designs are frequently altered later by the production engineers to facilitate production processes.

Consultant: Are they meeting their deadlines reasonably well?

Manager: No, that's the problem. What's worse is that they don't really seem too concerned about it.

Consultant: What financial rewards do you offer them?

Manager: These people are all well-paid — some of the best salaries for mechanical engineers that I know of anywhere. Base pay is determined mainly on the basis of seniority, but there is also a company-wide profit sharing plan. At the end of each year, the company distributes 10 percent of its profit after taxes to the employees. The piece of the pie that you get is in proportion to your basic salary. This kind of plan was used in the company I used to work for, and it seemed to have a highly motivating effect for them. They also get good vacations, insurance plans, and all the other usual goodies. I know of no complaints about compensation.

Consultant: How about promotion possibilities?

Manager: Well, all I know is that I was brought in from the outside.

Consultant: If they are so lackadaisical, have you considered firing any of them?

Manager: Are you kidding? We need them too much, and it would be difficult and expensive to replace them. If I even threatened to fire any of them for anything short of blowing up the building, my boss would come down on me like a ton of bricks. We are so far behind on our work as it is. Besides, I'm not sure that it's really their fault entirely.

1. Why are the engineers not motivated?
2. What should management do to correct the situation?

Case 9–2

The key punch section

The purpose of the key punch section of the Que Company is to transfer information from printed or written forms to punched cards that are then used as input to a computer.

There are 15 women in this unit who are paid an hourly rate and who all report to one manager. They key punch a wide variety of work which is supplied by various departments and groups. Some jobs are small, while others amount to as many as 2,500 cards. Some work receives priority with the remainder being prescheduled on a routine basis subject to the computer's capacity.

The work is supplied to the key punch operators by an assignment clerk who reviews the work for errors and legibility. If the forms are accurate the clerk attempts to divide the work evenly among the key punch operators. If the incoming work is rejected, the clerk gives it to the manager of the key punch section who either clears the problem or returns the work to the originating department.

Usually each key punch operator is able to process between 700 and 800 cards each day. Because of the exactness of the work and the expense of computer time, the work is also checked by key punch verifiers.

The error rate is high and many due dates and schedules are not met. Absenteeism is serious, and employee morale is low.

1. Analyze this situation in terms of the motivation theories presented in this chapter.
2. What can the Que Company do to raise the low morale of its key punch employees?

Objectives

1. To define leadership and its relationship to the management process.
2. To review research that has been conducted on the leadership process.
3. To provide a perspective on several different leadership styles and processes.
4. To emphasize that the most appropriate style of leadership depends on the situation in which the leader is functioning.

GLOSSARY OF TERMS

Autocratic leader A leader who dictates decisions to the group.

Contingency theory of leadership A theory of leadership, developed by Fred Fiedler, which contends that the most effective style of leadership depends on the situation in which the leader is functioning.

Democratic leader A leader who guides and encourages the group to make decisions.

Laissez faire leader A leader who provides little guidance and allows individuals in the group to make their own decisions.

Leader A person who has the ability to influence the behavior of other people according to the leader's desires in a given situation.

Leader Behavior Description Questionnaire (LBDQ) A questionnaire developed by researchers at Ohio State University and designed to determine how successful leaders carry out their activities.

Leadership A process whereby one person influences the behavior of members of a group.

Path-goal theory of leadership States that the role of the leader in eliciting goal-directed behavior is to increase personal payoffs to subordinates for work-goal attainment, to make the path to payoffs easier to travel, and to increase the opportunities for satisfaction in route, and that the effectiveness of the leader's efforts depends on the particular situation.

Managerial Grid® A technique developed by Robert Blake and Jane Mouton which uses a two-dimensional grid, based on concern for people and concern for production, for classifying leadership styles.

Traitist theory of leadership Assumes that leadership effectiveness is a function of certain physical and psychological characteristics of the leader.

10

Leadership behavior

Concern with leadership is as old as recorded history. Plato's Republic, *to give but one early example, speculates about the proper education and training of political leaders, and most political philosophers since that time, have attempted to deal with this problem. Leadership has been a particular concern in democracies, which, by definition, cannot rely upon the accident of birth for the recruitment of leaders. Where there is no hereditary aristocracy, every man is potentially a leader, and society has to give thought to the identification and proper training of men who will be able to guide its institutions.*

Fred E. Fiedler*

EACH YEAR new research is published that explores various facets of leadership. Checklists have been established to determine the style of leadership used by individuals. Questionnaires have been developed to determine the style of leadership used within a particular organization. New teaching aids and devices appear which are designed to improve one's leadership abilities. All of this activity should indicate that today's practicing manager knows a great deal about the leadership process; however this is not true. Many managers appear to experience difficulty performing effectively in leadership roles. As the above quote states, leadership is and must be a concern of society and organizations. This chapter is designed as a review of some of the leadership research and is intended to provide a perspective on leadership styles and processes.

---

* *A Theory of Leadership Effectiveness* New York: McGraw-Hill Book Company, 1967, p. 3

215

LEADERSHIP — CAN IT BE DEFINED?

"Leadership," observes Northwestern University political scientist Louis Masotta, "is one of those things you don't know you need until you don't have it."[1] Peter Drucker has described leadership as follows:

> Leadership is the lighting of man's vision to higher sights, the raising of a man's performance to a higher standard, the building of man's personality beyond its normal limitations.[2]

Alan C. Filley and Robert J. House define leadership and leader in the following manner:

> Leadership . . . is a process whereby one person exerts social influence over the members of a group. A leader, then, is a person with power over others who exercises the power for the purpose of influencing their behavior.[3]

Edwin P. Hollander and James W. Julian expand the concept of leadership in the following discussion:

> An early element of confusion in the study of leadership was the failure to distinguish it as a process from the leader as a person who occupies a central role in the process. Leadership constitutes an influence relationship between two, or usually more, persons who depend upon one another for the attainment of certain mutual goals within a group situation. This situation not only involves the task but also comprises the group's size, structure, resources, and history, among other variables.[4]

All of the above definitions provide insight into the leadership process. In summary, leadership is a process in which one person influences the behavior of members of a group.

Leadership and motivation are complementary processes. In most instances, motivation is influenced by leader effectiveness. Thus, both effective leadership and effective motivation are essential for good management and good performance.

SOURCE OF AUTHORITY

The emergent leader of a group is the one that is perceived by the group as being the one that is most capable of satisfying the group's

[1] "In Quest of Leadership," *Time*, July 15, 1974, p. 21.

[2] Peter F. Drucker, *The Practice of Management* (New York: Harper & Row, 1954), pp. 159–60.

[3] Alan C. Filley and Robert J. House, *Managerial Process and Organizational Behavior* (Glenview, Ill.: Scott, Foresman and Co., 1969), p. 391.

[4] Edwin P. Hollander and James W. Julian, "Contemporary Trends in the Analysis of Leadership Processes," *Psychological Bulletin*, vol. 71 (1969), pp. 387–97.

needs. The authority of the leader can be removed, reduced, or increased depending on the group's perceived progress toward its goal. The authority of the leader may also be threatened by the emergence of different or additional goals.

The following simple example illustrates this point. Suppose a group of people were shipwrecked on a desolate island. The group's first goal would probably be to ensure their security by obtaining food, water, and shelter. Using the definition of leadership that has been previously developed, the person selected by the group as the leader would be the person perceived by the group as the one who can best help the group to achieve the essentials for survival. However, after satisfying this need, other needs will emerge. The need to escape from the island would probably emerge rather quickly. The person originally selected for the leadership position may not necessarily be the person perceived by the group as most capable in directing the attainment of these new, emerging needs. In this case, the group might select a new leader. The leadership position might continue to change depending on the group's needs and perceptions.

The role of the manager and the role of the leader in the previous example are different. The example illustrated more of an elective or emergent style of leadership. Under this system, the leader must perceive the needs of the group and must be perceived by the group as being most capable in achieving those needs. In other words, the source of authority for the leader is the group being led. In most organizations, however, the source of authority comes from above rather than below. As was discussed in Chapter 6 lower levels of management are usually appointed by higher levels of management. Thus a manager's source of authority does not come from the group being managed. Obviously a manager is in a leadership position, although the manager is appointed to that position.

It would seem that the source of a leader's authority would constitute a significant element in the leadership process. However, little research has been performed regarding this relationship. One research study demonstrated that the continuity of leadership is better maintained in groups where leaders are elected than in groups where leaders are appointed.[5] Another study indicated that a leader's source of authority is perceived and reacted to as an important element in the leadership process.[6]

---

[5] A. M. Cohen and Warren G. Bennis, "Continuity of Leadership in Communication Networks," *Human Relations*, vol. 14 (1961), pp. 351–67.

[6] J. W. Julian, E. P. Hollander, and C. R. Regula, "Endorsement of the Group Spokesman as a Function of His Source of Authority, Competence, and Success," *Journal of Personality and Social Psychology*, vol. 11 (1969), pp. 42–49.

TRAITIST THEORY

The traitist theory of leadership focuses on the leader. This theory assumes that leadership effectiveness can be explained by isolating the physical and psychological characteristics or traits that differentiate the leader from the group. Some of the most frequently listed traits of a good leader are (1) honesty, (2) truthfulness, (3) open-mindedness, (4) courage, and (5) perseverance.

All of these traits are considered virtues within our ethical system. Since the traitist theory purports that the degree to which a leader possesses these qualities determines effectiveness, a person occupying a leadership position would be expected to have these traits. How then does one explain the overwhelming power of a leader such as Adolph Hitler?

Numerous other examples can be cited of famous leaders who possessed few, if any, of the above traits. Alvin Gouldner reviewed much of the evidence relating to traits and concluded; "At this time there is no reliable evidence concerning the existence of universal leadership traits."[7] A study by Gordon Lippitt relating to the traitist theory showed that in 106 studies on the traitist theory only five percent of all traits listed appeared in four or more of the studies.[8]

The inherent flaw in the traitist theory is that it views leadership as merely being a one-dimensional process. In truth, leaders do not emerge or function in a vacuum. The cultural, social, and physical environment plays a complex role in the development and existence of a leader.

BASIC LEADERSHIP STYLES

Studies conducted by Kurt Lewin, Ronald Lippitt, and Ralph K. White at the University of Iowa in 1938 and 1940 focused attention on styles of leadership.[9] They identified three basic leadership styles— autocratic, laissez faire, and democratic. The location of the decision-making function emerged from these studies as the main difference among the leadership styles. In general, the autocratic leader makes all decisions; the laissez faire leader allows individuals in the group to make all decisions; and the democratic leader guides and encourages the group to make decisions. Leland P. Bradford and Ronald

---

[7] Alvin W. Gouldner ed., *Studies in Leadership* (New York: Harper & Row, 1950), pp. 31–35, esp. p. 34.

[8] Gordon L. Lippitt, "What Do We Know about Leadership?" *NEA Journal*, December 1955. Reprinted in *Leadership in Action*, Gordon L. Lippitt ed., National Training Laboratories—National Education Association, 1961, pp. 7–11.

[9] Ralph White and Ronald Lippitt, *Leader Behavior and Member Reactions in Three "Social Climates" in Group Dynamics* (Evanston, Ill.: Row, Peterson, 1953).

Lippitt[10] have described each of these leaders and their groups as follows:

Autocratic leader and group:
1. He is very conscious of his position.
2. He has little trust and faith in his subordinates.
3. He feels that pay is a just reward for work and is the only reward that will motivate the worker.
4. He gives orders and demands that they be carried out. No questions are allowed and no explanations given.
5. Group members assume no responsibility for performance and merely do what they are told.
6. Production is good when the leader is present, but drops in his absence.

Laissez faire leader and group:
1. He has no confidence in his leadership ability.
2. He does not set goals for the group.
3. Decision making is performed by whoever in the group is willing to accept it.
4. Productivity is generally low and work is sloppy.
5. The group has little interest in their work.
6. Morale and teamwork are generally low.

Democratic leader and group:
1. Decision making is shared between the leader and the group.
2. Criticism and praise are objectively given.
3. New ideas and change are welcomed.
4. A feeling of responsibility is developed within the group.
5. When the leader is forced to make a decision, his reasoning is explained to the group.
6. Quality and productivity are generally high.
7. The group generally feels successful under the democratic leader.

In summary, the importance of the studies by Lewin, Lippitt, and White lies in the fact that they were the first to study leadership in a scientific fashion. Their studies showed that different styles of leadership produced different reactions from the group. However, it is important to note that their research was conducted in hobby clubs for ten-year-old boys. No attempt was made to relate leadership style to productivity. Their primary contribution was that they identified three different leadership styles—autocratic, laissez faire, and democratic.

The descriptions of the three different leadership styles developed by Bradford and Lippitt went much further in that they attempted to relate leadership style to productivity. Their description of the

---

[10] Leland P. Bradford and Ronald Lippitt, "Building a Democratic Work Group," *Personnel*, vol. 22, no. 3 (November 1945).

leadership styles implies that the democratic style is the most desirable and productive for most situations. However, as will be shown later in this chapter, the style of leadership that is the most productive depends on the situation in which the leader is operating.

OHIO STATE LEADERSHIP STUDIES

Beginning in 1945, a series of studies were conducted at Ohio State University to further investigate leadership. These studies started with the assumption that no satisfactory theory or definition of leadership was currently available. The researchers further decided that previous research had regarded "leadership" as being synonymous with "good leadership." They felt that this assumption contaminated the previous research. They then decided to study leadership, however defined, as to its effectiveness.

One of the primary goals of the research project was to determine how successful leaders carry out their activities. The research staff was composed of psychologists, sociologists, and economists. In approaching the problem the group decided to develop a leader description instrument to aid in determining "how the leader does it." Agreeing that the instrument should be applicable to a wide cross-section of situations, the research team developed an instrument known as the Leader Behavior Description Questionnaire (LBDQ). This questionnaire has been used on commanders and crew members of bomber crews in the Department of the Air Force; commissioned officers, noncommissioned personnel, and civilian administrators in the Department of Navy; foremen in a manufacturing plant; executives in regional cooperative associations; college administrators; school superintendents, principals, and teachers; and leaders in a wide variety of student and civilian groups and organizations.[11]

One of the first problems which faced the researchers was identifying the dimensions of leader behavior. The researchers finally agreed on the following dimensions of leader behavior.

1. Initiation—Frequency of originating, facilitating, or resisting new ideas.
2. Membership—Frequency of mixing with the group, stressing informal interaction between himself and members, and interchanging personal services with members.
3. Representation—Frequency of defending his group against attack, advancing the interests of his group, and acting in behalf of his group.

---

[11] Ralph M. Stodgill and Alvin E. Coons eds., *Leader Behavior: Its Description and Measurement* (Columbus, Ohio: College of Administrative Science, College Communications, 1957), p. vii.

4. Integration—Frequency of subordinating individual behavior, encouraging pleasant group atmosphere, reducing conflicts between members, or promoting individual adjustment to the group.

5. Organization—Frequency of defining or structuring his own work, the work of other members, or the relationship among members in the performance of their work.

6. Domination—Frequency of restricting the behavior of individuals of the group in action, decision making, or expression of opinion.

7. Communication—Frequency of providing information to members, seeking information from them, facilitating exchange of information; or showing awareness of affairs pertaining to the group.

8. Recognition—Frequency of engaging in behavior which expresses approval or disapproval of the behavior of group members.

9. Production—Frequency of setting levels of effort or achievement, or prodding members for greater effort or achievement.[12]

Communication was divided into Communication Up and Communication Down, resulting in a total of ten dimensions of leader behavior.

The Leader Behavior Description Questionnaire (LBDQ) was formed by selecting 150 items of leader behavior that were classified by dimension. The items were randomized and disguised such that the respondent could not identify the various dimensions of leader behavior. A multiple choice format was used for the questionnaire. For example, the first item was:

1. He plans his day's activities in detail.
   a. Always *b.* Often *c.* Occasionally *d.* Seldom *e.* Never[13]

It should be remembered that the LBDQ was designed to determine how a leader performs. In applying the questionnaire, two areas of leader behavior emerged consistently. These were membership and organization. Frequently the name "consideration" is applied to the dimension of membership and the name "initiating structure" is applied to the dimension of organization. Thus the dimensions of leader behavior that emerged from the Ohio State studies were goal-directed behavior (organization or initiating structure) and recognition of individual needs (membership or consideration).

The real value of the Ohio State studies was their attempt to determine scientifically how a leader operates. These studies were the first to point out the importance of goal-directed behavior and the recognition of individual needs in leader behavior.

---

[12] Ibid., pp. 11–12.
[13] Ibid., p. 14.

THE MANAGERIAL GRID

Working independently of the Ohio State studies and under actual operating circumstances, Robert Blake and Jane Mouton developed a technique for classifying leadership styles.[14] Basically, the Man-

FIGURE 10–1
The Managerial Grid

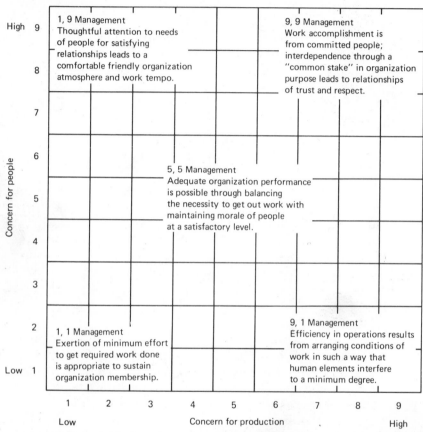

Source: The Managerial Grid figure from *The Managerial Grid*, by Robert R. Blake and Jane Srygley Mouton (Houston, Texas: Gulf Publishing Company, © 1964), p. 10. Reproduced with permission.

agerial Grid uses the questionnaire method to locate a particular style of leadership or management on a two-dimensional grid. Reaching conclusions similar to the Ohio State studies, Blake and Mouton labeled the dimensions of leadership as Concern for People and Con-

---

[14] Robert R. Blake and Jane Srygley Mouton, *The Managerial Grid* (Houston, Tex.: Gulf Publishing Company, 1964).

cern for Production. The horizontal axis on the grid represents concern for production while the vertical axis represents concern for people.

Using the grid, Blake and Mouton have described five basic styles of management which are shown in Figure 10–1. Task management, which is described in the lower right-hand corner (9,1 position), takes the view that efficiency in operations results from properly arranging the conditions of work with minimum interference from the human elements. The opposite view, country club management, which is located in the upper left-hand corner (1,9 position), assumes that proper attention to human needs leads to a comfortable organization atmosphere and work pace. Team management combines a high degree of concern for people with a high degree of concern for production and is located in the 9,9 position, or upper right-hand corner of the grid.

UNIVERSITY OF MICHIGAN STUDIES

The Institute for Social Research of the University of Michigan was granted a contract in April 1947 by the Office of Naval Research.[15] The purpose of the contract was to discover principles contributing both to the productivity of a group and to the satisfaction derived by group members. The study was conducted at the home office of the Prudential Insurance Company, Newark, New Jersey.

A nondirective interview technique was used to interview 24 section heads or supervisors and 419 nonsupervisory personnel. The interviewer did not know whether the employee being interviewed was in a high- or low-producing section. Interviewees were assigned on a random basis. The following areas were explored with supervisory personnel:

1. Job content.
2. Job aspiration.
3. Attitudes toward company.
4. Relationships with staff.
5. Employee's evaluation of his or her job and section.
6. Attitude toward company policies and practices.
7. General attitudes.[16]

---

[15] Daniel Katz, Nathan Maccoby, and Nancy C. Morse, *Productivity, Supervision and Morale in an Office Situation* (Ann Arbor: Institute for Social Research, University of Michigan, 1950).

[16] Ibid., pp. 68–74.

The types of questions asked were as follows:

Job Aspiration

What are your plans and ambitions now? (What is the relation of your present job to these plans?)

a.   Do you think anything you are doing is leading up to that?
b.   What do you think will really happen about those plans? (What is the highest job here at Prudential you can expect to get?)[17]

The nonsupervisory employees were asked the following questions:

3.   When you are at work, does the time *usually* pass slow or fast?
10. Why did you decide to come to work for Prudential?[18]

Results of the interviews showed that supervisors of high-producing sections were more likely:

1.   To receive general, rather than close, supervision from their superiors.
2.   To like the amount of authority and responsibility they have in their job.
3.   To spend more time in supervision.
4.   To give general, rather than close, supervision to their employees.
5.   To be employee-oriented rather than production-oriented.[19]

Supervisors of low-producing sections had basically opposite characteristics and techniques. They were production-oriented and gave close supervision.

In 1961, Rensis Likert, then director of the Institute for Social Research at the University of Michigan, published the results of his years of research. His book, *New Patterns of Management*, is a classic in its field.[20] Basically, Likert feels that the patterns or styles of leadership or management employed by a particular organization can be categorized into four styles. He has identified and labeled these styles as follows:

1.   System 1—Exploitive authoritative—Authoritarian form of management that attempts to exploit subordinates.
2.   System 2—Benelovent authoritative—Authoritarian form of management but is paternalistic in nature.

---

[17] Ibid., p. 69.

[18] Ibid., pp. 76–77.

[19] Ibid., p. 69.

[20] Rensis Likert, *New Patterns of Management* (New York: McGraw-Hill Book Company, 1961).

3. System 3—Consultative—Manager requests and receives inputs from subordinates, but maintains the right to make the final decision.

4. System 4—Participative—Manager gives some direction but decisions are made by consensus and majority based on total participation.

There is a close resemblance of this categorization system to the earlier system developed by Lewin, Lippitt, and White.

Likert used a questionnaire to determine the style of leadership and management pattern employed in the organization as a whole. The questionnaire measures the following operating characteristics of an organization: motivation, communication, interaction, decision making, goal setting, control, and performance. Figure 10–2 illustrates a portion of the questionnaire.[21]

Likert summarized his research findings as follows:

> Those firms or plants where System 4 is used show high productivity, low scrap loss, low costs, favorable attitudes, and excellent labor relations. The converse tends to be the case for companies or departments whose management system is well toward System 1.[22]

Thus Likert feels that the most effective style of management is System 4 and that organizations should strive to develop a management pattern analogous to this system.

A THREE-DIMENSIONAL APPROACH

The relationships among the Ohio State studies, the Managerial Grid, and Likert's work can be more easily understood using a three-dimensional graph (Figure 10–3). The horizontal axis of the graph represents concern for the task or production; the vertical axis represents concern for people; the third axis represents the degree of participation.

Blake and Mouton's five basic leadership styles and Likert's Systems 1 through 4 are represented on the three-dimensional graph in Figure 10–4.

The three-dimensional approach stresses the often misunderstood difference between participation and concern for people. A manager who is only concerned with people is not necessarily a participative manager, but may simply possess a laissez faire attitude and let people do as they please.

---

[21] Rensis Likert, *The Human Organization* (New York: McGraw-Hill Book Company, 1967).

[22] Ibid., p. 46.

FIGURE 10–2
Likert's profile of organization characteristics

Instructions:

1. On the lines below each organizational variable (item), please place an *n* at the point which, *in your experience*, describes your organization at the present time (*n* = now). Treat each item as a continuous variable from the extreme at one end to that at the other.
2. In addition, if you have been in your organization one or more years, please also place a *p* on each line at the point which, *in your experience*, describes your organization as it was one to two years ago (*p* = previously).
3. If you were not in your organization one or more years ago, please check here _____ and answer as of the present time, i.e., answer only with an *n*.

Organizational variable				*Item no.*
1. Leadership processes used				
a. Extent to which superiors have confidence and trust in *subordinates*	Have no confidence and trust in subordinates	Have condescending confidence and trust, such as master has in servant	Substantial but not complete confidence and trust; still wishes to keep control of decisions	Complete confidence and trust in all matters
				1
b. Extent to which subordinates, in turn, have confidence and trust in *superiors*	Have no confidence and trust in superiors	Have subservient confidence and trust, such as servant has to master	Substantial but not complete confidence and trust	Complete confidence and trust
				2
c. Extent to which superiors display supportive behavior toward others	Display no supportive behavior or virtually none	Display supportive behavior in condescending manner and situations only	Display supportive behavior quite generally	Display supportive behavior fully and in all situations
				3

FIGURE 10-3
Three-dimensional approach to leadership

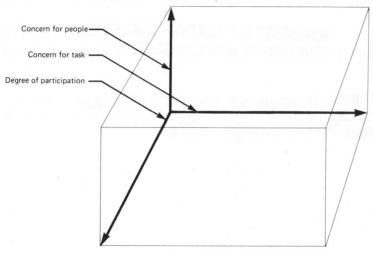

FIGURE 10-4
Relationships of various leadership styles

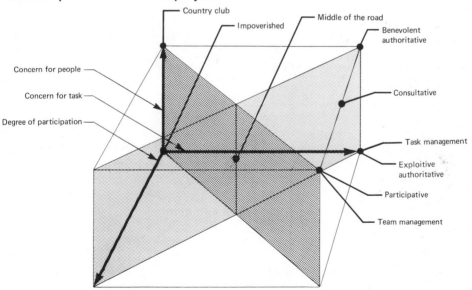

THE CONTINGENCY MODEL

In 1967, Fred E. Fiedler published the results of 15 years of re-search on leadership.[23] Going at least one step further than previous works, Fiedler's research was an attempt to define the particular style of leadership that is appropriate for a given leadership situation. As a result, Fiedler's approach seems to be the most promising work to date for developing guidelines for effective leadership.

The contingency theory postulates that there are two basic styles of leadership: the task-motivated leadership style and the relation-ship-motivated leadership style. The task-motivated style satisfies

FIGURE 10–5
Partial listing of questions for measuring leadership style

Pleasant	8	7	6	5	4	3	2	1	Unpleasant
Friendly	8	7	6	5	4	3	2	1	Unfriendly
Rejecting	8	7	6	5	4	3	2	1	Accepting
Helpful	8	7	6	5	4	3	2	1	Frustrating

Source: Fred E. Fiedler *A Theory of Leadership Effectiveness* (New York: McGraw-Hill Book Company, 1967), p. 41.

the leader's need to gain satisfaction from the performance of a task. The relationship-motivated style is oriented toward the leader's need to achieve good interpersonal relations within the group and toward satisfying the leader's need to assume a position of prominence in the group.

Fiedler developed a unique method for measuring the leadership style employed by a leader. He asked the individual being surveyed to think of the person with whom the leader could work least effec-tively. The respondent was then asked to describe this person on the form shown in Figure 10–5. The resulting descriptions were called the Least-Preferred Coworker (LPC).

The respondent was then asked to describe the person with whom the respondent could work most effectively. The same form as shown in Figure 10–5 was used to record the answers. These descriptions were called the Most-Preferred Coworker (MPC).

---

[23] Fred E. Fiedler, *A Theory of Leadership Effectiveness* (New York: McGraw-Hill Book Company, 1967).

The scores on the LPC and MPC were then used to calculate what Fiedler called the Assumed Similarity Between Opposites (ASO). A low ASO score indicates that the individual being analyzed perceives the most- and least-preferred coworkers as being quite dissimilar. A high ASO score indicates that the individual perceives the most-preferred and the least-preferred coworkers as being quite similar.

Working under the assumption that a person who describes the least-preferred coworker in relatively favorable terms is basically motivated to have close interpersonal relations with others, Fiedler classified persons with a high ASO score as relationship-motivated leaders. In contrast, by assuming that persons who reject someone with whom they cannot work are basically motivated to accomplish or achieve the task, persons with a low ASO score were classified as task-oriented leaders.

After analyzing the leadership style, Fiedler turned his attention to the situation in which the leader was operating. He classified leadership situations along a favorable-unfavorable continuum by taking into account three major dimensions: leader-member relations, task structure, and position power. Leader-member relations refer to the degree of trust, respect, and congeniality of the leader. Task structure refers to the degree to which the job tasks are structured. Position power refers to the power and influence inherent in the job. Leaders have more position power if they are able to hire, fire, discipline, and so forth. Using the three dimensions described above, an eight-celled classification scheme was developed. Figure 10–6 illustrates this classification scheme along the favorable-unfavorable continuum.

Figure 10–7 summarizes the results of Fiedler's work. In both highly favorable and highly unfavorable situations, a task-motivated leader was more effective. In moderately favorable situations, a relationship-motivated leader was more effective. In Situation 7 (moderately poor leader-member relations, unstructured task, and strong leader position power) the task and relationship style of leadership were equally effective.

Implications of the contingency model

Fiedler's contingency model has many general implications. First, the model can be used for the selection and training of managers to fit a given situation. Second, Fiedler's model indicates that performance can be affected by changing either the leader's style or the situation. Generally, it is easier to change the situation (one or more of the three situational factors) than it is to change the leader.

Prior to Fiedler's work, most of the studies on leadership had con-

FIGURE 10–6
Fiedler's classification of situations

	1	2	3	4	5	6	7	8
Leader-member relations.........	Good	Good	Good	Good	Poor	Poor	Poor	Poor
Task structure.........	Structured	Structured	Unstructured	Unstructured	Structured	Structured	Unstructured	Unstructured
Position power.........	Strong	Weak	Strong	Weak	Strong	Weak	Strong	Weak

Favorable for leader ———→ ———→ Unfavorable for leader

FIGURE 10–7
Relationship of leadership style to situation

Situation	1	2	3	4	5	6	7	8
Leader-member relations.........	Good	Good	Good	Good	Moderately Poor	Moderately Poor	Moderately Poor	Moderately Poor
Task structure.........	Structured	Structured	Unstructured	Unstructured	Structured	Structured	Unstructured	Unstructured
Leader position power.........	Strong	Weak	Strong	Weak	Strong	Weak	Strong	Weak
	Favorable for leader ———→						———→ Unfavorable for leader	
Most productive leadership style	Task	Task	Task	Relation	Relation	No data	Task or relation	Task

cluded that a democratic or participative style of leadership was appropriate for all situations. Fiedler's work demonstrates that other styles of leadership can be more effective in certain situations. However, the problem of defining the most appropriate leadership style for any particular situation is still one of the most controversial issues relating to the study of leadership.

PATH-GOAL THEORY OF LEADER EFFECTIVENESS

The path-goal theory of leader effectiveness is basically an extension and combination of the Ohio State Studies and Fiedler's work. Under this theory, the role of the leader in eliciting goal-directed behavior consists "of increasing personal payoffs to subordinates for work-goal attainment, and making the path to these payoffs easier to travel by clarifying it, reducing road blocks and pitfalls, and increasing the opportunities for personal satisfaction en route."[24] Thus, the role of the leader is to clarify goals, provide rewards for goal attainment, facilitate goal attainment, and provide opportunities for achieving personal satisfaction in the goal attaining process.

Additionally, the path-goal theory implies that the degree to which the leader can be effective in eliciting goal-directed behavior depends on the situation. The leader can have positive effects in those situations where there is role ambiguity or the leader controls the reward/punishment system. In situations where tasks are routine and the reward/punishment system is relatively fixed, attempts by the leader to clarify path-goal relationships can increase performance but generally at the cost of decreased satisfaction. Finally, leader behavior that reflects concern for people can result in increased performance only to the extent that it facilitates the accomplishment of goals.

LEADERSHIP DEVELOPMENT FOR MANAGERS

Generally management development programs include some form of leadership development training. Subject material includes human relations skills, communication skills, decision-making skills, and so on. These programs are often designed to influence a manager's style toward participative or team management. However, a more logical approach to leadership development is to determine the system or style of leadership that a manager or organization is presently using. Many of the previously described research instruments could be used

---

[24] Robert J. House, "A Path-Goal Theory of Leader Effectiveness," *Administrative Science Quarterly*, vol. 16, no. 3 (September 1971), p. 324.

to determine the style of leadership presently employed. Identifying the present style of leadership employed by a particular manager is the first step in becoming a more effective leader.

The next step involves analyzing the situation in which the leader is operating. Once these questions have been answered, leadership performance can be improved by either changing the leadership style or changing the leadership situation. Because it is difficult to alter an individual's personality, it is fallacious to think that a lasting change in leadership style can be accomplished in a short time. Thus if a manager or an organization determines that the leadership style that is presently being used is ineffective, then a change to a more effective style of leadership would require a long and determined effort. The alternative is to change the situation. This can be accomplished by changing the leader-member relationship, the structure of the task, or the position power of the leader. Both the contingency theory and path-goal model offer promise for developing a better understanding of leadership development.

Many of the theories and concepts discussed in this chapter and the previous chapter of motivation will be applied in Section Four, which is concerned with obtaining individual performance in an organizational setting.

SUMMARY

This chapter was designed to familiarize the student with some of the important concepts and supporting research in the area of leadership. Leadership, as defined in this chapter, is a process in which one person influences the behavior of the members of a group. Several important research studies were reviewed. The Lewin, Lippitt, and White studies were the first to identify three basic styles of leadership—autocratic, laissez faire, and democratic. The Ohio State studies then attempted to describe the behavior of leaders. These researchers found that consideration for people and initiating structure (goal direction) were key dimensions of leadership behavior. The University of Michigan studies were designed to study the relationship between leadership style and productivity. Basically they concluded that the employee-oriented manager had more productive workers. Using leadership dimensions similar to the Ohio State studies, Blake and Mouton developed the managerial grid, which uses a two-dimensional grid for classifying leadership styles.

Fred Fiedler demonstrated in his research that the situation or situational variables are important in determining the effectiveness of a particular leadership style. His model can be used for the selection and training of managers to fit a given situation. In addition, his studies suggest that performance can be affected by changing either the leader's style or the situation.

Finally the path-goal theory of leader effectiveness was discussed. This theory states that the role of the leader in eliciting goal-directed behavior consists of increasing personal payoffs to subordinates for work-goal attainment, making the path to these payoffs easier to travel by reducing road blocks, and increasing the opportunities for personal satisfaction en route to the goal. The theory also implies that the effectiveness of the leader's efforts depends on the particular situation in which the leader is functioning.

REVIEW QUESTIONS

1. Define leadership. What is the source of a leader's authority?

2. Describe in detail the following three leadership styles: $P219$
    a. Autocratic
    b. Laissez faire
    c. Democratic

3. What was the purpose of the Ohio State leadership studies? What were the areas of leader behavior investigated in these studies? What were the results of the Ohio State studies? $P220-21$

4. Describe the Managerial Grid. $P222-23$

5. What was the purpose of the University of Michigan leadership studies? Explain the results of the Michigan studies.

6. Explain the relationship between the three-dimensional approach to leadership, the Managerial Grid, and Rensis Likert's work on leadership.

7. What is the contingency theory of leadership?

8. What is the path-goal theory of leader effectiveness?

DISCUSSION QUESTIONS

1. Discuss the following statement: "Leaders are born and cannot be developed."

2. "Leaders must have courage." Do you agree or disagree? Why?

3. What is meant by the statement: "We need strong leadership?"

4. Do you think the variance in leadership styles of such people as Adolph Hitler, Franklin D. Roosevelt, and Martin Luther King, Jr. can be explained by one of the theories discussed in this chapter? Elaborate on your answer.

SELECTED READINGS

Administrative Science Quarterly. The entire March 1971 issue of this
   journal is devoted to organizational leadership.

Bennis, Warren G. "Revisionist Theory of Leadership." *Harvard Business
   Review,* vol. 39, no. 1 (January–February 1961), pp. 26–40.

Blake, R. R., and Jane S. Mouton. "Managerial Facades," *Advanced Management Journal* (July 1966), pp. 30–37.

———. "The Developing Revolution in Management Practices," *Journal
   of the American Society of Training Directors* (now *Training and Development Journal*), vol. 16, no. 7 (July 1962), pp. 29–52.

Davis, K. *Human Behavior at Work.* 4th ed. New York: McGraw-Hill
   Book Company, 1972.

Evans, M. G. "Leadership and Motivation: A Core Concept," *Academy of
   Management Journal* (March 1970), pp. 91–102.

Fiedler, Fred E. *A Theory of Leadership Effectiveness.* New York: McGraw-
   Hill Book Company, 1967.

———. "Style or Circumstance: The Leadership Enigma," *Management
   Review,* vol. 58, no. 8 (August 1969), pp. 25–31.

Gouldner, Alvin W., ed. *Studies in Leadership.* New York: Harper and Row,
   1950.

House, R. J. "A Path-Goal Theory of Leader-Effectiveness," *Administrative
   Science Quarterly,* vol. 16 (1971), pp. 321–28.

Likert, Rensis. *New Patterns of Management.* New York: McGraw-Hill
   Book Company, 1961.

———. *The Human Organization.* New York: McGraw-Hill Book Company,
   1967.

Mann, R. D. "A Review of the Relationship between Personality and Performance in Small Groups," *Psychological Bulletin,* vol. 56, no. 4 (July
   1959).

Reddin, W. J. *Managerial Effectiveness.* New York: McGraw-Hill Book
   Company, 1970.

Tannenbaum, R., and W. R. Schmidt. "How to Choose a Leadership Pattern," *Harvard Business Review* (May–June 1973), pp. 162–180.

Case 10–1

Does the congregation care?

Situation: You are talking with a young minister of an independent
church with about 300 adult members. The minister came directly
to the church after graduating from a nondenominational theological
school. He has been in the job for eight months.

Minister: I don't know what to do. I feel as if I have been treading water ever since the day I got here, and frankly, I'm not sure that I will be here much longer. If they don't fire me, I may leave on my own. Maybe I'm just not cut out for the ministry.

You: What has happened since you came to this church?

Minister: When I arrived I was really full of energy and wanted to see how much this church could accomplish. The very first thing I did was to conduct a questionnaire survey of the entire adult membership to see what types of goals they wanted to pursue. Unfortunately, I found that the members had such mixed (and perhaps apathetic) feelings about the goals, that it was hard to draw any conclusions. There were a few who felt very strongly that we should be doing much more in the area of evangelism and charitable service. There were also a few who strongly favored more emphasis on internal things, such as remodeling the sanctuary, developing our music program, and setting up a day care center for the use of the members. Most of the members, however, didn't voice any strong preferences. A lot of people didn't return the questionnaire, and a few even seemed to resent my conducting the survey.

You: What have you done since you took the survey?

Minister: To be honest about it, I have kept a pretty low profile, concentrating mainly on routine duties. I haven't tried to implement or even push any major new programs. One problem is that I have gotten the impression through various insinuations that my being hired was by no means an overwhelmingly popular decision. Evidently a fairly substantial segment of the congregation was skeptical of my lack of experience and felt that the decision to hire me was railroaded through by a few members of the Pastoral Search Committee. I guess I am just reluctant to assume a strong leadership role until some consensus has developed concerning the goals of the church and I have had more time to gain the confidence of the congregation. I don't know how long that will take though, and I'm not sure I can tolerate the situation much longer.

1. Can you analyze and explain the situation using any of the theories of leadership discussed in this chapter?
2. What would you recommend that the young minister do?

Case 10–2

Taking a new job

The Motor Transport Division of the municipal government of a small northern city was responsible for maintaining all motorized equipment and establishing minimum acceptable standards for purchases of new equipment. After an extensive study, the city administration decided to divide the department into three divisions, one for automotive equipment, one for heavy equipment, and one for trucks and tractors. As a result of this new reorganization, three new field manager positions were created.

When Joe Kelly was appointed as a manager of the truck division there was much skepticism among the people working there. Mr. Kelly had been an office manager in an administrative division of the municipal government and according to one employee "Couldn't change a tire if his life depended on it." After Mr. Kelly had been working there a short time, he noticed that absenteeism and tardiness were increasing and the quality of work had slackened considerably in one of the maintenance crews. After some investigation he found that the foreman of the crew, Joe Smith, had been in his present position for five years and had been doing a satisfactory job previously. He also learned that Mr. Smith had been an applicant for the field manager's job and had expressed resentment to several employees following Kelly's appointment.

1.   What style of leadership should Mr. Kelly use?
2.   How should Mr. Kelly handle Mr. Smith?

OBJECTIVES

1. *To develop an understanding of the types of conflict that can occur in organizations.*
2. *To identify the positive and negative effects of conflict in organizations.*
3. *To explore several possible methods of resolving conflict in organizations.*
4. *To present a general model for managing conflict.*

GLOSSARY OF TERMS

Dissonance A feeling of disharmony within an individual.

Frustration A form of intrapersonal conflict which results when a drive or motive is blocked before the goal is reached.

Functional conflict A form of conflict which exists as a result of the organizational structure and is relatively independent of the individuals occupying the roles within the organizational structure.

Goal conflict A form of intrapersonal conflict which results when a goal that an individual is attempting to achieve has both positive and negative features or when two or more competing goals exist.

Interpersonal conflict A form of conflict between two or more individuals which can be caused by many factors.

Intrapersonal conflict A form of conflict which is internal to the individual and relates to the need-drive-goal motivational sequence.

Strategic conflict A form of conflict which usually results from the promotion of self-interests on the part of an individual or a group and is often deliberately planned.

11

Causes and patterns of conflict in organizations

As conflict—difference—is here in the world, as we cannot avoid it, we should, I think use it. Instead of condemning it, we should set it to work for us. Why not? What does the mechanical engineer do with friction? Of course his chief job is to eliminate friction, but it is true that he also capitalizes friction. The transmission of power by belts depends on friction between the belt and the pulley. The friction between the driving wheel of the locomotive and the track is necessary to haul the train. All polishing is done by friction. The music of the violin we get by friction. We left the savage state when we discovered fire by friction. We talk of the friction of mind on mind as a good thing. So in business, too, we have to know when to try to eliminate friction and when to try to capitalize it, when to see what work we can make it do.

Mary Parker Follett*

CONFLICT in organizations is often assumed to be an unnatural and undesirable situation that is to be avoided at all costs. Conflict can lead to rigidity in the system in which it operates, can distort reality, and can debilitate the participants in the conflict situation.[1] Therefore, many organizations approach the management of conflict based on the following assumptions:

1. Conflict is avoidable.
2. Conflict is the result of personality problems within the organization.

---

* "Constructive Conflict" in *Dynamic Administration* edited by Henry C. Metcalf and L. Urwick, Harper & Brothers Publishers, 1940, pp. 30–31.

[1] Richard E. Walton, *Interpersonal Peacemaking* (Reading, Mass.: Addison-Wesley, 1969), p. 5.

3. Conflict produces inappropriate reactions by the persons involved.
4. Conflict creates a polarization of perception, sentiments, and behavior within the organization.[2]

Recent studies in the behavioral sciences have caused a reexamination of the assumptions concerning organizational conflict. These studies suggest that conflict is perfectly natural and should be expected to occur. The key point in the study of conflict, however, is not that it is natural or unavoidable, but that, as Mary Parker Follett stated in the introduction to this chapter, management must know when to eliminate conflict and when to build on it.

The private enterprise system itself is based on competition which is a form of conflict. This new attitude toward conflict has led to the emergence of the following set of assumptions regarding conflict:

1. Conflict is unavoidable.
2. The causes of conflict can be found only in the total situation.
3. Conflict is a vital element in change.
4. Conflict can be advantageous to an organization.[3]

Today's management should accept the existence of conflict and realize that attempting to eliminate all conflict is a mistake. The goal of management should be to understand and manage conflict in order to obtain the maximum benefits at a cost which is acceptable.

Conflict can be analyzed from two basic perspectives. One approach is to analyze conflict as a process that is internal to an individual. The other approach is to view conflict as a process that is external to the individual—individual versus individual, group versus group, organization versus organization, or any combination of these. External conflict can be categorized into three general types: functional, interpersonal, and strategic.

INTRAPERSONAL CONFLICT

Intrapersonal conflict is internal to the individual and is probably the most difficult form of conflict to analyze. Basically, intrapersonal conflict relates to the need-drive-goal motivational sequence that was discussed in Chapter 9.

---

[2] Joe Kelly, *Organizational Behavior* (Homewood, Ill.: Richard D. Irwin, Inc., and The Dorsey Press, 1969), p. 501.

[3] Ibid., pp. 503–5.

FIGURE 11–1
The motivation sequence

Need $\longrightarrow$ Drives or motives $\longrightarrow$ Achievement of goals

Intrapersonal conflict can result when barriers exist between the drive and goal. This form of conflict may also result when goals have both positive and negative aspects and when competing and conflicting goals exist. Figure 11–2 illustrates these types of conflict.

FIGURE 11–2
Sources of intrapersonal conflict

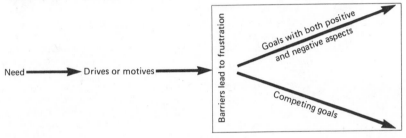

Frustration

Frustration results when a drive or motive is blocked before the goal is reached. Barriers can be either overt (rules and procedures) or covert (mental hangups). When a drive is blocked, people tend to react with defense mechanisms, which are the behaviors that individuals use to cope with frustration. Figure 11–3 enumerates some typical examples of defense mechanisms used when an individual is frustrated.

Goal conflict

Goal conflict results when a goal that an individual is attempting to achieve has both positive and negative features, or when two or more competing goals exist. Basically there are three forms of goal conflict. These are as follows:

1. Mutually exclusive positive goals—This type of goal conflict results when an individual is simultaneously motivated toward two or more positive, mutually exclusive goals. The decision a student makes in selecting an academic major is an example of this type

FIGURE 11–3
Reactions to frustration

Adjustive Reactions	Psychological process	Illustration
Compensation ...	Individual devotes himself to a pursuit with increased vigor to make up for some feeling of real or imagined inadequacy.	Zealous, hard-working president of the Twenty-five Year Club who has never advanced very far in the company hierarchy.
Conversion........	Emotional conflicts are expressed in muscular, sensory, or bodily symptoms of disability, malfunctioning, or pain.	A disabling headache keeping a staff member off the job, the day after a cherished project has been rejected.
Displacement.....	Re-directing pent-up emotions toward persons, ideas, or objects other than the primary source of the emotion.	Roughly rejecting a simple request from a subordinate after receiving a rebuff from the boss.
Fantasy............	Day dreaming or other forms of imaginative activity provides an escape from reality and imagined satisfactions.	An employee's day dream of the day in the staff meeting when he corrects the boss' mistakes and is publicly acknowledged as the real leader of the industry.
Negativism	Active or passive resistance, operating unconsciously.	The manager who, having been unsuccessful in getting out of a committee assignment, picks apart every suggestion that anyone makes in the meetings.
Rationalization...	Justifying inconsistent or undesirable behavior, beliefs, statements and motivations by providing acceptable explanations for them.	Padding the expense account because "everybody does it."
Regression........	Individual returns to an earlier and less mature level of adjustment in the face of frustration.	A manager having been blocked in some administrative pursuit busies himself with clerical duties or technical details, more appropriate for his subordinates.
Repression........	Completely excluding from consciousness impulses, experiences, and feelings which are psychologically disturbing because they arouse a sense of guilt or anxiety.	A subordinate "forgetting" to tell his boss the circumstances of an embarrassing situation.
Resignation, apathy, and boredom	Breaking psychological contact with the environment, withholding any sense of emotional or personal involvement.	Employee who, receiving no reward, praise, or encouragement, no longer cares whether or not he does a good job.
Flight or withdrawal	Leaving the field in which frustration, anxiety, or conflict is experienced, either physically or psychologically.	The salesman's big order falls through and he takes the rest of the day off; constant rebuff or rejection by superiors and colleagues, pushes an older worker toward being a loner and ignoring what friendly gestures are made.

Source: Timothy W. Costello and Sheldon S. Zalkind, *Psychology in Administration: A Research Orientation,* © 1963, pp. 148–49. Reprinted by permission of Prentice-Hall, Inc., Englewood Cliffs, N.J.

of conflict. Business administration, law, and medicine may all have positive aspects, but all cannot be pursued simultaneously. Generally this form of conflict can be resolved by making a decision rather quickly and eliminating the conflict.

2. Positive-negative goals—In this form of goal conflict, the individual attempts to achieve a goal that has both positive and negative effects. For example, in pursuing a top management position individuals frequently must make personal sacrifices of their own time and time with their family. Thus, the goal of being a successful business leader has both positive and negative aspects.

3. Negative-negative goals—Here the individual attempts to avoid two or more negative, mutually exclusive goals. Under these circumstances, the individual may choose to abandon the situation and therefore not select either one of the goals. This form of conflict may also exist when the individual does not have the opportunity to leave. For example, an individual may dislike his job, but the alternative of quitting and looking for another job may be even less attractive.

Goal conflict forces the individual to make a decision. Decision making often creates a feeling of conflict within the individual. An individual experiencing such a feeling of disharmony, called dissonance, will always attempt to reduce it. Some methods used in reducing dissonance and, hence, goal conflict are summarized below:

> . . . changing a behavioral element, changing an environmental cognitive element, and adding new cognitive elements. For example, suppose that a person owns a car that his friends call a "lemon." One way of reducing or eliminating dissonance would be to sell the car (changing a behavioral element). But perhaps he cannot find a buyer, or he must take a large financial loss. In this case, it might be preferable to try to convince his friends that the car is really a fine piece of machinery (changing an environmental cognitive element). Friends, however, are not always easily convinced; so perhaps he would fail there also. He might then seek favorable opinions of others regarding the quality of the car (adding new cognitive elements). Of course, it is not proposed that an individual is more prone to use one mode of reduction rather than another nor that he systematically tries all methods of dissonance reduction.[4]

FUNCTIONAL CONFLICT

Functional conflict exists as a result of the organizational structure and is relatively independent of the individuals occupying the roles

---

[4] Marvin E. Shaw and Philip R. Costanzo, *Theories of Social Psychology* (New York: McGraw-Hill Book Company, 1970), p. 210.

FIGURE 11–4
Functional organization structure

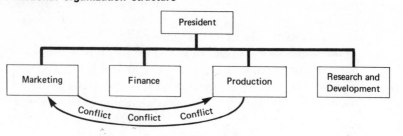

within the organizational structure. For example, the marketing department and the production department in Figure 11–4 may experience functional conflict. The marketing department, being customer-oriented, may believe that some exceptions can and should be made in production for the sake of sales and the generation of future sales. The production department may view such exceptions as completely unreasonable and certainly not in the best interests of the organization. Hence a functional conflict occurs. Various types of functional conflict are discussed in the following sections.[5]

Mutual department dependence

When two departments or units within an organization are dependent on one another for the accomplishment of their respective goals, a potential for functional conflict is present. For instance, the marketing department's sales are dependent on the volume of production from the production department, at the same time the production department's quotas are dependent on the sales of the marketing department. This type of mutual dependence exists in many organizations and thus creates a potential for conflict.

Unequal departmental dependence

Frequently organizational structures exist which cause the departmental dependence to be unequal. A situation of unequal dependence fosters conflict. For instance, in most organizations staff groups are generally more dependent on line groups. The staff generally must understand the problems of the line, must cooperate with the line,

---

[5] Much of the material from this section is drawn from Richard E. Walton and John M. Dutton, "The Management of Interdepartmental Conflict: A Model and Review," *Administrative Science Quarterly*, vol. 14, no. 1 (March 1969), pp. 73–84.

and must sell their ideas to the line. However, the line does not have to reciprocate.

One tactic that is used in this form of conflict is an attempt by the more dependent unit to interfere with the work performance of the independent group. Here the more dependent group hopes that the independent group will cooperate once they realize how the dependent group can hinder their progress.

Goal segmentation and rewards

Each functional unit of an organization has different functional goals. These differences can be the basis for conflict which, when it emerges, may appear to result from "personality clashes." The classical problem of inventory levels illustrates this dilemma. The marketing department would like to keep finished goods inventories high so that they can supply all of the customers' needs on short notice. The finance department would like to keep inventories low because of the cost incurred in maintaining these inventories.

Another illustration of this dilemma concerns the product line. Marketing would like to carry a product line composed of all shapes, sizes, and colors. Because of the problems involved in producing multiple shapes, sizes, and colors, the production department would prefer one basic product. The end result in either case is often a conflict between departments.

Richard Walton and John Dutton suggest that the reward system is the key to reducing this type of conflict.[6] They believe that a reward system that emphasizes the separate performance of the conflicting departments will encourage the conflict. However, a reward system which remunerates the combined efforts of the conflicting departments will reduce the conflict.

Functional unit and the environment

Functional units obviously perform different tasks and cope with different segments of the environment. Research has shown that the more the environments served by functional units differ, the greater the potential for conflict. Paul R. Lawrence and Jay W. Lorsch developed four basic dimensions for describing these differences: (1) structure—this refers to the basic type of supervisory style employed; (2) environment orientation—this refers to the orientation of the unit to the outside world. The three environments studied were competitive action (market), processing costs (technical-economic), and de-

---

[6] Ibid., p. 75.

TABLE 11–1
Differences related to environment of departments

Departments	Degree of formality in departmental structure	Orientation toward environment	Orientation toward time	Interpersonal orientation†
Fundamental research...	Medium (4)	Techno-economic and scientific	Long	Task (2)
Applied research	Medium (3)	Techno-economic	Long	Relationship (3)
Sales........................	High (2)	Market	Short	Relationship (4)
Production..................	Highest (1)*	Techno-economic	Short	Task (1)

* Numbers refer to the relative ranking of the departments.
† Fiedler's questionnaire discussed in Chapter 10 was used in this analysis.
Source: P. R. Lawrence and J. W. Lorsch, "Differentiation and Integration in Complex Organizations," *Administrative Science Quarterly*, vol. 12 (1967), pp. 16–22.

veloping new knowledge (scientific); (3) time-span orientation—this refers to the unit's planning time perspectives; (4) interpersonal orientation—this refers to the openness and permissiveness of interpersonal relationships.[7]

Lawrence and Lorsch applied the above scheme to six organizations in the plastics industry and reported the results shown in Table 11–1.

The environmental differences outlined in Table 11–1 are a primary cause of functional conflict. Coordinating the activities of departments such as applied research, sales, and production is made more difficult due to these differences.

Role dissatisfaction

Role dissatisfaction may produce conflicting situations. Professionals in an organization unit who receive little recognition and have limited opportunities for advancement may initiate conflict with other units. Purchasing agents in organizations often experience this form of conflict.

Role dissatisfaction and conflict often result when one group that has less perceived status sets standards for another group. For example, within academic institutions, administrators, who may be viewed by the faculty as having less status, frequently set standards of performance and make administrative decisions that affect the faculty.

---

[7] P. R. Lawrence and J. W. Lorsch, *Organization and Environment* (Boston: Division of Research, Harvard Business School, 1967).

Ambiguities

Ambiguities in the description of a particular job can lead to functional conflict. When the credit or blame for a particular assignment cannot be determined between two departments, conflict is likely to result. For instance, improvements in production techniques require the efforts of the engineering and production departments. However, after the improvements are made, credit is difficult to assign.

Common resource dependence

When two organizational units are dependent on common but scarce resources, potential for conflict exists. This type of conflict often occurs when two departments are competing for computer time. Each department obviously feels that its projects are more important.

Communication barriers

Semantic differences can cause conflict. For instance, purchasing agents and engineers generally use different language to describe similar materials, and this can lead to conflict.

Another cause of communication-related conflict occurs when a physical or organizational barrier to effective communication exists. Relationships between company headquarters and branch offices frequently suffer from this problem. The role of communication in the management process will be discussed in depth in Chapter 13.

INTERPERSONAL CONFLICT

Interpersonal conflict may result from conflicting personalities as well as from functional conflict and may be caused by many factors. Interpersonal conflicts most assuredly arise when personal obstacles to communication exist. Such barriers are often more difficult to overcome than the obstacles mentioned earlier under functional conflict. Communication barriers can give rise to what is called pseudoconflict.[8] Pseudoconflict results from an inability on the part of the participants to reach a group decision because of their failure to exchange information, opinions, or ideas. Although the group may actually be in complete agreement, the situation has all the symptoms of a conflict caused by differences of opinion.

A second major cause of interpersonal conflict occurs when indi-

---

[8] E. Rhenman, L. Stromberg, and G. Westerlund, *Conflict and Cooperation in Business Organizations* (London: Wiley–Interscience, 1970), pp. 7–8.

viduals are dissatisfied with their roles as compared with the roles of others. For example, an employee may be compatiable with his or her manager and fellow employees. But, when one of the employee's peers is promoted to a management job the employee can no longer accept his or her position in relation to the former peer.

Many times opposing personalities cause conflict situations. Some people simply rub each other the wrong way. The extrovert and the introvert, the boisterous and the reserved, the optimist and the pessimist, the impulsive and the deliberate are but a few possible combinations that might bother each other.

Finally there are special prejudices based on personal background or ethnic origin that cause conflict. This, of course, includes racial and religious conflicts, but also other, more subtle, prejudices. Possible examples include the college graduate versus the person without a college education, or the married woman versus the divorcee.

Unlike functional conflicts in which both parties are actively involved, interpersonal conflicts may be one-sided, with one of the parties totally unaware that the conflict exists.

STRATEGIC CONFLICT

Intrapersonal, functional, and interpersonal conflicts are usually not planned. They simply develop as a result of existing circumstances. Strategic conflicts are often deliberately instigated and are sometimes fought with an elaborate battle plan. Such conflicts usually result from the promotion of self-interests on the part of an individual or group. There is a clear objective to be attained, and those who stand in the way of reaching the objective are identified as the adversary. The goal is usually to obtain an advantage over the opponent within the performance appraisal and reward system. The potential reward may be a bonus or commission, a choice assignment, a promotion, or an expansion of power. Whatever the reward may be, the situation is usually such that only one of the participants will receive the reward or the greatest portion of it.

The vice presidents of an organization may find themselves in a strategic conflict as the president's time of retirement approaches. An overly ambitious vice president, in an attempt to better his chances for the presidency, may create a strategic conflict with one or more of the other vice presidents.

Strategic conflict does not necessarily imply that the participants are dishonest or unethical. Indeed, rewards are established to be pursued vigorously. Sometimes, however, such conflicts degenerate into unfair play because of the participant's inability to resist temptation.

Because it is usually impossible to isolate a single cause, few conflicts fit neatly into one of the above categories. Nevertheless, these classifications do provide a useful framework for analyzing conflict.

EFFECTS OF CONFLICT

The effects of conflict may be constructive, destructive, or both. The favorableness of the conflict often depends on the particular participant's point of view; however, the results of a conflict should also be evaluated from the organization's point of view. For example, in a struggle between two men to gain a promotion, the winner will generally feel that the conflict was most worthwhile, while the loser will probably reach the opposite conclusion. However, the impact of the conflict on the organization is of primary importance. If the conflict ends in the selection and promotion of the better man, then from the organization's viewpoint the effect is good. If, as a result of the competition, the parties have produced more or made improvements within their areas of responsibility, then the effect is also positive. At the same time, there may be several destructive effects which offset the good. The overall work of the organization may have suffered during the conflict. The loser may resign or withdraw as a result of his failure. The struggle may turn into continuous conflict and inhibit the work of the organization. In extreme cases, the health of one or both of the participants may be adversely affected.

The destructive effects of conflict are generally obvious. The constructive effects may be more subtle. It is essential that the manager be able to recognize these constructive effects and to weigh their benefits against the costs. A summary of the useful effects of conflict is presented below.[9]

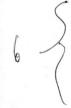

1. Conflict energizes people. Even if not all of the resulting activity is constructive, it at least wakes people up and gets them moving.

2. A functional or strategic conflict usually involves a search for a resolution of the underlying issue. In resolving the conflict, needed changes in the organizational system may be discovered and implemented.

3. Conflict is a form of communication, and the resolution of conflict may open up new and lasting channels.

4. Conflict often provides an outlet for pent-up tensions resulting in catharsis. With the air cleared, the participants can again concentrate on their primary responsibilities.

---

[9] Jane Templeton, "For Corporate Vigor, Plan a Fight Today," *Sales Management*, vol. 102, no. 13 (June 15, 1969), pp. 32–36. Dr. Templeton draws heavily upon George R. Bach and Peter Wyden, *The Ultimate Enemy* (New York: Morrow, 1969). Also, Joseph A. Litterer, "Conflict in Organizations: A Re-Examination," *Academy of Management Journal*, vol. 9 (September 1966), pp. 178–86.

5. Conflict may actually be an educational experience in that the participants may become more aware and more understanding of their opponents' functions and the problems with which they must cope.

PROGRESSIVE STAGES OF THE CONFLICT CYCLE

It is important that the manager be aware of conflict's dynamic nature. Conflict does not usually appear suddenly. It passes through a series of progressive stages as tensions build. These stages of development are as follows:[10]

1. Latent conflict—At this stage the basic conditions for potential conflict exist but have not yet been recognized.
2. Perceived conflict—The cause of the conflict is recognized by one or both of the participants.
3. Felt conflict—Tension is beginning to build between the participants, although no real struggle has yet begun.
4. Manifest conflict—The struggle is under way, and the behavior of the participants makes the existence of the conflict apparent to others who are not directly involved.
5. Conflict aftermath—The conflict has been ended by resolution or suppression. This establishes new conditions that will lead either to more effective cooperation or to a new conflict that may be more severe than the first.

Conflict does not necessarily pass through all of the above stages. Furthermore, each participant in a conflict may not be at the same stage. One participant could be at the manifest stage of conflict while the other participant could be at the perceived stage.

SOLUTION OF CONFLICT

The methods of solving conflict are summarized below:[11]

1. Withdrawal of one or more of the participants.
2. Smoothing the conflict and pretending that it does not exist.
3. Compromise for the sake of ending the conflict.
4. Forcing the conflict to a conclusion by third-party intervention.
5. Confrontation between the participants in an effort to solve the underlying problem.

---

[10] Louis R. Pondy, "Organizational Conflict: Concepts and Models," *Administrative Science Quarterly,* September 1967, pp. 296–320.

[11] Ronald J. Burke, "Methods of Resolving Interpersonal Conflict," *Personnel Administration,* vol. 32, no. 4 (July–August 1969), pp. 48–55.

Only the last method, confrontation for problem solving, will yie
the permanent and constructive results that an organization shou
seek to obtain from its inevitable conflicts. The manager must aid the
participants in this effort but must always be aware of the costs of
conflict and take whatever actions are necessary if these costs become too great.

A MODEL FOR CONFLICT MANAGEMENT

Richard Walton and John Dutton have developed a general model,
as shown in Figure 11–5, for managing conflict in organizations. This
model views the conflict situation from two perspectives. The first

FIGURE 11–5
Model for conflict management

Source: Richard E. Walton and John M. Dutton, "The Management of Interdepartmental
Conflict: A Model and Review," *Administrative Science Quarterly*, vol. 14, no. 1 (March 1969),
p. 74.

perspective views the manager as an intervening force in the conflict
cycle. The second perspective involves the response patterns of
higher-level managers.

The conflict interface

Management of the conflict interface is based on monitoring the
behavior of the participant(s) as the conflict develops. The objective
of the manager is not to resolve the conflict but to act as a referee and
counselor in helping the participant(s) reach an acceptable solution.
Understanding the type of conflict—intrapersonal, functional, interpersonal, or strategic—and the stage of the conflict cycle will aid the
manager in the conflict situation.

The manager should also be aware of the following ground rules
for verbal confrontations to maximize the constructive aspects of the

conflict and to speed its resolution while minimizing the destructive consequences:[12]

1.   Review past actions and clarify the issues before the confrontation begins.
2.   Communicate freely; do not hold back grievances.
3.   Do not surprise the opponent with a confrontation for which he is not prepared.
4.   Do not attack the opponent's sensitive spots that have nothing to do with the issues of the conflict.
5.   Keep to specific issues; do not argue aimlessly.
6.   Maintain the intensity of the confrontation but ensure that all participants say all that they want to say. If the basic issues have been resolved at this point, agree on what steps will be taken next toward reaching a solution.

Besides acting as a referee in enforcing the above rules, the manager of the conflict interface can give valuable assistance to the participant(s) without interfering in the struggle or relieving the participant(s) of the responsibility to resolve it. The manager can help the participant understand why the conflict exists and what underlying issues must be resolved. The manager can also help obtain information that may be necessary in order to reach a solution. In interpersonal conflict, the manager can, to some extent, regulate the frequency of contacts between the participants and perhaps establish a problem-solving climate when they meet. The manager's most important contribution, however, is to keep them working toward a true resolution of the conflict. Confrontation of conflict within the guidelines developed above should encourage constructive conflict within the organization.

Responses of higher-level managers

The second level of conflict management concerns the responses of higher level managers to the consequences of the conflict as it affects the ongoing work of the organization. If the conflict itself, or the nature of its aftermath, have produced conditions that are considered intolerable, management must step in and make whatever decisions and changes they deem necessary to restore order. The resulting actions either force a resolution to the conflict or change the solution that has been reached. This intervention is often regarded as arbitrary by the participant(s), especially by those who do not receive a favorable decision. In such cases it is important that the intervening

---

[12] Henry Assael, "Constructive Role of Interorganizational Conflict," *Administrative Science Quarterly*, December 1969, pp. 573–82; Richard E. Walton, "Third-Party Roles in Interdepartmental Conflict," *Industrial Relations*, vol. 7, no. 1 (October 1967), pp. 29–43.

authority not give the impression that the action has been taken because either or both of the participants have failed but rather because an immediate or different solution is in the best interest of the organization. There should be no doubt that the solution is final and that the conflict has been concluded.

SUMMARY

Conflict in organizations is often assumed to be an unnatural and undesirable situation that is to be avoided at all costs. Management must realize that conflict exists in all organizations and is not necessarily negative. The goal of management should be to understand and manage conflict in order to obtain the maximum benefits.

Conflict was analyzed from two basic perspectives—internal or intrapersonal conflict and external conflict. External conflict can be further divided into three types: functional, interpersonal, and strategic.

In a model presented by Richard Walton and John Dutton, conflict management is viewed from two perspectives. The first perspective views the manager as an intervening force in the conflict cycle. The second perspective concerns the responses of higher-level managers to the consequences of the conflict as it affects the ongoing work of the organization.

REVIEW QUESTIONS

1. What are two basic viewpoints that can be used to analyze conflict? *P240*
2. What causes intrapersonal conflict? What are some typical defense mechanisms used when an individual is frustrated? Describe three forms of intrapersonal goal conflict. *P24-43*
3. Name at least four types of functional conflict.
4. What are some of the causes of interpersonal conflict?
5. What is strategic conflict?
6. Describe some of the useful effects of conflict.
7. Identify the five stages of conflict.
8. What are some methods that can be used to resolve conflict?
9. Describe in detail a model for managing conflict in organizations.

DISCUSSION QUESTIONS

1. Discuss the following statement: "Every manager should attempt to avoid conflict at all times."

2. How can managers reduce destructive role conflict in organizations?

3. Describe how you would handle the situation in which you have two people working for you who "just rub each other the wrong way."

4. "Conflict is inevitable." Do you agree or disagree? Discuss.

SELECTED READINGS

Aldrich, Howard. "Organizational Boundaries and Interorganizational Conflict," *Human Relations* (August 1971), pp. 279–93.

Bass, Bernard M. *Organizational Psychology*. Boston: Allyn and Bacon, Inc., 1965.

Burke, Ronald J. "Methods of Resolving Interpersonal Conflict," *Personnel Administration*, vol. 32, no. 4 (July–August 1969), pp. 48–55.

Henderson, Hazel. "Toward Managing Social Conflict," *Harvard Business Review* (May–June 1971), pp. 82–90.

House, Robert J. "Role Conflict and Multiple Authority in Complex Organizations," *California Management Review* (Summer 1970), pp. 53–60.

Kelly, Joe. "Make Conflict Work for You," *Harvard Business Review* (July–August 1970), pp. 103–13.

Litterer, Joseph A. "Managing Conflict in Organizations," *Proceedings of the 8th Annual Midwest Management Conference*. Southern Illinois University, Business Research Bureau, 1965.

Pondy, Louis R. "Organizational Conflict: Concepts and Models," *Administrative Science Quarterly* (September 1967), pp. 296–320.

Walton, Richard E. *Interpersonal Peacemaking*. Reading, Mass.: Addison-Wesley, 1969.

Walton, Richard E., and John M. Dutton. "The Management of Interdepartmental Conflict: A Model and Review," *Administrative Science Quarterly*, vol. 14, no. 1 (March 1969), pp. 73–84.

Williams, Frederick P., and Raymond L. Read. "Contemporary Approaches to the Control of Organizational Conflict," *Business Studies—North Texas State University* (Fall 1969), pp. 78–84.

Case 11–1

Problems at the hospital

Smith County is a suburban community near a major midwestern city. The county has experienced such a tremendous rate of growth during the past decade that local governments have had difficulty providing adequate service to the citizens.

The Smith County Hospital has a reputation of being a first-class facility, but it is inadequate to meet local needs. During certain periods of the year the occupancy rates exceed the licensed capacity. There is no doubt in anyone's mind that the hospital must be expanded immediately.

At a recent meeting of the Hospital Authority the hospital administrator, Sam Austin, presented the group with a proposal to accept the architectural plans of the firm of Watkins and Gibson. This plan calls for a 100-bed expansion adjacent to the existing structure. Sam announced that after reviewing several alternative plans, he believed the Watkins and Gibson plan would provide the most benefit for the expenditures.

At this point, Randolph (Randy) Lewis, the board chairman, began questioning the plan in such a manner that Sam became defensive. Randy made it clear that he would not go along with the Watkins and Gibson plan. He stated that the board would look for other firms to serve as the architects for the project.

The pursuing arguments became somewhat heated and a ten-minute recess was called to allow those attending to get coffee as well as to allow tempers to calm down. Sam was talking to John Rhodes, another member of the Hospital Authority Board, in the hall and said, "Randy seems to fight me on every project."

Randy, who was talking to other members of the board was saying, "I know that the Watkins and Gibson plan is good, but I just can't stand for that guy Austin to act like it is his plan." I wish that _____ would leave so we would get a good administrator from the community who we can identify with."

1. Is Randy's reaction uncommon? ~ no
2. What type of conflict exists between Randy and Sam? person mason
3. What methods would you use to reduce or resolve the conflict?

Case 11–2

The young college graduate and the old superintendent

SITUATION: You are a consultant to the manager of a garment manufacturing plant in a small southern town. The manager has been having trouble with two of his employees: Ralph, the plant superintendent, and Barbara, the production scheduler. Ralph is 53 years old and has been with the company since he was released from military duty after World War II. He started as a warehouseman with a sixth-grade education and worked his way up through the ranks. Until recently, Ralph handled the production scheduling function himself along with his many other duties. He was proud of the fact that he could handle it all "in his head." As the volume of production and the number of different products grew, however, the plant manager felt that significant savings could be attained through a more "scientific" approach to scheduling. He believed that he could save on raw materials by purchasing in larger lots and on production set-up time by making longer runs. He also wanted to cut down on the frequency of finished good stock-outs, and when backlogs did occur, he wanted to be able to give customers more definite information as to when goods would be available. He wanted to have a schedule documented for at least two months into the future with daily updates.

Barbara is 24 years old, and grew up in the Chicago area. This is her first full-time job. She earned a Master of Science in Industrial Engineering from an eastern engineering school. She jumped right into the job and set up a computer-assisted scheduling system using a time-sharing service with a teletype terminal in her office. The system is based on the latest production scheduling and inventory control technology. It is very flexible and has proven to be very effective in all the areas that were of interest to the plant manager.

Plant Manager: Sometimes I just want to shoot both Ralph and Barbara. If those two could just get along with each other, this plant would run like a well-oiled machine.

Consultant: What do they fight about?

Manager: Anything and everything that has to do with the production schedule. Really trivial things in a lot of cases. It all seems so completely senseless!

Consultant: Have you tried to do anything about it?

Manager: At first I tried to minimize the impact of their feuds on the rest of the plant by stepping in and making decisions that would eliminate the point of controversy. I also tried to smooth things over as if the arguments were just friendly disagreements. I thought that after they had a chance to get accustomed to each other the problem would go away. But it didn't. It got to the point that I was spending a good 20 percent of my time stopping their fights. Furthermore, I began to notice that other employees were starting to take sides. The younger women seemed to support Barbara; everybody else sided with Ralph. It began to look as if we might have our own little war.

Consultant: What's the current situation?

Manager: I finally told them both that if I caught them fighting again, I would take "very drastic action" with both of them. I think that move was a mistake though, because now they won't even talk to each other. Barbara just drops the schedule printouts on Ralph's desk every afternoon and walks away. Ralph needs some help in working with those printouts, and Barbara needs some feedback on what's actually going on in the plant. Frankly, things aren't going as well production-wise now as when they were at each other's throats. And the tension in the plant as a whole is even worse. They are both good people and outstanding in their respective jobs. I would really hate to lose either one of them, but if they can't work together, I may have to let one or both of them go.

1. Why is this conflict occurring? *Barb & Ralph don't get along*
2. What method did the manager use in dealing with this conflict situation? Was it effective? *negative*
3. Recommend an approach for resolving the conflict.

Objectives

1. *To examine the nature of groups in organizations.*
2. *To explore the reasons why groups form in organizations.*
3. *To define the concepts of conformity and creativity.*
4. *To discuss the impact that groups can have on individual conformity and creativity.*

GLOSSARY OF TERMS

Brainstorming A process designed to produce creative ideas by presenting a group with a problem and then eliciting their ideas for solutions. No criticisms of solutions are allowed so as not to inhibit the group members.

Conformity Refers to the degree to which the members of a group accept and abide by the norms of the group.

Creative process A process that involves developing something new. The process involves four basic stages: preparation, incubation, illumination, and verification.

Formal work groups Groups in organizations which generally have a defined structure and established goals and are formally recognized by the organization.

Gordon technique An aid in producing creative ideas relating to technical problems which uses a key word to describe the problem area and then uses the key word as a starting point for exploring the problem area.

Group A number of persons who interact with one another often over a span of time, communicate with all the other members on a face-to-face basis, and perceive themselves to be a group.

Group cohesiveness The degree of attraction that each member has for the group.

Idiosyncracy credit A form of credit or liberties which a group gives to certain members of the group who have made or are making significant contributions to the group's goals.

Informal work groups Groups in organizations which generally do not have a defined structure and established goals and are not formally recognized by the organization.

Linking-pin concept A concept proposed by Rensis Likert which views managers as a potential force for linking together the different groups within the organization.

Primary group A group that meets all of the characteristics of an ordinary group but which must also have feelings of loyalty, comradeship, and a common sense of values among its members.

Work groups A term used to describe groups in organizations.

12

Work groups, conformity, and creativity

When the individual has become associated with a cooperative enterprise he has accepted a position of contact with others similarly associated. From this contact there must arise interactions between these persons individually, and these interactions are social. It may be, and often is, true that these interactions are not a purpose or object either of the cooperative systems or of the individuals participating in them. They nevertheless cannot be avoided. Hence, though not sought, such interactions are consequences of cooperation, and constitute one set of social factors involved in cooperation. These factors operate on the individuals affected; and, in conjunction with other factors, become incorporated in their mental and emotional characters. This is an effect which makes them significant. Hence, cooperation compels changes in the motives of individuals which otherwise would not take place. So far as these changes are in a direction favorable to the cooperative system they are resources to it. So far as they are in a direction unfavorable to cooperation, they are detriments to it or limitations of it.

Chester I. Barnard*

PEOPLE are members of a wide range of organizations, such as business organizations, governmental organizations, labor unions, religious organizations, and so forth. As the introductory quote states, other groups invariably form within these organizations. Furthermore, these smaller groups can have a significant impact on organization performance. The purpose of this chapter is to examine the nature of groups in organizations and their impact on individual conformity and creativity.

° *The Functions of the Executive,* Cambridge: Harvard University Press, 1938, p. 40.

259

WORK GROUPS DEFINED

There are many ways of defining a group. However, when referring to groups in organizations, what is needed is a definition which facilitates an understanding of how individuals work together in organizations.

Edgar Schein has described a group as "any number of people who (1) interact with one another, (2) are psychologically aware of one another, and (3) perceive themselves to be a group."[1] George Homans further refined the definition of a group as "a number of persons who communicate with one another often over a span of time, and who are few enough so that each person is able to communicate with all the others, not at secondhand, through other people, but face-to-face."[2] Thus, small size, physical and psychological awareness, and interaction are all characteristics of groups.

Sociologists have further refined the definition by distinguishing between a small group and a primary group. A small group must merely meet all of the characteristics outlined in the previous paragraph. A primary group in addition to meeting the above characteristics must also have feelings of loyalty, comradeship, and a common sense of values among its members. Thus, all primary groups are small groups, but all small groups are not necessarily primary groups. Both types of groups exist within organizations.

For the purposes of this chapter, the term *work groups* will be used to describe groups in organizations. A further distinction will be made between formal and informal work groups. Formal work groups result primarily from the organizing function of management. Generally, formal work groups are defined by formally prescribed relationships between the members and a prescribed plan of effort directed toward the attainment of specific objectives. On the other hand, informal work groups are the result of personal contacts and interactions and the associated groupings of people working within the formal organization. The structure of informal work groups is not formally and consciously designed.

Two popular forms of formal work groups are command and task groups.[3] These groups can be either small or primary. Command groups can be seen on the organization chart. The vice presidents reporting to the president comprise a command group. The depart-

---

[1] Edgar H. Schein, *Organizational Psychology* (Englewood Cliffs, N.J.: Prentice-Hall, Inc., 1965), p. 67.

[2] George C. Homans, *The Human Group* (New York: Harcourt, Brace & World, Inc., 1950), p. 1.

[3] Leonard R. Sayles, "Work Group Behavior and the Larger Organization," in *Research in Industrial Human Relations,* Industrial Relations Research Association publication no. 17 (New York: Harper and Brothers, Publishers, 1957), pp. 131–45.

FIGURE 12–1
Potential benefits from informal groups

1. Informal groups blend with the formal organization to make a workable system for getting work done.
2. Informal groups lighten the workload for the formal manager and fill in some of the gaps in the manager's abilities.
3. Informal groups provide satisfaction and stability to the organization.
4. Informal groups provide a useful channel of communication in the organization.
5. The presence of informal groups encourages managers to plan and act more carefully than they would otherwise.

Source: Keith Davis, *Human Behavior at Work,* 4th ed. (New York: McGraw-Hill Book Company, 1972), pp. 257–59.

ment heads reporting to a vice president comprise another command group. A task group is formed by employees that collaborate in order to accomplish a work task assigned by the organization. Engineers working on a particular project and committees are both examples of task groups. Since Chapter 6 dealt at length with formal work groups, this chapter will be primarily concerned with informal work groups.

Mutual interests, friendships, and the need to fulfil social needs lead to the formation of informal work groups. Informal work groups are usually primary because of the fact that members of the group generally have feelings of loyalty, comradeship, and a common sense of values.

Many managers view informal work groups as being negative in their orientation toward organizational goals. However, as summarized in Figure 12–1, informal work groups can be beneficial to the organization.

IMPORTANCE OF WORK GROUPS

Management as defined in Chapter 1 gives an indication of the importance of groups. Management was defined as a process or form of work that involved the guidance or direction of a *group* of people toward organizational goals or objectives. Thus even the definition of management recognizes that groups exist within organizations.

As was true of our look at conflict in Chapter 11, group pressures can have both positive and negative influences on the individuals in the group. Groups can also have a significant impact on total organizational performance. Thus, understanding the nature of work groups and the interaction between formal and informal work groups is a vital element in effective management.

The Hawthorne Studies which were introduced in Chapter 2 first highlighted the importance of work groups. The major conclusion reached by the Hawthorne researchers was that workers react to the psychological and social conditions at work as well as to the physical conditions, and that group pressures directly effect individual responses. One significant benefit of the studies was the recognition that an organization consists of individuals, groups, and intergroup relationships, and that these components can greatly influence the productivity and stability of the organization.

THE FORMATION OF WORK GROUPS

Work groups form for many reasons. The following paragraphs outline some of these reasons.

The organization structure provides the primary force behind the formation of command and task groups. The organization structure requires department heads who are reporting to a vice president to interact and thus to form groups. As was pointed out earlier, command groups are generally small groups and may or may not be primary. Comradeship and loyalty are not necessary in these groups. Likewise, task groups are generally defined by the organization structure. Again they are small and not necessarily primary groups.

Maslow's need hierarchy theory, which was discussed in Chapter 9, can be used to explain the formation of many work groups. The safety or security need is concerned with protection, comfort and peace, elimination of threats or danger, and orderly, neat surroundings. When these needs are not met by the formal organization, informal work groups will form in an attempt to satisfy these needs. The threatening nature of the formal organization structure to the individual can cause that person to join an informal work group. This is especially true for new employees. The informal work group provides the security that is frequently lacking with the new surroundings.

Probably the most important reason for the formation of informal work groups is the social need for affiliation. It has been said that "some form of social contact appears necessary for the normal physical and personality development of the human infant; and total isolation is virtually always an intolerable situation for the human adult—even when physical needs are provided for."[4] Furthermore, research has

---

[4] Bernard Berelson and Gary A. Steiner, *Human Behavior* (New York: Harcourt, Brace, & World, Inc., 1964), p. 252.

shown that employees who are isolated from other employees find their jobs to be less satisfying than employees who can interact with other employees.[5]

Esteem needs also encourage individuals to join both formal and informal work groups. Groups that have a high status in an organization—junior boards of directors, executive committees, union shop steward committee, and so on—often influence the behavior of organization members who wish to join the group.

Finally, the self-actualization needs can promote group formation. Chris Argyris has argued in his incongruity model discussed in Chapter 9 that groups form when the self-actualization needs of employees cannot be satisfied by the organization.

In addition, work groups tend to form among people who are in close proximity on the job. People in close proximity to each other are almost forced to interact with each other, and a natural impetus exists to form work groups. The formal organization concepts of departmentation and functionalization contribute to this process of group formation. For example, schools of business administration group accounting professors, management professors, and so on, and thus encourage the formation of groups.

There are many reasons for group formation within organizations, and the reasons discussed above are by no means all inclusive. An effective manager must realize that groups exist and that they can have a significant impact on individual and organizational performance.

STAGES OF WORK-GROUP DEVELOPMENT

A major determinant of performance of a work group depends on how well the group learns to use its resources. This learning process basically involves four stages.[6] First, group members must learn to not only accept others but also themselves. Members of a group initially mistrust each other. The group members fear not only the inadequacies of other group members but also their own inadequacies. This distrust leads to defensive behaviors. Only after these initial fears have been resolved will the group develop mutual acceptance and a feeling of belonging to the group.

Mutual acceptance and cohesiveness allows the group to enter the communication and decision-making stage in a more productive way. Open communication replaces caution. Problem solving re-

---

[5] Elton Mayo, *The Human Problems of an Industrial Civilization* (Boston: Division of Research, Harvard Business School, 1946), pp. 42–52.

[6] Bernard Bass, *Organizational Psychology* (Boston: Allyn and Bacon, 1965), pp. 197–98.

places the gimmicks and tricks that are frequently used in the early stage of group work.

The third stage is characterized by the growing awareness that creativity can be maintained over long periods of time, members are involved in their work, extrinsic rewards are not needed to maintain productivity, and members cooperate instead of compete.

The final stage involves control and organization. A successful group allocates work according to the abilities of the individuals and by agreements among the individuals. Informality, flexibility, and spontaneity are stressed rather than the structure of the organization.

The development of all groups does not necessarily follow the above four stages in a step-by-step sequence; however, the development of most groups does follow such a sequential process. The mature, effective group that emerges has the following characteristics:

1. The members function as a unit. The group works as a team. The members do not disturb each other to the point of interfering with their collaboration.

2. The members participate effectively in group effort. They work hard when there is something to do. Members do not loaf if they get the opportunity.

3. The members are oriented toward a single goal. They work for common purposes.

4. The members have the equipment, tools, and skills necessary to attain the group's goals. The group members are taught various parts of their jobs by experts. The group is not short-handed.

5. Members ask and receive suggestions, opinions, and information from each other. If a member is uncertain about something, he stops working and finds out. The members talk to each other frequently.[7]

GROUP COHESIVENESS

A variable that plays an important role in the achievement of group goals is group cohesiveness. Cohesiveness basically refers to the degree of attraction that each member has for the group, or the stick-togetherness of the group. This is important because the greater the cohesiveness of the group, the more likely it will be that members will pursue the group goals and not individual goals.

An important variable affecting the cohesiveness of the group is its size. As discussed earlier, individuals in the group must interact in order for the group to exist. This interaction requirement limits the

---

[7] Ibid., p. 199.

size of the group.[8] In other words, group cohesiveness decreases as the size of the group increases.

1) It is impossible to specify an upper limit on the size of work groups. However, the interaction requirement generally limits the size of the work group to a maximum of 15 to 20 members. Generally, if the work group becomes larger than 20, subgroups begin to form.

2) Success also plays an important part in group cohesiveness. The more successful a group is in achieving its goals, the more cohesive is the group. The relationship is circular in that success breeds cohesiveness and cohesiveness in turn breeds more success.

Highly cohesive groups whose goals are incongruous with those of the formal organization can be disruptive to the organization. On the other hand, highly cohesive groups whose goals support those of the formal organization are generally very productive and efficient for the organization. Naturally, management should provide an environment which fosters the formation of work groups that have goals compatible to those of the organization.

Managers can also influence group cohesiveness. If demands or requests made by management are perceived as threats by work groups, group cohesiveness may increase to offset the perceived threat.

Stanley Seashore studied the relationship between group cohesiveness and worker attitudes and production in a large, heavy-equipment manufacturing company.[9] Seashore found that workers in highly cohesive groups had less anxiety about job-related matters. In other words, workers in highly cohesive groups felt less pressure on the job. Seashore also found that highly cohesive groups are more likely to have output records that diverge in either direction from plant averages. Thus, if the goals of a highly cohesive group are compatible with the organization's productivity goals, then the group's output will be above average. However, if the group's goals are incompatible with the organization's performance goals, the group's output will be below average.

INFLUENCE OF WORK GROUPS ON ORGANIZATIONAL CHANGE

In the late 1940s. Lester Coch and John R. P. French conducted studies at a textile firm, Harwood Manufacturing Company, in Marion, Virginia. Figure 12–2 illustrates a major finding of their study. In this

---

[8] Stanley E. Seashore, *Group Cohesiveness in the Industrial Work Group* (Ann Arbor: University of Michigan, Institute for Social Research, 1954), pp. 90–95.

[9] Ibid., pp. 90–95.

case, a woman textile worker started to exceed the group norm of 50 units per day. On the 13th day, the group exerted pressure on the woman in the form of scapegoating, and thus, the woman's output was quickly reduced to conform with the group norm. On the 20th day, the group was disbanded by moving all group members, except the woman, to other jobs. Once again, her production quickly climbed to almost double the group norm.

Coch and French also investigated the relationship between participation in the decision-making process and work group productivity. Before the study was undertaken, workers at the Harwood Manufacturing Company had shown a strong resistance to changes

FIGURE 12–2
Effect of group expectations on member productivity

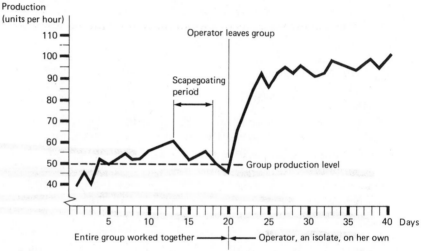

Source: Lester Coch and J. R. P. French, Jr., "Overcoming Resistance to Change," *Human Relations*, 1948, pp. 519–20.

in their jobs. Coch and French designed a study in which there were basically three different types of groups. One group was not allowed to participate in planning new work methods. Another group was allowed limited participation by selecting certain members of the group to participate in improving and implementing new methods. These selected members then trained the remainder of the group in the new method. The final group was designed so that all members of the group participated in designing the new method. The researchers found a strong positive relationship between the degree of participation in planning and implementing new methods and actual productivity.

Coch and French concluded:

> It is impossible for management to modify greatly or to remove completely group resistance to changes in methods of work and the ensuing piece rates. This change can be accomplished by the use of group meetings in which management effectively communicates the need for change and stimulates group participation in planning the changes.[10]

Thus, as consistent with the leadership theories discussed in Chapter 10, Coch and French found the degree of participation by the group had an important impact on behavior—especially when introducing change.

THE LINKING-PIN CONCEPT

Rensis Likert has proposed several new ideas relating to work groups. Likert suggests that as an individual interacts with the organi-

FIGURE 12–3
Linking-pin concept

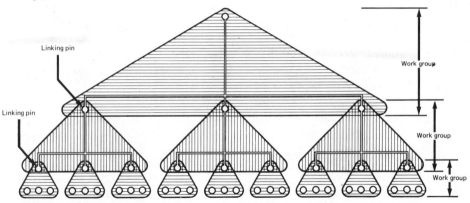

Source: Rensis Likert, *New Patterns of Management* (New York: McGraw-Hill Book Company, 1961), p. 104.

zation, these interactions should contribute to maintaining the sense of personal worth and importance. An important source of satisfaction in maintaining an employee's sense of personal worth and importance is the work group. Thus, Likert concludes:

> Management will make full use of the potential capacities of its human resources only when each person in an organization is a member of one or more effectively functioning work groups that have a high degree

---

[10] Lester Coch and J. R. P. French, Jr., "Overcoming Resistance to Change," *Human Relations*, 1948, pp. 519–20.

of group loyalty, effective skills of interaction, and high performance goals.[11]

Likert further contends that management should consciously attempt to build these groups. Managers who have overlapping group memberships link these groups to the total organization. Thus the manager is viewed as a linking pin in the organization. The linking-pin concept is depicted in Figure 12–3.

CONFORMITY AND WORK GROUPS

The earlier sections of this chapter were designed to give an understanding of the nature of work groups in organizations. The purpose of this section is to examine the role of work groups in obtaining individual conformity.

Conformity refers to the degree to which the members of a group accept and abide by the norms of the group. Conformity in one situation might be viewed as deviant behavior in another situation; therefore, conformity is situationally determined. Probably the most important variable in the situation is the individual's relationships with other people and their relationships with each other. Thus the group defines conformity for any given situation.

Knowing that the group defines conformity does not offer much help to the practicing manager. The manager needs to know how the group establishes conformity and the effect it has on the individual in the group. The following sections explore these concerns.

Group pressures on the individual

Solomon Asch has conducted research on group pressure and its effect on individual behavior.[12] Asch placed college students in groups ranging in size from seven to nine people. The members of the groups were told that they would be comparing lengths of lines on white cards. Figure 12–4 illustrates the cards and lines. The individuals in the study were then asked to pick the line on the second card that was identical in length to the line on the first card.

In the experiment, all but one member of each group was told to pick one of the two wrong lines on card 2. In addition, the uninformed member of the group was positioned so that he or she was always one of the last individuals to respond. Under ordinary circumstances, individuals make mistakes on the line selection less than 1 percent

---

[11] Rensis Likert, *New Patterns of Management* (New York: McGraw-Hill Book Company, New York: 1961), p. 104.

[12] Solomon Asch, "Opinions and Social Pressure," *Scientific American*, November 1955, pp. 31–34.

of the time. However, in this experiment the uninformed member made the wrong selection in 36.8 percent of the trials.

The study further showed that when an uninformed member was confronted with only a single individual who contradicted the choice, the uninformed member continued to answer correctly in almost all trials. When the opposition was increased by two, incorrect responses increased to 13.6 percent. When the opposition was increased to three, incorrect responses increased to 31.8 percent.

The experiment demonstrated that the group's behavior affected the behavior of the individual members; although some individuals remained independent in their judgments, others acquiesced on almost every judgment. Overall group pressure caused individuals to make incorrect judgments in over one third of the cases. The experi-

FIGURE 12–4
Cards in Asch experiment

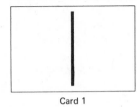

Card 1

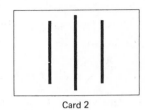

Card 2

ment also showed that the more members that disagree with the individual, the more likely is the individual to succumb to the judgment of the group.

Richard S. Crutchfield conducted a similar experiment which called for various types of judgments—lengths of lines, areas of figures, logical completion of number series, vocabulary items, estimates of the opinions of others, expression of own attitudes on issues, expression of personal preferences for line drawings, and so on.[13] The results of this study were similar to Asch's results. Crutchfield, however, went one step further in that he attempted to define the personal characteristics of conformers and nonconformers. He defined the conformist as "having less ego strength, less ability to tolerate his own impulses and to tolerate ambiguity, less ability to accept responsibility, less self-insight, less spontaneity and productive originality, and as having more prejudiced and authoritarian attitudes, more idealization of parents, and greater emphasis on external and socially approved values."[14]

---

[13] Richard S. Crutchfield, "Conformity and Character," *American Psychologist*, vol. 10 (1955), pp. 191–98.

[14] Ibid., p. 196.

Idiosyncrasy credit

Each member of a group gives to and takes from the group. This process does not have to be balanced; some give more than they take; others take more than they give. One way in which the group pays its overgiving members is by extending to them a form of credit. That is, the group allows certain members who have made or are making significant contributions to the group's goals to take certain liberties within the group. E. P. Hollander has called this phenomenon idiosyncrasy credit.[15] Thus any group member's behavior that is allowed by the group to deviate from group norms is an example of idiosyncrasy credit.

People who contribute a great deal to the group also play a major role in developing group norms. Consequently, the group's norms largely reflect the attitudes of the major givers. This means that those who accumulate the most idiosyncrasy credit do not have to use it because the group norms largely reflect their own attitudes. Therefore, people who make large contributions to the group are allowed to deviate from the group norms, but they are not likely to do so because of the similarity between their norms and group norms. Conversely, those members who make little or no contribution to the group must learn to conform to norms which they had little or no part in establishing. Conformity, therefore, may be more difficult and more rigorously demanded for these members.

Producing conformity

Certain basic steps can be taken to produce and develop a high degree of conformity within work groups. These are listed below:

1. Staff the group with people who are submissive, compliant, overly accepting, perform prescribed acts, have a narrow range of interests, are inhibited, vacillate or delay in making decisions, are suggestible and lack self-insight.
2. Have a group size of about 6 to 15.
3. Discourage all deviations from group norms.
4. Control the development of idiosyncrasy credit.

The above suggestions for producing conformity are viewed negatively by most individuals. However, organizations must have some conformity in order to achieve organizational goals. The problem is that a fine line exists between enough conformity and too much con-

---

[15] E. P. Hollander, "Conformity, Status, and Idiosyncrasy Credit," *Psychological Review*, vol. 65 (1958), pp. 117–27.

formity. Managers and organizations also need creativity, and too much conformity stifles creativity. Creativity is discussed in the next section to help provide the manager with the perspective for properly balancing conformity and creativity.

CREATIVITY IN ORGANIZATIONS

Creativity is a process that involves developing something new. This definition makes no distinction between good and bad creativity. No distinction is made between discovering a new pain-relieving drug and devising new methods for torturing people. Both actions are creative, although their social values are different. In addition, this definition makes no distinction regarding the degree of creativity, since this also requires a value judgment.

The creative process   *STUDY*

The creative process can be outlined in four basic stages: (1) preparation, (2) incubation, (3) illumination, and (4) verification.[16]

Preparation involves the hard, conscious, systematic, and often fruitless examination of a problem or area of study. The preparation stage involves getting ready to solve a particular problem. Preparation requires not only being aware of a problem area but also requires study of the problem area. The stage during which the individual or group is not consciously thinking about the problem forms the incubation stage. Unconscious mental exploration of the problem occurs during incubation. The illumination stage occurs with the appearance of the solution and is generally a very sudden occurrence. Finally, the verification stage of creativity involves testing and refining the solution.

For most people, the above four stages overlap each other as different problems are explored. A business executive reading the morning mail may be accumulating knowledge in preparation for solving one problem, may be incubating on another problem, and may also be verifying another problem.

Aids in creativity

Several techniques exist which can serve as aids in encouraging group creativity. Two of the more widely used techniques are brainstorming and the Gordon technique.

---

[16] Graham Wallis, *The Art of Thought* (New York: Harcourt, Brace and Company, 1926), p. 80.

Alex F. Osborn developed brainstorming as an aid in producing creative ideas for an advertising agency. Basically, brainstorming involves presenting a problem to a group of people and allowing them to present ideas for solution to the problem. No criticisms of solutions are allowed. The assumption made under this technique is that criticism of solutions will inhibit the generation of new ideas.

William J. J. Gordon developed a technique to spur creative problem solving for the consulting firm of Arthur D. Little, Inc. The technique was devised to get creative ideas on technical problems. The Gordon technique differs from brainstorming in that the participants are not aware of the specific problem that is being explored. A key word is used to describe a problem area and the group then explores the problem area using the key word as a starting point. For instance, the word *conservation* might be used to start a discussion on energy conservation. The key word would direct discussion and suggestions on conservation in other areas in addition to the one under question. Proponents of the Gordon technique argue that it gives better quality ideas because the discussion is not limited to one particular area as with the brainstorming technique. Some rules and suggestions for conducting sessions using brainstorming and the Gordon technique are also summarized in Figure 12–5.

Larry Cummings has developed an excellent summary of the characteristics of a creative organization. These are summarized in Figure 12–6.

Conformity and creativity are both required in organizations. Providing an environment that fosters a healthy mix of conformity and creativity is difficult at best. But the manager who is cognizant of the components of both characteristics is better able to recognize the trade-off involved and better prepared to manage successfully this trade-off.

SUMMARY

Small size, physical and psychological awareness, and interaction are all characteristics of groups. Sociologists distinguish between a small group and a primary group. A small group meets all of the requirements given above. A primary group in addition to meeting the above requirements must also have feelings of loyalty, comradeship, and a common sense of values among its members. Both types of groups exist within organizations.

The term *work groups* was used to describe groups in organizations. Both formal and informal work groups exist in organizations. The primary difference between these two types of groups is that the

FIGURE 12–5
Rules and suggestions for brainstorming and the Gordon technique

Osborn brainstorming
Rules:
1. Judicial thinking or evaluation is ruled out.
2. Freewheeling is welcomed.
3. Quantity is wanted.
4. Combinations and improvements are sought.

Suggestions for the Osborn technique:
1. Length: 40 minutes to one hour, sessions of 10 to 15 minutes can be effective if time is short.
2. Do not reveal the problem before the session. An information sheet or suggested reference material on a selected subject should be used if prior knowledge of a general field is needed.
3. Problem should be clearly stated and not too broad.
4. Use a small conference table which allows people to communicate with each other easily.
5. If a product is being discussed, samples may be useful as a point of reference.

Gordon technique
Rules:
1. Only the group leader knows the problem.
2. Free association is used.
3. Subject for discussion must be carefully chosen.

Suggestions for the Gordon technique:
1. Length of session: two to three hours are necessary.
2. Group leader must be exceptionally gifted and thoroughly trained in the use of the technique.

General suggestions that apply to both techniques
1. Selection of personnel: a group from diverse backgrounds helps. Try to get a balance of highly active and quiet members.
2. Mixed groups of men and women are often more effective, especially for consumer problems.
3. Although physical atmosphere is not too important, a relaxed pleasant atmosphere is desirable.
4. Group size: groups of from 4 to 12 can be effective. We recommend 6 to 9.
5. Newcomers may be introduced without disturbing the group, but they must be properly briefed in the theory of creative thinking and the use of the particular technique.
6. A secretary or recording machine should be used to record the ideas produced. Otherwise they may not be remembered later. Gordon always uses a blackboard so that ideas can be visualized.
7. Hold sessions in the morning if people are going to continue to work on the same problem after the session has ended; otherwise hold them late in the afternoon. (The excitement of a session continues for several hours after it is completed, and can affect an employee's routine tasks.)
8. Usually it is advisable not to have people from widely differing ranks within the organization in the same session.

Source: Reprinted by permission of the publisher from Charles S. Whiting, "Operational Techniques of Creative Thinking," *S.A.M. Advanced Management Journal*, October 1955, © 1955 by Society for Advancement of Management, p. 28. All rights reserved.

FIGURE 12–6
Characteristics of a creative organization

1. A relatively small degree of formalization of relationships among the organizational positions, (Flexibility of structure may be a necessary quality of the truly creative organization).

2. Careful attention given to *not* overspecifying the human resources needed for a specific task.

3. A flexible power-authority-influence structure or network oriented primarily toward the task at hand.

4. Relatively large areas of discretion and healthy amounts of participation and autonomy for those who are expected to exhibit creativity.

5. Perhaps broadened spans of control to decrease the likelihood of management by direction and control. (This will probably mean flatter or at least nonpyramidally shaped structures.)

6. Measurement of results and the associated evaluation of personnel based on the longest time span compatible with economic survival.

7. A tendency to utilize actual results accomplished within this time span, rather than the adherence to minutely prescribed procedures, as the standard for evaluation and measurement.

8. A tendency to organizationally or at least conceptually separate the idea generation function from the idea evaluation function.

9. A tendency toward the maximum number of open communication channels interconnecting all those knowledgeable units relevant to a particular problem area.

10. A conscious attempt to institutionalize an organizational reward system, basically intrinsic in character, which appeals to the needs of the creative individual. Suggestive mechanisms here might be considerable self-selection of task assignments, given some broadly defined constraints; increased freedom of work scheduling; increased autonomy concerning work methods; enhanced opportunities for professional growth and recognition; and, perhaps, differential extrinsic reward systems for professionals and nonprofessionals involving parallel promotional chains based on different but appropriate criteria.

11. Of primary importance, but somewhat intangible, a managerial philosophy and attitudinal climate which projects the assumption that employees are generally capable, well-trained and able to exert creative efforts in the pursuit of organizational goals.

Source: Larry Cummings, "Organizational Climate for Creativity," *Academy of Management Journal,* vol. 8, no. 3 (September 1965), p. 226.

formal group generally has a defined structure and established goals while the informal group does not.

Two popular forms of formal work groups are command and task groups. Command groups are generally determined by the organization chart. A task group is formed by employees that must collaborate if the work task assigned by the organization is to be completed. Mutual interests, friendships, and the need to fulfil social needs lead to the formation of informal work groups.

Group cohesiveness decreases as the size of the group increases. Highly cohesive groups whose goals are incongruous with those of the formal organization can be disruptive to the organization. On the other hand, highly cohesive groups whose goals support those of the formal organization are generally very productive for the organization.

Conformity refers to the degree to which the members of a group accept and abide by the norms of the group. Thus groups play an important role in establishing conformity. In order to produce conformity, individuals must be selected that have the proper personal characteristics, idiosyncrasy credit must be controlled, and deviations from group norms must be discouraged.

On the other hand, creativity is a process that involves developing something new. The four stages in the creative process are preparation, incubation, illumination, and verification. Brainstorming, the Gordon technique, and a suggested organizational climate for creativity were also described.

REVIEW QUESTIONS

1. Define the following terms:
   a. Group.
   b. Small group.
   c. Primary group.
   d. Work group.

2. Distinguish between formal and informal work groups.

3. Describe some beneficial effects of informal work groups in organizations.

4. Outline some of the reasons why work groups exist in organizations.

5. Describe the stages of work group development.

6. What factors influence group cohesiveness?

7. What did the Coch and French studies indicate?

8. What is conformity? How does the group influence conformity?

9. What is idiosyncrasy credit?

10. What is creativity? Describe the creative process.

11. What is brainstorming? What is the Gordon technique? Distinguish between the two.

12. Outline some of the characteristics of a creative organization.

DISCUSSION QUESTIONS

1. Do you think it is possible to eliminate entirely the need for informal work groups?

2. Many lower level managers believe that they are often the last to know of impending changes. Do you feel that this is true in most organizations?

3. "Creativity is born in an individual and cannot be developed." Do you agree?

4. Discuss the following statement: "Goals of informal work groups will never be congruent with the goals of the formal organization."

SELECTED READINGS

Bucklow, M. "A New Role for the Work Group," *Administrative Science Quarterly*, vol. 7 (1962), pp. 236–57.

Cartwright, Dorwin, and Alvin Zander eds. *Group Dynamics*. 2d ed. Evanston, Ill.: Row, Peterson and Company, 1960.

Cummings, Larry. "Organizational Climate for Creativity," *Academy of Management Journal*, vol 8, no. 3 (September 1965), pp. 220–32.

Davis, James H. *Group Performance*. Reading, Mass.: Addison-Wesley Publishing Company, 1969.

Hare, A. Paul. *Handbook of Small Group Research*. New York: The Free Press of Glencoe, 1962.

Hinton, Bernard L., and H. Joseph Reitz eds. *Groups and Organizations*. Belmont, Calif.: Wadsworth Publishing Company, 1971.

Hollander, E. P. *Leaders, Groups, and Influence*. New York: Oxford University Press, 1964.

Homans, G. C. *The Human Group*. New York: Harcourt, Brace and World, 1950.

Levitt, Theodore. "Creativity Is Not Enough," *Harvard Business Review*, vol. 41, no. 3 (May–June 1963), pp. 72–83.

Olmstead, Michael S. *The Small Group*. New York: Random House, Inc., 1959.

Sayles, Leonard R. "Work Group Behavior and the Larger Organization," *Research in Industrial Human Relations*, Industrial Relations Research Association, No. 17. New York: Harper and Brothers, 1957, pp. 131–45.

Wallis, Graham. *The Act of Thought.* New York: Harcourt, Brace and Company, 1926.

Whiting, Charles S. "Operational Techniques of Creative Thinking," *Advanced Management* (October 1955), pp. 24–30.

Case 12–1

Company man or one of the gang?

Recently Gary Brown was appointed as the supervisor of a group of machine operators in which he was formerly one of the rank and file. When he was selected for the job, the department head told him the former supervisor was being transferred because he could not get sufficient work out of the group. He said also that the reason Gary was selected was because he appeared to be a natural leader, that he was close to the group, and that he knew the tricks they were practicing in order to restrict production. He told Gary that he believed he could lick the problem and that he would stand behind him.

He was right about Gary knowing the tricks. When he was one of the gang, not only did he try to hamper the supervisor, but he was the ringleader in trying to make life miserable for him. None of them had anything personally against the supervisor, but all of them considered it a game to pit their wits against his. There was a set of signals to inform the boys that the supervisor was coming so that everyone would appear to be working hard. As soon as he left the immediate vicinity, everyone would take it easy. Also the operators would act dumb to get the supervisor to go into lengthy explanations and demonstrations while they stood around. They complained constantly and without justification about the materials and the equipment.

At lunchtime the boys would ridicule the company, tell the latest fast one they had pulled on the supervisor, and plan new ways to harass him. All this seemed to be a great joke. Gary and the rest of the boys had a lot of fun at the expense of the supervisor and the company.

Now that Gary has joined the ranks of management, it is not so funny. He is determined to use his managerial position and his knowledge to win the group over to working for the company instead of against it. Gary knows that, if this can be done, he will have a topnotch group. The operators know their stuff, have a very good team spirit, and if they would use their brains and efforts constructively, they could turn out above average production.

Gary's former buddies are rather cool to him now, but this seems to be natural, and he believes he can overcome this in a short time. What has him concerned is that Joe James is taking over his old post as ringleader of the group, and the group is trying to play the same tricks on him as they did on the former supervisor.

1. Did the company make a good selection in Gary?
2. What suggestions would you make to Gary?
3. Are work groups necessarily opposed to working toward organizational goals? Explain.

Case 12–2

Talkative Mike

Mike was an exceptionally friendly and talkative man to the extent that he bothered his supervisor by frequently stopping his whole work crew to tell them a joke or story. It didn't seem to bother Mike that it was during working hours or that somebody other than his crew might be watching. He just enjoyed telling stories and being the center of attention. The trouble was that the rest of the crew enjoyed him too.

The supervisor had just recently taken over the department and he was determined to straighten the crew out. He felt that he would have no problem motivating Mike, since he was such a friendly person. The crew was on a group incentive, and the supervisor felt that he could get them to see how much they were losing by standing around and talking. But there was no question about it, Mike was the informal leader of the crew, and they followed him just as surely as if he was the plant manager.

Mike's crew produced extremely well. When they worked, and that was most of the time, they couldn't be equaled in their output. But the frequent nonscheduled breaks for storytelling did bother the supervisor. Not only could their nonproductive time be converted into badly needed production but also they wouldn't be setting a poor example for the other crews and the rest of the department.

The supervisor called Mike in and discussed the situation with him. But the primary emphasis was on the fact that Mike's crew could be making more money by better using their idle time. Mike's contention was, "What good is money if you can't enjoy it. You sweat your whole life away to rake in money and then all you've got is a lot of miserable years and no way of knowing how to enjoy what's left. Life's too short to spend every minute of it trying to make more money." This discussion ended with Mike stating that the group would quiet down, and if their production didn't keep up to let him know.

Things did improve for a while, but within a week or so the old pattern was right back where it had been so the supervisor arranged to talk with the other members of the crew individually. Their reactions were the same as Mike's, and as before, some improvements were noted at first. Then they gradually reverted back to their old habits.

1. Do you agree with Mike and his group?
2. Does the supervisor really have a complaint in light of the fact that Mike's group produces well above average?
3. If you were the supervisor what would you do next?

Objectives

1. *To develop an appreciation for the importance of communication in organizations.*
2. *To present a model of the communication process.*
3. *To describe upward, downward, and lateral communication systems in organizations.*
4. *To emphasize the importance of listening and feedback.*
5. *To discuss several methods for improving organizational communication.*

GLOSSARY OF TERMS

Communication The transfer of commonly meaningful information.

Fayol's gangplank or bridge An idea developed by Henri Fayol which says that under certain circumstances, shortcuts can be taken in the scalar chain to allow for direct communication between individuals at lower levels in the organization.

Feedback The final step in the communication process which involves determining whether the receiver has received the intended message and produced the intended response.

Grapevine An informal communication network that exists in most organizations.

Information theory An approach to the communication process that uses mathematical relationships to express the technical aspects of information transmission.

Management information system A system that is designed to provide information for managerial decision making.

Perception The manner in which any one individual views a particular situation.

Semantics The science of the meaning and study of words and symbols.

13

Communication in organizations

Good communication aids in coordinating activities. For instance, it is important to know promptly whether operations are proceeding in accordance with plan so that adjustments can be made when necessary. Moreover, there are a wide variety of activities, particularly those of a detailed nature, that it is impractical to plan for in advance, and coordination of these is achieved only as the people directing and performing them have current information regarding related work.

Communication of information on operating conditions and anticipated changes is also vital in preparing programs for the future. So, often when something goes wrong we hear the comments. "Why didn't somebody tell me?" "How was I to know?" Communication systems should provide, as a normal matter of business, for the flow of the bulk of this information needed for coordination.

William H. Newman*

FIGURE 1-1 in Chapter 1 outlines the activities involved in performing the functions of management—planning, organizing, motivating, and controlling. The final activity listed for each of the functions is related to coordination. As the introductory quote states, good communication greatly facilitates coordination in organizations. On the other hand, poor communication is said to cause divorces, wars, racial problems, business failures, and other problems too numerous to mention. Within organizations there are endless places where poor communication can be costly, if not disastrous.

Studies have shown that managers spend the largest portion of

---

* *Administrative Action*, Prentice-Hall, Inc., 1951, p. 396

their working day in communicating—speaking, listening, writing, and reading.[1] It is, therefore, not surprising that poor communication is often named the culprit when any problem arises. Poor communication may very well be the cause of the problem, but it is sometimes only a symptom of a more complex problem. Thus poor communication can be used and is sometimes used as a scapegoat for other problems. Good communication is not a panacea for all organizational problems. Nevertheless, communicating is a very important skill required in the management process, and its significance cannot be understated.

COMMUNICATION—WHAT IS IT?

Communication is a word frequently used by virtually everyone in our society. Unfortunately, there is no universally accepted definition. The Latin word *communis*, meaning "common," is the root word for the word communication. Communication can be defined as "the transfer of commonly meaningful information."[2] Leon Megginson has described the process of communication in organizations as transmitting company policies and orders downward; getting suggestions, opinions, and feelings upward; and securing interest, goodwill, and cooperation from all employees.[3] Communication from top to bottom, bottom to top, and laterally is an important component in effectively managing an organization.

Before a manager initiates a communication, it should have a well-defined purpose. All too often a manager devotes too much attention to the *how* and not enough to the *why* of communications.[4] A second factor that should be considered is the person or persons to whom the communication is directed. How is the recipient likely to interpret the communication? What atmosphere exists between the communicator and the recipient? A third consideration is the quality of the communication. Clarity, sincerity, and simplicity are the keys to good quality.

---

[1] Milton M. Mandell and Pauline Duckworth, "The Supervisor's Job: A Survey," *Personnel*, vol. 31 (1955), pp. 456–62.

[2] Fred Luthans, *Organizational Behavior* (New York: McGraw-Hill Book Company, 1973), p. 236.

[3] Leon C. Megginson, *Personnel: A Behavioral Approach to Administration* (Homewood, Ill.: Richard D. Irwin, Inc., 1967), p. 519.

[4] E. T. Eggers, "The Essence of Understanding," *Atlanta Economic Review*, September 1971, pp. 38–39.

A MODEL OF THE COMMUNICATION PROCESS

Claude Shannon and Warren Weaver have developed a widely accepted model of the communication process.[5] A modified version of their model is shown in Figure 13–1. An explanation of each component in this model is given below to aid in understanding the total communication process.

FIGURE 13–1
Model of communication process

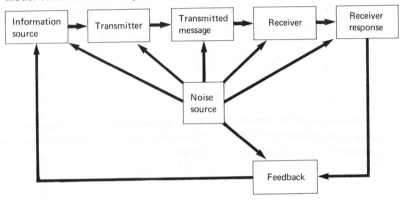

Information source

The information source serves as the beginning of the communication process. The source can be individuals, machines, or organizational systems. The primary requirements necessary to begin the communication process are ideas or information that have some form of intent and purpose for the communication. This creates the message.

Transmitter

The transmitter takes the message, encodes it, and transmits it to the receiver. The encoding can take many forms—facial expressions, verbal expression, written documents, computer signals, and numerous other forms. Encoding merely provides a form in which the message can be transmitted. Thus the transmitter creates a signal called the transmitted message. If correctly encoded, the transmitted message is identical to the original message.

---

[5] Claude E. Shannon and Warren Weaver, *The Mathematical Theory of Communication* (Urbana: The University of Illinois Press, 1949), pp. 5, 98.

Noise source

Noise sources cause interference in the communication process. Shannon and Weaver define noise to be those factors that reduce or distort the quality of the signal. Within organizations, noise can result from a wide range of factors. Some examples of these factors include:

1. Semantic problems—The sender and receiver assign different meanings to the same word.
2. Status differences—Messages transmitted from one level in the hierarchy to another level often are distorted.
3. Time pressures—Lack of time often leads to distortions of messages.

Receiver

In this step of the communication process, decoding takes place. The receiver interprets the received signal in terms of personal experience and frame of reference. Listening, knowledge, and perception are all important facets of the receiving process. Ideally, the received message is identical to the transmitted message.

Receiver response

Since the information source has a purpose for transmitting the message, it should produce a response from the receiver. The response can range from doing nothing to undertaking specific activities within the organization. Ideally, the response from the receiver is identical to what the transmitter intended.

Feedback

The final step in the communication process involves determining whether the receiver has received the intended message and whether the intended response has been produced. Feedback can range from facial expressions to elaborate and costly organizational reporting systems.

INTERPERSONAL COMMUNICATION

Interpersonal communication can be described as a behavioral approach to communication because it emphasizes the importance of communication between individuals. It incorporates the processes of language perception, motivation, and learning into the communication process. The importance of listening and feedback are also emphasized.

Semantics

Semantics is often defined as the science of the meaning and study of words and symbols. The basic idea in semantics is that meanings are in people and their reactions to words and not in the words themselves. Words have numerous definitions. In fact, the 500 most commonly used words in the English language have over 14,000 dictionary definitions. In interpersonal communication, words are the most commonly used form of communication and must be carefully chosen so that the communication is as clear as possible.

Perception

Perception plays an important role in interpersonal communication. People often perceive the same situation in entirely different ways:

> A woman of 35 came in one day to tell me that she wanted a baby but that she had been told that she had a certain type of heart disease which might not interfere with a normal life but would be dangerous if she ever had a baby. From her description I thought at once of mitral stenosis. This condition is characterized by a rather distinctive rumbling murmur near the apex of the heart, and especially by a peculiar vibration felt by the examining finger on the patient's chest. The vibration is known as the "thrill" of mitral stenosis.
>
> When this woman had been undressed and was lying on my table in her white kimono, my stethoscope quickly found the heart sounds I had expected. Dictating to my nurse, I described them carefully. I put my stethoscope aside and felt intently for the typical vibration which may be found in a small but variable area of the left chest.
>
> I closed my eyes for better concentration, and felt long and carefully for the tremor. I did not find it, and with my hand still on the woman's bare breast, lifting it upward and out of the way, I finally turned to the nurse and said: "No thrill."
>
> The patient's black eyes snapped open, and with venom in her voice she said: "Well, isn't that just too bad? Perhaps it's just as well you don't get one. That isn't what I came for."
>
> My nurse almost choked, and my explanation still seems a nightmare of futile words.[6]

Obviously the words used caused the two individuals to have completely different perceptions of the situation.

---

[6] Frederic Loomis, *Consultation Room* (New York: Alfred A. Knopf, 1939), p. 47.

FIGURE 13–2
Perception development in communication

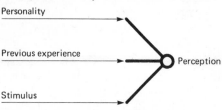

Perception in the communication process is primarily dependent on three factors: individual personality, previous experience, and a stimulus (see Figure 13–2). The combination of these factors creates perception which is unique for each individual.

In perception development, the stimulus refers to the information received whether it be written, oral, or otherwise. The individual receives the information and modifies it based on individual personality and previous experience. In the example given earlier, the word *thrill* was viewed quite differently by the doctor and patient due to the difference in their personalities and previous experiences. Thus the patient's perception of the communication was completely different from the doctor's intended message.

Listening—An important factor

A study conducted several years ago by Dr. Paul Rankin of Ohio State University found that "communication time is devoted 9 percent to writing, 16 percent to reading, 30 percent to speaking, and 45 percent to listening."[7] Yet, how many people have formal education in listening?

Empirical studies have revealed listening efficiency as measured by retention of the transmitted information to be approximately 25 percent.[8] Given that a person can think four times as fast as he can talk, why is listening efficiency so low and how can it be improved? Good listening skills do not come naturally to most people, but they can be developed. Effective listening can be taught. Ralph Nichols has listed three mental manipulations that should be present in any listening training.[9]

1. Anticipate the speaker's next point—If the listener guesses correctly his learning is reinforced. If he guesses wrong he learns by comparison. Either way the listener benefits.

---

[7] Ralph Nichols, "Listening Is Good Business," *Management of Personnel Quarterly,* vol. 1, no. 2 (Winter 1962), p. 2.

[8] Ibid., p. 3.

[9] Ibid., pp. 8–9.

2. Identify supporting elements — Learn to sort out the facts from the emotions.

3. Make mental summaries — Whenever the speaker pauses or breaks, make mental summaries of what has been covered.

The ten commandments for good listening shown in Figure 13–3 enumerate some additional ways for improving listening habits.

STUDY

FIGURE 13–3
Ten commandments for good listening

1. STOP TALKING!
   You cannot listen if you are talking.
   Polonius (in *Hamlet*): Give every man thine ear, but few they voice.

2. PUT THE TALKER AT EASE.
   Help him feel that he is free to talk.
   This is often called a "permissive environment."

3. SHOW HIM THAT YOU WANT TO LISTEN.
   Look and act interested. Do not read your mail while he talks.
   Listen to understand rather than to reply.

4. REMOVE DISTRACTIONS.
   Don't doodle, tap, or shuffle papers.
   Will it be quieter if you shut the door?

5. EMPATHIZE WITH HIM.
   Try to put yourself in his place so that you can see his point of view.

6. BE PATIENT.
   Allow plenty of time. Do not interrupt him.
   Don't start for the door or walk away.

7. HOLD YOUR TEMPER.
   An angry man gets the wrong meaning from words.

8. GO EASY ON ARGUMENT AND CRITICISM.
   This puts him on the defensive. He may "clam up" or get angry.
   Do not argue: Even if you win, you lose.

9. ASK QUESTIONS.
   This encourages him and shows you are listening.
   It helps to develop points further.

10. STOP TALKING!
    This is first and last, because all other commandments depend on it. You just can't do good listening while you are talking.

Source: Keith Davis, *Human Relations at Work* (New York: McGraw-Hill Book Company, 1962), p. 360.

Individual feedback

As explained earlier, effective communication is a two-way process. Information must flow back and forth between the transmitter and the receiver. The flow of information from the receiver to the transmitter is called feedback. It allows the transmitter to know if the receiver has received the correct message and also lets the receiver know if he or she has the correct message.

Harold Leavitt and R. A. H. Mueller conducted an experiment which illustrated the importance of feedback.[10] In their experiment, an individual described a series of rectangles (see Figure 13–4) to a group of individuals. The experiment was conducted under two distinct conditions. First, the transmitter described the rectangles and

FIGURE 13–4
Rectangles in communication experiment

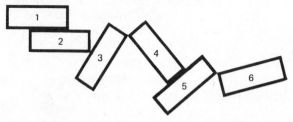

Source: Harold J. Leavitt, *Managerial Psychology* (Chicago: University of Chicago Press, 1972), p. 116.

the listeners could not ask questions or see the transmitter. Thus feedback was nonexistent. In the second trial, the transmitter could see the listeners, and the listeners could ask questions. Thus feedback was present.

The results showed that lack of feedback increased the speed of transmission. However, feedback caused the accuracy and the degree of confidence the listeners had in the accuracy to improve significantly. In summary, the results showed that feedback in the communication process takes more time but significantly improves the quality of the communication.

ORGANIZATIONAL COMMUNICATION

Analyzing the communication process from an organizational perspective views the organizational structure as a network through which the communication process functions.

---

[10] Harold J. Leavitt and R. A. H. Mueller, "Some Effects of Feedback on Communications," *Human Relations*, vol. 4 (1951), pp. 401–10.

Communication patterns

Figure 13–5 shows several different communication patterns which can exist in an organization.[11] Each of the patterns in Figure 13–5 falls into one of two classes depending on the presence or lack of feedback. No pair of individuals can exchange messages in Patterns A, B, and C. In other words, no feedback can occur. Any pair of individuals in Patterns D, E, and F can exchange messages either directly or indirectly. Thus feedback can occur. Patterns A, B, and C do not lend themselves to good coordination or the exchange of ideas.

FIGURE 13–5
Communication patterns

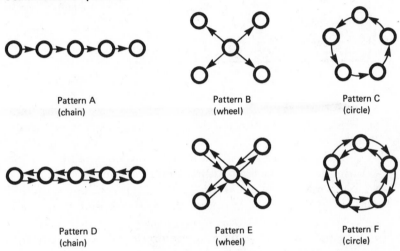

| Pattern A | Pattern B | Pattern C |
| (chain) | (wheel) | (circle) |

| Pattern D | Pattern E | Pattern F |
| (chain) | (wheel) | (circle) |

Patterns which allow feedback or two-way communication (Patterns D, E, and F in Figure 13–5) have advantages and disadvantages as outlined in Figure 13–6.

The following conclusions can be drawn from Figure 13–6.

1. The pattern of the communication network affects the accuracy and speed of messages.

2. The pattern of the communication network affects the task performance of the groups.

3. The pattern of the communication network affects the satisfaction of group members.[12]

---

[11] Alex Bavelas and Dermot Barrett, "An Experimental Approach to Organizational Communication," *Personnel*, vol. 27, no. 5 (March 1951), pp. 366–71.

[12] James L. Gibson, John M. Ivancevich, and James H. Donnelly, Jr., *Organizations: Structure, Processes, Behavior* (Dallas, Tex.: Business Publications, Inc., 1973), p. 174.

FIGURE 13–6
Advantages and disadvantages of communication patterns

Characteristics	Chain	Wheel	Circle
Speed	Fast	Fast	Slow
Accuracy	Good	Good	Poor
Organization	Slowly emerging but stable organization	Almost immediate and stable organization	No stable form of organization
Emergence of leader	Marked	Very pronounced	None
Morale	Poor	Very poor	Very good

Thus no one communication pattern is best for all situations. The most effective communication pattern for a given situation depends on the required speed, accuracy, morale, and organization structure. For instance, the wheel pattern is most desirable in situations requiring a clear-cut leader and rapid decisions.

Numerous research studies have been conducted on the relationships between the pattern of the network and the communication process. Primarily, these studies have indicated that the network configuration is important in determining the effectiveness of the communications process.

Two early approaches to organizational communication

The management pioneer Henri Fayol, who was discussed in Chapters 2 and 6, was one of the first writers to analyze the communication process. Fayol recognized that communication via the formal chain of command could produce unnecessary distortion. In Figure 13–7, suppose that F would like to transmit a message to G. Following the formal chain of command the message would go from F-B-C-G. It is easy to see from the number of steps in the process the potential for distortion. Fayol proposed that a short-cut be taken between F and G. Called Fayol's gangplank or bridge, this concept is illustrated in Figure 13–7. Fayol summarized the need for the gangplank as follows:

> allow the two employees . . . to deal at one sitting, and in a few hours, with some question or other which via the scalar chain would . . . inconvenience many people, involve masses of paper, lose weeks or

FIGURE 13–7
Fayol's gangplank concept

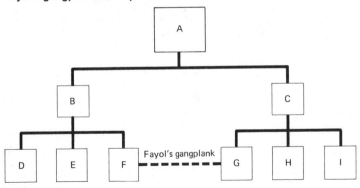

months to get to a conclusion less satisfactory generally than the one which could have been obtained via direct contact.[13]

Chester Barnard also stressed the importance of the communication process in organizations.[14] In fact, he felt that communication was one of the basic elements necessary for the existence of an organization. Barnard felt that the communication process was essential for establishing the authority structure of the organization. His contention was that an individual can and will accept a communication as authoritative only if four conditions are met: The individual (1) understands the communication, (2) believes it to be consistent with the purpose of the organization, (3) believes it to be compatible with his or her personal interest as a whole, and (4) is physically and mentally able to comply with the communication. Barnard's coupling of authority with the communication process led to his development of the acceptance theory of authority which was discussed in Chapter 6.

Downward communication systems

Traditional views of the communication process in organizations are dominated by downward communication systems. In a downward communication system, communication with subordinates takes place in the form of orders and directives with very little, if any, direct feedback from the subordinate to the superior.

Because downward communications systems are essentially one-way processes, they are highly subject to breakdowns due to misin-

---

[13] Henri Fayol, *General and Industrial Management*, Constance Storrs, trans. (London: Sir Isaac Pitman and Sons, 1949), p. 35.

[14] Chester I. Barnard, *The Functions of the Executive* (Cambridge, Mass.: Harvard University Press, 1938).

TABLE 13–1
Agreement between superior-subordinate on subordinate's job

Job factors	Almost no agreement	Agreement on less than half	Agreement on about half	Agreement on more than half	Agreement on all or almost all
Job duties........................	3.4%	11.6%	39.1%	37.8%	8.1%
Job requirements	7.0	29.3	40.9	20.5	2.3
Future changes................	35.4	14.3	18.3	16.3	18.7
Job performance obstacles.....................	38.4	29.8	23.6	6.4	1.7

Source: Norman R. F. Maier, Richard Hoffman, John J. Hoover, and William H. Reed, *Superior-Subordinate Communication in Management* (New York: American Management Association, AMA Research Study 52, 1961), p. 10.

terpretation. Norman R. F. Maier has conducted a study which vividly illustrates the potential inefficiencies of a system which depends heavily on downward communication. Maier independently asked both the superior and subordinate to describe the subordinate's job with regard to the different job factors listed in Table 13–1. The figures clearly indicate a communication problem.

Frequently downward communication systems are assumed to be better than they actually are. When policy manuals, bulletins, company magazines, job descriptions, and so on are printed and distributed throughout organizations, management often assumes that the information has been received. The previous example illustrates that this may be a fallacious assumption.

Upward communication systems

Ideally, the organizational structure should provide a basis for an upward communication system as well as a downward system. In other words, communication should flow in both directions through the formal organizational structure. Unfortunately, communication from the bottom does not flow as freely as communication from the top.

Some of the deterrents to upward communication are:

1. Management fails to respond to communication from the bottom. When subordinates bring information or problems to management, failure to respond will ultimately result in the termination of communication.
2. Managers tend to be defensive about their actions which have been less than perfect. When subordinates recognize that a man-

ager is being defensive about his actions, information will be withheld.

3. The manager's attitude plays a critical element in the upward communication process. If the manager is really concerned and really listens, then communication upward will improve.

4. Physical barriers also can inhibit the upward communication process. Physically separating a manager from immediate subordinates creates communication problems.

5. Time lags from the time of the communication to the time of action can inhibit upward communication. For example, if an employee makes a suggestion and it takes months for the various levels of management to approve the suggestion, upward communication is harmed.

Fred Luthans has outlined some methods that can help in the upward communication system. These are summarized in Figure 13–8.

Horizontal or lateral communication system

Committee meetings can be used to improve horizontal communications within organizations. However, it is important to recognize that committee meetings can become quite dysfunctional in organizations. Everyone has heard the old joke that a camel is a horse that was developed by a committee. Three good guidelines for ensuring the effective performance of committees are:

1. A specific purpose for the meeting—In other words, the meeting should have specific objectives for accomplishment.

2. An agenda prepared in advance—This ensures that the people who are to attend the meeting will know in advance the items to be covered.

3. A specific time schedule—Meetings tend to drag and participants lose interest if time schedules are not established.

Because some temporary committees have a way of becoming permanent, the need for a committee should be periodically reviewed.

Another method for improving lateral communication is to distribute written communications across departmental lines. This also must be done with caution. Too many memos and reports create a paperwork factory which can in itself create new communication problems.

Grapevine

An organization also has informal communication channels called the grapevine. The grapevine is a primary means of communication

FIGURE 13–8
Aids for upward communication system

1. *The grievance procedure.* Provided for in most collective bargaining agreements, the grievance procedure allows an employee to make an appeal upward beyond his immediate supervisor. It protects the individual from arbitrary action from his direct superior and encourages upward communication.

2. *The open-door policy.* Taken literally, this means that the superior's door is always open to subordinates. It is a continuous invitation for a subordinate to come in and talk about anything that is troubling him. Unfortunately, in practice the open-door policy is more fiction than fact. The boss may slap his subordinate on the back and say, "My door is always open to you," but in many cases both the man and his boss know the door is really closed. It is a case where the adage that actions speak louder than words applies.

3. *Counseling, attitude questionnaires, and exit interviews.* The personnel department can greatly facilitate upward communications by conducting nondirective, confidential counseling sessions, periodically administering attitude questionnaires, and holding meaningful exit interviews for those who leave the organization. Much valuable information can be gained from these forms of upward communication.

4. *Participative techniques.* The participative-decision techniques can generate a great deal of upward communication. This may be accomplished by either informal involvement from subordinates or by formal participation programs such as the junior boards, union-management committees, and suggestion boxes.

5. *The ombudsman.* A largely untried but potentially significant technique to enable management to obtain upward communication is the use of an ombudsman. The concept has been used primarily in Scandinavia to provide an outlet for persons who have been treated unfairly or in a depersonalized manner by large, bureaucratic government. It has more recently gained popularity in American state governments, military posts, and universities. Although it is just being introduced in a few business organizations, if set up and handled properly it may work where the open-door policy has failed. As business organizations become larger and more depersonalized, the ombudsman may fill an important void which exists under these conditions.

Source: Fred Luthans, *Organizational Behavior* (New York: McGraw-Hill Book Company, 1973), pp. 253–54.

used by informal work groups which were discussed in Chapter 12. Although the grapevine is not generally sanctioned by the formal organizational structure, it always exists. One fallacious assumption frequently made by management is that the grapevine generally carries only gossip and is not very reliable. The grapevine does carry gossip, but its reliability may be better than is generally thought. Recent research has revealed that between 75 and 95 percent of grapevine information is correct, even if most of the messages are incomplete in detail.[15] Figure 13–9 represents some characteristics of the grapevine.

As the name indicates, the grapevine does not follow the organizational hierarchy. It may go from secretary, to vice president, to stockroom clerk, to plant manager. The grapevine is not limited to nonmanagement personnel; it is just as active among managers.

FIGURE 13–9
Characteristics of the grapevine

1. People talk most when the news is recent.
2. People talk about things that affect their work.
3. People talk about people they know.
4. People working near each other are likely to be on the same grapevine.
5. People who contact each other in the chain of procedure, tend to be on the same grapevine.

Source: Keith Davis, "Communication within Management." Reprinted by permission of the publisher from *Personnel*, November 1954, p. 212, © 1954 by American Management Association, Inc.

During periods of excitement and insecurity, the grapevine will be very active. Reorganizations and reductions in personnel are examples which may cause the grapevine to increase its activity. The grapevine is often much faster than formal communication channels. One complaint frequently expressed by a manager is that "I am the last to know." This can occur when the manager is excluded from the grapevine and depends solely on formal communication channels.

Rumors and distortions can occur in the grapevine. If rumors do surface, they must be dealt with by managers; otherwise future actions will be interpreted in light of the rumor. Rumors must be handled firmly and consistently. However, managers should be careful

---

[15] Keith Davis, "The Care and Cultivation of the Corporate Grapevine," *Dun's* (New York: Dun and Bradstreet Publications, Inc., July 1973).

not to attack everything in the grapevine because their credibility can be damaged, especially if the rumor or even a portion of it is true.

INFORMATION THEORY

A final approach to the communication process is the information theory or mathematical theory of communication. Under this approach, mathematical relationships are used to express the technical aspects of information transmission. Primarily, information theory is useful in such fields as computer technology, cryptology, modeling, systems analysis, language, and statistical mechanics. The important area of interest for management is its use in computer technology and systems analysis.

Computers and systems analysis play a key role in the development of management information systems. A management information system is designed to provide the information necessary for managerial decision making. The role of decision making in the management process was discussed in Chapter 3.

IMPROVING COMMUNICATION WITHIN ORGANIZATIONS

As discussed at the beginning of this chapter, poor communication within organizations occurs frequently. Improving communication within the organization should be an objective of all managers.

FIGURE 13–10
Ten commandments of good communication

1. Seek to clarify your ideas before communicating.
2. Examine the true purpose of each communication.
3. Consider the total physical and human setting.
4. Consult with others, where appropriate, in planning communications.
5. Be aware of the overtones as well as the basic content of the message.
6. Take the opportunity, when it arises, to convey something of help or value to the receiver.
7. Follow up the communication.
8. Communicate for tomorrow as well as today.
9. Be sure that actions support communications.
10. Last, but by no means least: Seek not only to be understood but to understand.

Source: Adapted from "Ten Commandments of Good Communication," American Management Association, New York, 1955. © 1955 American Management Association, Inc.

The American Management Association has presented what it calls the Ten Commandments of Good Communication. These are summarized in Figure 13–10.

SUMMARY

Communication is defined as the transfer of commonly meaningful information. The process involves an information source, a transmitter, noise sources, a receiver response, and feedback. Three different approaches to the communication process were analyzed: interpersonal communications, organizational communications, and information theory.

Interpersonal communication involves the behavioral approach and emphasizes the importance of person-to-person communication. Perception, listening, semantics, and feedback are all included in this approach.

Analyzing communication from an organizational perspective involves viewing the organizational structure as the primary network through which the communication process functions. This approach to communication was analyzed from four different perspectives: downward communication, upward communication, lateral communication, and the grapevine. Management must realize that all these communication systems exist and operate within an organization.

Information theory is a relatively technical approach to communication and involves the use of mathematical relationships. Computer technology and systems analysis have greatly facilitated the development of management information systems which are designed to provide the information necessary for managerial decision making.

This chapter emphasizes the importance of improving one's communication skills. Most managers have the potential to improve their communication skills. By working on the Ten Commandments of Good Communication presented in this chapter a manager should be able to elicit a better response to directions and at the same time improve relationships with subordinates.

REVIEW QUESTIONS

1. What is communication?

2. Describe in detail a model of the communication process and its various components.

3. What is semantics?

4. What is perception and what role does it play in communication?

5. Give some suggestions for improving listening.

6. Describe some of the advantages and disadvantages of the chain, wheel, and circle communication patterns.

7. Identify the contributions of Henri Fayol and Chester Barnard to the communication process.

8. Describe the following organizational communication systems:
    a. Downward communication system.
    b. Upward communication system.
    c. Horizontal or lateral communication system.
    d. Grapevine.

9. What is information theory?

10. Give some methods for improving communication within organizations.

DISCUSSION QUESTIONS

1. Describe some ways in which the grapevine can be used effectively in organizations.

2. Explain why the following question is raised frequently by many managers: "Why didn't you do what I told you to do?"

3   Discuss the following statement: "Meanings are in people not words."

4. "Watch what we do, not what we say." Is this a good practice? Explain.

5   Poor communication of the organization's goals is often given as the reason for low performance of the organization. Do you think that this is usually a valid explanation?

SELECTED READINGS

Athanassiades, J. C. "The Distortion of Upward Communication in Hierarchial Organizations," *Academy of Management Journal* (June 1973), pp. 207–26.

Berlo, David K. *The Process of Communication.* New York: Holt, Rinehart & Winston, Inc., 1960.

Boyd, B. B., and J. M. Jensen. "Perceptions of the First-Line Supervisor's Authority: A Study in Superior-Subordinate Communication," *Academy of Management Journal* (September 1972), pp. 331–42.

Davis, Keith. *Human Relations at Work.* New York: McGraw-Hill Book Company, 1962.

Gemmill, Gary. "Managing Upward Communication," *Personal Journal* (February 1970), pp. 107–10.

Hall, J. "Communication Revisited," *California Management Review* (Spring 1973), pp. 56–67.

Leavitt, Harold J., and R. A. H. Mueller. "Some Effects of Feedback on Communications," *Human Relations,* vol. 4 (1951), pp. 401–10.

Maier, Norman R. F., Richard Hoffman, John J. Hoover, and William H. Reed, *Superior-Subordinate Communication in Management.* New York: AMA Research Study 52.

Nichols, Ralph G. "Listening Is Good Business," *Management of Personnel Quarterly,* vol. 1 (Winter 1962), pp. 2–9.

Shannon, Claude E., and Warren Weaver. *The Mathematical Theory of Communication.* Urbana: University of Illinois Press, 1947.

Wickesberg, A. K. "Communication Networks in the Business Organization Structure," *Academy of Management Journal* (September 1968), pp. 253–62.

Case 13–1

The National Bank of Glenville

The National Bank of Glenville is the oldest and largest bank in that city. The bank has enjoyed a reputation as one of the most progressive banks in the state. Although the bank has been profitable, the president recently requested all officers to look for methods to cut costs.

Just prior to the president's request, Hal Roberts, the operations officer, had implemented a study to look for areas where costs could be cut. A systems analyst working on the project recommended that the customer service department be moved from the first floor to the sixth floor.

Roberts found this to be a sound idea and wasted no time in making the change. Within two weeks it was discovered that the department staff could be reduced by 50 percent since fewer customers "dropped by" to check their balances or to obtain other account information.

A few weeks later Roy Atkins, the director of public relations, stormed into Hal Robert's office in a rage. "What do you think you are doing," he asked. "I spend years trying to create an image of being concerned about the customer and you come around creating problems. I want the customer service department moved back to the first floor, or I'm taking this matter to the president."

1. What is the real problem?
2. Do you think that Roy Atkins has a legitimate complaint?
3. Should Hal Roberts have handled the situation any differently?

Case 13-2

Management training program?

Bill Crane was recently hired by the Accounting Department of the Ace Company and placed in the department's management training program. Bill had no desire to pursue accounting as a career but accepted the offer of employment with the understanding that he would be considered for positions in other departments when appropriate. During his preemployment interviews, Bill had been told that the principal purpose of the assignment in the accounting department was to prepare qualified candidates for assignments in other areas of the company as openings occurred.

At various times during his tenure with the company, there were anywhere from three to six people in the management training program. They all had similar career expectations. Time passed and there was no movement among the trainees except laterally. One enterprising young trainee had cultivated a friendship with a woman who was in a position of responsibility in the personnel department. He asked her if there was any particular reason why there had been no reassignments of trainees into other departments or whether they were simply experiencing a period in which no vacancies were being created. The answer was not what he wanted to hear. He was told that on several occasions other department heads or their representatives had requested to speak with one or more trainees to determine their qualification for a position in their department. In each instance the reply from the head of the accounting department had been that the individual "could not be spared." This had occurred so frequently that representatives from other departments no longer came to the accounting department for needed personnel. Consequently, the management training program had been quietly dissolved and all of the trainee job classifications had been changed from trainee positions to accounting positions.

Shortly thereafter, all of the management trainees resigned.

1. What happened?
2. What went wrong? Why?

section four

Individual performance

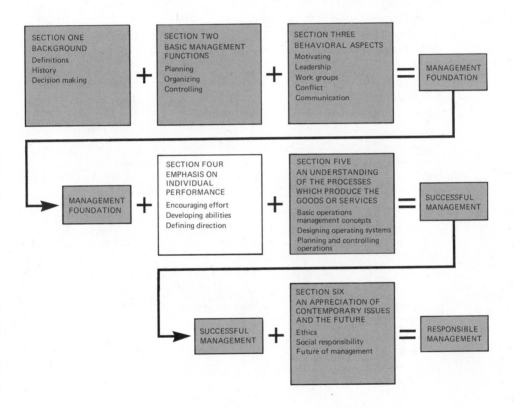

14 Recognizing and measuring individual performance

15 Encouraging effort

16 Developing abilities and traits

17 Defining direction

The first three sections of this text were designed to provide the reader with a sound management foundation by outlining what managers do, discussing the basic functions that managers perform in doing their jobs, and developing an understanding of human behavior in organizations. Building on this management foundation, Section Four is based on the realization that if a manager is to be successful he or she must be able to integrate and apply his or her knowledge *through individuals*. In fact, the success of a manager depends largely on the performance of subordinates. Thus a manager must know how to elicit high levels of performance from subordinates. Section Four shows how to apply the management concepts and principles developed in the earlier sections in such a manner as to attain high individual performance.

Individual performance is discussed and presented as dependent on three major factors — effort, ability, and task direction. A chapter is devoted to each factor.

Chapter 14 is devoted to a discussion of performance in general. What determines performance and how to measure it are two questions that are addressed. Several different methods and techniques are presented for setting performance standards in organizations.

Chapter 15 deals with the effort component of performance. The emphasis of this chapter is on integrating and applying the motivation and leadership theories discussed in Section Three. Worker satisfaction is investigated in depth. The organizational reward system is presented as the key to attaining high individual effort.

Chapter 16 stresses the importance of analyzing and developing individual abilities. The relationship of staffing, which was discussed in Section Two, to analyzing and developing individual abilities is discussed. The role of training in modern organizations is explored. Alternative methods for training individuals are presented.

Chapter 17, Defining Direction, is concerned with the problem of clearly defining what organization members should be doing. Performance appraisal and management by objectives are presented and discussed in detail.

Objectives

1. *To identify the major determinants of individual performance.*
2. *To develop an appreciation for the importance of measuring individual performance.*
3. *To describe the essential requirements of good performance measures.*
4. *To discuss several methods of establishing standards and expected performance levels.*

GLOSSARY OF TERMS

Abilities and traits An individual's personal characteristics which are used in performing a job.

Activity trap A trap that many managers fall into by focusing on the effort component of performance rather than on performance itself.

Conceptual criterion A verbal statement of important or socially relevant outcomes or performance levels based on the general aims of the organization.

Effort The amount of energy (physical and/or mental) used by an individual in performing a job.

Job A grouping of work tasks.

Job analysis The process of determining, through observation and study, the pertinent information relating to the nature of a specific job.

Job evaluation A systematic method of appraising the value of each job in relation to other jobs in the organization.

Management by objectives (MBO) A management system in which the superior and subordinate jointly define the objectives and responsibilities of the subordinate's job and then use them as criteria in evaluating the subordinate's performance.

Performance The degree of accomplishment of the tasks that make up an individual's job.

Performance criteria Standards used to measure success on the job.

Performance evaluation A process used to determine how well an employee is performing.

Position An aggregate of duties, tasks, and responsibilities requiring the services of an individual.

Reliability Refers to the reproducibility of results or the degree to which a measuring instrument is consistent or stable.

Role or task perception Refers to the direction(s) in which individuals believe they should direct their efforts on the job.

Standard A value used as a point of reference for comparing other values.

Task Created whenever human effort must be expended for a specific purpose; a grouping of tasks creates a job.

Time study A method used to determine the time an individual with ordinary qualifications, working with normal effort, should take to do a specified task.

Work sampling A statistical technique for setting standards based on random sampling.

14

Recognizing and measuring individual performance

The Chairman: *Is it not true that a man who is not a good workman and who may not be responsible for the fact that he is not a good workman, has to live as well as the man who is a good workman?*

Mr. Taylor: *Not as well as the other workman; otherwise, that would imply that all those in the world were entitled to live equally well whether they worked or whether they were idle, and that certainly is not the case. Not as well.**

IN THE final analysis, a manager's success is dependent on the performance of those individuals working for the manager. The above introductory statement made by Frederick W. Taylor in 1912 suggests that individuals should be rewarded according to their level of performance. One problem is that many managers do not understand the basic factors that determine an individual's performance. A second major problem is that many managers either do not know how or refuse to measure performance and thus distinguish between high and low performers. This chapter is designed to help the manager become aware of and avoid both of the above problems.

Performance refers to the degree of accomplishment of the tasks that make up an individual's job. It reflects how well an individual is fulfilling the requirements of the job. Often confused with effort, which refers to energy expended, performance is measured in terms

---

* Hearings before Special Committee of the House of Representatives to investigate The Taylor and other systems of Shop Management under authority of House Resolution 90, Washington, D.C.: U.S. Government Printing Office, 1912, pp. 1452–53.

of results. For example, a student may exert great effort in preparing for an examination and still make a poor grade. In such a case, the effort expended was high yet the performance was low.

DETERMINANTS OF PERFORMANCE

Lyman Porter and Edward Lawler have defined job performance as "the net effect of a person's effort as modified by his abilities and

FIGURE 14–1
Determinants of performance

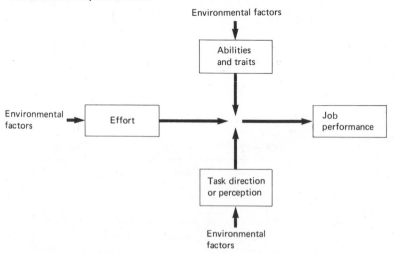

Source: Adapted from Lyman W. Porter and Edward E. Lawler, III, *Managerial Attitudes and Performance* (Homewood, Ill.: Richard D. Irwin, Inc., and The Dorsey Press, 1968), p. 17.

traits and by his role perceptions."[1] This definition implies that performance in a given situation can be viewed as resulting from the interrelationships between effort, abilities and traits, and role (or task) perceptions (see Figure 14–1).

Effort refers to the amount of energy (physical and/or mental) used by an individual in performing a task. Abilities and traits are the individual's personal characteristics which are used in performing the task. Abilities and traits do not fluctuate widely over short periods of time. Role or task perceptions refer to the direction(s) in which individuals believe they should direct their efforts on the job. The ac-

---

[1] Lyman W. Porter, and Edward E. Lawler, III, *Managerial Attitudes and Performance* (Homewood, Ill.: Richard D. Irwin, Inc., and The Dorsey Press, 1968), p. 28.

tivities and behaviors that people believe are necessary in the performance of their jobs define their role perceptions.

In order to obtain an acceptable level of performance, a minimum level of proficiency must exist in each of the performance components. Similarly the level of proficiency in any one of the performance components can place an upper boundary on performance. If an individual puts forth tremendous effort and has great abilities but lacks a good understanding of his or her role, performance will probably not be good in the eyes of his or her superiors. A lot of work will be produced, but it will be misdirected. Likewise, an individual who puts forth an above average effort, understands the job, but lacks ability, will rate low on performance. A final possibility is the individual who has good ability and understands his or her role but is lazy and expends little effort. His or her performance will also be low. Of course, an individual can compensate up to a point for a weakness in one area by being above average in one or both of the other areas.

ENVIRONMENTAL FACTORS AS PERFORMANCE OBSTACLES

Other factors beyond the control of the subordinates can also stifle performance. Although such potential obstacles are sometimes used as mere excuses, they are often very real and should be recognized by management.

Some of the more common potential performance obstacles include a lack of time or conflicting demands on the subordinate's time, inadequate work facilities and equipment, restrictive policies, lack of authority, insufficient information about other activities that affect the job, lack of cooperation from others, type of supervision, timing, and even luck.[2]

A skillful and motivated machine operator cannot be productive without good machinery and proper raw materials. A great salesperson's performance may be hindered by overly restrictive and outdated policies. A research and development project may prove to be fruitless because a competitor perfected the idea first. It is obvious that the individual worker does not have total control over performance in the above situations.

The dynamics of the work group as discussed in Chapter 12 can also inhibit performance. This occurs when the group goals and norms are counterproductive to the organizational goals. In such instances,

---

[2] Charles N. Greene, "The Satisfaction-Performance Controversy," *Business Horizons*, October 1972, p. 36.

FIGURE 14–2
Environmental factors that modify performance

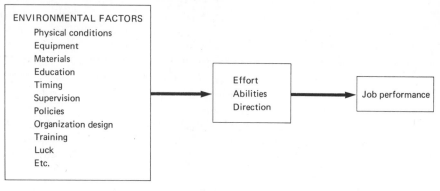

the performance of an individual is influenced by his or her attraction to the group.

Many performance obstacles can be overcome by following good organization principles. In other instances it may be necessary to re-define the job. However, the first step in overcoming performance obstacles is for management to recognize that real performance ob-stacles can exist.

Environmental factors should not be viewed as direct determinants of individual performance but rather as modifying the effects of effort, ability, and direction (See Figure 14–2). For example, a poor physical environment or worn-out equipment might very easily affect the effort exerted by an individual. Unclear policies or poor supervision can easily produce misdirected effort. Similarly, a lack of training could result in under-utilized abilities. One of management's greatest re-sponsibilities is to provide employees with adequate working condi-tions and a supportive environment in order to eliminate or minimize performance obstacles.

THE ACTIVITY TRAP

One major problem in organizations today is that managers tend to focus on the effort component of performance rather than on perform-ance itself. George Odiorne has referred to this as "the activity trap."[3] Odiorne has offered the following explanation of what goes wrong in many organizations:

---

[3] George S. Odiorne, *Management and the Activity Trap* (New York: Harper and Row, Publishers, 1974).

> Most people get caught in the Activity Trap! They become so enmeshed in activity they lose sight of why they are doing it, and the activity becomes a false goal, and end in itself. Successful people never lose sight of their goals, the hoped-for outputs.[4]

The activity described by Odiorne may supplant the effort component of performance. As an activity becomes entrenched, it becomes more meaningful than actual performance. Managers become supervisors of activity rather than performance. Looking busy and generating activity become more important than producing results.

As Odiorne explains, the activity trap is a self-feeding mechanism. Top management can lose sight of its purpose and start to enforce activity controls which become increasingly unrelated to any useful purpose. All the while, this increased activity consumes more and more resources (money, labor, materials, and so on) and produces less and less. Style and conformity become more important than performance. "It does not matter whether or not you get results as long as you do it my way" becomes a prevalent attitude.

Causes of the activity trap

In many organizations, the appraisal process fosters activity orientation. Such is the case when people are rewarded for activity and not performance. The most common system of this type is the one that bases promotions and salary increases on seniority. Another familiar type is the appraisal system that rewards people on the basis of personalities. Any system that does not base rewards on actual performance is inviting activity orientation and the activity trap.

Falling into the activity trap is not the result of stupidity. As Odiorne points out, "the most intelligent, highly educated people tend to be those most likely to become entrapped in interesting and complex activities."[5] Professional people often become attached to a family of techniques which they attempt to apply in all situations, whether applicable or not. The end result is often the generation of meaningless activity and low performance.

Costs of the activity trap

The physical costs (wasted materials, labor, and so on) of activity orientation are rather obvious. Less obvious and perhaps more costly is the effect the activity trap has on people. It causes people to shrink rather than to grow. Employees, rather than seeking responsibility,

---

[4] Ibid., p. 6.

[5] Ibid., p. 7.

become dependent on rules, regulations, and methods. The end result is that as subordinates become more and more dependent they also become more and more narrow in their mode of operations. Hence, they lose all imagination and enthusiasm for their jobs.

The key to avoiding the activity trap is to emphasize and reward performance, and this requires the ability to accurately measure performance.

MEASURES OF PERFORMANCE — CRITERIA

Aside from avoiding the activity trap there are many other reasons for measuring individual performance:

1. As a basis for setting objectives and planning work schedules.
2. As a basis for rewarding workers.
3. As a basis for promotions, separations, and transfers.
4. As a means for evaluating different work methods, different tools and equipment, and different conditions of work.
5. As a basis for estimating and allocating costs.
6. As a means of determining when and if a problem arises.

As evidenced by the foregoing list, measures of job performance are needed in most, if not all, phases of management.

The idea of evaluating individual performance is not new. The problem is that relatively few organizations utilize procedures for measuring individual performance which are scientifically developed. Many organizations still use activity-centered methods for measuring performance.

One of the most difficult jobs a manager faces is locating or creating satisfactory measures of job success, called criteria. The difficulties of obtaining satisfactory criteria arise from a variety of problems. There are many jobs that do not readily lend themselves to objective measurement. But even in cases that do, job performance is often influenced by many factors outside the individual's control. For example, a salesperson's performance is not only a function of his or her own effectiveness but also of the particular sales territory. Similarly, a punch press operator's performance may be affected by the physical condition of the punch press or the lighting conditions.

Robert Thorndike and Elizabeth Hagen have listed four qualities that should be sought when selecting criteria.[6] Listed in order of importance they are (1) relevance, (2) freedom from bias, (3) reliability, and (4) availability. Relevance is the primary and absolutely funda-

---

[6] Robert L. Thorndike and Elizabeth Hagen, *Measurement and Evaluation in Psychology and Education* (New York: John Wiley & Sons, Inc., 1955), p. 118.

FIGURE 14–3
Criterion relevance

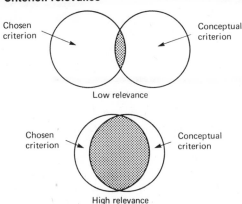

Chosen criterion
Conceptual criterion

Low relevance

Chosen criterion
Conceptual criterion

High relevance

mental requirement of a criterion measure. A criterion is relevant if the knowledge, skills, and basic aptitudes required for success on it are the same as those required for performance of the ultimate task.[7] In other words, to what degree does the criterion represent the characteristics of the job it purports to measure? Unfortunately, relevance can rarely be empirically proven. Therefore, the relevance of a particular criterion usually must be estimated on rational grounds using professional judgment.

Ordinarily, some "ultimate" or "conceptual" criterion exists. A conceptual criterion is a verbal statement of important or socially relevant outcomes based on the general aims of the organization.[8] Because the conceptual criterion is rarely directly measurable, substitutes must frequently be used. For example, a conceptual criterion might be to appraise the success of a production foreman. A substitute that might be used for the conceptual criterion is the output of the foreman's department. Therefore, most criteria represent only a part of the conceptual criterion.[9] The major problem in criteria selection is choosing the criteria which are most representative of the conceptual criterion.

Figure 14–3 depicts a chosen criterion which is not very relevant to the conceptual criterion and a chosen criterion which is highly relevant. The more overlap there is between the chosen criterion and the conceptual criterion, the more relevant is the chosen criterion.

---

[7] Robert L. Thorndike, *Personnel Selection* (New York: John Wiley & Sons, Inc., 1949), p. 125.

[8] Alexander W. Astin, "Criterion-Centered Research," *Educational and Psychological Measurement*, 1964, p. 809

[9] Thorndike and Hagen *Measurement and Evaluation*, p. 125.

The second desirable quality of a criterion measure, freedom from bias, requires that each person be provided an equal opportunity to make a good score. For instance, if widgets per hour is the criterion used in evaluating the performance of a certain set of workers, each worker should have equal equipment. If some workers have faster machines than others, then the criterion measure is biased.

Reliability refers to the reproducibility of results. Reliability answers the question of how consistently the criterion measures whatever it does measure. A criterion measure is reliable to the extent that the same person working under the same conditions produces approximately the same results. If a machine operator's output is highly dependent on a fluctuating supply of raw materials, then output would probably not be a reliable measure of the worker's performance.

Finally, the criterion measure must be reasonably convenient and available. Practicality in terms of time and cost must be considered and may dictate the choice of the criterion.

SUBJECTIVE CRITERIA

As was pointed out in the previous section, objective performance measures should be used wherever and whenever possible. However, objective measures are not feasible or even possible in many situations. One method of handling such situations is to measure performance on the basis of larger and larger groups until objective measures can be established.[10] For example, it is difficult to measure objectively the contribution of any one member of a rowing team, but it is not difficult to measure objectively the performance of the entire team. A second approach is to use subjective measures on an indi-

FIGURE 14–4
Relationship of trust and objectivity of performance measure to success of the program

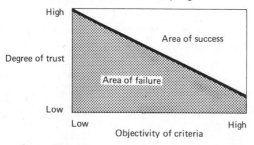

Source: Edward E. Lawler, III, *Pay and Organizational Effectiveness: A Psychological Review* (New York: McGraw-Hill Book Co., 1971), p. 172.

---

[10] Edward E. Lawler, III, *Pay and Organizational Effectiveness: A Psychological Review* (New York: McGraw-Hill Book Co., 1971), p. 171. This section draws heavily on Lawler's work.

vidual or small group level. The key factor in determining the feasibility of using subjective measures is the degree of trust between the superior and the subordinate. As Edward Lawler has stated, "The more subjective the measure, the higher the degree of trust needed. . . ."[11] Using subjective performance measures increases the likelihood that the subordinate will not believe that rewards are based on performance unless a high degree of trust exists. Figure 14–4 illustrates the relationship between trust and subjectivity of the performance measure. It should be noted in Figure 14–4 that some amount of trust is required for even the most objective system.

SETTING STANDARDS

As defined and used in Chapter 8, a standard is a value used as a point of reference for comparing other values. In practice standards are established criteria which are used to measure performance. Generally speaking, output standards should reflect the "normal output of a normal person." Such standards attempt to answer the question "What is a fair day's work?" or "How good is good enough?" Output standards for production workers and for lower levels in the organizational hierarchy are usually expressed as pieces per time or as time per unit. Although designed to reflect normal output, standards include more than just work. Output standards include allowances for rest, delays that occur as part of the job, time for personal needs, and, where necessary, an allowance for physical fatigue.[12] Standards for managers and staff employees are generally broader and much harder to define.

Setting any type of standard also involves subjective elements of judgment. Determining what is normal and reasonable requires judgment. However, the degree of subjective judgment required varies with the particular method used in setting the standard. Generally standards for managers require more subjective judgment.

Certain inherent human problems are also associated with setting output standards. A manager may avoid setting a standard or set it too low for fear of offending subordinates or due to a lack of experience. On the other hand, a manager may set standards unrealistically high. In both cases, the standard acts as a deterrent to productivity.

PERFORMANCE STANDARDS

Standards provide data that are used in making many management decisions. In addition to decisions concerning performance evalua-

---

[11] Ibid.

[12] Elwood S. Buffa, *Modern Production Management*, 4th ed. (New York: John Wiley & Sons, Inc., 1973), pp. 417–18.

tions and remuneration, standards provide data for making decisions regarding equipment acquisition, process selection, and scheduling. Performance standards also provide a basis for determining labor costs as well as for incentive wage payment systems.

Average group production as a standard

The use of average group production as a standard works best when the tasks performed by all individuals are the same or approximately the same but where certain factors cause a difference in output for certain groups.[13] For example, the output of machine operators using newer and faster machines would not be directly comparable to the output of similar operators using older and slower machines. However, adjustments in individual output can be made by expressing each individual's output as a ratio of the average output of all the individuals in that respective group. In this case one group would be the operators of the newer, faster machines, and the other group would be the operators of the older, slower machines.

Standards based on the performance of specially selected individuals

Certain individuals whose work is expected to be "free from bias" can be selected to form the basis of a standard. A specially selected individual may not be representative of ordinary workers on the job. In such instances, a "leveling" or correction factor may be applied so that the resulting standard better describes a "normal" worker. While there are several methods that attempt to level the differences in skill and effort between the specially selected individuals and the other workers, none of the methods has proven totally successful.

Time study

Time study was popularized in the early 1900s and became the traditional method used by industrial engineers for setting standards. Edwin Ghiselli and Clarence Brown have stated that "In general, the purpose of time study can be said to be the determination of the time an individual with ordinary qualifications, working with normal effort, should take to do a specified task."[14] Once the standard time for performing a task or group of tasks has been determined, it is a simple

---

[13] Drawn from Edwin E. Ghiselli and Clarence W. Brown, *Personnel and Industrial Psychology,* 2d ed. (New York: McGraw-Hill Book Co., 1955), pp. 69–77.

[14] Ibid., p. 74.

matter to evaluate any individual by comparing his or her time to the standard.

Although the exact method may vary with the practitioner, time study involves the following six steps:

1. The fractionation of the task into its elemental parts, each of which is timed.
2. The determination of those elements which are essential for completion of the task.
3. The determination of an operation time for each element by selection or correction of the original data.
4. The determination of the operation time of the total task by adding together the operation times of all the elements.
5. The determination of extra time allowances.
6. The determination of the standard time for the task by adding together operation time and extra time allowances.[15]

Time study is not as objective as many people like to believe. Subjective judgments are required at many points in the process. The choice of operation times of the elements, inferences concerning worker effort, and the selection of extra time allowances are all inputs that require a certain amount of subjective judgment.

Experimentally determined times

This method of establishing standards is based on the assumption that a complex task can be broken down into a group of elemental movements, each of which has a predetermined standard time. In other words, standard times are independently determined for certain basic motions and movements. A task is then analyzed to determine all of its basic motions. The predetermined standard times for the basic motions of the task are then summed. The method of using experimentally determined times is subject to the same shortcomings as the time study method. Convenience is its only advantage over the time study method.

The use of experts

A group of recognized experts or interested parties may be used to set standards. The idea is to have a group of experts exchange ideas and eventually arrive at a consensus. The acceptance or rejection of such standards by the work force depends on its perceptions of the group of experts.

---

[15] Ibid., p. 76.

Work sampling

Work sampling is a statistical technique for setting standards based on random sampling. A number of random observations are made of an individual performing a task. The state of the individual is recorded for each observation, indicating whether the individual was idle or working. By making an adequate number of observations, inferences can be drawn from the sample to determine the percentages of working time and idle time required in the job. Standards can then be established from the resulting data.

Work sampling is most applicable for measuring noncyclical types of work where many different tasks are performed and where there is no set pattern or cycle. For example, most office and staff work lends itself to work-sampling methods.

Management by objectives (MBO)

MBO is a system of management that can be used for measuring performance of managers. MBO requires that the subordinate and superior *jointly* set the objectives (standards) by which the subordinate will be evaluated. After the objectives have been set, the superior and subordinate periodically review the subordinate's performance relative to the agreed-upon objectives. MBO is discussed in depth in Chapter 17.

JOB EVALUATION

Job evaluation is a systematic method of appraising the value of each job in relation to other jobs in the organization.[16] It determines the relative worth of jobs. Job evaluation is concerned with jobs, not performance, personalities, or individuals. A job evaluation should never be intended to appraise the performance of the individual performing the job.

A job is a grouping of work tasks. A task is created whenever human effort must be expended.[17] A position is an aggregate of duties, tasks, and responsibilities requiring the services of an individual.[18] Thus an organization employing 500 people must have 500 positions. However, the same organization may have only 50 jobs, and each job could be composed of several tasks.

---

[16] David W. Belcher, *Wage and Salary Administration*, 2d ed. (Englewood Cliffs, N.J.: Prentice-Hall, Inc., 1962), p. 177.

[17] Charles W. Brennan, *Wage Administration*, rev. ed. (Homewood, Ill.: Richard D. Irwin, Inc., 1963), p. 63.

[18] Ibid.

The process of job evaluation has several essential elements.[19] The first element involves a study of the jobs in the organization. This is accomplished through a job analysis. Job analysis is defined as the process of determining, through observation and study, the pertinent information relating to the nature of a specific job. The end product of a job analysis is a job description which identifies and describes the job and specifies the requirements of the job.

FIGURE 14–5
Potential job evaluation benefits

1. To provide a more workable internal wage structure in order to simplify and make rational the relatively chaotic wage structure resulting from chance, custom, and such individual factors as favoritism or aggressive tendencies.

2. To provide an agreed-upon device for setting rates for new or changed jobs.

3. To provide a means whereby realistic comparisons may be made of the wage and salary rates of employing organizations.

4. To provide a base for measuring individual performance.

5. To reduce grievances over wage and salary rates by reducing the scope of grievances and providing an agreed-upon means of solving disputes.

6. To provide incentive values to employees to strive for higher level jobs.

7. To provide facts for wage negotiations.

8. To provide facts on job relationships for use in selection, training, transfers, and promotion.

Source: David W. Belcher, *Wage and Salary Administration*, 2d ed. © 1962, p. 180. Reprinted by permission of Prentice-Hall, Inc., Englewood Cliffs, N.J.

The second step in the job evaluation process is to determine the factor or factors to be used in determining the worth of the job to the organization. In other words, what factors are used in determining the pay scale of the job? Some factors frequently used are skill, responsibility, and working conditions. The factors are then used to describe the minimum qualifications necessary for the successful performance of a job.

The third step in the job evaluation process involves developing and implementing a system that uses the chosen factors for evaluating

[19] For an in-depth discussion see Belcher, *Wage and Salary Administration*, pp. 178–79.

the relative worth of the jobs to the organization. Such a system should consistently place jobs requiring more of the factors at a higher level in the job hierarchy than jobs requiring less of the factors. Several existing methods for comparing jobs are available.[20]

The final step in the job evaluation process is the "pricing" of the jobs. Wages and salaries are assigned to jobs according to their position in the job hierarchy. Wage data from other organizations in the same labor market plays an important role in arriving at the final price tag for each job.

While the overriding purpose of job evaluation is to establish the relative worth of jobs, a number of other goals may be attained. Figure 14–5 presents a list of potential job evaluation benefits.

Ideally, job evaluation should result in a wage range for each job. Performance evaluation is then used to position an individual within the established range. High performers should be placed at the upper end of the range while lower performers should be placed in the middle and lower end of the range. Thus, an individual's compensation should be determined by both the value of the job to the organization and the individual's performance of that job.

SUMMARY

In the final analysis, a manager's success is dependent on the performance of those individuals working for that manager.

Job performance refers to the accomplishment of tasks that compose the individual's job and results from a person's effort, abilities and traits, and role (task) perceptions. Effort is the amount of energy, either physical or mental, used by an individual in performing a task. Abilities and traits represent the individual's personal characteristics used in performing the task. Role perceptions refer to the direction of effort. In order to obtain an acceptable level of performance, a minimum level of proficiency must exist in each of the above-described components of performance.

One major problem in organizations is that managers tend to focus on the effort component of performance rather than in performance itself. George Odiorne has referred to this as the activity trap. Organizations that become activity-oriented rather than performance-oriented waste resources and people.

Measures of job performance are used throughout an organization. Criteria are the standards used to measure success on the job. A cri-

---

[20] For an in-depth discussion of such methods see Brennan, *Wage Administration*, pp. 108–80.

terion measure should have four major qualities: (1) relevance, (2) freedom from bias, (3) reliability, and (4) availability.

Job performance can be evaluated using objective measures, such as actual output, or by subjective measures, such as ratings made by others or ratings made by the individual.

Standards are established criterion against which actual results can be measured. A standard should reflect the normal output of a normal person. Setting standards necessarily involves some subjective judgment; however, the amount varies with the method used.

Job evaluation is a systematic method of appraising the value of each job in the organization in relation to other jobs in the organization. A job evaluation program should result in a fair day's pay for a fair day's work.

REVIEW QUESTIONS

1. What is performance? Describe a model that outlines the determinants of performance.

2. How can environmental factors affect performance?

3. What is the activity trap?

4. What are some reasons for measuring performance in organizations?

5. Discuss in detail the four qualities that should be sought when selecting performance criteria?

6. What is a performance standard?

7. Describe the following methods for setting performance standards:
    a. Average production.
    b. Performance of specially selected individuals.
    c. Time study.
    d. Experimentally determined times.
    e. Use of experts.
    f. Work sampling.

8. What is management by objectives (MBO)?

9. What is job evaluation? Describe the essential elements of job evaluation.

DISCUSSION QUESTIONS

1. Do you think that most organizations attempt to measure individual performance?

2. Why do you think that many managers shy away from distinguishing high performers from low performers?

3. Is it possible to accurately measure job performance in all instances? Elaborate and give examples where appropriate.

4. Why do you think that the term "standard" has bad connotations among many workers?

SELECTED READINGS

Belcher, David. *Wage and Salary Administration.* 2d. ed. Englewood Cliffs, N.J.: Prentice-Hall, Inc., 1962.

Cummings, L. L., and Donald P. Schwab. *Performance in Organizations: Determinants and Appraisal.* Glenview, Ill.: Scott, Foresman and Company, 1973.

Ferguson, George A. "Human Abilities," *Annual Review of Psychology,* vol. 16 (1965), pp. 39–62.

Fleishman, Edwin A. "Human Abilities," *Annual Review of Psychology,* vol. 20 (1969), pp. 349–80.

Lawler, Edward E., III. *Pay and Organizational Effectiveness: A Psychological Review.* New York: McGraw-Hill Book Company, 1972.

Odiorne, George S. *Management and the Activity Trap.* New York: Harper and Row, Publishers, 1974.

Case 14–1

The Christmas season

Sally Perry works as a methods analyst for a large mail order company. In the past the company has experienced extreme difficulty in getting all of the Christmas card orders out on time. Sally, who is an industrial engineering graduate, was assigned the job of developing a system to ensure that all orders are processed in time for the Christmas season.

The first department that Sally worked with in developing this system was the printing department. Sally discussed the problem with the printers, and they agreed in principle to establishing production standards. A bonus was to be paid on a monthly basis for all performance above the standard. A time study was conducted to establish the standard. The standard was tested for four days and seemed to work well. Output increased during the test period, fewer errors were made, and the unit cost was reduced. Sally was pleased with her work.

However, at the end of the first month of operation of the system, the printers made more bonus money than they did salary. Sally's boss ordered her to "Go back and straighten out that bonus."

1. What would you do if you were Sally?
2. What are some of the things that could have gone wrong?
3. Can Sally raise the standards without adversely affecting production?

Case 14–2

Promotions at the university

Dan Andrews, an assistant professor of management at the state university, has just received a call from the Dean. Dan had written a letter to the Dean asking whether promotions were based on seniority or performance.

The letter had been written because Dan had just been notified that he had not been promoted to associate professor because he did not have five years in grade as an assistant professor. Dan was extremely upset because he had over 20 articles published, had a book in process that was to be published by a leading textbook publisher, and was always rated high on student evaluations.

The Dean had told Dan in the telephone conversation that he understood how Dan felt and promised that Dan would be promoted next year when he had the time in grade. In fact, the Dean had told Dan that measuring the performance of college professors is extremely difficult and should not be the sole basis for promotion. He asked that Dan meet with him in the near future to discuss the problems of measuring the performance of a faculty member.

1. Do you agree with the Dean's analysis of the situation?
2. What suggestions, if any, would you make to the Dean?
3. Can you think of any situation where you would suggest "a promotion based on seniority" system?

Objectives

1. *To explore the relationship between employee satisfaction and employee performance.*
2. *To develop an understanding of the importance of organizational reward systems.*
3. *To present a model which relates effort, performance, rewards, and other key variables.*
4. *To discuss how the organization can get maximum benefit from its compensation package.*

GLOSSARY OF TERMS

Achievement motivation Pioneered by David McClelland, and refers to the need of an individual to advance and achieve success.

Attitude An individual's mental set or readiness to act which serves as a frame of reference for opinions and potential actions.

Effort The amount of energy (physical and/or mental) used by an individual in performing a task.

Job enlargement Involves making a job structurally larger by giving a worker more similar operations or tasks to perform.

Job enrichment Upgrading a job with factors such as more meaningful work, more recognition, more responsibility and more opportunities for advancement.

Job rotation The practice of periodically changing or rotating job assignments.

Job satisfaction An individual's general attitude about the job.

Level of aspiration The level of performance that an individual expects or hopes to attain.

Morale Refers to the feeling of an individual of being accepted by and belonging to a group of employees through common goals, confidence in the desirability of these goals, and progress toward these goals.

15

Encouraging effort

*All you have to do is look around you to see that modern
organizations are only getting people to use about 20 percent
—the lower fifth—of their capacities. And the painful part is that
God didn't design the human animal to function at 20 percent. At
that pace it develops enough malfunctions to cause a permanent
shortage of psychoanalysts and hospital beds.*

Robert Townsend*

As Robert Townsend suggests in the above quote, most organizations
are getting far less than maximum effort from their employees. This
phenomenon is not the result of chance and can be explained in most
instances. This chapter is designed to provide an understanding of
what can and cannot be done to encourage effort from individuals
within the organization.

Effort was defined in Chapter 14 and refers to the amount of energy,
either physical or mental, expended by an individual in performing
a task. Effort is the product of motivation. A motivated employee puts
forth effort; it may be misdirected or inefficient but it will exist. Chapters 9 and 10 presented a detailed discussion on current motivation
and leadership theories. The purpose of this chapter is to integrate
the more theoretical concepts of those chapters with the practical
aspects of organization life.

JOB SATISFACTION

Job satisfaction refers to an individual's general attitude about the
job. Philip Applewhite has listed the five major components of job
satisfaction as "(1) attitude toward work group, (2) general working

---

* *Up the Organization*, New York: Alfred A. Knopf, Inc., 1970, p. 140.

323

conditions, (3) attitude toward company, (4) monetary benefits, and (5) attitudes toward supervision."[1] Other major components that should be added to these five are the individual's attitudes toward the work itself and toward life in general. The individual's health, age, level of aspiration, social status, and political and social activities can all contribute to job satisfaction. Therefore, job satisfaction is an attitude that results from other specific attitudes and factors.

Psychologically, an attitude is an individual's mental set or readiness to act which serves as a frame of reference for opinions and potential actions. Attitudes are acquired or learned and may be rational or irrational. An individual may not recognize that he or she possesses a certain attitude. Usually attitudes are developed over relatively long time periods.

Job satisfaction refers to an individual's mental set about his or her job. This mental set may be positive or negative depending on the individual's mental set concerning the major components of job satisfaction. Job satisfaction is not synonymous with organizational morale. Organizational morale refers to the feeling of an individual of being accepted by and belonging to a group of employees through common goals, confidence in the desirability of these goals, and progress toward these goals. Morale is related to group attitudes while job satisfaction is more of an individual attitude. However, the two concepts are interrelated in that job satisfaction can contribute to morale and morale can contribute to job satisfaction.[2]

THE SATISFACTION-PERFORMANCE CONTROVERSY[3]

> As Ben walked by smiling on the way to his office, Ben's boss remarked to a friend: "Ben really enjoys his job and that's why he's the best damn worker I ever had. And that's reason enough for me to keep Ben happy." The friend replied: "No, you're wrong! Ben likes his job because he does it so well. If you want to make Ben happy, you ought to do whatever you can to help him further improve his performance."[4]

Since the Hawthorne Studies were concluded in the 1930s, managers have believed, for the most part, that a satisfied worker is necessarily a good worker. In other words, if management could keep all the workers happy, then good performance would automatically

---

[1] Philip B. Applewhite, *Organizational Behavior* (Englewood Cliffs, N.J.: Prentice-Hall, Inc., 1965), p. 22.

[2] Milton L. Blum, *Industrial Psychology and Its Social Foundations* (New York: Harper and Brothers, 1956), p. 126.

[3] Much of the section is based on Charles N. Greene, "The Satisfaction-Performance Controversy," *Business Horizons*, October 1972, pp. 31–41; and Donald P. Schwab and Larry L. Cummings, "Theories of Performance and Satisfaction: A Review," *Industrial Relations*, October 1970, pp. 408–29.

[4] Greene, "The Satisfaction-Performance Controversy," p. 31.

follow. While such beliefs were never explicitly stated by the Haw-thorne researchers, they nevertheless resulted from the studies.[5] Charles Greene has suggested that many managers subscribe to this belief because it represents the path of least resistance.[6] Greene's thesis is that increasing the employees' happiness is far more pleasant than confronting them with their performance if a performance prob-lem exists. The work of Herzberg and his colleagues, discussed in Chapter 9, provides a good illustration of motivation theory based on the view that satisfaction leads to performance. Before exploring this question further it might be wise to point out that there are subtle but real differences between being satisfied and being happy. Al-though happiness eventually results from satisfaction, satisfaction goes much deeper and is far less tenuous than happiness.

The incident at the beginning of this section presented two propo-sitions concerning the satisfaction-performance relationship. The first is the traditional view that satisfaction causes performance. The second proposition is that satisfaction is the effect rather than the cause of performance. In the second proposition performance leads to rewards which result in a certain level of satisfaction. Thus rewards constitute a necessary intervening variable in the relationship. A closely related position considers both satisfaction and performance to be functions of rewards. This position not only views satisfaction as being caused by rewards but also postulates that current perform-ance affects subsequent performance if rewards are based on current performance.

Recent research evidence generally rejects the more popular view that satisfaction causes performance. The evidence does, however, provide moderate support for the view that performance causes satisfaction. The evidence also provides strong indications that (1) rewards constitute a more direct cause of satisfaction than does performance and (2) rewards based on current performance cause subsequent performance.[7]

As Greene has pointed out, "the finding that rewards based on cur-rent performance affect subsequent performance does, however, offer a strategy for increasing subordinates' performance."[8] The strategy is to grant rewards based directly on current performance. Unfortunately such a system is not the path of least resistance for

---

[5] In fact, F. J. Roethlisberger, a primary member of the research team, noted that ". . . the factors which make for efficiency in a business organization are not necessarily the same as those factors that make for happiness, collaboration, teamwork, morale, or any other word which may be used to refer to cooperative situations." In F. J. Roethlis-berger, *Management and Morale* (Cambridge, Mass.: Harvard University Press, 1941).

[6] Greene, "The Satisfaction-Performance Controversy," p. 32.

[7] Ibid., p. 40.

[8] Ibid., p. 34.

the manager. Subordinates will express varying degrees of satisfaction with the manager's assessments of performance. Low performers will criticize the system as being unfair. It is also true that many managers do not like to be placed in an evaluating role. However, the potential benefits (mainly increased performance) of such a system greatly overshadow the liabilities.

REWARDS AND EFFORT

The precise relationship between rewards and performance is complex. Effort is the key element which links rewards to perform-

FIGURE 15–1
Reward-effort-performance relationship

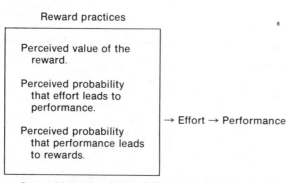

Source: Adapted from Charles N. Greene, "The Satisfaction-Performance Controversy," *Business Horizons* (October 1972), p. 37.

ance. Figure 15–1 demonstrates the complexity of the reward-effort-performance relationship. As suggested by the preference-expectancy theory discussed in Chapter 9, three major factors influence the effort put forth by an individual: (1) the perceived value of the reward; (2) the perceived probability that increased effort will result in increased performance; and (3) the perceived probability that increased performance will lead to increased rewards.

Value of the reward

The rewards associated with any job are either intrinsic or extrinsic (see Figure 15–2). Intrinsic rewards are internal to the individual and are normally derived from involvement in an activity. Job satisfaction and feelings of accomplishment are examples of intrinsic rewards. Most extrinsic rewards are controlled by the organization and are more tangible than intrinsic rewards. Fringe benefits and pay are examples of extrinsic rewards. In general extrinsic rewards appeal more to the lower levels of Maslow's need hierarchy while intrinsic rewards appeal more to the upper levels of Maslow's need hierarchy (Maslow's need hierarchy was discussed at length in Chapter 9).

Although an individual may strongly believe that hard work in the form of increased effort will lead to increased rewards, the individual must value the rewards before working harder. Therefore, the organization should determine the rewards that are most desired by the employees. Frequently, rewards which the organization considers to be valuable are evaluated differently by many of the employees. In the final analysis, the employee's views of the rewards are of primary

FIGURE 15–2
Extrinsic and intrinsic rewards

Extrinsic Rewards	Intrinsic Rewards
Formal recognition	Achievement
Fringe benefits	Feeling of accomplishment
Incentive payments	Informal recognition
Pay	Job satisfaction
Promotion	Personal growth
Social relationships	Status
Work environment	

importance. The magnitude of the reward also contributes to the value placed on the reward by the recipient. A $10 a week raise may motivate one individual but have little or no effect on another at the same salary level. The value of a reward increases as its ability to satisfy needs increases. Because individuals have different and changing needs and desires, an organization must periodically evaluate the nature and strength of these needs. If an organization is going to distribute rewards (and all do), why not get the maximum benefit? This can only be achieved if the organization knows the needs and desires of the recipients. Recently Edward Lawler has suggested a "cafeteria style" reward plan where employees are allowed to select their own individual combination of cash and fringe benefits.[9] Under this plan each employee is given "X" amount of total compensation which can be collected from a number of fringe benefits and cash. Not only does such a plan better suit the individual employee, but it also reduces the

[9] Edward E. Lawler, III, *Pay and Organizational Effectiveness: A Psychological Review* (New York: McGraw-Hill Book Co., 1971), pp. 198–99.

waste in funds allocated by the organization to fringe benefits not valued by its members.

The effort-performance contingency

The extent to which workers believe that harder work will improve their performance is largely a function of their confidence in their own abilities and their previous personal experiences in similar situations. As explained in Chapter 14, the transformation of an individual's effort into performance is affected by his or her abilities and the direction of efforts. Through experience, every individual becomes aware of the less than perfect spare relationship between effort and performance. This relationship then becomes a factor in determining effort. Generally, the higher a person's self-esteem and the more effectively he or she has been able to perform in similar situations, the more confident he or she will be that increased effort will result in increased performance.[10] Obviously this type of confidence is desirable.

The performance-reward contingency

Ideally performance is accompanied by commensurate rewards. However, the relationship between performance and rewards is often nebulous or indirect. At least three factors inhibit organizations from providing rewards which discriminate according to performance.[11] The first limiting factor is the organization's inability to differentiate among individual differences in performance. If the manager is unable to distinguish between the good and the poor performing employee, then it is obviously impossible for the employees to receive rewards commensurate with their performance. Differentiating performance is most difficult when there is little or no objective criteria for evaluation. In such instances, the manager is forced to make purely subjective evaluations which are frequently difficult to substantiate and may be based on prejudice, nepotism, and so on.

The second inhibiting factor is the organization's capability to give rewards. It is not unusual for an organization and/or a superior to identify an outstanding performer but be unable to provide the deserved rewards. For example, the identified employee may deserve a promotion but no vacancies exist. The reward structure of the organization may be so rigid that pay raises can only be given at certain times. Of course some kind of reward can always be given,

---

[10] Ibid., p. 107.

[11] Lyman W. Porter and Edward E. Lawler, III, *Managerial Attitudes and Performance* (Homewood, Ill.: Richard D. Irwin, Inc., 1968), p. 35.

even if it is only a pat on the back or some other type of informal recognition. However, a pat on the back will lose its motivational benefits if it is not ultimately accompanied by a promotion or pay raise.

A third limiting factor is the organization's or the superior's willingness to give rewards. Even though capable of discriminating between the good and poor performers and even with the authority to grant appropriate rewards, the superior still may not be willing to dispense the rewards. The superior may believe that greater rewards might have a detrimental effect on performance (the intention is usually to give the reward at some later, indefinite date). The superior may be jealous of the subordinate's accomplishments and not want that person to move ahead so rapidly. The end result is that the deserving subordinate is not rewarded.

If the subordinate perceives a weak or nonexistent relationship between effort and rewards, the subordinate will soon adopt a lackadaisical attitude. This attitude will be reflected in work pace; the employee will put forth only the minimum effort necessary to maintain the job.

An integrative model

Figure 15–3 presents a model which relates effort, performance, rewards, and other key variables.[12] While no claims are made that the model provides a total explanation of the relationships between effort, performance, and rewards, the model does provide a vehicle for integrating the key concepts previously discussed.

Effort is shown to be dependent on the value placed on the reward by the individual, the perceived probability that performance is related to effort, and the perceived probability that rewards are related to performance. By either consciously or unconsciously combining the contingency relationship between effort and performance and between performance and rewards, the individual develops a feeling for the probability that effort will ultimately lead to rewards. Naturally, the greater the individual values the rewards and the higher the perceived probability that effort will ultimately lead to these rewards, the greater will be the effort. For example, suppose a young man, who is planning on getting married and thus places a high value on salary increases, believes that hard work results in high performance. If he also believes that pay increases are tied to actual performance, he would probably be motivated to work hard. On the other hand, if he believes that everyone will receive about the same

---

[12] The formulation of this model is attributed to Professor Thomas B. Clark, Georgia Institute of Technology.

FIGURE 15-3
Effort-performance-reward relationship

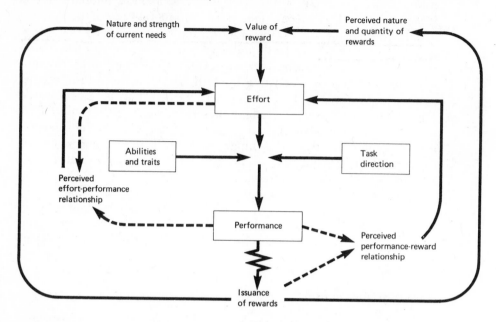

raise regardless of their performance, then he will probably not be motivated to work hard.

The model indicates that the relationship between effort and performance is modified by task direction and abilities and traits. This relationship was discussed at length in Chapter 14. The relationship between performance and rewards is depicted with a wavy line indicating that rewards often are not tied directly to performance.

As discussed in an earlier section of this chapter, the value of the reward is determined by the nature and strength of current needs and by the nature and quantity of the rewards. The young employee contemplating marriage in the previous example would probably place a high value on a pay increase. However, another employee might much rather have another week of vacation.

The model has four major feedback loops — one incorporating the effort-performance contingency, one incorporating the performance-reward contingency, and two relating the actual rewards received to the value placed on the reward. Loop 1 in Figure 15-4 indicates that past performance affects future effort through the effort-performance contingency. Loops 2, 3, and 4 show the impact of current rewards on future behavior. Loop 2 indicates that effort is related to rewards through the performance-reward contingency. Loops 3 and 4 show

FIGURE 15–4
Feedback relationships

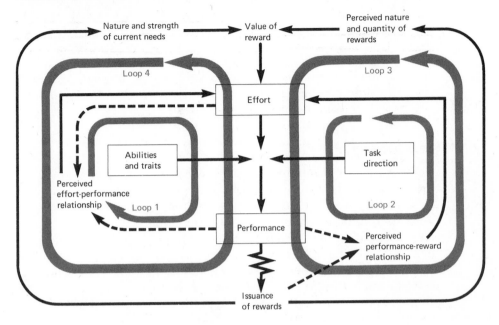

that current rewards affect the value placed on the reward by the individual. An individual's level of satisfaction is affected to the extent that the rewards received satisfy current needs (Loop 4). These feedback relationships emphasize that past experiences often affect future perceptions and actions.

The model in Figure 15–3 is, of course, subject to the same situational and performance obstacles that were discussed in Chapter 14. The entire effort-performance-reward relationship is further complicated by the different perceptions, values, and beliefs of the individuals involved.

COMPENSATION AND EFFORT

Many of the formal rewards of an organization are unrelated to performance. Most fringe benefits such as paid vacations, insurance plans, and the like are a function of organization membership and seniority. Rewards unrelated to performance may initially attract an individual and even keep that person from leaving the organization, but once on the job, they probably will not motivate the individual. Advancement in the form of promotion can be an effective reward. However, opportunities for advancement may be rare and, when available, may be filled on a seniority basis or by someone outside the organization. The primary organizational variable that can be used to reinforce performance is pay. Research has shown that pay is a reward that is able to satisfy higher order needs such as esteem and recognition as well as the lower order physical and security needs.[13] Because pay may serve a range of individual needs and because individual needs vary, pay is viewed with varying degrees of importance by different individuals. However, *if directly linked to performance*, pay can be an important motivator in almost all instances.

Equity theory

The problem of defining an employee's fair pay is not a new one. Frederick Taylor and his protégés attempted to answer the question through the use of motion and time studies. Wage surveys have also been used to determine fair wages. If an organization is to get maximum benefit from a compensation package, the package must be perceived as equitable by the recipients.

A wide range of actions may be taken by an individual who perceives wage inequities. One decision may be to terminate the relationship with the organization. Other less drastic actions include asking for more money or decreasing the effort exerted. It should be pointed out that an employee may perceive overcompensation as well as undercompensation. Such a situation can result in feelings of apprehension and general unrest.

Several remedies may be used by organizations to minimize real inequities and employees' perceptions of inequities.[14] First, organizations can adopt a policy covering pay differentials that reflects the dominant norms of equity of the employees.[15] This approach contrasts with the traditional view that compensation should reflect top management's judgment. This suggestion is based on the assumption that employees at all levels can agree on what constitutes a fair level of pay for their respective jobs. For instance, the employees must be able to agree that skilled workers are paid more than unskilled workers. The basic idea is to avoid a situation in which an individual intuitively feels unfairly compensated.

---

[13] See Edward E. Lawler, III and Lyman W. Porter, "Perceptions Regarding Management Compensation," *Industrial Relations*, October 1963, pp. 41–49; and M. S. Myers, "Who Are Your Motivated Workers?" *Harvard Business Review*, January–February 1964, pp. 73–88.

[14] Malcolm S. Salter, "What Is 'Fair Pay' for the Executive?" *Harvard Business Review*, May–June 1972, pp. 6–14, 144–46.

[15] For a detailed discussion of this idea see Elliott Jaques, *Equitable Payments* (London: Heinemann, 1961).

Another suggestion is to develop procedures for ensuring consistency of pay brackets for broad levels within the organization and with respect to similar levels within other organizations.[16] This procedure would enable organizations to avoid situations in which two employees in different departments are paid substantially different wages for doing basically the same work.

A third suggestion is to relate pay to performance. As has been shown earlier in this chapter, individuals make judgments concerning the relationship of rewards and performance. If an individual believes that pay is not related to performance, then pay will not serve as a motivator. It is not always easy to tie pay to performance especially for management and staff jobs. Traditionally, wherever efforts have been made, various types of merit systems have been used. One approach is management by objectives (MBO). MBO is explored in depth in Chapter 17.

A final suggestion is periodically to disclose the ranges of pay for the various levels within the organization. Pay secrecy makes it difficult for individuals to determine if pay is related to performance. Research has also shown that many employees have a tendency to overestimate the pay of their peers.[17] Obviously such a situation can create unwarranted problems. On the other hand, publishing individual salaries is often viewed as an invasion of privacy. One solution is to disclose the pay ranges for various job levels within the organization.

Pay incentives

Pay incentives gained wide acceptance in the early 1900s. It has been estimated that approximately two thirds of all companies listed on the stock exchanges use some type of pay incentives.[18] Incentive plans can be used on an individual or group basis. Normally, individual plans are preferred because of their direct link with the performer. However, many situations require a cooperative effort (such as an assembly line) and, therefore, lend themselves to group incentives.

Lower level incentive programs are usually a function of produc-

---

[16] For a detailed discussion of this idea see J. S. Adams, "Toward an Understanding of Inequity," *Journal of Abnormal and Social Psychology*, November 1963, pp. 422–36.

[17] Edward E. Lawler, III, "Managers' Perceptions of Their Subordinates' Pay and of Their Superiors' Pay," *Personnel Psychology*, Winter 1965, p. 413; and Lawler, "Should Managers' Compensation Be Kept under Wraps?" *Personnel*, January–February 1965, p. 17.

[18] Arch Patton, "Why Incentive Plans Fail," *Harvard Business Review*, May–June 1972, p. 59.

tion or time and are by definition related to performance. At such levels the only potential hazard is in setting the standard. A time standard has little validity if it was established using inefficient or improper methods. A standard set too high causes people to take a negative attitude and not attempt to achieve the standard. Management incentive programs present a different set of problems. Because subjective evaluations are often required decisions concerning managerial performance are often avoided. Such a course of action often results in everybody receiving the same bonus.

A well-administered incentive program can, under the right circumstances, benefit all parties. However, a poorly administered, inappropriate scheme can result in increased costs, output restriction, and hostility.[19] Because of the potential ill effects, the adoption of an incentive program requires careful planning.

WORK-RELATED SATISFACTION AFFECTORS

If an organizational variable is to influence individual behavior it must possess need-satisfying power, and the individual must perceive that the reward level is related to performance. The major sources of such rewards are the formal organization, the task itself, and the

FIGURE 15–5
Rewards and their potential impact on performance (work-related satisfaction affectors)

Source	Performance Contingency
Formal organization (extrinsic)	
Supervisory behavior	May be high
Incentive payments	High
Advancement	Low to moderate
Security	Low to moderate
Base wage	Low
Benefits	Low
Work environment	Low
Task (intrinsic)	
Stimulation and challenge	Variable
Accomplishment	Variable
Growth and development	Variable
Recognition	Variable
Work group (extrinsic)	
Social relationships	Variable

---

[19] Gene K. Groff, "Worker Productivity: An Integrated View," *Business Horizons,* April 1971, p. 84.

work group. Gene Groff has categorized various work-related "satisfaction affectors" as to their source and their potential impact on performance (see Figure 15–5).[20] Some of the more important of the satisfaction affectors that have not been discussed previously are discussed below.

Supervisory behavior

An often overlooked or mishandled but key variable affecting individual effort is the supervisor or superior. The supervisor's behavior often shapes the subordinates attitudes toward the organization and work. The superior's ability to plan, schedule, and solve problems has a direct influence on productivity. Because each individual and situation is different, the supervisor's sensitivity to the values and expectations of others is a key variable in determining supervisory effectiveness. An individual reacts to a certain set of perceived circumstances although this perception may or may not conform to reality. An effective supervisor attempts to understand the situation from not only his or her viewpoint but also from the subordinate's viewpoint.

Another potentially important variable is the supervisor's upward influence within the organization. It is only natural for subordinates to ignore a superior who is perceived to have very little upward influence. Reporting on some empirical studies Donald Pelz has stated ". . . the supervisory behaviors of 'siding with employees' and 'social closeness to employees' will tend to raise employee satisfaction only if the supervisor has enough influence to make these behaviors pay off in terms of actual benefits for employees."[21]

Job designs

Many potential intrinsic rewards are directly related to job design. Feelings of achievement and accomplishment are experienced more frequently when the individual genuinely likes the job.

Job designs are often dictated by the envisioned economic efficiencies of specialization and mechanization. As discussed earlier in Chapter 6, there is no doubt that specialization, up to a point, is desirable both from an economic and motivational viewpoint. It is possible for a job to be so broad and vaguely defined that it frustrates and demotivates the occupant. More frequently, however, the job is overly narrow and repetitive and therefore boring.

---

[20] Ibid., p. 81.

[21] Donald C. Pelz, "Influence: A Key to Effective Leadership in the First Line Supervisor," *Personnel*, November 1952, pp. 209–17.

In analyzing a job it is useful to separate the design into two functions: (1) the determination of efficient job methods and (2) specification of the set of tasks to be assigned to individual workers.[22] There is little controversy over the simplification of job methods. The elimination of inefficient methods and unnecessary steps does not make the job less satisfying. Changes in job methods do not affect the scope and depth of the job. Job scope and depth can only be altered by changing the basic job structure or the job content.[23]

Many methods have been suggested for creating "satisfying jobs" or jobs capable of providing intrinsic rewards. Among these methods are job rotation, job enlargement, and job enrichment. Job rotation is the practice of periodically changing job assignments. For example, job rotation occurs when assembly line workers temporarily switch jobs. A major criticism of job rotation is that changing from one unsatisfying job to another does not significantly reduce boredom or job dissatisfaction. Job rotation does not require that the jobs be redesigned. Job enlargement makes a job structurally larger by increasing its scope (the number of types of work performed). Like job rotation, job enlargement has been criticized as adding only more of the same type operations. Job enrichment goes beyond job enlargement by increasing not only the job scope but also the job depth (the freedom to plan and organize the work, to work at a self-determined pace, and to move around and communicate as needed).[24] The argument made for job enrichment is that it offers additional opportunities for personal responsibility and growth and that these are the factors that make the job more or less satisfying.

INTRAPERSONAL SATISFACTION AND EFFORT AFFECTORS

Certain variables internal to the individual can influence both satisfaction and effort. Although these variables cannot be directly controlled by the organization, they should be considered when selecting and attempting to motivate employees.

Level of aspiration

A person's level of aspiration has been defined as "the level of future performance in a familiar task which an individual, knowing his level of past performance in that task, explicitly undertakes to

---

[22] Groff, "Worker Productivity," p. 85.

[23] See Chapter 6 for a discussion of job scope and job depth.

[24] See Chapter 9 for an expanded discussion on job enrichment.

FIGURE 15–6
Determining one's level of aspiration

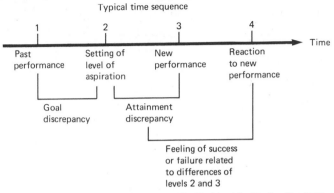

Source: Kurt Lewin, Tamara Dembo, Leon Festinger, and Pauline Snedden Sears, "Level of Aspiration," in *Personality and the Behavior Disorders*, edited by J. McV. Hunt. Copyright 1944, renewed © 1972, The Ronald Press Company, New York, p. 334.

reach."[25] Thus, a person's level of aspiration refers to the level of performance that he or she expects to attain. As brought out in the above definition, a person's level of aspiration is strongly influenced by his or her own past achievements. For example, a male athlete might have been very pleased to have thrown the shotput 45 feet at an early stage in his career. However, as he has matured and improved, he raises his expectations and is satisfied with nothing less than 50 feet.

Figure 15–6 shows the sequence of events which determine the level of aspiration. A person's past performance influences the setting of the level of aspiration. The difference between past performance and the current level of aspiration is referred to as the goal discrepancy. Goal discrepancy can be either positive or negative depending on whether the level of aspiration is set above or below the level of past performance. The difference between the level of aspiration and the level of new performance is called the attainment discrepancy, which can also be positive or negative. The attainment discrepancy in turn strongly influences the psychological reaction to the new performance. The psychological reaction to the new performance is also influenced by such things as the group's level of aspiration and any goals that may have been set for the individual by others. The resulting reaction to the new performance influences the next level of aspiration, and thus the cycle repeats itself.

Many managers assume that subordinates will work harder by al-

---

[25] J. D. Frank, "Individual Differences in Certain Aspects of the Level of Aspirations," *American Journal of Psychology*, January 1935, p. 119.

ways giving them goals that are just out of reach. The belief is that once employees have reached their objectives their work pace will slow or stop completely. Research does not support this view. In general, research has shown that not only does the level of aspiration drop with continued failure but so does the level of performance.[26]

Achievement motivation

The need of an individual to achieve is an integral part of a person's personality which affects drive and motivation. People who have a high need for achievement are impelled to advance and achieve success. Such people like to set their own goals and receive concrete

FIGURE 15–7
Characteristics of high need achiever

1. Focuses primarily on rewards of success.
2. Competes against some standard of excellence such as an objective goal.
3. Sets challenging but realistic goals for himself.
4. Seeks feedback. *information of results*
5. Takes moderate risks.
6. Prefers risk situations where he can affect the odds of succeeding.
7. Prefers a system where payoffs are related to the results achieved.
8. Likes entrepreneural roles.

feedback concerning their performance toward those goals; they like to know where they stand and therefore avoid situations that provide little or no feedback; they tend to set challenging but realistic goals; and they prefer situations of moderate risk. Figure 15–7 outlines the characteristics of a high need achiever.

Professor David McClelland has estimated that approximately 10 percent of the American population possess a high achievement motive.[27] However, McClelland's research has also shown that the achievement motive can be learned and developed. McClelland believes that certain measures (such as joint goal setting, personal responsibility, frequent appraisals, and so forth) encourage high

---

[26] Timothy W. Costello and Sheldon S. Zalkind, *Psychology in Administration* (Englewood Cliffs, N. J.: Prentice-Hall, Inc., 1963), pp. 72–73.

[27] David C. McClelland, "Achievement Motivation Can Be Developed," *Harvard Business Review*, November–December 1965, pp. 6–24, 178.

achievement on the job. Because a high achievement motive is desirable, managers should attempt to provide an environment which fosters and develops the employee's need to achieve.

PUTTING IT ALL TOGETHER

The top portion of Figure 15–8 shows the major factors which determine an individual's level of satisfaction (or dissatisfaction). The

FIGURE 15–8
Determinants of satisfaction and dissatisfaction

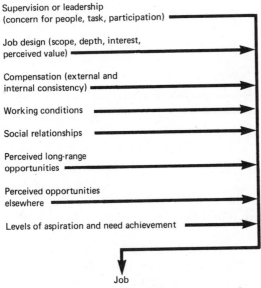

lower portion of the figure shows the organization behaviors generally associated with satisfaction and dissatisfaction. A wide range of both internal and external factors affect an individual's level of satisfaction. Individual satisfaction leads to organizational commitment while dissatisfaction results in behaviors detrimental to the organization (turnover, absenteeism, tardiness, accidents, and so forth). For example, employees who like their jobs, supervisors, and the job related factors will probably be very loyal and devoted employees. However, employees who strongly dislike their jobs or any of the job related factors will probably be disgruntled and will often exhibit these feelings by being late, absent, or by taking more covert actions to disrupt the organization.

It should be re-iterated that satisfaction and motivation are not synonymous. Motivation is a drive to perform while satisfaction reflects the individual's attitude or happiness with the situation. The factors that determine whether an individual is satisfied with the job differ from those that determine whether that individual is motivated. Satisfaction is largely determined by the comfort offered by the environment and the situation. Motivation, on the other hand, is largely determined by the value of rewards and their contingency on performance. The result of motivation is increased effort, which in turn increases performance as modified by abilities and task direction. The result of satisfaction is increased commitment to the organization which may or may not result in increased performance. All things being equal, a high level of satisfaction is definitely desired but this does not in itself guarantee high performance.

SUMMARY

Effort refers to the amount of energy, either physical or mental, expended by an individual in performing a task. Effort is the product of motivation and may be misdirected.

Job satisfaction is an individual's general attitude about the job and is influenced by many factors. The relationship between job satisfaction and job performance is complex and has been debated for years. Current theory holds that performance should determine rewards. Rewards, in turn, affect an individual's level of satisfaction through their impact on current needs and desires.

The relationship between effort and rewards is largely dependent on the value placed on the reward, the perceived probability that effort leads to performance, and the perceived probability that performance leads to rewards. The employee must value the reward if it is to produce motivation, and must also perceive definite relationships between effort and performance and between performance and rewards. A model presented in this chapter provides a vehicle for integrating effort, performance, rewards, and other key variables.

Pay, if directly linked to performance, can be an important motivator in almost all instances. However, if an organization is to get maximum benefit from a compensation package, the package must be perceived as being equitable by the recipients. The organization can take certain actions to minimize real and perceived inequities.

Many other variables internal to the organization besides compensation affect worker satisfaction. Supervisory behavior and job design are two of the most important.

Worker satisfaction is also affected by variables not directly controlled by the organization. Such external satisfaction affectors include a person's level of aspiration and achievement motive.

Encouraging individual effort is not a simple task. When attempting to encourage effort, the manager must deal with both controllable and uncontrollable variables and with individual differences in preferences and perceptions.

REVIEW QUESTIONS

1. What is job satisfaction? What are the major components of job satisfaction?

2. What is organizational morale?

3. What is the satisfaction-performance controversy?

4. What factors influence the effort put forth by an individual?

5. Describe the types of rewards that are associated with any job.

6. Describe the effort-performance contingency.

7. Describe the performance-reward contingency.

8. Describe in detail the reward-effort-performance relationships.

9. What is the relationship between pay and effort?

10. Describe the following work-related satisfaction affectors.
    a. Supervisory behavior.
    b. Job designs.

11. Describe the following intrapersonal satisfaction and effort affectors:
    a. Level of aspiration.
    b. Achievement motivation.

DISCUSSION QUESTIONS

1. Do you think that a very loyal employee is necessarily a good employee?

2. The XYZ Company has just decided to take all of its employees (200 in number) to Las Vegas for a three-day weekend to show its appreciation for their high level of performance this past year. What is your reaction to this idea?

3. Discuss the following statement: "A satisfied employee is one that is not being pushed hard enough!"

4. An employee of the ABC Company was overheard making the following statement: "Effort should be the sole determinant of rewards; an employee can't help it if he or she doesn't have above average ability or if his or her boss doesn't clearly explain the job!" Do you support the employee?

SELECTED READINGS

Blood, M. R. "Work Values and Job Satisfaction," *Journal of Applied Psychology*, vol. 52 (1968), pp. 456–59.

Greene, Charles N. "The Satisfaction-Performance Controversy," *Business Horizons* (October 1972), pp. 31–41.

Herzberg, F., B. Mausner, R. Peterson, and D. Capwell. *Job Attitudes: Review of Research and Opinion.* Pittsburgh: Psychological Services of Pittsburg, 1957.

Lawler, Edward E., III. *Pay and Organizational Effectiveness: A Psychological Review.* New York: McGraw-Hill Book Co., 1972.

Locke, E. A., N. Cartledge, and C. S. Kneer. "Studies in the Relationship Between Satisfaction, Goal-Setting, and Performance," *Organizational Behavior and Human Performance*, vol. 5 (1970), pp. 135–58.

McClelland, David C. "Achievement Motivation Can Be Developed," *Harvard Business Review* (November–December 1965), pp. 6–24, 178.

Roberts, Karlene H., and Frederick Savage. "Twenty Questions: Utilizing Job Satisfaction Measures," *California Management Review*, vol. 15, no. 3 (Spring 1973), pp. 82–90.

Schwab, Donald P., and Larry L. Cummings. "Theories of Performance and Satisfaction: A Review," *Industrial Relations*, vol. 9, no. 4 (October 1970), pp. 408–29.

Wanous, John P., and Edward E. Lawler, III. "Measurement and Meaning of Job Satisfaction," *Journal of Applied Psychology*, vol. 56, no. 2 (1972), pp. 95–105.

Case 15–1

Disappointing results at First National

The First National Bank of Melville had experienced a decline in its share of the banking market during its last three quarters. The bank president, Joseph Butler, assigned his assistant, Floyd James, to research the problem and make recommendations for solving the problem.

Floyd developed statistical studies on population trends, customer profiles, and economic conditions. He found little information that could explain First National's problem. However, he did discover one interesting fact. First National offered eight different services to customers. However, the average customer used only 1.3 of the services.

When Mr. Butler asked for Floyd's report, Floyd related his findings concerning the use of services. Floyd also recommended a program of instruction for all employees on selling additional services to new and existing customers. Mr. Butler agreed and requested immediate implementation.

Floyd devised a program of visual aids, catchy slogans, and helpful hints for the employees to use. After the program had been in effect for three months, Mr. Butler asked for a progress report. The results were disappointing—First National's share of the market had declined another 2 percent and there was no sign of an increase in the number of services being used by each customer.

1. Explain why you think the service promotion program has failed.
2. How could the bank make the service promotion program more successful?

Case 15–2

An informative coffee break

On a Monday morning, April 28, George Smith was given the news that effective May 1, he would receive a raise of 13 percent. This raise came two months before his scheduled performance appraisal. He was informed by his manager, Tom Weeks, that the basis for the raise was his performance over the past several months and his potential worth to the company. He was told that this was a very considerable increase.

On the next day, Tuesday, a group of fellow workers in George's office were engaging in their normal coffee break. The course of conversation swung to salary increases. One of the group had received a performance review in April, but no indication of an impending salary adjustment had been given to him. George made a comment concerning the amount of any such increases, specifically questioning the range of increase percentages. A third individual immediately responded by saying how surprised he was in getting an "across the board" 12 percent increase last Friday. A fourth individual confirmed that he too had received a similar salary increase. Definitely astounded, George pressed for information, only to learn that several people had received increases of "around" 11 to 13 percent. George broke up the gathering by excusing himself.

That evening, George wrestled with his conscience concerning the foregoing discussion. His first impression of his raise was that it had been given based on performance. His second impression was decidedly sour. Several questions were bothering him:

1. Why did his boss tender the raise as a merit increase?
2. Is job performance really a basis for salary increases in his department?
3. Did his superior hide the truth regarding the raise?
4. Can he trust his boss in the future?
5. Upon what basis will further increases be issued?

1. What effect do you think that this new information will have on the effort put forth by George Smith?
2. What can Tom Weeks do to regain the confidence of George Smith?

Objectives

1. To explore the process of developing individual abilities and traits within organizations.
2. To discuss several specific methods of developing individual abilities and traits in organizations.
3. To introduce the concept of organization development along with some methods for implementing it.

GLOSSARY OF TERMS

Abilities and traits An individual's personal characteristics which are used in performing a job.

Apprenticeship training Supervised training and testing for a minimum time period and until a minimum skill level is reached.

Employee development A process concerned with the improvement and growth of the capabilities of individuals and groups within the organization.

Grid training A form of training used in organization development which is designed to make managers and organizations more team-oriented.

Human asset accounting A proposed approach to accounting which involves an attempt to place a value on an organization's human assets and customer good will.

Management development A subset of employee development which is designed to improve managerial performance.

On-the-job training A form of training given by the employee's manager or a senior employee which involves actually showing the employee the job and explaining how it is to be done.

Organization development A process which uses behavioral techniques for improving the management of change and conflict within an organization.

Sensitivity training A form of training used in organization development which is designed to make one more aware of oneself and one's impact on others.

Training A process that involves the acquisition of skills, concepts, rules, or attitudes.

16

Developing abilities
and traits

*Few organizations would admit that they can survive without
it—yet some act as though they could.*

*Everyone knows what it is—yet management, unions, and workers
often interpret it in light of their own job conditions.*

It is going on all the time—yet much of it is done haphazardly.

*It is futile to attempt it without the needed time and facilities—
yet often those responsible for it lack either or both.*

*It costs money—yet at times there is not adequate budgetary
appropriation for it.*

*It should take place at all levels—yet sometimes it is limited
to the lowest operating levels.*

*It can help everyone do a better job—yet those selected for it
often fear it.*

*It is foolish to start it without clearly defined objectives—yet
this is occasionally done.*

*It cannot be ignored without costing the company money—yet
some managers seem blind to this reality.*

*It should permeate the entire organization and be derived from
the firm's theory and practice of management—yet sometimes
it is shunted off to one department that operates more or less
in isolation from the rest of the business.*

F. A. Philips, W. M. Berliner, and J. J. Cribbin*

ABILITIES and traits are an individual's personal characteristics used
in performing a job. These characteristics do not fluctuate widely over
short periods of time. Because abilities and traits place an upper
limit on the performance of an individual regardless of effort and task
direction, organizations should make a conscious attempt to develop
the abilities and traits of its employees. However, as the introductory

---

° *Management of Training Programs*, Homewood, Ill.: Richard D. Irwin, Inc., 1960,
pp. 5–6.

347

quote points out, there are problems associated with developing abilities and traits in organizations.

Staffing as discussed in Chapter 7 is part of the organizing function and involves securing and developing personnel for the jobs which are created in earlier phases of the organizing function. The purpose of this chapter is to explore in depth the process of developing the abilities and traits of the organization's personnel.

HUMAN ASSET ACCOUNTING

Human asset accounting is a relatively new idea and involves an attempt to place a value on an organization's human assets and customer goodwill. Rensis Likert, one of the pioneers in this area, defines human asset accounting as follows: "Human asset accounting refers to activity devoted to attaching dollar estimates to the value of a firm's human organization and its customer goodwill."[1] Basically, the proponents of human asset accounting feel that the quality of the personnel of an organization should be reflected on the balance sheet of the organization. If good, well-trained people join the organization, then the organization is worth more. If good, well-trained people leave the organization, then the organization is worth less.

Likert suggests that the following variables should be considered in determining a value for an organization's human assets: intelligence and aptitudes, training, level of performance goals and motivation, quality of leadership, quality of communication systems, degree of teamwork within the organization, and quality of coordination.[2]

Reflecting the value of an organization's human assets on its balance sheet is currently not an accepted practice in accounting and financial circles. However, its importance seems to be that it does reflect a growing concern about the value of the skills and abilities of an organization's human resources.

EMPLOYEE DEVELOPMENT

Employee development, which was introduced in Chapter 7, is a process that is concerned with the improvement and growth of the capabilities of individuals and groups within the organization. Figure 16–1 illustrates how the employee development process should work within any organization.

Chapter 4 discussed in detail the process of establishing organiza-

---

[1] Rensis Likert, *The Human Organization* (New York: McGraw-Hill Book Company, 1967), p. 148.

[2] Ibid., p. 148.

FIGURE 16–1
Employee development process

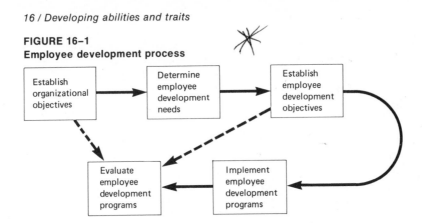

tional objectives. This essential step must be accomplished before an overall program of employee development can be implemented. Employee development must relate to the organization's objectives.

The employee development needs are then determined by comparing where the organization is headed with the present skills of its work force. The use of organizational objectives and a skills inventory aids management in forecasting the specific abilities and traits that are required. The results of this process enable management to establish objectives for the overall employee development program.

The overall employee development program can include many types of development programs such as: employee training, management development, counseling, and performance reviews.

After an employee development program has been implemented it should be periodically evaluated in light of the organizational objectives and the specific employee development objectives.

Employee training

Training is a process that involves the acquisition of skills, concepts, rules, or attitudes. The goal of training is to improve present and future performance. Training is and must be the responsibility of all managers. The training process begins on the first day of employment for an individual. This phase of training is known as orientation. Orientation should be designed to give new employees an understanding of their job, organization procedures and policies, as well as a general understanding of the organization's role in society. It is important to remember that all employees receive orientation whether or not there is a formal orientation program. The new employees will form impressions and attitudes about the organization through their daily contacts on the job. In order for the employee to form accurate impressions, it is desirable that every organization have a formalized orientation program. Generally the formalized orientation program is given by the personnel department. Orientation on the job is normally given by the new employee's manager. Both of these forms of orientation are important in shaping the new employee's attitude toward not only the job but also the organization as a whole. Unfortunately, many organizations underestimate the importance of an orientation program. All too often new employees are given a policy and procedures manual and told to study it until they are given another assignment. At this point the policies and procedures have little meaning to new employees and they are quickly bored. The unfortunate part is that the new employees are often not given another assignment for several days or even weeks in some cases. Obviously the new employee is off to a bad start.

Many organizations establish a training department to implement training programs. This department is normally located within the personnel or human resources department. The training department assists the managers of the organization in the following areas: (1) determining training needs; (2) organizing and scheduling formal training classes; (3) providing instructors for training classes; and (4) evaluating the formal training programs.

Training should be objective oriented. Regrettably, many training programs have no objectives at all. The adage "training for training's sake" seems to be appropriate for those situations. The following criteria should be considered as guideposts in defining training objectives: (1) Training objectives and organizational objectives should be compatible; (2) training objectives should be realistic; (3) training objectives should be clearly stated in writing; and (4) results should be measurable and verifiable.

In general, training programs are considered successful when participants respond enthusiastically to the program. The opinions and casual observations of participants comprise the extent of most training evaluation. However, enthusiasm cannot be taken as positive evidence of improved ability. Opinions do not always reflect the effectiveness of the training program. If training programs are to provide valuable services in the achievement of organizational objectives, they must be objectively evaluated and the results must be carefully analyzed by management.

When training results are measured objectively, a number of benefits accrue. Less effective programs can be withdrawn from consideration, which results in a saving of time and effort. Identified weaknesses within established programs can be strengthened. Finally, the results of effective training can be promulgated in a meaningful fashion and can be objectively evaluated by management.

Methods of training

Several different methods are available for achieving training objectives. Some of these include on-the-job training, apprenticeship training, classroom training, and programmed instruction.

On-the-job training is the most common method of training employees and is normally given by the employee's manager or a senior employee. It merely involves showing the employee the job and demonstrating or explaining how it is to be done. One commonly used

FIGURE 16-2
How to instruct (Practical methods to guide you in instructing a new man on a job, or a present worker on a new job or a new skill.)

First, here's what *you must* do to *get ready* to teach a job.
1. Decide what the learner must be taught in order to do the job efficiently, safely, economically, and intelligently.
2. Have the right tools, equipment, supplies, and material ready.
3. Have the work place properly arranged, just as the worker will be expected to keep it.

Then, you should *instruct* the learner by the following *four basic steps:*
Step I — Preparation (of the learner)
1. Put the learner at *ease.*
2. Find out what he already knows about the job.
3. Get him interested and desirous of learning the job.

Step II — Presentation (of the operations and knowledge)
1. *Tell, show, illustrate,* and *question* in order to put over the new knowledge and operations.
2. Instruct slowly, clearly, completely, and patiently, one point at a time.
3. Check, question, and repeat.
4. Make sure the learner really knows.

Step III — Performance try-out
1. Test learner by having him perform the job.
2. Ask questions beginning with *why, how, when,* or *where.*
3. Observe performance, correct errors, and repeat instructions if necessary.
4. Continue until you *know he knows.*

Step IV — Follow-up
1. Put him "on his own."
2. Check frequently to be sure he follows instructions.
3. Taper off extra supervision and close follow-up until he is qualified to work with normal supervision.

Remember — If the learner hasn't learned, the teacher hasn't taught.

Source: War Manpower Commission, *The Training within Industry Report* (Washington, D.C.: Bureau of Training, Training within Industry Service, 1945), p. 195.

TABLE 16–1
Length of apprentice training

	Years									
	2	2–3	2–4	3	3–4	3–5	4	4–5	5	5–6
Barber	X									
Cosmetician	X									
Brewer		X								
Painter-decorator		X								
Foundryman			X							
Ironworker			X							
Jeweler			X							
Stoneworker			X							
Baker				X						
Bricklayer				X						
Photographer				X						
Airplane mechanic					X					
Leatherworker					X					
Operating engineer					X					
Sheet metalworker					X					
Draftsman-designer						X				
Boilermaker							X			
Carpenter							X			
Machinist							X			
Printer							X			
Tailor							X			
Electrical worker								X		
Lithographer								X		
Tool and die maker								X		
Lead burner									X	
Patternmaker									X	
Electrotyper										X
Photoengraver										X
Stereotyper										X

Source: U.S. Department of Labor, *Apprentice Training* (Washington, D.C., 1969), p. 6.

method for structuring on-the-job training is the Job Instruction Training (JIT) system developed during World War II. Figure 16–2 summarizes the steps involved in applying JIT.

Apprenticeship training involves supervised training and testing for a minimum time period and until a minimum skill level is reached. This approach to training dates back to biblical times and is commonly used in skilled trades. Over a period of time, the apprentice has formal classroom training and practical on-the-job experience. During this time, the apprentice is normally paid somewhat less than the workers who have completed the apprentice period. Table 16–1 illustrates the length of some apprenticeship periods.

Formal classroom training is probably the most familiar type of training because almost everyone experiences this type of training through their own education. Lectures, movies, and exercises are the most commonly used methods of conducting classroom training.

Programmed instruction is one of the newest methods of providing training within organizations. With this method, material is presented in text form or on teaching machines. Regardless of the form in which the material is presented, programmed instruction involves such features as "active practice, a gradual increase in difficulty levels over a series of small steps, immediate feedback, learning at the individual's own rate, and minimization of error."[3] Programmed instruction generally does not require an instructor or training leader.

Management development

Formalized management development programs are a subset of the employee development process. Ideally they should be designed, conducted, and evaluated based on the objectives of the organization. They should also have the total support of top management, be designed around the needs of the organization and the individual needs of each manager, and be periodically evaluated.

Management development can take many forms. Techniques for management development include coaching and counseling, understudy assignments, job rotation, individual self-improvement programs, performance appraisals, in-house training programs, as well as training courses and programs sponsored by universities and other professional organizations.

Coaching and counseling are probably the most widely used techniques in management development. Under this system, a coach, generally a higher level manager, is assigned the responsibility of seeing that a manager-trainee learns the skills needed in becoming an effective manager. The assumption is made that the most effective method of teaching good management is for effective managers to teach what they are doing. Coaching and counseling often have good results, but they are not without their problems. First, this method of management development perpetuates current management practices and styles. This may or may not be desirable. In addition, frequently the coach does not have enough time to spend with the trainee and

---

[3] John B. Miner, and Mary Green Miner, *Personnel and Industrial Relations: A Managerial Approach*, 2d ed. (New York: The Macmillan Company, 1973), p. 365.

doesn't, therefore, allow the trainee to make mistakes and learn from experience. Presently, there has been little evaluation of this form of management development, and therefore, it is difficult to determine the effectiveness of the technique.

Job rotation is the practice of periodically changing job assignments. Job rotation was discussed in Chapter 15 in the context of encouraging effort with emphasis on the lower level jobs in the organization. In Chapter 15, job rotation was criticized on the grounds that changing from one unsatisfying job to another does not significantly reduce boredom or job satisfaction. Similarly, job rotation can be ineffective in management development if the trainee is merely shifted from department to department within the organization doing jobs that require little skill and lead to no development. Job rotation can lead to effective management development, but if it is not properly used, it can do more harm than good.

Individual self-improvement programs merely involve the self-development activities of a manager. These include home study courses or any other related activity that is designed to improve job performance. Ideally, counseling, understudy assignments, and job rotation would provide the perceptive manager with information and problems that could be used for home study. Obviously this approach to management development is very unstructured, and the effectiveness of such a program is difficult to determine.

Performance appraisals are discussed in detail in Chapter 17 as they relate to defining direction. However, performance appraisals can also play an important role in management development. The purpose of performance appraisal is to evaluate actual performance compared to planned performance. Analyzing the results of performance appraisals aids in increasing future performance by identifying both the strengths and weaknesses of the individual. Performance appraisal should involve the following basic components: (1) mutual establishment of performance objectives by superior and subordinate; (2) mutual review of the subordinate's performance; and (3) mutual discussion of development needs necessary to improve performance.

Organizational training programs are generally conducted by the training department. They are generally designed to give classroom instruction in such topics as planning, motivating, leadership, communication, and so on. Lectures, movies, games, exercises, role playing, and case studies are frequently used in this form of management development.

Organizational training programs may be supplemented by courses offered by educational or professional groups. Universities and colleges offer a wide range of programs designed to increase the skills of managers. Professional groups such as the American Management Association also offer a wide range of courses.

In summary, it is unrealistic to assume that the very difficult job of managing complex organizations can be accomplished by untrained managers. Peter Drucker explains the future of management as follows:

> We have, in other words, a great deal to learn about management. Indeed the great age of management as a discipline is probably still ahead. But the "heroic age" in which the discipline was founded is behind us. It lay in the quarter century before World War II. Then the basic thinking was being done by such men as the Frenchman Fayol, the Britishers Ian Hamilton and Urwick, and the American Alfred Sloan at General Motors, to name only a few of the pioneers. They made possible the great organizing feats of World War II in all combatant countries. Since then, in business and government as well as in the military, we have, by and large, only refined what was first learned in the 20s and 30s and first applied in the early 40s.[4]

There are some managers who have an intuitive and workable approach to the management process. Unfortunately, only a few of these managers exist. Thus the only realistic method of acquiring managerial skills is through management development. However, management development has yet to be perfected and is not without its problems. Robert J. House, executive director of the McKinsey Foundation for Management Research, examined over 400 programs concerned with management development and concluded as follows: "These programs have contributed little or no demonstrable or measurable effects on business performance or manager behavior."[5]

The major problem associated with developing managers is defining exactly what should be taught. Myles Mace has summarized the situation as follows:

> For the purposes of developing executives in individual organizations, no universally applicable list of quantities or qualities was found during the course of this study. . . . The executive capacities and skills required in each situation will vary, and the determination of what is required must be arrived at in terms of the working environment in which they are exercised.[6]

---

[4] Peter F. Drucker, *The Age of Discontinuity* (New York: Harper and Row Publishers, 1969), pp. 198–99.

[5] Robert J. House, "Most Management Training Misses the Mark," *Iron Age*, July 7, 1966, p. 43.

[6] Myles L. Mace, *The Growth and Development of Executives* (Boston: Division of Research, Harvard Business School, 1950), pp. 189–90.

ORGANIZATION DEVELOPMENT

In recent years, the term organization development (OD) has become widely used to describe the use of behavioral techniques for improving the management of change and conflict. Specifically, OD is: (1) A planned, systematic program initiated by an organization's management; (2) with the aim of making the organization more effective; (3) through the use of a variety of methods designed to change organizational behavior; (4) and based upon the assumption that organizational effectiveness is enhanced to the extent that the program facilitates the integration of individual and organizational objectives.[7]

Sensitivity training is frequently used in OD programs and is designed to make one more aware of oneself and one's impact on others. Sensitivity training involves a group, normally called a Training group or T-group, which meets and has no agenda or particular focus. As each member engages in dialogue with the group, he or she is encouraged to learn about himself or herself and others. The objectives of sensitivity training are to:

1. Increase self-insight and self-awareness concerning the participant's behavior and its meaning in a social context.

2. Increase sensitivity to the behavior of others.

3. Increase awareness and understanding of the types of processes that facilitate or inhibit group functioning and the interactions between different groups.

4. Heighten diagnostic skill in social, interpersonal, and intergroup situations.

5. Increase the participant's ability to intervene successfully in inter- or intragroup situations so as to increase member satisfactions, effectiveness, or output.

6. Increase the participant's ability to analyze continually his or her own interpersonal behavior for the purpose of helping himself or herself and others achieve more effective and satisfying interpersonal relationships.[8]

Although sensitivity training sessions have no agenda, there is a desired pattern of events. First, the group meets with no directive leadership patterns, no authority positions, no formal agenda, and no power and status positions. Therefore, a vacuum exists. Next feedback

---

[7] James L. Gibson, John M. Ivancevich, and James H. Donnelly, Jr., *Organizations: Structure, Processes, Behavior*, rev. ed. (Dallas: Business Publications, Inc., 1973), p. 371.

[8] John P. Campbell and Marvin D. Dunnette, "Effectiveness of T-Group Experiences in Managerial Training and Development," *Psychological Bulletin*, vol. 70, no. 2 (August 1968), pp. 73–104. Copyright 1968 by the American Psychological Association. Reprinted by permission.

on the present behavior of the group occurs. From this feedback and from limited guidance given to the group by the trainer, a feeling of mutual trust follows. In the third stage, openness and mutual trust emerge as the members of the group serve as resources to one another. Collaborative behavior develops in the third stage. Finally the group explores the relevance of the experience as it relates to their own individual organization.

Sensitivity training has suffered many misconceptions and misunderstandings. Chris Argyris attempted to correct some of the misunderstandings by outlining what sensitivity training is not. Basically he feels that sensitivity training is not:

1. A set of hidden, manipulative processes used to brainwash individuals into thinking, believing, and feeling the way someone might want them to without realizing what is happening to them.
2. An educational process guided by a leader who is covertly in control and hides this fact from the participants by some means.
3. Designed to suppress conflict and get everyone to like one another.
4. An attempt to teach people to be callous, disrespectful of society, and to dislike those who live a less open life.
5. Psychoanalysis, nor intensive group therapy.
6. Necessarily dangerous, but must focus on feelings.
7. A guarantee that a participant who attends a session will change behavior.[9]

In order for sensitivity training to be effective, some guidelines need to be followed in its use. These are summarized below:

1. The trainer(s) providing the training should be closely evaluated.
2. Trainees should be carefully screened.
3. Trainees should know in advance the nature of the training.
4. The training should be administered to each individual participant outside the normal work group.

Finally, sensitivity training has been emotionally criticized and defended as to its relative value for organizations. Research findings are both positive and negative. Marvin Dunnette and John Campbell summarize the present state of research on sensitivity training as follows:

> Laboratory education has not been shown to bring about any marked change in one's standing on objective measures of attitudes, values, outlooks, interpersonal perceptions, self-awareness, or interpersonal sensitivity. In spite of these essentially negative results on objective

---

[9] Chris Argyris, "T-Groups for Organizational Effectiveness," *Harvard Business Review*, March–April 1964, pp. 68–70.

FIGURE 16–3
The Managerial Grid

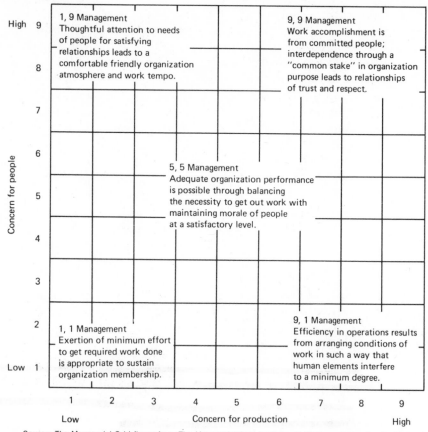

Source: The Managerial Grid figure from *The Managerial Grid*, by Rober R. Blake and Jane Srygley Mouton. Houston: Gulf Publishing Company, Copyright © 1964, p. 10. Reproduced with permission.

measures, individuals who have been trained by laboratory education methods are more likely to be seen as changing their job behavior than are individuals in similar job settings who have not been trained.[10]

Dunnette and Campbell use the word laboratory training to be synonymous with sensitivity training. At the present, more research is needed before a final judgment can be made on the value of sensitivity training.

Another approach used in OD is grid training. Grid training is an extension of the Managerial Grid which was discussed in Chapter 10. The Managerial Grid is shown again in Figure 16–3.

[10] Marvin D. Dunnette, and John P. Campbell, "Laboratory Education Impact on People and Organizations," *Industrial Relattons*, October 1968, p. 23.

The methodology used in grid training can be divided into six phases which are summarized below:

1. Laboratory-seminar training—This phase is designed to introduce the participant to the Managerial Grid concepts and material. Each manager determines where he or she falls on the Managerial Grid.
2. Team development—Work groups determine the ground rules and relationships necessary for 9,9 management.
3. Intergroup development—This phase involves establishing the ground rules and relationships necessary for 9,9 management for group-to-group working relationships.
4. Organizational goal setting—Management by objectives which will be discussed in detail in Chapter 17 is used to establish individual and organizational goals.
5. Goal attainment—Goals established in Phase 4 are pursued.
6. Stabilization—Changes brought about by the other phases are evaluated, and an overall evaluation of the program is made.[11]

As with sensitivity training, grid training has had mixed success in organizations. Again, more research is needed before determinations can be drawn regarding the effectiveness of grid training.

It should be pointed out that traditional training programs can also be used in OD programs.

SUMMARY

Abilities and traits are an individual's personal characteristics used in performing a job and as such they place upper limits on the performance of an individual. Therefore, organizations should make a conscious effort to develop the abilities and traits of its employees.

Human asset accounting is a relatively new idea and involves an attempt to place a value on an organization's human assets and customer goodwill.

Employee development is concerned with the improvement and growth of the capabilities of individuals and groups within the organization. The employee development process involves establishing organizational objectives, determining employee development needs, establishing employee development objectives, conducting employee development programs, and evaluating the employee development programs. Employee development programs should be evaluated based on organizational objectives, employee development objectives, and the results produced by the development programs.

Training is a process that involves the acquisition of skills, con-

---

[11] Robert R. Blake, Jane S. Mouton, Louis B. Barnes, and Larry E. Greiner, "Breakthrough in Organization Development," *Harvard Business Review*, vol. 42, no. 6 (November–December 1964), pp. 137–38.

cepts, rules, or attitudes. Training, as a supportive function of the organization, must be objective-oriented. Some of the methods available for achieving training objectives are on-the-job training, apprenticeship training, classroom training, and programmed instruction.

Management development is a subset of the employee development process and can take many forms including coaching and counseling, understudy assignments, job rotation, individual self-improvement programs, performance appraisals, in-house training programs, and educational and professional training courses.

Organization development (OD) is a process which uses behavioral techniques for improving the management of change and conflict. Sensitivity training is frequently used in OD programs and is designed to make one more aware of oneself and one's impact on others. Grid training, which is an extension of the managerial grid, is another approach used in OD.

REVIEW QUESTIONS

1. What are abilities and traits?

2. What is human asset accounting?

3. Describe the employee development process.

4. What is training? What are some guideposts in defining training objectives?

5. Describe the following methods of training:
    a. On-the-job.
    b. Apprenticeship.
    c. Formal classroom training.
    d. Programmed instruction.

6. Describe the following techniques for management development:
    a. Coaching and counseling.
    b. Job rotation.
    c. Performance appraisals.
    d. Organizational training programs.
    e. Educational and professional training courses.

7. What is organization development?

8. What is sensitivity training?

9. What is grid training?

DISCUSSION QUESTIONS

1. "Today's financial statements do not accurately reflect an organization's assets." Do you agree with this statement? Discuss in detail your reasons.

2. Discuss the following statement: "Managers are born not made."

3. "Why should we train our workers? It is a waste of money because they soon leave and another organization gets the benefit." Discuss.

4. "Everyone needs sensitivity training." Do you agree? Explain.

SELECTED READINGS

Argyris, Chris. "Puzzle and Perplexity in Executive Development." *Personnel Journal*, vol. 39 (1961), pp. 463–65; 483 ff.

Beckhard, R. *Organizational Development: Strategies and Models.* Reading, Mass.: Addison-Wesley, 1969.

Bennis, W. G. *Organizational Development: Its Nature, Origins, and Prospects.* Reading, Mass.: Addison-Wesley, 1969.

Blake, Robert, and Jane Mouton. *The Managerial Grid.* Houston, Tex.: Gulf Publishing Company, 1964.

Crockett, W. J. "Team Building: One Approach to Organizational Development," *Journal of Applied Behavioral Science*, vol. 6 (1970), pp. 291–306.

Haas, Frederick. *Executive Obsolescence.* New York: AMA Research Study 90, American Management Association, 1968.

Kepner, Charles, and Benjamin Tregoe. *The Rational Manager.* New York: McGraw-Hill Book Company, 1965.

Likert, Rensis. *The Human Organization.* New York: McGraw-Hill Book Company, 1967.

Maier, Norman, et al. *Supervisory and Executive Development.* New York: John Wiley and Sons, 1957.

Patten, Thomas H., Jr. *Manpower Planning and the Development of Human Resources.* New York: John Wiley and Sons, 1971.

Trills, Marvin. "Current Activities in Management Training," *Training and Development Journal*, vol. 22 (June 1968), pp. 42–47.

Case 16–1

Development—for what?

The Matlock Corporation began an extensive management development program several years ago. The company's personnel director felt that this program would benefit the company by providing a ready source of promotable individuals for filling vacancies as they occurred in the company. Up until this point, promotions had often been filled by personnel from outside the company.

Managers at all levels of the organization became involved in the management development program. They participated in in-company classes on subjects such as general management and time management. In addition, they were encouraged to improve other skills by taking night courses at the local college at company expense. Many of the managers did in fact enroll in several of the courses offered at the college.

At the time the program was initiated and at subsequent management development meetings, the managers were advised by top management that the management development program was designed to improve their management skills and to qualify them for future promotions within the company.

Paul Martin, a section supervisor, has been with the company for over ten years. He has diligently participated in the management development program and has completed several night courses at the local college. Paul originally felt that this diligence on his part would be rewarded by a promotion when an opening developed. However, twice during the last year outsiders had been hired to fill supervisory positions within Paul's department. In each case, Paul and the other section supervisors had applied for the vacancy and felt that their experience plus the additional knowledge gained through the management development program made them better qualified than the outsider who was hired.

At a recent appraisal interview, Paul brought up this problem for discussion with his department manager. He was told that in each case no supervisor within the company was considered to be qualified for the managerial opening. Paul expressed the opinion that the company management development program was a waste of time for the supervisors if the knowledge and experience gained are not recognized by higher level management. Paul's department manager explained that it takes time to develop a supervisor for higher level responsibility. He also reminded Paul that individuals are rewarded for their self-improvement efforts by extra merit salary increases during the annual performance appraisals.

1. Do you think that Paul has a legitimate complaint?
2. Do you think the organization is "training for training's sake?"
3. How do you think that Paul's supervisor should have handled the problem?

Case 16–2

The frustrated banker

Mr. Albert Tiech is a graduate of a well-known university. After graduation he entered the military service and performed admirably as a combat officer, receiving the Bronze Star in recognition of his achievements. Mr. Tiech received an honorable discharge upon completion of his tour of duty.

Returning to civilian life, he accepted a position of Management Trainee with Suburbia Bank. A relatively small banking enterprise, Suburbia serves the local community in the checking, savings, and loan areas.

The organizational structure of Suburbia Bank consists of the president, vice president, Loan Department, Teller Department, and Bookkeeping Department. The president is Mr. Shy, a paternal individual, who has been successful in satisfying the wants and needs of the employees. Mr. Right serves as vice president. He joined Suburbia Bank many years ago on graduation from high school and has gained much banking experience over the years. He displays an aggressive and arrogant attitude, both on and off the job, and has been given the authority to discipline and terminate employees as necessary. Mr. Shy and Mr. Right have been good friends since their high school days.

The Loan Department, Teller Department, and Bookkeeping Department are managed by middle-aged women who are high school graduates and have been employed by the bank from one to six years.

When Mr. Tiech joined the bank, he believed his training program would be personally handled by the president. His initial assignment was with the Bookkeeping Department, where he was to become familiar with all its functions, while working directly with the department supervisor. For three months, he spent 90 percent of his time filing cancelled checks. The remaining time was devoted to conferences with the supervisor on departmental procedures. Although Miss Jones, the supervisor, was able to efficiently carry out the functional aspects of her position, she was unable to effectively communicate to Mr. Tiech how or why certain policies and procedures were formulated. Mr. Tiech had very little contact with Mr. Shy during this time, and any encounters between them were usually paternal in nature.

At the conclusion of this three-month detail, Mr. Tiech received a message from Mr. Shy's secretary indicating that he was invited to have lunch with the president at the local country club. At lunch, Mr. Tiech was informed that as a result of his evaluation from the supervisor of the Bookkeeping Department his training program would be accelerated. The supervisor's evaluation indicated that Mr. Tiech got along well with the people and answered telephone inquiries effectively. The president informed Mr. Tiech that his next assignment was to be with the Teller Department, where he could observe and learn the functions of that important activity.

Mr. Tiech was assigned a position directly behind the head teller and observed transfer of monies, checks, and deposits. The head teller was very busy and showed Mr. Tiech how things were done but could not, or would not, take the time to explain why. Mr. Tiech was then assigned to a teller post, where he worked for a period of four months, carrying out the same activities as other tellers in the department.

Mr. Tiech began to become frustrated, and his frustration manifested itself by frequent trips to the water fountain and to the restroom. Later this pattern was accelerated, manifesting itself by late arrival for work and extended lunch periods.

At the conclusion of this work assignment, Mr. Tiech requested a conference with the president. He explained to the president that he felt he had sufficient training in the Teller Department and requested an assignment involving more direct management training. Mr. Shy indicated that he was extremely pleased with Mr. Tiech's performance in both previous assignments but felt that he should continue in the Teller Department for a "few more months." He informed Mr. Tiech he would consider his request and give him a decision in a few days. Approximately a week later Mr. Tiech observed that a room which had been used to store office supplies and equipment was being remodeled. Subsequently, he was called by the president and informed that the remodeled room was to be his office. Within a week, Mr. Tiech occupied his new office and was assigned a new function involving the collection of bad debts, including the repossession of automobiles and other items involving delinquent loans. This task required about 20 percent of Mr. Tiech's time, the balance was to be spent working directly with Vice President Right, who would teach him all he knew about banking.

Mr. Right has had occasional meetings with Mr. Tiech during which he expounded on his golf game and various aspects of his personal life. Mr. Tiech attempted to steer these discussions toward banking matters; however, Mr. Right continually put off answering them until a "later time." Currently, Mr. Tiech is sitting in his newly decorated office pondering his dilemma.

1. What do you think of Mr. Tiech's training program?
2. How can a person in Mr. Tiech's position change the situation?
3. Do you think that Mr. Tiech's situation is an exaggeration of the "average training program?"

Objectives

1. *To develop an appreciation for the importance of defining direction for individual organization members.*
2. *To explore some of the methods that can be used for defining direction within the organization.*
3. *To discuss and illustrate how to implement management by objectives.*

GLOSSARY OF TERMS

Hot stove rule A set of guidelines used for constructive discipline which call for administering disciplinary policy quickly, consistently, and impersonally.

Job analysis The process of determining, through observation and study, the pertinent information relating to the nature of a specific job.

Job description Written statement outlining the content and essential requirements of a job.

Management by objectives (MBO) A management system in which the superior and subordinate jointly define the objectives and responsibilities of the subordinate's job and then use these as criteria in evaluating the subordinate's performance.

Objective A statement (used interchangeably with goal) designed to give an organization and its members direction and purpose.

Performance appraisal or evaluation A process used to determine how well an employee is performing.

Performance criteria Standards used to measure success on the job.

Policies Broad, general guides to action which relate to goal attainment.

Procedures A series of related steps or tasks expressed in chronological order to achieve a specific purpose.

Rules Guidelines that require that specific and definite actions be taken or not taken with respect to a given situation.

Strategy A mix of goals and major policies which results in a specific action usually requiring the deployment of scarce resources.

17

Defining direction

> *. . . They are real people in every way except one: they are unclear to what they are trying to accomplish . . .*
>
> *It's like finding an opponent's sword sticking out of your chest, then discovering that a duel has been underway for ten minutes and that you have lost.*
>
> *It's like running in a race with none of the contestants knowing how long it is to be. They can only wonder if it is time to sprint for the wire—it may be a 100-yard dash or it may be the Boston Marathon.*
>
> *It's like being hit by a falling tree, after which the ax man leans over your broken body to whisper TIMBER!*
>
> George S. Odiorne*

THE analogies given above were used by George S. Odiorne in explaining the dilemmas an employee faces when he or she doesn't understand what is expected on the job. The activities and behaviors that an individual believes are necessary in the performance of the job define his or her role perceptions. Defining direction such that the employee properly perceives the job requirements and what is expected is an important element in the management process. The purpose of this chapter is to explore some of the methods that can be used for successfully defining direction within the organization.

OBJECTIVES, POLICY, AND STRATEGY

Objectives, policy, and strategy were discussed in depth in Chapter 4. Objectives or goals are designed to give an organization and its

---

* *Management and the Activity Trap,* New York: Harper & Row, Publishers, 1974, p. 29.

members direction and purpose. Policies are broad, general guides to action which relate to goal attainment. Policies indicate the intentions of the top levels of management.

Policies aid in preventing deviation from the desired course of action. Policies provide communication channels between the organizational units, thus facilitating the delegation process. Policies ensure that the different elements within the organization are all operating under the same ground rules and within the same boundaries.

Procedures and rules are both subsets of policies. A procedure is a series of related steps or tasks expressed in chronological order to achieve a specific purpose. Procedures define in step-by-step fashion the methods by and through which policies are achieved. Rules require that specific and definite actions be taken or not taken with respect to a given situation. Unlike procedures, rules do not specify sequence.

Finally, strategy is a mix of goals and major policies which results in a specific action usually requiring the deployment of scarce resources. Strategies outline the basic approach to be followed in reaching goals.

Objectives, policies, procedures, rules, and strategy are all used to define direction for the organization. They provide a framework for defining managerial and individual employee direction. It is important to remember that motivation is goal-directed behavior. Thus, the possibilities of improved motivation and increased performance are enhanced by defining direction. The following sections present specific approaches for defining individual direction in the organization.

JOB DESCRIPTIONS

A job description is the end result of job analysis. Job analysis is the process of determining, through observation and study, the pertinent information relating to the nature of a specific job. A job description is a written statement outlining the contents and essential requirements of a job. Most job descriptions contain three general parts: "a summary statement of duties, responsibilities, and working conditions; the details of the key tasks and responsibilities; and the qualification requirements for employees in that job."[1]

Job descriptions have been greatly criticized for their use in or-

---

[1] Donald P. Crane, *Personnel Management: A Situational Approach* (Belmont, Calif.: Wadsworth Publishing Company, Inc., 1974), p. 330.

ganizations. Many managers claim that they already know the requirements of the jobs they are managing and, therefore, do not need
formalized, written requirements. A research study conducted by
Norman R. F. Maier was presented in Chapter 13 which illustrates
the fallacy of this type of managerial thinking. The results of that study
are again presented in Table 17–1 for emphasis and convenience.
Maier's study demonstrates major discrepancies between the superior's and the subordinate's definition of the subordinate's job.

However, some criticisms of job descriptions are justified. Many
organizations have made them overly formal and meaningless in content. Furthermore, job descriptions can be misused in order to limit
the scope of the job. "It's not part of my job description" is too frequently expressed in organizations. In addition, many organizations

TABLE 17–1
Agreement between superior-subordinate on subordinate's job

Job factors	Almost no agreement	Agreement on less than half	Agreement on about half	Agreement on more than half	Agreement on all or almost all
Job duties	3.4%	11.6%	39.1%	37.8%	8.1%
Job requirements	7.0	29.3	40.9	20.5	
Future changes	35.4	14.3	18.3	16.3	18.7
Job performance obstacles	38.4	29.8	23.6	6.4	1.7

Source: Norman R. F. Maier, Richard Hoffman, John J. Hoover, and William H. Reed, *Superior-Subordinate Com-munication in Management* (New York: American Management Association. AMA Research Study 52, 1961), p. 10.

do not keep job descriptions current. In order to provide direction,
the job description must be relevant in terms of the information it
provides, and this requires periodic review and updating. One approach designed to minimize many of the above problems is for the
employee, rather than management, to write the job description.

PERFORMANCE CRITERIA

Performance criteria can also be used to define direction for individuals in an organization. Performance criteria are the standards
used to measure success on the job. The difficulties and potential
methods of establishing performance criteria were discussed in depth
in Chapter 14. The value of establishing performance criteria for jobs
is that they establish the expected level of performance. Implement-

ing job descriptions and performance standards for jobs is the first step in defining direction.

PERFORMANCE APPRAISAL

Performance appraisal systems are normally designed to meet three basic purposes:

1. They provide systematic judgments to support salary increases, promotions, transfers, and sometimes demotions or terminations.
2. They are a means of telling a subordinate how he is doing, and suggesting needed changes in his behavior, attitudes, skills, or job knowledge; they let him know "where he stands" with the boss.
3. They also are being increasingly used as a basis for the coaching and counseling of the individual by the superior.[2]

Ideally, performance appraisal should be directly related to the performance criteria of the job. Under this ideal situation, performance appraisal would be relatively simple, requiring only that actual performance be compared to the criteria or standard. However, as was discussed in Chapter 14, setting relevant and objectively measurable criteria is very difficult for many jobs. In such situations performance appraisals are often based on personal characteristics and other subjective criteria.

The assumption made in this type of performance appraisal is that there are certain personal characteristics which lead to increased performance. It is further assumed that these characteristics can be perceived and isolated; they can be evaluated; and they should be rewarded. Some of these characteristics are integrity, dependability, work quality, attitude, initiative, judgment, responsibility, attendance, potential for growth, and others.

The difficulties of a performance appraisal system based on personal characteristics are numerous. Managers resist the process. The underlying reason seems to be that it places the manager in the position of being the judge and the employee in the position of being the defendant. Another problem is the temptation of the appraiser to favor friends and close associates. Because it is natural for one to perceive favorable characteristics in friends, the appraiser may never realize favoritism is interfering. Despite all the problems, the fact remains that performance appraisal systems based on personal characteristics and subjective evaluations are still in widespread use.

Figure 17–1 summarizes many of the more commonly used methods of performance appraisal.

---

[2] Douglas McGregor, "An Uneasy Look at Performance Appraisal," *Harvard Business Review*, September–October 1972, pp. 133–34.

FIGURE 17–1
Selected methods of performance appraisal

Method of appraisal	Description of method
1. Critical incident appraisal	Reviewer keeps records of actual incidents of positive and negative behaviors. These records are then reviewed with the employee during the performance review.
2. Essay appraisal	Reviewer writes a paragraph describing strengths, weaknesses, and so on, of the individual.
3. Forced choice rating	Under this method, the reviewer must choose one statement from a group of statements that best describes an employee's performance in a particular area.
4. Graphic rating scale	A scale (outstanding, above average, or unsatisfactory) is used to evaluate an individual on various factors.
5. Management by Objectives	The employee's performance is evaluated relative to the attainment of certain pre-agreed-upon objectives. MBO is discussed in detail in the following sections of this chapter.
6. Ranking methods	This method involves comparing the performance of individuals and is highly subjective.
7. Work-standards technique	Techniques described in Chapter 14 are used to set performance standards that are subsequently used for evaluation.

MANAGEMENT BY OBJECTIVES (MBO)

One approach to resolving the problems of performance appraisal based on subjective data is the concept of management by objectives. Peter Drucker was one of the first to popularize management by objectives.[3] Drucker proposed that organizations should set objectives and measure the results of its performance in the following areas: market standing, innovation, productivity, physical and financial resources, profitability, manager performance and development, worker performance and attitude, and public responsibility.

MBO is a philosophy of management that is based on converting organizational goals into personal goals. It is based on the assumption

---

[3] Peter Drucker, *The Practice of Management* (New York: Harper & Brothers, 1954).

FIGURE 17–2
The MBO process

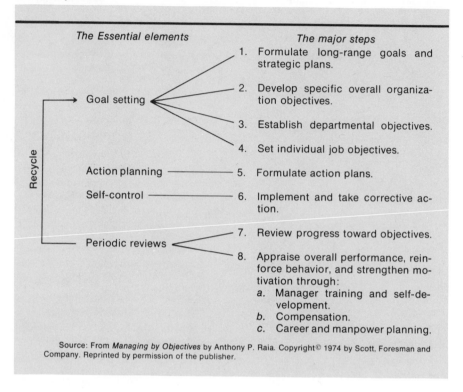

Source: From *Managing by Objectives* by Anthony P. Raia. Copyright© 1974 by Scott, Foresman and Company. Reprinted by permission of the publisher.

that establishing personal goals elicits employee commitment, which leads to performance. The MBO process is summarized in Figure 17–2.

MBO has been called "management by results," "goals and controls," "work planning and review," and "goals management." Drucker actually called the system "management by objectives and self-control." However, all these programs are similar and follow the same basic process.

Goal setting

The goal setting process in MBO is best accomplished by using the cascade approach to goal setting that was discussed in Chapter 4. Figure 17–3 summarizes that process.

Establishing objectives from the top to bottom creates an integrated hierarchy of objectives throughout the entire organization. It ensures

FIGURE 17–3
Cascade approach to objective setting

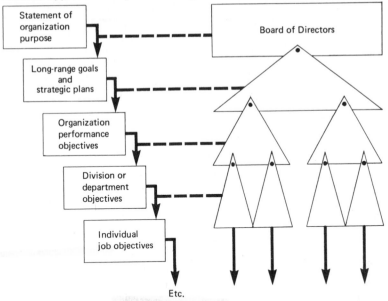

Source: From *Managing by Objectives* by Anthony P. Raia. Copyright© 1974 by Scott, Foresman and Company. Reprinted by permission of the publisher.

that the various levels within the organization have a common direction.

In MBO, the objective-setting process requires a high degree of participation and collaboration among the various levels of the organization. This results in several benefits. First, the individuals at each level in the organization become more aware of overall goals and objectives. The better one understands the overall goals and objectives, the better will be one's understanding of his or her role in the total organization. MBO also requires that the goals for an individual be jointly set by the individual and the superior. Such an approach results in "give and take" negotiating sessions between the individual and the superior. Furthermore, achieving self-formulated objectives can improve motivation and, thus, job performance.

In setting goals for individual managers, four separate areas of managerial performance must be addressed. The first area includes the routine or regular duties and responsibilities of the manager. Performance in these duties is usually measured on the basis of exceptions (management by exception) or through periodic reviews. For example, if there are constant errors occurring in the routine duties

FIGURE 17–4
Types of goals in MBO

Type	How to measure	When to measure
Routine or regular duties and responsibilities	By exception	When exceptions occur or with an annual review
Problem solving..............	Solutions as promised in time	At the promised solution date
Innovative	By stages of commitment	As each stage is completed
Personal development.....	By stages of commitment	As each stage is completed

and responsibilities, then the manager would be evaluated poorly. The job description should define most of the objectives in this area.

The second area is concerned with the problem-solving activities of a manager. Performance is measured here on the basis of promised solution dates.

The third area covers innovative activity. This area includes such things as projects which raise performance, new ideas, new systems or developmental programs. Projects in this area are generally long-term and should be measured by stages of commitment as each stage is completed.

The final area for setting individual managerial objectives is personal development objectives. Potential personal development objectives might be aimed at improving technical competence or increasing managerial skills. The first three areas of goal setting — routine, problem-solving, innovative — are largely aimed at organizational goals. Including personal development objectives integrates individual needs with organizational goals. This leads to a higher degree of motivation and commitment. Thus the importance of personal development objectives lies "in their potential to improve current performance, to combat technological and managerial obsolescence, to prepare the individual for additional responsibility and advancement, and to increase his level of motivation and commitment to his total set of job objectives."[4] Personal development goals should be measured by stages of commitment as each stage is completed. Figure 17–4 summarizes the four classes of goals for individual managers.

Goal setting in MBO is difficult, and problems occur frequently.

---

[4] Anthony P. Raia, *Managing by Objectives* (Glenview, Ill.: Scott, Foresman and Company, 1974), p. 51.

FIGURE 17–5
Guidelines for establishing goals

1. Adapt your objectives directly to organizational goals and strategic plans. Do not *assume* that they support higher level management objectives.

2. Quantify and target the results whenever possible. Do not formulate objectives whose attainment cannot be measured or at least verified.

3. Test your objectives for challenge and achievability. Do not build in cushions to hedge against accountability for results.

4. Adjust the objectives to the availability of resources and the realities of organizational life. Do not keep your head either in the clouds or in the sand.

5. Establish reliable performance reports and milestones that measure progress toward the objective. Do not rely on instinct or crude benchmarks to appraise performance.

6. Put your objectives in writing and express them in clear, concise, and unambiguous statements. Do not allow them to remain in loose or vague terms.

7. Limit the number of statements of objectives to the *most* relevant key result areas of your job. Do not obscure priorities by stating too many objectives.

8. Communicate your objectives to your subordinates so that they can formulate their own job objectives. Do not demand that they do your goal setting for you.

9. Review your statements with others to assure consistency and mutual support. Do not fall into the trap of setting your objectives in a vacuum.

10. Modify your statements to meet changing conditions and priorities.

11. Do not continue to pursue objectives which have become obsolete.

Source: From *Managing by Objectives* by Anthony P. Raia. Copyright © 1974 by Scott, Foresman and Company. Reprinted by permission of the publisher.

The guidelines offered in Figure 17–5 should help in establishing meaningful goals.

Action planning

Outlining how the established goals are going to be achieved by the individual is the purpose of action plans. The steps required by an action plan are as follows:

1. Determine the major activities necessary to accomplish the objective.
2. Establish subactivities necessary for accomplishing the major activities.
3. Assign primary responsibility for each activity and subactivity.
4. Estimate time requirements necessary to complete each activity and subactivity.
5. Identify additional resources required for each activity and subactivity.

Self-control

After establishing goals and developing an action plan, each individual is allowed to pursue his or her goals in his or her own manner. Therefore MBO is largely a system of self-control. Obviously, there are policy constraints on the individual, but basically a person achieves the goals through his or her abilities and effort.

Support is provided from the upper levels of management by allocating necessary resources and by providing support services such as training. Generally when MBO is used by an organization, MacGregor's Theory Y assumptions are required. Proponents of MBO argue that Theory Y assumptions are necessary to create a motivating environment. Furthermore, MBO appeals to the higher order needs in Maslow's need hierarchy and provides the motivational factors in Herzberg's maintenance-motivation theory. MBO is also consistent with most of the other modern theories of motivation (which were discussed in Chapter 9).

Periodic progress reviews

Periodic progress reviews are an essential ingredient of MBO. Personal feedback is provided on actual performance as compared to planned performance (objectives). The importance of this personal feedback cannot be underestimated.

In a study of one organization, it was determined that individuals who received periodic progress reviews improved their average performance, while other individuals in the same organization who received no feedback on their performance actually decreased in performance.[5] In a series of studies at the General Electric Company, it was determined that increasing the amount of feedback from foremen to their subordinates increased the subordinates' performance. These same studies further revealed that the more specific, relevant, and

---

[5] J. A. Weitz, J. Antoinetti, and S. R. Wallace, "The Effect of Home Office Contact on Sales Performance," *Personnel Psychology*, vol. 7 (1954), pp. 381–84.

FIGURE 17-6
Guidelines for improving performance appraisals

1. Performance tends to improve when specific objectives are established for the job.
2. The participation of a subordinate in setting his own performance objectives yields favorable results.
3. Mutual goal setting by the superior and the subordinate produces positive results.
4. Criticism tends to have a negative impact on the attainment of objectives. As a consequence, defensiveness can result in inferior performance.
5. Praise has little, if any, effect on the achievement of goals.
6. Coaching is best done on a day-to-day basis when related to specific behavior and results, not once a year.
7. Interviews intended primarily to improve performance should not at the same time deal with salary and promotion.
8. Separate performance evaluations are generally required for different purposes.

Source: From *Managing by Objectives* by Anthony P. Raia. Copyright © 1974 by Scott, Foresman and Company. Reprinted by permission of the publisher.

timely the feedback, the greater the positive effects on performance.[6]

Anthony P. Raia has provided some specific guidelines for improving performance appraisals which are listed in Figure 17-6.

The manner in which the feedback is given is important. If the manager provides the feedback in a hostile manner, then performance may be reduced. The purpose of performance appraisal is to compare planned performance to actual performance and should not be used to degrade the individual. The results of performance appraisals should aid in increasing future performance.

The periodic performance reviews should reflect the individual's performance under the MBO system. This appraisal is based on his performance toward specified objectives. Although it depends on the specific situation, MBO performance appraisals are generally suggested for two or three times a year.

Individual performance reviews

Individual performance reviews include not only an individual's performance under the MBO system, but they also include an assess-

---

[6] L. Miller, "The Use of Knowledge of Results in Improving the Performance of Hourly Operators," General Electric Company, Behavioral Research Service, 1965.

ment of the individual's potential for advancement, performance as a manager if already a manager, and personal qualifications and characteristics. This type of review should serve as a basis for personal development, compensation, and career and human resource planning.

There are many reasons why individual performance reviews should not be based solely on the MBO system. First, luck or misfortune can play a significant role in the attainment of specific objectives. Second, defining all the duties of an individual in terms of specific objectives is almost impossible. Third, the MBO system emphasizes performance in the present job. Human resource planning requires an evaluation of future potential. Finally, MBO emphasizes

FIGURE 17–7
Individual performance reviews

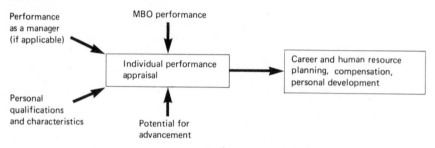

the accomplishment of specific, short-term goals. Long-term implications of short-term accomplishments must also be evaluated.

Figure 17–7 depicts graphically the total relationships that exist in the individual performance review. It is generally recommended that individual performance reviews be given on an annual basis.

Salary recommendations

Studies have also shown that it is undesirable to deal with salary and promotion recommendations during the individual performance review.[7] Primarily the reason for this recommendation is that it places the individual who is being evaluated in a defensive position and prohibits or blocks learning. As previously stated, the individual performance appraisals should be used as part of the development process. This does not imply that salaries and promotions should not be based on performance but that annual salary review sessions should be held separately from the individual performance review.

_____
[7] Ibid.

Implementing MBO

George S. Odiorne has presented three approaches to implementing MBO within an organization—authoritarian, persuasion, and education.[8] No one method seems to fit all situations. The total organizational climate including such factors as power and authority, the organization structure, and the people involved determine the optimum method of implementation.

Under the authoritarian method of implementation, the top manager merely decides that MBO should be used and dictates that it will be used. Several conditions must exist in order for this approach to be successful. First, the top manager must have the power to implement MBO and be willing to use this power. Second, the lower levels of management must be more dependent on the top manager than the top manager is on them. Third, the lower levels of management must be accustomed to working with unexplained directives from top management. Regardless of the value judgments placed on authoritarian management, implementation of MBO using this method has been successful under the conditions mentioned above.

Persuasion is the technique that Odiorne says has led to the most failures of MBO systems. Basically, persuasion involves an over-selling of the MBO process to management. Speakers or consultants convince management of the benefits of MBO without conveying a clear understanding of the time, effort, and commitment required to install MBO successfully. Persuasion is probably helpful in the initial stages of MBO. However, since the management team usually does not understand the total commitment required, MBO generally fails when persuasion is the only method used.

Education is the most successful method of installing MBO. The features of this method of installing MBO are summarized by Odiorne as follows:

> Training should produce behavior change, and training in MBO is measurable. It can be readily determined if the training worked: Did the trainees set objectives or didn't they?
>
> The quality of the results can be noted clearly. The course may suggest, for example, that a manager should establish three classes of objectives. The effect on the manager can be checked by examining sample goals statements.
>
> MBO comprises a sound basis for relating training to the job. Some training sessions require students to set objectives on their job as part of the course; they learn by doing what they are being taught.
>
> MBO provides a vehicle for teaching more general management

---

[8] George S. Odiorne, "The Politics of Implementing MBO," *Business Horizons*, June 1974, pp. 13–21.

education. It can be the framework for teaching motivational methods, management functions (organizing, planning, and controlling), and such interpersonal skills as coaching, counseling, and listening.

MBO can teach interpersonal skills that can be applied on the job, rather than skills which the boss will not permit or endorse when the trainee returns to the desk or plant floor. This is especially true if the boss attends the session or is used as a trainer.

MBO can reinforce company objectives rather than become, as it does in many behavioral courses, an internal reform movement to overcome the organization's autocratic or bureaucratic tendencies or to produce some new kind of organizational form.

MBO is capable of maintaining a high level of trainee interest, since it deals with the real world of work and world problems, and with interpersonal and group relations problems.

Conceptually, it is easy to learn, for MBO training courses ask people to "talk shop"; they have a tendency to do this whether they are in training or not. Except for courses in which the trainers have worked hard at obscuring the obvious, the language is operational and practical.

The basic framework of MBO permits it to take a behavioral or logical systems direction without appearing contradictory or mutually exclusive. This means that it can appeal to the personnel and training men in the organization, as well as to the engineer, controllers, and dollar-centered managers.

Both insiders and outsiders can be used as trainers. The insiders have more knowledge of the business and can deal with real world problems, and the outsiders can be briefed sufficiently to relate to the world of the trainee.[9]

Successful implementation of MBO requires an understanding of such factors as the power structure in the organization, the organization form — centralized or decentralized, the reward systems, the informal organization structure, and the total organizational climate.

Real MBO

Before departing from the subject of MBO, its basic requirements should be summarized. Many organizations proudly proclaim to have successfully implemented MBO when, in fact, they have met very few of the actual requirements. In its simplest form an MBO system must meet the following three minimum requirements:

1. Individuals are evaluated by results (objectives).
2. Individual objectives are known in advance.
3. Individual objectives are jointly set by the subordinate and the superior.

---

[9] Ibid., pp. 15–16.

Frequently the joint goal setting process is successfully completed only to have the individual evaluated on the basis of personality characteristics. In addition, superiors can set objectives and then ask the subordinate "You agree don't you?" However, if all of the minimum requirements are not met, then MBO will probably fail.

CONSTRUCTIVE DISCIPLINE

Constructive discipline is another method of defining direction for individuals within organizations. This method is often not effec-

FIGURE 17–8
Hot stove rule

1. The hot stove burns immediately. Disciplinary policies should be administered quickly. There should be no question of cause and effect.
2. The hot stove gives a warning and so should discipline.
3. The hot stove consistently burns everyone that touches it. Discipline should be consistent.
4. The hot stove burns everyone in the same manner regardless of who they are. Discipline must be impersonal. People are disciplined for what they have done and not because of who they are.

tively used because the disciplinary policies are applied in a primitive manner. Correcting behavior should be the primary purpose of discipline, not administering punishment for the sake of punishment.

Constructive discipline uses light penalties for the first offense and progressively harsher penalties for repetitions. Generally, after a certain number of offenses — regardless of whether they are the same offense — the employee is discharged. A suggested schedule of steps to be used as a policy for dealing with employees who repeatedly require discipline is shown below.

1. Oral warning that is not recorded in employee's personnel records.
2. Oral warning that is recorded in employee's personnel records.
3. Written reprimand.
4. Suspension.
5. Discharge.

Of course, exceptions occur in the above steps in that some offenses, such as fighting or drinking on the job, are subject to immediate termination. Furthermore, labor organizations play an important role in establishing disciplinary policies.

Several specific guidelines for administering discipline are contained in the so-called Hot Stove Rule shown in Figure 17–8.

If the Hot Stove Rule is followed and discipline is applied in a constructive manner, it can serve as an excellent method of defining or at least correcting direction.

SUMMARY

One of the components necessary for good performance is employees' understanding of their jobs. Objectives, policies, and strategy serve to define direction for the total organization. Procedures and rules also define direction for individuals within the organization.

Job analysis is the process of determining, through observation and study, the pertinent information relating to the nature of a specific job. A job description is a written statement outlining the contents and essential requirements of a job and is the end result of job analysis.

Performance criteria are the standards used to measure success on the job. Implementing job descriptions and performance standards for jobs is the first step in defining direction. Performance appraisals let the subordinate know where he or she stands with his or her superior and, if properly used, can improve performance.

Management by objectives (MBO) is a philosophy of management that is based on converting organizational goals into personal goals. It assumes that commitment which leads to performance is established by the superior and subordinate jointly setting individual goals. The basic elements of the MBO process are goal setting, action planning, self-control, and periodic reviews. In its simplest form a MBO system must meet the following requirements: Individuals must be evaluated by results (objectives); individual objectives must be known in advance; and individual objectives must be jointly set by the subordinate and the superior.

The final method for defining direction is constructive discipline.

Constructive discipline should have as its primary purpose correcting behavior. Under constructive discipline lighter penalties are used for the first offense and progressively harsher penalties are used for repetitions. The Hot Stove Rule provides specific guidelines for administering discipline.

REVIEW QUESTIONS

1. What role do objectives, policies, procedures, rules, and strategy play in defining direction in the organization?

2. Define job analysis and job description. How are they used in defining direction?

3. Describe the three basic purposes of performance appraisal systems.

4. Develop in detail the steps in the MBO process.

5. What are the types of goals in MBO? How and when are these goals measured?

6. Describe three approaches to implementing MBO.

7. What are the three minimum requirements of an MBO system?

8. What is the Hot Stove Rule and what role does it play in defining direction?

DISCUSSION QUESTIONS

1. Do you think MBO would work in an academic institution? Discuss.

2. "People work harder if they have specific and personal goals." Do you agree or disagree?

3. Discuss the following statement: "Job descriptions for management jobs are a waste of time."

4. Should performance appraisals and salary reviews be held simultaneously?

5. Can you think of some potential reasons why MBO might fail in a given organization?

SELECTED READINGS

Bryan, J. F., and E. A. Locke. "Goal Setting as a Means of Increasing Motivation," *Journal of Applied Psychology*, vol. 51 (1967), pp. 274–77.

Carroll, Stephen J., Jr., and Henry L. Tosi, Jr. *Management by Objectives Applications and Research.* New York: Macmillan Company, 1973.

Cummings, L. L., and Donald P. Schwab. *Performance in Organizations: Determinants and Appraisal.* Glenview, Ill.: Scott, Foresman and Company, 1973.

Drucker, Peter. *The Practice of Management.* New York: Harper and Brothers, 1954.

House, R. *Management Development: Design, Evaluation, and Implementation.* Ann Arbor, Mich.: Bureau of Industrial Relations, University of Michigan, 1967.

Maier, N. R. *The Appraisal Interview: Objectives, Methods, and Skills.* New York: John Wiley & Sons, Inc., 1958.

McGregor, Douglas. "An Uneasy Look at Performance Appraisal," *Harvard Business Review* (September–October 1972), pp. 133–38.

Odiorne, George S. "The Politics of Implementing MBO," *Business Horizons* (June 1974), pp. 13–21.

Raia, Anthony P. *Managing by Objectives.* Glenview, Ill.: Scott, Foresman, and Company, 1974.

Wickens, J. D. "Management by Objectives: An Appraisal," *Journal of Management Studies* (October, 1968), pp. 365–79.

Case 17–1

Can MBO work?

Situation: You are a consultant to the president of a marketing company. It is fairly small and has not grown very rapidly over the years, though it has gained a reputation for innovative and effective approaches to market research and advertising. The organization consists mainly of intelligent and creative people who seem to love their work. The current president was brought in a year ago. The previous president, who was also the founder and sole owner of the firm, had died and left the company to his two sons. The sons were not interested in getting actively involved with the business, but they wanted to hire someone who had proven his ability to stimulate and guide rapid growth of the organization. The current president had previously managed a shoe manufacturing company through a period of fantastic growth. He enjoys a reputation as an extremely effective manager.

President: I am really frustrated and baffled by my inability to meet my objectives since I came here. My goal for the first year was a 25-percent increase in revenue, which I thought would be easily attainable if we combined some good solid management with the talent and fine reputation of our staff. Instead of a 25-percent increase, we suffered an 8-percent decrease, and that's the first decrease this company has ever had. On top of that, morale around here is at a low ebb right now. I just can't understand it. I know I'm a darn good manager; I've proven that. I have been using the same management philosophies and techniques that have worked so well for me in the past.

Consultant: What sorts of philosophies and techniques have you been applying?

President: The very first thing I did when I took over was to get the whole staff together and talk over our objectives for the year. The main objective, of course, was growth. The 25-percent figure was an understanding between the two owners of the company and myself. Looking back on that staff meeting, I must admit that the staff did not seem overly awed or inspired by that objective, but they didn't fight it either.

Consultant: What did you do next?

President: Well, I knew that if I was to be effective in managing this bunch, we needed to get organized. I could find no written documentation of the organization structure, so I decided to start from scratch. I asked every member of the staff to write his or her own job description. The results were really disappointing. Most of them didn't even know what a job description should consist of, and nobody seemed to put much effort into it. Anyway, the job descriptions showed that the individuals perceived themselves as having very broad and vague responsibilities. There was a lot of overlap, as if everybody thought he or she should be involved in just about everything.

Consultant: What did you do about it?

President: I decided that if we were going to get organized, I would have to develop the structure myself. I put a lot of time and thought into it and came up with a functional division of labor. I set up a Client Development Department (which is really our sales effort), a Market Research Department, and a Media Systems Department (which is really advertising). I assigned individual staff members to the three departments based on my perceptions of their interests and talents and our needs. I designated one person in each department to serve as departmental manager and report directly to me.

Consultant: How was that accepted by the staff?

President: Hard to tell. Nobody said very much at the time.

Consultant: What else have you done?

President: I worked directly with each of the department managers in writing their new job descriptions and had them do the same thing with each person in their departments. Then I introduced an MBO program in which every individual worked with his or her immediate superior in setting personal goals for the remainder of this year that would contribute to the overall goal of 25-percent growth. I also developed a procedure for following up on performance for each individual on a quarterly basis.

Consultant: How did that work out?

President: Not too well so far I'm afraid. I can't seem to get the departmental managers to deal in objectively measurable goals for themselves or their subordinates. Everything seems so darn vague. I would really like your help with some training on the proper application of MBO, and then maybe we can develop some sort of incentive program based on performance measured against objectives.

1. Why do you feel that this MBO program is going wrong?
2. What type of training would you recommend to the president?
3. What can be done to correct this situation?

Case 17–2

What is the real problem?

In the early part of April, Dick Bradley, the manager of the Adjustment Desk at the First National Bank requested assistance from the Management Consulting Department of the bank, hoping to find how to motivate his employees. The Adjustment Desk is involved in the correction of errors between banks, particularly on cash letter items. It seems the Adjustment Desk's production had fallen steadily since February. Dick had not asked for assistance sooner because he had initially thought that this was just a temporary lull. The consultant assigned to this project knew Dick and knew his style of management which was strictly "being fair to all people and getting the work out." Dick was a likeable fellow and easy to work with. Therefore it was assumed the problem was not with Dick. At the start of the project, the consultant met with Dick and the following conversation resulted:

Dick: Come on in, have a seat.

Consultant: Hey, Dick, how are you today?

Dick: Fine. I guess you're here to look us over.

Consultant: Yeah, seems your production is down, and has been for awhile.

Dick: Yes, it started down in February and has yet to go back up. That's why I called for you guys.

Consultant: Do you know what the problem might be?

Dick: At first, I thought it was me, but now I believe very strongly that it is the job content. I am hoping you will suggest some job enrichment or whatever it's called.

Consultant: If we decide that it is needed, we can show you how to implement it.

Dick: Well, I sure hope something can be done. The VP is really jumping on me, and I don't know what it is. I'm not a bad guy. Production was pretty good, holding through the end of the year. Then, as you know, I got involved in performance appraisals of the people, and maybe I wasn't devoting enough time to supervision. I don't know what it is, but I sure hope you can help.

Consultant: I'll give it a good look.

The consultant then observed the employees, learned their jobs, and held extensive interviews with all of them. A sample interview with Sam Martin, an employee, is below:

Martin: Well, what are you guys up to now?

Consultant: We're trying to see why production is down in this area. Are you tired of your job or what?

Martin: I am not tired of it. As a matter of fact, it is fairly challenging. You have to know a lot about banking and debits and credits to work in this department.

Consultant: Do you have any idea why the department's production has dropped?

Martin: Frankly, I didn't know it had. I hadn't noticed. I just keep plugging along doing what is "expected" of me. I think all of us do what is really "expected" of us.

Consultant: Think about it and if anything comes up, give me a buzz.

Martin: All right.

It seems that the job is challenging enough and the employees are not really dissatisfied. The manager is fairly likeable and is not causing the employees to "slough off."

1. What is the real problem?
2. How should Dick correct the problem?
3. Do you think that motivation is a scapegoat in this situation?

section five

Operations management

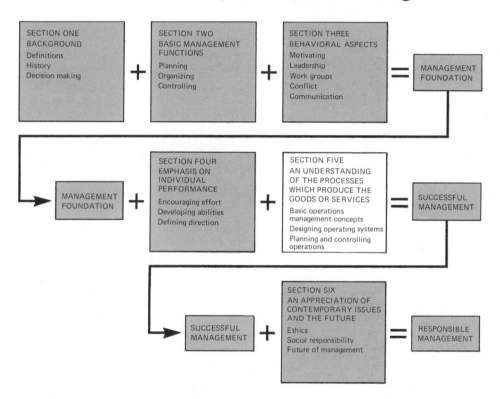

The first three sections of this text concentrated on building a sound foundation for understanding the management process. Section Four, which emphasized individual performance, added to that foundation.

The final tier which must be added to the foundation in order to provide the ingredients necessary for successful management is an understanding of the goods and/or services producing function of the organization—the operations function. The operations function includes the design, operation, and control of the facilities and resources that are directly involved in the production of the organization's goods and/or services. Because most management personnel are either a part of or interact with the operations phase of the organization, and because the operations phase usually involves the largest portion of an organization's financial assets, personnel, and expenditures, it behooves all managers to have a basic understanding of the operations function.

Chapter 18 introduces the topic of operations management. The operations function and its relationship to the other parts of the organization are defined. The concept of productivity and its importance are discussed.

Chapter 19 concentrates on the design of operating systems. The argument is made that the operating system must first be properly designed if the organization is to be efficient. Product service design, process selection, site location, physical layout, and job design are all discussed along with several methods and techniques for accomplishing these tasks.

The final chapter in this section, Chapter 20, is concerned with the planning and controlling of operations. The point is stressed that the operating system must not only be properly designed but that the day-to-day operations must be properly planned and controlled. Production control, inventory control, and quality control are all covered.

Objectives

1. *To introduce the major concepts relating to operations management.*
2. *To explain the role of the operations manager in the organization.*
3. *To define productivity, develop an appreciation for its importance, and explain specific strategies for achieving high organizational productivity.*

GLOSSARY OF TERMS

Operating capabilities Refers to the production capacities and abilities of the organization.

Operating system A system consisting of the processes and activities necessary to transform various inputs into goods and/or services.

Operations management The application of the basic concepts and principles of management to those segments of the organization that produce the goods and/or services.

Productivity Units of output per worker-machine hour or total output/total input.

18

Operations management

Productivity is something of a vogue word in our society today. The President has appointed a commission on productivity; Congress right now is conducting hearings on productivity. Economists measure productivity; they analyze it; they record it. Management traditionally urges more productivity; and labor leaders at times seem to resist it, even though they publicly advocate it. The effect of productivity on the daily lives of everyone is nothing less than enormous; yet few people appreciate it, or even understand it—and even fewer are trying to do anything to increase it.

Richard C. Gerstenberg[*]

AS THE above quote implies, productivity and production are concerns of all areas of society. Operations management which evolved from the field of production or manufacturing management is concerned with the application of the basic concepts and principles of management to those segments of the organization that produce the goods and/or services of the organization. Traditionally the term *production* brings to mind such things as smoke stacks, machine shops, and the manufacture of real goods. Operations management is concerned with the management of the producing function in any organization, whether it is private or public, profit or nonprofit, manufacturing or service. Specifically operations management involves designing the systems of the organization that produce the goods or services and with the planning and controlling of the day-to-day operations which take place within these systems. The overall focus of operations man-

---

[*] "Productivity: Its Meaning for America," *Michigan Business Review* (July 1972), p. 1.

393

agement is the effective integration of resources in the pursuit of organizational goals.[1]

OPERATING SYSTEMS AND ACTIVITIES

Operating systems consist of the processes and activities necessary to transform various inputs into goods and/or services. Operating systems exist in all organizations and are composed of people, material, facilities, and information. The end result of an operating system is to add value by improving, enhancing, or rearranging the inputs. Often this involves bringing inputs together into a new arrangement in such a manner that the inputs can do something that they could not do separately.[2]

The assembly of an automobile represents a combination of separate parts to form a more valuable whole. At other times the operating system involves breaking something down from a larger quantity to smaller quantities which hold more value. A metal shop which fabricates smaller parts from larger sheets of metal or a butcher who produces steaks, hamburger, and other cuts from a side of beef both break down a larger quantity into smaller quantities with more value. A third type of operating system is one which produces services by transforming inputs into more useful outputs. In producing services emphasis is usually placed more on labor and less on materials. For example, a television repair shop uses some materials but the primary value added results from the repairman's labor. Figure 18–1 presents a simplified model of an operating system.

As can be seen in Figure 18–1 the operating system is broader and more inclusive than just the conversion or transformation process. The operating system includes not only the design and operation of the transformation process but also many of the activities necessary to get the various inputs into the transformation process (such as product design and scheduling) and many of the activities necessary to get the outputs out of the transformation process (such as inventory control and materials distribution).

The activities required to manage an operating system can be categorized into two main areas: (1) system design and (2) operations planning and control. The design of an operating system starts with the product design. Product design largely determines the production capabilities needed. Equipment and process selection, site location,

---

[1] Wickham Skinner, "New Directions for Production and Operations Management," *Academy of Management P/OM Division Communication 2,* ed. George J. Gore, July 1972, p. 5.

[2] John A. Reinecke, and William F. Schoell, *Introduction to Business* (Boston: Allyn Bacon, Inc., 1974), p. 183.

FIGURE 18–1
Simplified model of an operating system

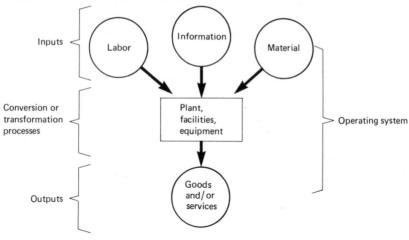

physical layout, and design of work methods are all part of the design phase of operations management. It is obviously impossible to design efficient and effective production systems and facilities without knowing the short- and long-range plans, policies, and strategies of the organization. Therefore, all of the design-related activities of the operating system must be closely coordinated with the overall planning process of the organization.

The operations planning and control phase includes planning and maintaining control over the day-to-day operations. This includes production control (aggregate output planning, resource allocation, and activity scheduling), inventory control, quality control, cost control and improvement, and facility maintenance. The operations planning and control activities must be closely coordinated with the design activities. For instance, the design objectives of the operating process would most likely dictate the most appropriate control system. Figure 18–2 relates specific operations activities to the basic management functions.

The relative importance of the various operating activities varies considerably depending on the nature of the specific operating system. For example, quality control is a much more important factor in producing pharmaceuticals or mechanical parts with close tolerances than when producing toys. Furthermore, not all operations managers work with every component of an operating system. In fact, many operations managers do not come in contact with the operating system until the system has been designed and is already in operation. Of

FIGURE 18–2
Operations activities related to the basic management functions

Basic management function	Related operations activity
Planning.............	Activity scheduling
	Aggregate output planning
	Equipment selection
	Physical layout
	Process selection
	Product design
	Resource allocation
	Site location
Organizing..........	Equipment selection
	Physical layout
	Process selection
	Resource allocation
Motivating	Job design
	Work methods
	Work incentives
Controlling	Cost control and improvement
	Facility maintenance
	Inventory control
	Production control
	Quality control

course, this does not prohibit a redesign of portions of the system. For instance, new work methods might be established or a new scheduling system installed after the operating system has been designed and is functioning. Figure 18–3 shows in detail the components of an operating system.

RELATIONSHIP OF OPERATIONS MANAGEMENT TO OTHER AREAS

In addition to the operations function, most organizations require a marketing function and a finance function. The marketing function generally centers around the sale and distribution of the goods or services produced by the operating system. The function of finance is to provide the funds necessary to support the operations and marketing activities. Not only do these funds come from the sale of the organization's goods and services but also may be acquired through loans, sale of stock, investment income, retained earnings, and so on.

FIGURE 18-3
The operating system

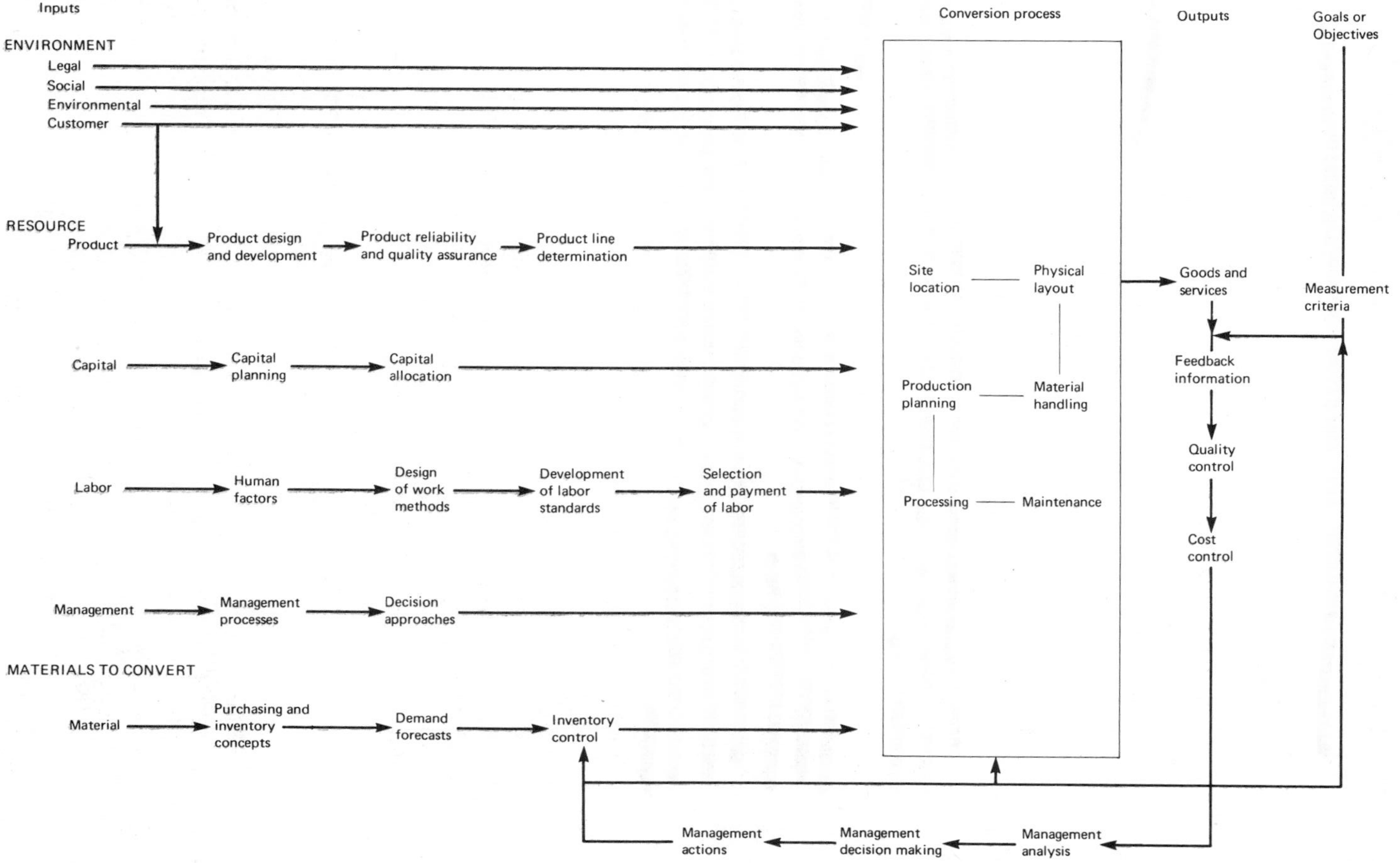

Source: Adapted from Leonard J. Garrett and Milton Silver, *Production Management Analysis*, 2d ed. Copyright 1966, 1973 by Harcourt Brace Jovanovich, Inc., and reproduced with their permission, pp. 24–25.

Many of the activities of the above three functions overlap. For example, product design and packaging are operations functions that directly relate to marketing. Process design and equipment acquisition are operations activities which cannot be undertaken independently of finance. Thus the operations manager must continually coordinate and communicate with the other functional areas of the organizations. In effect, the operations manager must take a "systems view" of the organization when performing his or her activities.

THE IMPORTANCE OF OPERATIONS MANAGEMENT

The production of goods and/or services ordinarily involves the largest portion of an organization's financial assets, personnel, and expenditures. The operations process which produces a good or service also usually consumes an appreciable amount of time. Thus, because of the resources and time consumed by the operations function, the management of this function plays a critical role in achieving the organization's goals.

One direct influence on worker output is the effectiveness of operations managers in (1) building group cohesiveness and individual commitment and (2) making sound technical and administrative decisions. Both of these problems have increased in complexity and importance in recent years. Society wants not only improved productivity but also an enriched work environment, and at the same time, social changes have increased the cultural gap between the new workers and established managers. Thus the human problems confronting operations management have become increasingly important and more difficult.

Most operations managers no longer manage in a stable environment with standard products. Changing technology and a dominant emphasis on low costs have changed the technical and administrative problems confronting the operations manager. The modern operations manager must be concerned not only with low costs but also with product diversity, high quality, short lead times, improved supply dependability, and a rapidly changing technology. As a result, the problems confronting operations managers are more difficult and require substantially greater managerial talent.

In the past the operations area has suffered from an unglamorous image which has made it difficult for organizations to attract, develop, and retain managers capable of high performance. Management cannot wait for these problems to disappear or diminish; positive action including increased attention and emphasis on operations management is necessary.

BASIC TYPES OF OPERATING SYSTEMS

There are two basic types of operating systems. One is based on continuous flows; whereas, the other is based on intermittent flows. Examples of continuous flow systems include assembly lines, chemical plants, paper plants, petroleum refineries, and fast food outlets with standardized products (such as McDonald's). Examples of intermittent flow systems would be special order fabrication shops, hospitals, and dental offices.

The basic type of operating system is generally determined by the certainty of the product or service specifications and by the volume demanded.[3] If a standardized product or service will meet the needs

TABLE 18-1
Type of operating system, volume, and product specification

		Low market volume	High market volume
Certainty of product specification	High	Intermittent production	Continuous production to stock
	Low	Intermittent production to customer orders	Continuous production to customer orders

Source: Adapted from Howard L. Timms and Michael F. Pohlen, *The Production Function in Business*, 3d ed. (Homewood, Ill.: Richard D. Irwin, Inc., 1970), p. 23.

and the desires of the organization's customers, then the product or service lends itself to a continuous flow operating system. On the other hand, if the product or service must be customized, an intermittent system is usually desirable. High volumes are best accommodated by continuous flow systems while low volumes are best handled by intermittent flow systems. Table 18–1 depicts the relationships between type of operating system, volume, and product specification.

Because of economies of scale, specialization of labor, and high equipment utilization, the continuous flow system usually results in lower unit costs than the intermittent flow system. However, continuous flow systems usually require special-purpose equipment which is less flexible and usually more expensive than general-purpose equipment. A continuous flow system therefore usually requires a larger capital investment than does an intermittent flow system.

---

[3] Howard L. Timms and Michael F. Pohlen, *The Production Function in Business*, 3d ed. (Homewood, Ill.: Richard D. Irwin, Inc., 1970), pp. 23–24.

DETERMINING OPERATING CAPABILITIES

The capabilities developed within an operating system should match the requirements of an organization.[4] The organizational requirements are determined by the organization goals and resources and by the environment. Organization purpose and goal setting were discussed in Chapter 4. Because almost all organizations (including service and nonprofit organizations) must operate within certain budgetary constraints, they are all concerned with costs. The extent of their concern for cost is determined for the most part by the technological and competitive characteristics of the firm's environment. Many public service organizations have recently become more cost conscious as private organizations have started to provide direct competition. For example, the number of private hospitals has been increasing. The efficient utilization of resources must be a primary concern of operations managers.

Gene Groff and Jack Muth have outlined three general types of operating environments for firms.[5] The first type of environment is the noncompetitive, monopolistic environment in which success is easily achieved. Even with operating inefficiencies, an organization can thrive in such an environment. Businesses producing patented products often operate in such an environment.

The second type of environment is relatively stable and is characterized by pure competition, a relatively stable technological base, and undifferentiated product designs. The packaging industry, lumber mills, banks, and insurance companies all represent organizations operating in a relatively stable environment. Success in this environment is highly dependent on operating efficiencies.

In the third type of environment, organizations are confronted with rapid change and multifirm competition. Survival depends on innovation and not solely on short-run operating efficiency. Because of the rapid rate of change, the operations area must continually improve current capabilities in order to stay competitive. The development of new products and new methods is also essential. The electronics industry, the plastics industry, and generally the more technical industries operate in this type of environment.

Operating capabilities for a stable environment

Environments characterized by stable designs and price competition still exist for many organizations. In such environments the focus

---

[4] Gene K. Groff, and John F. Muth, *Operations Management: Analysis for Decisions* (Homewood, Ill.: Richard D. Irwin, Inc., 1972), p. 4.

[5] Ibid., pp. 4–10.

of the operations manager is on efficiency in the form of high productivity. High productivity is attained through task specialization. Products are standardized wherever possible in order to keep costs low. High volume production runs are encouraged in order to minimize "changeover" costs. Methods are continually analyzed and perfected. All costs are closely scrutinized and periodically evaluated. In summary, the operations manager in a stable environment is primarily concerned with efficiency and cost reducing activities.

Operating capabilities for a changing environment

Organizations operating in a rapidly changing environment must also change if they are to maintain a competitive position. Change in such an environment normally means new products and new processes as well as improving existing products and services. All of this must be accomplished while maximizing quality and minimizing costs. Thus, organizations operating in a rapidly changing environment must not only be concerned with efficiency but also with product value as measured by the customers. The value attached to a product by the customer is affected by its quality, dependability, delivery time, and its level of technology. In order to attain high product value, emphasis should be placed on research and development and product improvement. The added concern for product value makes the operations manager's job much more complex in a rapidly changing environment than in a stable environment. Figure 18–4 shows specific operating capabilities required by stable and changing environments.

FIGURE 18–4
Operating capabilities for stable and changing environments

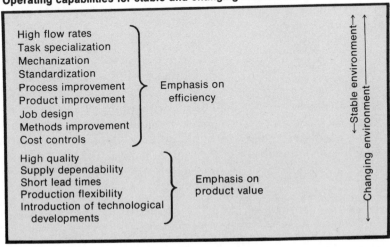

WHY PRODUCTIVITY?

Productivity may be defined as units of output per worker-machine hour. Management and labor leaders alike publicly urge higher productivity yet many people do not understand what it is or why it is important. Referring to his activities as former chairman of the Price Commission, Jackson Grayson, Jr., stated, "I've been actually aston-

FIGURE 18–5
Output per worker-hour

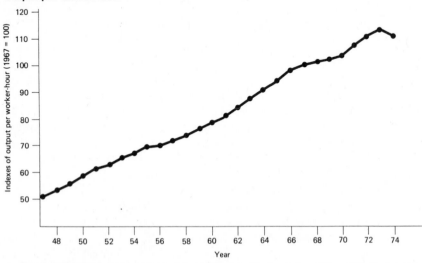

Source: *National Commission on Productivity and Work Quality, Fourth Annual Report* (Washington, D.C., March 1975), p. 40.

ished at how few of the major companies that we've met with even know what productivity is. . . ."[6]

Historically, this country has enjoyed very high productivity relative to other countries. However, in the post-Vietnam era, this nation's previously unmatched production capabilities have become a matter of national concern.[7] The economy has changed from one of affluence and surplus to one of decreasing competitive effectiveness and more frequent scarcities. Costs have risen dramatically, the balance of trade has deteriorated, the value of the dollar has decreased, and the quality of output has been variable at best. Figures 18–5 and 18–6 illustrate the decline of productivity in this nation and relative to

[6] Richard C. Gerstenberg, "Productivity: Its Meaning for America," *Michigan Business Review*, July 1972, p. 1.

[7] Wickham Skinner, "After Seven Lean Years," *Proceedings, 33d Annual Meeting, Academy of Management*, eds. Thad B. Green and Dennis F. Ray, August 1973, p. 557.

other nations. In attempting to explain the nation's productivity problems, Professor Wickham Skinner outlined three environmental factors which have had a powerful impact on U.S. organizations: (1) accelerating foreign competition, (2) technological changes in production and information-handling equipment, and (3) social changes in the work force.[8]

FIGURE 18–6
Decreasing gap in the productivity level between United States and other countries

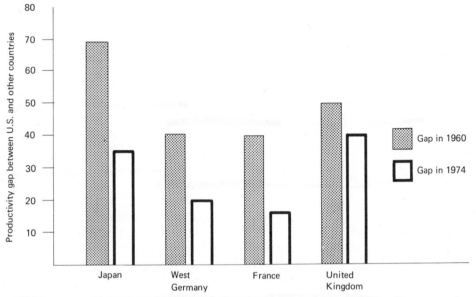

Source: *National Commission on Productivity and Work Quality, Fourth Annual Report* (Washington, D.C., March 1975), p. 14.

Productivity determinants

Unfortunately, when the term *productivity* is mentioned, many people automatically assume that it only means harder work. This is not necessarily the case. As indicated in Figure 18–7, productivity is the result of three separate components—efficiency of technology (equipment, methods, materials, and so on), efficiency of labor, and the effectiveness of management.

Technology as defined here includes new ideas, inventions, innovations, techniques, methods, and materials. Efficiency of labor is a function of the general level of services offered and the motivation

[8] Wickham Skinner, "The Anachronistic Factory," *Harvard Business Review,* January–February 1971, p. 61.

FIGURE 18–7
Determinants of productivity

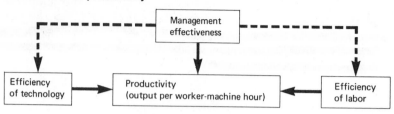

to work. Services as used here includes health, education, research, and so forth. Given high efficiencies of technology and labor, these inputs must be effectively combined by management if high productivity is to result. Thus productivity is not simply a matter of making employees work longer and harder. The desire to work, which is often referred to as the puritan work ethic, must not be absent; however, it represents only one of several requirements for high productivity. Richard Gerstenberg, chief executive officer for General Motors, has said that the real meaning of productivity is "To produce more with the same amount of human effort."[9] Gerstenberg's statement is based on the fact that, over the long run, far greater gains in productivity come from efficiency of technology and effective management than from efficiency of labor. For example, the average factory worker in the United States currently produces more than six times as much in an hour as that worker's grandfather produced at the turn of the century and with less effort in most cases.[10]

Management is the force that integrates the technology and labor to produce outputs. Management can greatly affect the level of technology through its willingness to invest capital, to take risks, and to engage in research. The management style and policies employed affect the efficiency of labor. Thus productivity is one reflection of management's efficiency.

Productivity and standard of living

Figure 18–8 diagramatically shows the basic relationship between productivity and standard of living. Total production depends on the rate of productivity, the quantity of equipment, and the quantity of people willing and able to work. New capital equipment, consumer goods, and services are the results of production. The new equipment

---

[9] Gerstenberg, "Productivity," p. 2.
[10] Ibid., p. 5.

FIGURE 18–8
Productivity and standard of living

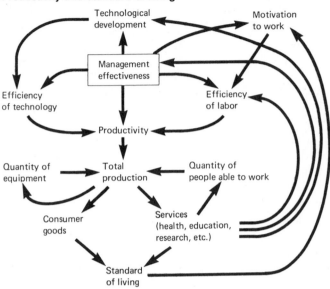

is cycled back to industry, while the goods and services are used by the consumer. The level of goods and services used and available to the consumer determines the overall standard of living. Thus productivity is central to the quality of our daily lives.

SUMMARY

Operations management is the application of the basic concepts and principles of management to the operating systems of an organization. Operating systems consist of the processes and activities necessary to transform various inputs into goods and/or services. Operating systems exist in all organizations and are composed of people, material, facilities, and information. The end result of an operating system is to add value to the inputs by improving, enhancing, or rearranging them.

The activities undertaken while managing an operating system can be categorized into two main areas: (1) systems design and (2) operations planning and control. Product design and selection, equipment and process selection, site location, physical layout and design of work methods are all part of the design phase. Production control (aggregate output planning, resource allocation, and activity scheduling), inventory control, quality control, cost control and improvement, and facility maintenance are all part of the operations planning and control phase of operations management.

Operations management overlaps with other functional areas of an organization, and therefore, many of the operations activities should be coordinated with the other functional areas.

There are two basic types of operating systems: one is based on continuous flows while the other is based on intermittent flows.

The capabilities developed within an operating system should match the requirements of the organization. One factor which influences these requirements is the environment. The operations manager in a stable environment is primarily concerned with efficiency and cost-reducing activities. The operations manager in a changing environment is concerned not only with cost but also with increasing the value of the product to the consumer.

Because of the relatively large amount of resources and time consumed by the operations function, the management of this function plays a critical role in achieving the organization's goals.

Productivity is a central concern of the operations manager. Productivity also has a direct relationship to the standard of living in a society.

REVIEW QUESTIONS

1. What is operations management?

2. Describe an operating system.

3. What are the activities required to manage an operating system?

4. How does operations management relate to the other functional areas of an organization?

5. Describe the two basic types of operating systems.

6. What are the operating capabilities required for a stable environment? A changing environment?

7. What are the main determinants of productivity?

8. How is productivity related to the standard of living?

DISCUSSION QUESTIONS

1. Explain how you might take a production-line approach (transferring the concepts and methodologies of operations management) to a service organization such as a fast food restaurant.

2. Why should a marketing manager be concerned with the operations or production function of the organization?

3. What in your opinion are the reasons that the rate of increase in productivity has begun to slow in this country?

4. How does the organization's environment affect the needed capabilities of the organization's operating system?

SELECTED READINGS

Burch, E. Earl. "Productivity: Its Meaning and Measurement," *Atlanta Economic Review* (May–June 1974), pp. 43–47.

Chase, Richard B., and Aquilano, Nicholas J. *Production and Operations Management.* Homewood, Ill.: Richard D. Irwin, Inc., 1973.

Garrett, Leonard J., and Milton Silver. *Production Management Analysis.* 2d ed. New York: Harcourt, Brace, Jovanovich, Inc., 1973.

Gerstenberg, Richard C. "Productivity: Its Meaning for America,"*Michigan Business Review* (July 1972), pp. 1–7.

Kast, Fremont E., and James E. Rosenweig. *Organization and Management: A Systems Approach.* New York: McGraw-Hill Book Company, 1970.

Levitt, T. "Production-Line Approach to Service," *Harvard Business Review* (September–October 1972), pp. 41–52.

Skinner, Wickham. "The Anachronistic Factory," *Harvard Business Review* (January–February 1971), pp. 61–70.

———. "Production under Pressure," *Harvard Business Review*, vol. 44, no. 6 (November–December 1966), pp. 139–46.

Work in America. Report of a Special Task Force to the Secretary of Health, Education, and Welfare. Cambridge, Mass.: The M.I.T. Press, 1973.

Case 18–1

The lines at Sam's

Sam Baker owns and manages a cafeteria on Main Street in Dawsonville. Sam has been in business for almost two years. During his two years of operation, Sam has identified several problems that he has not been able to solve. One major problem is the line that always seems to develop at the check-out register during the rush hour. Another problem is that customers are constantly complaining that the size of the helpings and the size of the pie slices vary tremendously from customer to customer. A third problem that has been disturbing Sam is the frequency with which the cafeteria runs out of "choice dishes." The final problem perplexing Sam is the fact that every Sunday at noon, when a large crowd arrives after church, Sam invariably runs short of seating space.

Sam has worked at other food establishments for the past 15 years and most of them have experienced similar problems. In fact, these and other related problems have come to be expected and are, therefore, accepted practice for the industry. After all, Sam's former boss used to say, "You can't please everybody all the time." Sam is wondering if he should take the industry's position and just accept these problems as an inherent part of the business.

1. Do you have any suggestions for Sam? If so, what are they?
2. Can you think of other service-oriented industries that seem to take the same view as Sam's industry toward their problems?

Case 18–2

"*Milking*" *the business*

Mickey "Mick" Lang is operations manager for the Tremble Company. Tremble was started by Joseph Went, Sr., in 1910 and is still privately owned by the Went family. In fact, Joseph Went III, is now president of Tremble. In recent years, the Went family has been "milking" the profits from the company and has refused to modernize in any respect. For example, Tremble has been in the same building employing the same basic equipment for the past 40 years. The company has also been reluctant to grant any employee benefits beyond the minimum requirements of the law.

Recently, the productivity of Tremble began to slip. This, coupled with rising labor and material costs and a soft market, has put Tremble in a precarious position for the first time in its history. As a result, Joseph Went III has approached Mick and suggested that Mick is not properly motivating his employees. After explaining that numerous machine breakdowns had occurred, Mick received the following reply from Mr. Went: "This equipment has done a good job for the past 40 years and there is no reason why it won't for the next 40 years! You obviously don't understand that motivation is what causes high productivity."

1. Do you agree with Mr. Went?
2. In light of the situation, what should Mick do?
3. How do the long-term prospects look for Tremble?

Objectives

1. *To emphasize the importance of the operating system design to the overall success of the organization.*
2. *To discuss the activities involved in designing an operating system.*

GLOSSARY OF TERMS

Assembly charts Depict the sequence and manner in which the various components of a product or service are assembled.

Flow process chart Outlines what happens to the product as it progresses through the facility.

Job design Specifies the specific work activities of an individual or group of individuals.

Job methods Refer to the manner in which the human body is used, the arrangement of the work place, and the design of the tools and equipment which are used.

Physical layout The process of planning the optimum physical arrangement of facilities which includes personnel, operating equipment, storage space, office space, materials handling equipment, and room for customer or product movement.

Process physical layout A type of physical layout in which equipment or services of a similar functional type are arranged or grouped together.

Process selection Specifies in detail the processes and sequences required to transform inputs into products or services.

Product physical layout A type of physical layout in which equipment or services are arranged according to the progressive steps by which the product is made or the customer is serviced.

19

Designing operating systems

As Some Men See Us

The Designer bent across his board
Wonderful things in his head were stored
And he said as he rubbed his throbbing bean
"How can I make this thing tough to machine?
If this part here were only straight
I'm sure the thing would work first rate,
But 'twould be so easy to turn and bore
It never would make the machinists sore.
I better put in a right angle there
Then watch those babies tear their hair
Now I'll put the holes that hold the cap
Way down in here where they're hard to tap,
Now this piece won't work, I'll bet a buck
For it can't be held in a shoe or chuck
It can't be drilled or it can't be ground
In fact the design is exceedingly sound."
He looked again and cried—"At last—
Success is mine, it can't even be cast."

Ken Lane*

THE SPECIFIC product or service produced by an organization establishes both opportunities and limitations on the design of its operating systems. If the design of the product or service causes extensive systems redesign, equipment alteration, new personnel, and so on, it can drastically alter the attractiveness of the product or service. As suggested by the above introductory story, the design of the product or service can be functionally sound yet unproducible. Certainly specific functional design objectives must be achieved; however,

---

° As quoted by J. P. Hahir, "A Case Study on the Relationships Between Design Engineering and Production Engineering" Proceedings, Fifth Annual Industrial Engineering Institute University of California Berkeley—Los Angeles, 1953, p. 22.

several alternative designs are often available for attaining these objectives. When such alternatives exist, production costs should certainly be one criterion used in evaluating the alternatives.

Designing an operating system involves selecting the process that is going to be used in producing the product or service, determining the location and layout of the physical facilities, and designing the jobs necessary to produce the product or service.

Process selection, like product design, can have a great impact on the costs and quality of the product or service. Process selection specifies in detail the processes and sequences required to transform the inputs into products or services. When goods or products are produced the emphasis of process selection is usually on the specific equipment that is to be used and how it fits together. With service industries the major emphasis shifts to the procedures used.[1]

The location and layout of the physical facilities are also important decisions that affect the organization's capabilities. Not only can site location affect overall costs in terms of wages paid, transportation costs, energy costs, and so on, but it can also affect the ability to service customers adequately and thus affect employee satisfaction. The primary objective of physical layout is to develop an operating system that meets the productive and quality requirements of the organization in the most economical manner.[2]

Job design specifies the specific work activities of an individual or group of individuals. Job design determines the depth and scope of the job and is, therefore, influenced by the physical layout and the process selection. As discussed in Chapters 7 and 14, job design can have a significant impact on employee motivation.

There are important interdependencies among each of the different design phases. The operations manager must serve as an integrating force for design decisions and thus ensure that the final design is effective from a total production standpoint.

PRODUCT OR SERVICE DESIGN

Usually the operations manager becomes involved with product or service design after many of the preliminary design decisions have been accomplished. Traditionally, after the design engineers and marketing specialists have worked out the basic specifications so that the product or service meets its functional requirements, the operations

---

[1] Richard B. Chase and Nicholas J. Aquilano, *Production and Operations Management: A Life Cycle Approach* (Homewood, Ill.: Richard D. Irwin, Inc., 1973), p. 81.

[2] Elwood S. Buffa, *Basic Production Management*, 2d ed. (New York: John Wiley & Sons, Inc., 1975), p. 271.

manager becomes involved. At this point the operations manager begins to select the materials, basic configurations, and the processes that will be used to minimize the production costs. Possible alterations to the design may be necessary due to cost considerations. Experience has shown that in many situations more than one basic design is functionally acceptable. The operations manager and the design engineer must work closely at this point to ensure that a sound design from both a functional and cost standpoint is found.

Traditionally conflict has existed between design engineers and operations managers. Design engineers are technically oriented and sometimes have little concern for production methods and costs. On the other hand, operations managers are more concerned with production costs and requirements than with the functional requirements of the product. Such potentially destructive conflict can be minimized through good communication which fosters an appreciation by both the engineer and the manager of the common objective of producing a functionally sound product or service at the minimum cost.

PROCESS SELECTION

Process selection encompasses a wide range of decisions including the feasibility of the product design, the basic type of configuration of the process system that is to be used, equipment selection, and product routing. Richard Chase and Nicholas Aquilano have classified process selection desisions into four different categories: (1) major technological, (2) minor technological, (3) specific component, and (4) specific process flow.[3] Figure 19-1 outlines the scope of each type of process selection decision. Major technological decisions answer the basic question of whether or not the product or service can be produced. These decisions do not address the question of whether or not the product can be economically produced. Major technological decisions deal primarily with the physical sciences.

Minor technological decisions choose between the alternative transformation processes available. These decisions include the choice between the use of general purpose and special-purpose equipment, make or buy decisions, or the degree of automation. The overall organizational objectives and plans must be considered in making minor technological decisions. This requires input from not only technical specialists but also from other areas of management.

Specific component decisions refer to the selection of equipment

---

[3] Chase and Aquilano, *Production and Operations Management*, p. 91.

FIGURE 19–1
Decisions in process selection

General-process decision	Decision problem	Decision variables	Decision aids
Major technological decisions	Transformation potential	Product choice Laws of physics, chemistry, etc. State of scientific knowledge	Technical specialists
Minor technological decisions	Selecting among alternative transformation processes	State of the art in equipment and techniques Environmental factors such as ecological and legal constraints Primary task of organization General financial and market strength	R&D reports Technical specialists Organizational objectives Long-run market forecasts Mathematical programs Simulation
Specific component decisions	Selecting specific equipment	Existing facilities Cost of equipment alternatives Desired output level	Industry reports Investment analysis, including make-or-buy, break-even, and present-value methods Medium-range forecasts
Specific process flow decisions...........	Selecting production routings	Existing layout Homogeneity of products Equipment characteristics	Product specifications Assembly charts Route sheets Flow process charts Equipment manuals Engineering handbooks

Source: Richard B. Chase and Nicholas J. Aquilano, *Production and Operations Management: A Life-Cycle Approach* (Homewood, Ill.: Richard D. Irwin, Inc., 1973), p. 91.

and procedures. Obviously equipment and procedures decisions should not be made independent of the minor technological decisions. Beyond the normal cost considerations, the following other factors should be evaluated in making specific component decisions:

1. Training required for the operators.
2. Maintenance record and potential.

3. Availability of parts and service.
4. Supplier assistance in installation and debugging.
5. Compatibility with existing equipment.
6. Flexibility of equipment in handling product variation.
7. Safety of equipment.
8. Delivery date expected.
9. Warranty coverage.

Specific process flow decisions route the materials and product through the facility. These decisions are highly dependent on the available equipment and space. Although the process flow may appear to be fixed because of certain physical limitations, it should always be carefully analyzed.

Flow charting and diagrams are used to aid in detecting and eliminating inefficiencies in a process by analyzing a certain sequence of operations in a step-by-step fashion. Most charting procedures classify the actions which occur during a given process into five classifications known as operations, transportations, inspections, delays, and storages. Figure 19–2 defines each of these types of actions. Two common charts used are assembly charts and flow process charts.

Assembly charts depict the sequence and manner in which the

FIGURE 19–2
Flow-charting activities

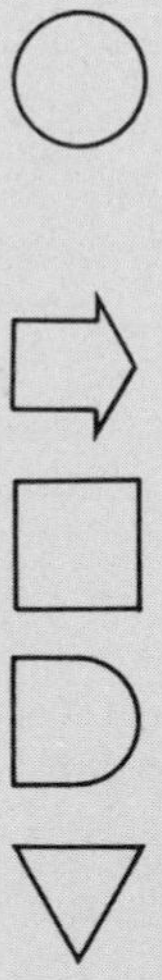

Operation. An operation occurs when an object is intentionally changed in any of its physical or chemical characteristics, is assembled or disassembled from another object, or is arranged for another operation, transportation, inspection, or storage. An operation also occurs when information is given or received or when planning or calculating takes place.

Transportation. A transportation occurs when an object is moved from one place to another, except when such movements are a part of the operation or are caused by the operator at the work station during an operation or an inspection.

Inspection. An inspection occurs when an object is examined for identification or is verified for quality or quantity in any of its characteristics.

Delay. A delay occurs to an object when conditions, except those which intentionally change the physical or chemical characteristics of the object, do not permit or require immediate performance of the next planned action.

Storage. A storage occurs when an object is kept and protected against unauthorized removal.

Source: William R. Mullee and David B. Porter, "Process-Chart Procedures," in H. B. Maynard (ed.), *Industrial Engineering Handbook*, 2d ed. (New York: McGraw-Hill Book Co., Inc., 1963), pp. 2–21.

FIGURE 19-3
Flow process chart representing the processing of a sales order

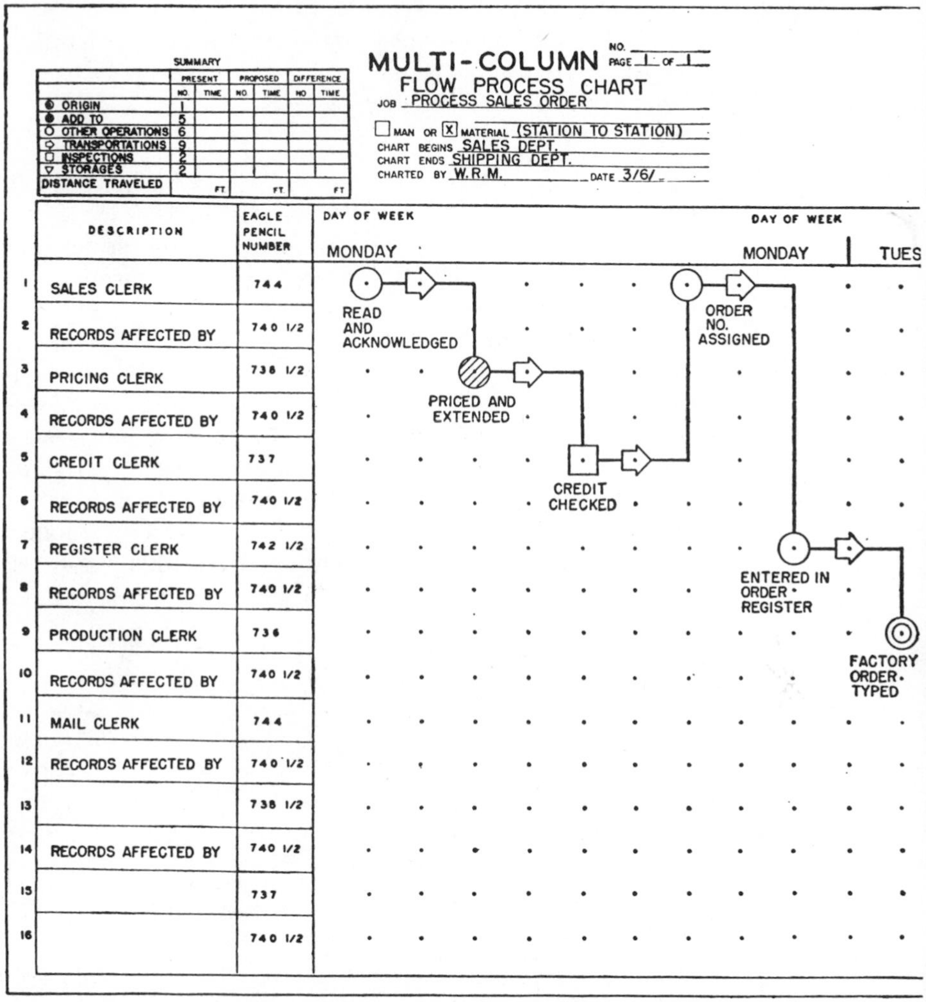

various components of a product or service are assembled. A flow process chart outlines what happens to the product as it progresses through the operating facility. Flow process charts can also be used to map the flow of customers through a service facility. Figure 19-3 is an example of a flow process chart representing the processing of a sales order.

Designed, 1950, by William Robert Mullee
Published by Work Simplification Round Tables – New York University, I.T.C.
A-PURPOSE: For a-bird's-eye view of a number of events and their chronological relationships. To develop a better product or procedure at a lower cost.
B-CONSTRUCTION: Use A.S.M.E. symbols ◯▷☐▽ (MODIFICATIONS ⦾ ORIGIN OF RECORD, ⨀ ADD TO RECORD)
  1-Material Type Chart (use passive voice, i.e., Typed, Data entered, Checked, etc.)
    a-Multicopy or Multiproduct. Chart each on a separate line   Use the 740½ line for posting to other papers, etc
    b-Single Copy or product: Use a separate line for each station and indicate movement from station to station.
  2-Man Type (use active voice, i.e., Types, Enters data, Checks, etc.)
    a-Multi-Person: Use a separate line for each person, and chart like a chronological series of snap shots
    b-Single Person: Chart from station to station to show travel.
C-IDENTIFICATION: To dramatize different items, fill out symbols with colors
D-ANALYSIS: Steam shovel approach. Use 6 questions (why, what, where, when, who, how) to get the actions (eliminate, combine change sequence, simplify). If detailed analysis is required, prepare a regular Flow Process Chart for each paper, material, or man.

| DAY OF WEEK | | DAY OF WEEK | | |
| DAY | WEDNESDAY | THUR. | FRI. | MONDAY |

(FROM THIS POINT THE MULTICOPY FORM IS USED)

SALES COPY

SCHEDULE CLERK COPY — PROMISE DATE ENTERED

CUSTOMER ORDER STAPLED TO SALES COPY — 5 COPIES

PROCESS CLERK COPY — PRODUCTION DATA ENTERED

MAILED TO FACTORY — FACTORY ENGINEERING DEPARTMENT — MFG. INSTRUCT. ADDED — INSPECTOR COPY — CHECKED FOR SHIPMENT

FINISHING CLERK COPY — FINISHING DATA ENTERED

SHIPPING CLERK COPY — SHIPPED

Source: William R. Mullee and David B. Porter, "Process-Chart Procedures" in H. B. Maynard (ed.), *Industrial Engineering Handbook*, 2d ed. (New York: McGraw-Hill Book Co., 1963), pp. 2–36, 2-37.

The different phases of process selection described above are all interdependent and overlapping. They should not be carried out in a distinct step-by-step fashion but rather in an integrative manner. The overriding objective of process selection is to specify in detail the most economical processes and sequences required to transform the inputs into the desired product or service.

SITE LOCATION

Management should give careful consideration to site-location decisions. It is easy to become overly engrossed in the operating details and techniques and to ignore the importance of site location. Location is an ongoing question and does not occur only when a facility is outgrown or becomes obsolete. Location decisions relate

FIGURE 19-4
Factors to be considered in site location

1. Revenue
   a. Location of customers and accessibility.
   b. Location of competitors.
2. Operating costs
   a. Price of materials.
   b. Transportation costs: materials, products, people.
   c. Wage rates.
   d. Taxes: income, property, sales.
   e. Utility rates.
   f. Rental rates.
   g. Communication costs.
3. Investment
   a. Cost of land.
   b. Cost of construction.
4. Other limiting factors
   a. Availability of labor with appropriate skills.
   b. Availability of materials, utilities, supplies.
   c. Union activity.
   d. Community attitudes and culture.
   e. Political situation.
   f. Pollution restrictions.
   g. Climate.
   h. General living conditions.

to offices, warehouses, service centers, and branches as well as the main facility. Each site selection decision should consider the total production-distribution system of the organization. Therefore the location of new facilities should not be the only locations examined. The location of present facilities should also be periodically examined to determine the most effective production-distribution system.

Several possibilities exist for expanding capacity when the existing facility is overcrowded. These are:

1. Subcontract work.
2. Add another shift.
3. Work overtime.
4. Move operation to a larger facility.
5. Expand present facility.
6. Keep current facility and add another facility elsewhere.

If the decision has been made to move the entire operation to a larger facility or to keep the current facility and add another facility elsewhere, then management is faced with a location decision. Figure 19–4 lists several factors which should be considered by management when locating a new facility. The final site choice will, by necessity, represent a compromise among the items in Figure 19–4.

PHYSICAL LAYOUT

Physical layout is essentially the process of planning the optimum physical arrangement of facilities which includes personnel, operating equipment, storage space, office space, and materials handling equipment or room for customer service and movement. Physical layout integrates all of the previous planning of the design process into one physical system. Physical layout decisions become necessary for a number of different reasons:

1. Construction of a new or an additional facility.
2. Obsolescence of current facilities.
3. Changes in demand.
4. The development of a new or redesigned product or process.
5. Personnel considerations: frequent accidents, poor worker environment, or prohibitive supervisory costs.

Demand forecasts for the product or service must be considered in establishing the productive capacity of the organization. Management must balance the costs of running short on space and equipment with the costs of having idle space and equipment. Generally the space requirements are matched with estimates of future demand, but equipment is purchased only as it is needed. Such an approach provides for quick capacity expansion and avoids the costs of the idle equipment.

Basic layout classifications

Most layouts can be classified as either process-oriented or product-oriented. Process layouts are generally used in intermittent flow operating systems which were discussed in Chapter 18. In a process layout, equipment or services of a similar functional type are arranged or grouped together. A process layout is followed when all x-ray machines are grouped together, all reproduction equipment is grouped together, all drilling machines are grouped together, and so forth. Custom fabrication shops, hospitals, and restaurants are usually arranged in this fashion. Under a process layout a product or customer travels from area to area according to the desired sequence of functional operations. When the product or service is not standardized or when the volume of similar products or customers in service at any one time is low, a process layout is preferred because of its flexibility.

Product layouts are usually employed in continuous flow operating systems which were discussed in Chapter 18. In a product layout, equipment or services are arranged according to the progressive steps by which the product is made or the customer is serviced. A product layout is generally used when a standardized product is made in large quantities. The assembly line is the ultimate example of a product layout. Automobile assembly plants, cafeterias, and standardized testing centers are examples which normally are product layout-

FIGURE 19–5
Advantages of process and product layout

Advantages of Process Layout

A. Lower investment in equipment and personnel because of less duplication (do not need the same machine or person doing the same thing in two different areas).

B. Adaptable to demand fluctuations.

C. Worker jobs are not as repetitive or routine.

D. Layout is conducive to incentive pay systems.

E. Allows for the production of greater variety of products with a smaller capital base.

F. Failures of equipment or people do not hold up a succession of operations.

Advantages of Product Layout

A. Relatively unskilled labor may be utilized.

B. Training costs are low.

C. Materials handling costs are usually low.

D. Smaller quantities of work in process.

E. Operations control and scheduling is simplified.

oriented. In a product layout, all the equipment or services necessary to produce a product or completely serve a customer are located in one area. Figure 19–5 summarizes the major advantages of both process and product layouts.

Computer assisted physical layout

Various computer programs have been developed to aid in designing physical layouts. Most of the computer approaches to designing a process-oriented layout attempt to optimize the relative placement of like components subject to some predetermined criterion or criteria. Materials handling cost is the most frequently used criterion. Computer programs for product-oriented layouts generally attempt to determine the optimum number of work stations to meet certain criteria. This approach is known as *line balancing*. Processing cost is normally the criterion used for line balancing.

JOB DESIGN

Job design specifies the specific work activities of an individual or group of individuals. Job design answers the question of how the job is to be performed, who is to perform it, and where it is to be performed. As shown in Figure 19–6 the ultimate job structure is the product of job design.

FIGURE 19–6
Factors in job design

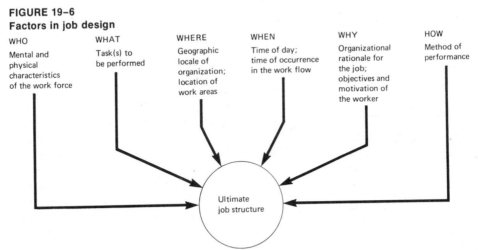

WHO	WHAT	WHERE	WHEN	WHY	HOW
Mental and physical characteristics of the work force	Task(s) to be performed	Geographic locale of organization; location of work areas	Time of day; time of occurrence in the work flow	Organizational rationale for the job; objectives and motivation of the worker	Method of performance

Ultimate job structure

Source: Richard B. Chase and Nicholas J. Aquilano, *Production and Operations Management: A Life-Cycle Approach* (Homewood, Ill.: Richard D. Irwin, Inc., 1973), p. 415.

The job design process can generally be divided into three phases:

1. The specification of individual tasks.
2. The specification of the method of performing each task.
3. The combination of individual tasks into specific jobs to be assigned to individuals.[4]

Phase one and three determine the content of the job (which includes both job scope and job depth) while phase two indicates how the job is to be performed. Job scope and job depth were both briefly discussed in Chapter 6.

Job content

Until recently, the prevailing practice in designing the content of jobs has been to rely on the criterion of minimizing short-run costs by minimizing the unit operation time. This approach resulted in the application of the following rules:

For specifying the content of individual tasks:

1. Specialize skills.
2. Minimize skills requirements.
3. Minimize learning time.
4. Equalize workloads and make it possible to assign full workloads.
5. Provide for worker's satisfaction.
6. Conform to the layout of equipment or facilities or, where they exist, to union restrictions on work assignments.

For combining individual tasks into specific jobs:

1. Limit the number and variety of tasks in a job.
2. Make the job as repetitive as possible.
3. Minimize training time.[5]

The obvious problem with this process-centered approach is that the job can become overly routine and repetitive, which leads to motivational problems in the form of boredom, absenteeism, turnover, and possibly low performance. Various worker-centered approaches have been suggested which are aimed at overcoming those problems by broadening the job content. These approaches, which were discussed in relation to job satisfaction in Chapter 15, include more participation by the worker in designing the job as well as job enlargement and job enrichment. Although many of the concepts de-

---

[4] Louis E. Davis, "Job Design and Productivity: A New Approach," *Personnel*, March 1957, p. 420.

[5] Davis, "Job Design and Productivity," p. 420.

signed to increase job content have been accepted, they are not without their critics. In a critical review of several studies relating to job enlargement and job enrichment, Charles Hulin and Milton Blood state:

> The studies reviewed appear to be of two types. Those which have used acceptable methodology . . . have generally not yielded evidence which could be considered as supporting the job enlargement thesis. Those studies which do appear to support such a thesis frequently contain a number of deviations from normally accepted research practice.[6]

Hulin and Blood further state that "the case for job enrichment has been drastically overstated and overgeneralized.[7] In an attempt to explain the rather mixed evidence relating to job content Donald Schwab and Larry Cummings have suggested a situational approach to job scope.[8] Their contention is that a given employee's reaction to the scope of the job is dependent on several situational factors. This approach would explain why different individuals react differently to jobs of a similar scope. The situational approach to job scope also emphasizes the importance of the staffing process and matching the individual to the job.

Job methods

The optimum method of performing a job is a function of the manner in which the human body is used, the arrangement of the work place, and the design of the tools and equipment which are used.[9] The overriding objective of job method design is to find the "one best way" of performing a particular job. Normally job methods are determined after the basic process and physical layout have been determined.

Motion study is the primary approach used in designing jobs. Basically, motion study involves determining the necessary motions and movements for performing a job or task and then designing the most efficient method for putting these motions and movements together. Figure 19–7 presents a list of motion-economy principles.

Charts similar to those used in process design are also useful in methods design. The difference is that charts used in methods design

---

[6] C. L. Hulin and M. R. Blood, "Job Enlargement, Individual Differences and Worker Responses," *Psychological Bulletin*, vol. 69 (1968), p. 50.

[7] Ibid.

[8] Donald P. Schwab and Larry L. Cummings, "A Theoretical Analysis of the Impact of Task Scopes on Employee Performance," *Academy of Management Review*, Forthcoming.

[9] Richard A. Johnson, William T. Newell, and Roger C. Vergin, *Production and Operations Management: A Systems Concept* (Atlanta: Houghton-Mifflin Company, 1974), p. 204.

FIGURE 19-7
Principles of motion economy

A check sheet for motion economy and fatigue reduction

These 22 rules or principles of motion economy may be profitably applied to production and office work alike. Although not all are applicable to every operation, they do form a basis or a code for improving efficiency and reducing fatigue.

Use of the human body

1. The two hands should begin as well as complete their motions at the same time.
2. The two hands should not be idle at the same time except during rest periods.
3. Motions of the arms should be made in opposite and symmetrical directions, and should be made simultaneously.
4. Hand and body motions should be confined to the lowest classification with which it is possible to perform the work satisfactorily.
5. Momentum should be employed to assist the worker wherever possible, and it should be reduced to a minimum if it must be overcome by muscular effort.
6. Smooth continuous curved motions of the hands are preferable to straight-line motions involving sudden and sharp changes in direction.
7. Ballistic movements are faster, easier, and more accurate than restricted (fixation) or "controlled" movements.
8. Work should be arranged to permit easy and natural rhythm wherever possible.
9. Eye fixations should be as few and as close together as possible.

Arrangement of the work place

10. There should be a definite and fixed place for all tools and materials.
11. Tools, materials, and controls should be located close to the point of use.
12. Gravity feed bins and containers should be used to deliver material close to the point of use.
13. Drop deliveries should be used wherever possible.
14. Materials and tools should be located to permit the best sequence of motions.
15. Provisions should be made for adequate conditions for seeing. Good illumination is the first requirement for satisfactory visual perception.
16. The height of the work place and the chair should preferably be arranged so that alternate sitting and standing at work are easily possible.

Figure 19–7 (Continued)

17. A chair of the type and height to permit good posture should be provided for every worker.

Design of tools and equipment

18. The hands should be relieved of all work that can be done more advantageously by a jig, a fixture, or a foot-operated device.
19. Two or more tools should be combined wherever possible.
20. Tools and materials should be prepositioned whenever possible.
21. Where each finger performs some specific movement, such as in typewriting, the load should be distributed in accordance with the inherent capacities of the fingers.
22. Levers, crossbars, and hand wheels should be located in such positions that the operator can manipulate them with the least change in body position and with the greatest mechanical advantage.

Source: Ralph M. Barnes, *Motion and Time Study*, 6th ed. (New York: John Wiley and Sons, Inc., 1968), p. 220.

show more detailed work elements than do process charts which represent entire operations.

Traditionally, job methods designers have concentrated their efforts on manual activities. However, the basic concept of "finding the one best way" is applicable to most jobs.

The physical work environment

The physical work environment, which includes factors such as temperature, humidity, ventilation, noise, light, and color, can have an impact on worker performance and safety. While there are studies which clearly show that adverse physical conditions do have a negative effect on performance, the degree of influence varies from individual to individual.

The importance of safety considerations in the design process was magnified by the passage of the Occupational Safety and Health Act of 1970 (OSHA). Designed to reduce the incidence of job injuries, the Act outlines very specific federal safety guidelines which must be followed by all U.S. organizations.

In general, the work environment should allow for normal lighting, temperature, ventilation, and humidity. Baffles, acoustical wall materials, and sound absorbers should be used where necessary to reduce unpleasant noises. If workers must be exposed to less than ideal conditions, it is wise to limit these exposures to short periods of time so as to minimize the probability that the worker will suffer any permanent physical or psychological damage.[10]

Sociotechnical approach

The concept "sociotechnical" was first introduced in the 1950s by Eric Trist and his colleagues at the Tavistock Institute of Human Relations in London, England.[11] The thrust of the concept is that both the technical system and the accompanying social system should be considered when designing jobs. Under the sociotechnical concept, jobs should be designed by taking a "holistic or systems" view of the entire job situation including its physical and social environment. The sociotechnical approach is very situational because few jobs have identical technical requirements and social surroundings. Specifically, the sociotechnical approach requires that the job designer carefully consider the role of the worker in the sociotechnical system, the nature of the task boundaries, and the autonomy of the work group. Using the sociotechnical approach, Louis Davis has developed the following guidelines for job design:

1. The need for the content of a job to be reasonably demanding for the individual in terms other than sheer endurance and yet provide some variety (not necessarily novelty).
2. The need for being able to learn on the job and to go on learning.
3. The need for some minimum area of decision making that the individual can call his own.
4. The need for some minimal degree of social support and recognition at the work place.
5. The need to be able to relate what the individual does and what he produces to his social life.
6. The need to feel that the job leads to some sort of desirable future.[12]

SUMMARY

The specific product or service produced by an organization establishes limitations on the design of its operating system. Generally operations managers become involved with product or service design

---

[10] Johnson, Newell, and Vergin, *Production and Operations Management*, p. 206.

[11] Peter B. Vaill, "Industrial Engineering and Socio-Technical Systems," *Journal of Industrial Engineering*, September 1967, p. 535.

[12] Louis B. Davis, *Job Satisfaction—A Socio-Technical View*, report 515-1-69 (Los Angeles: University of California, 1969), p. 14.

after much of the preliminary design has been accomplished by engineering. At this point, the operations manager and the design engineer must work closely to ensure that the optimal design from a functional and production standpoint is found.

Process selection encompasses a wide range of decisions including the feasibility of product design, the basic type and configuration of the process system that is to be used, equipment selection, and product routing. The overriding objective of process selection is to specify in detail the most economical processes and sequences required to transform the inputs into the desired product or service.

The location and layout of the physical facilities are important decisions which also affect the success of the product or service. Plant location has an impact on employee morale as well as on costs. The physical layout integrates all of the planning of the design process into one physical system. Process-oriented and product-oriented are the basic forms of physical layout.

Job design specifies the specific work activities of an individual or group of individuals and answers the questions of how the job is to be performed, who is to perform it, and where it is to be performed. Job content is determined by the specification of individual tasks and by the manner in which these individual tasks are combined into a specific job. Job methods specify the precise method of performing each task.

Unlike the more traditional approach to job design, which assumes that the job content is fixed by the requirements of the process or by the organization structure, the sociotechnical approach advocates considering both the task and social environment in designing jobs.

REVIEW QUESTIONS

1. Outline the different phases involved in designing operating systems.

2. Identify the four major categories of process selection decisions.

3. What charting procedures are available to aid in process selection?

4. Discuss several factors that should be considered in site location.

5. What is a process-oriented layout? A product-oriented layout?

6. What is the sociotechnical approach to job design? Give some guidelines for job design using the sociotechnical approach?

DISCUSSION QUESTIONS

1. Does process selection in service industries such as restaurants and hotels differ from process selection in manufacturing? If so, how?

2. How do the problems of organizing facilities for a service organization differ from those of laying out the facility for a manufacturing or goods-producing organization?

3. Why should all of the phases involved in designing an operating system be integrated?

4. Discuss the following statement made by a senior engineer: "Why should we be concerned with the product or process design since we know management will make us do it again anyway?"

SELECTED READINGS

Buffa, Elwood S. *Basic Production Management.* 2d ed., New York: John Wiley and Sons, Inc., 1975.

Chase, Richard B., and Nicholas J. Aquilano. *Production and Operations Management: A Life Cycle Approach.* Homewood, Ill.: Richard D. Irwin, Inc., 1973.

Hulin, C. L., and M. R. Blood. "Job Enlargement, Individual Differences and Worker Responses," *Psychological Bulletin,* vol. 69 (1968), pp. 41–55.

Ignall, Edward J. "A Review of Assembly Line Balancing," *The Journal of Industrial Engineering,* vol. 16, no. 4 (July–August 1965), pp. 244–54.

Vaill, Peter B. "Industrial Engineering and Socio-Technical Systems," *Journal of Industrial Engineering,* vol. 16, no. 9 (September 1967), pp. 530–38.

Vollmann, Thomas E., and Elwood S. Buffa. "The Facilities Layout Problem in Perspective," *Management Science,* vol. 12, no. 10 (June 1966), pp. 3450–68.

Case 19–1

A new building for Tot-Two

The Tot-Two Company manufactures clothes for children up to five years old. Tot-Two has been growing rapidly for the past several years and is planning to build a new plant in the city's recently developed industrial park on the north side of town. Charles "Chubby" Shaver, the plant's operations manager, has been assigned the task of drawing up a new physical layout subject to the constraints that the new building cannot exceed 7,000 square feet including the office space and that it must be a perfect rectangle in order to minimize the construction costs. Chubby developed the following list of departments with their respective approximate space requirements:

Shipping (400 sq. ft.)—area for shipping all finished goods.

Receiving (400 sq. ft.)—area for receiving all materials and supplies.

Materials Supply Room (300 sq. ft.)—storage area for all incoming materials.

Spreading and Cutting Area (1,600 sq. ft.)—area containing three 40-foot tables for spreading and then cutting the cloth. Many layers of cloth are spread on top of each other and cut at the same time with large portable cutters.

Pattern Making Area (300 sq. ft.)—area in which patterns are made.

Assembly Area (1,200 sq. ft.)—area for sewing together the various clothing parts.

Packing Area (400 sq. ft.)—area for packing the finished goods into boxes for shipping.

Finished Goods Storage (500 sq. ft.)—area for storing finished goods prior to shipping.

Design Area (200 sq. ft.)—area occupied by designers.

Office Space (800 sq. ft.)—space for secretaries and company officers.

Wash Facilities (300 sq. ft.)—area containing men and women's bathrooms.

Lunch/Break Area (400 sq. ft.)—area with vending machines and lunch tables.

Chubby then drew up an initial layout:

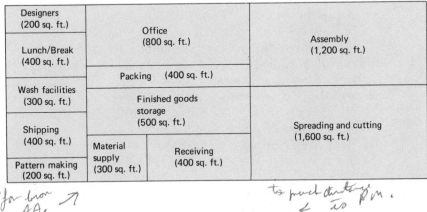

1. What are the strong points of Chubby's layout? What are the weak points?
2. Redesign the layout based on your answers to Question 1.

Case 19–2

Allocation of office and work space

The Burr Corporation has an office which audits the various divisions and offices of the Corporation throughout the northwestern United States. The Audit Office occupies one entire floor of a relatively small building in a large centrally located city in the Northwest. Much of the audit work is done outside of the city in which the Audit Office is located. When the auditors are on travel status, they are provided office and working space by the divisions and offices being audited.

The Audit Office is run by a director who has four deputy directors. Additionally, the Audit Office has 16 audit managers assigned about equally under the deputy directors. Audit staffs are assigned to the audit managers from a pool of about 125 auditors. Naturally, the job supervisors who work under the audit managers have usually spent a number of years with the office while the other staff members are relatively new.

The floor of the building where the office is located is in a rectangular shape with the director's office toward the center with an open entrance hall leading into it. A receptionist and two secretaries are positioned at desks in the open space leading to the director's office. Two of the secretaries do work for one of the deputy directors whose office is positioned directly across from the director's office. In addition to being responsible for directing about 25 percent of the audits, this deputy director is responsible for making audit assignments. The other three deputy directors are assigned to three larger offices in three of the corners of the floor.

In addition to the offices of the deputy directors, there are 22 other sizeable offices around the perimeter of the floor. Nineteen of the offices are occupied by the 16 audit managers, a training coordinator, a recruiter, and a computer specialist. The remaining three offices around the perimeter of the office are left for use by audit teams.

The inner portion of the floor is partitioned into 18 small cubicles, a conference room, a mail and file room, and a library. Therefore there are only the 18 cubicles and the three team rooms for the audit staffs to use when they are working in the office. These spaces are available to the auditors on a first-come first-served basis, without regard to whether the auditor is a first-year employee or a ten-year supervisor. At times the number of auditors overflows into the library and other areas. Another drawback is that the auditors sometimes lose productive time looking for a cubicle that is not being occupied.

There have been complaints from the auditors about the situation. Some of the job supervisors also consider it degrading that after many years with the office they do not have even a desk in the office for permanent use.

The director has recognized that space is a problem but has said that the office would have to do the best with what it has. For one thing, there was still a short-term lease on the building.

1. What impact could the described situation have on the morale of the audit staff and the performance of audits?
2. How should the director handle the situation? Has everything been done to help the situation or are there any other options?

1) low morale + performance because they will feel that if the co. doesn't care about them + won't give the best to them; then they won't do their best for the co.

2) try to renovate the floor to utilize all the space effectively. Get rid of 1 of the secretaries if they aren't really needed. Shorten the office space of the deputy director + the other 22 officers. Get rid of the cubicals to save time.

Objectives

1. *To emphasize the importance of properly implementing and controlling operating systems.*
2. *To apply the control concepts and principles learned in Chapter 8 to operating systems.*
3. *To introduce and discuss production control, inventory control, and quality control.*

GLOSSARY OF TERMS

ABC classification system A method of managing inventories based on their values.

Acceptance sampling A statistical method of predicting the quality of a batch or large group of products from the inspection of a sample or group of samples.

Activity scheduling Develops the precise timetable to be followed in producing the product or service.

Aggregate output planning A process of determining work force requirements, production rates, and inventory levels over a specified time period for the entire operating system.

Economic Order Quantity (EOQ) The optimum number of units to order.

Inventory A quantity of raw materials, in-process goods, or finished goods on hand.

Process control chart A time-based graphic display which shows whether a machine or process is producing items that meet certain preestablished specifications.

Production control A form of planning and control concerned primarily with aggregate output planning, resource allocation, and activity scheduling.

Quality control A process of ensuring or maintaining a certain level of quality with regard to materials, products, or services.

Resource allocation Refers to the efficient allocation of people, materials, and equipment in order to meet the demand requirements of the operating system.

Safety stocks Inventory stocks maintained for the purpose of accommodating unexpected changes in demand and supply and to allow for delivery time.

20

Planning and controlling operations

*The design of the operating system establishes the potential
productivity levels of an organization. However, the managerial
planning and controlling decisions that determine how resources
are utilized must be effectively accomplished if these potential
productivity levels are to be reached.*

Gene K. Groff[*]

PRODUCT design, physical layout, and other design-related topics
were discussed in Chapter 19. Unfortunately, designing an effective
operating system does not in itself ensure that the system will operate
efficiently. As indicated in the introductory quote, after the system
has been designed, the day-to-day operations must be properly
planned and controlled. The products or services must be guided
and scheduled through the system, the system processes must be
monitored, quality must be maintained, inventories must be managed,
and all of this must be accomplished within cost constraints.

Effective operations planning and control are attained by applying
the planning and control concepts and principles discussed in Chapters 5 and 8 to the operations function of the organization and can be
a substitute for resources. For example, good inventory control can
reduce the investment cost in inventories and physical layout. Similarly, good quality control can reduce scrap and wasted materials and
thus reduce costs.

[*] Fuller E. Callaway Professor of Management, Georgia State University.

PRODUCTION CONTROL

Production control is in reality a form of planning and control and is concerned with aggregate output planning, resource allocation, and activity scheduling. The overriding purpose of production control is to maintain a smooth, constant flow of work from start to finish so that the product or service will be completed in the desired time at the lowest possible cost. Aggregate output planning is a broad level of planning which determines the general personnel requirements, production rates, and inventory levels over a specified time period for the entire operating system. Detailed routing and scheduling through the production facility are undertaken after the production rates have been determined by the aggregate plan.

Aggregate output planning

Aggregate output planning is concerned with the overall operations and with balancing the major segments of the operating system. The primary objective of aggregate output planning is to match the organization's resources with the demands for its goods or services. Specifically, the aggregate output plan should determine the production rates which satisfy demand requirements while minimizing the costs of work force and inventory fluctuations.

The first step in developing an aggregate output plan is to obtain a demand forecast for the organization's goods or services. The second step involves evaluating the impact of the demand forecasts on the organization's resources. The final step in the process is to develop the best plan for using the organization's current and expected resources for meeting the forecasted demand. Thus the aggregate output plan results in the determination of production rates, work force requirements, and inventory levels for the entire operating system over a specified time period.

Resource allocation

Resource allocation refers to the efficient allocation of people, materials, and equipment in order to meet the demand requirements of the operating system. The materials needed in the system must be determined and ordered, the work must be distributed to the different departments and work stations, personnel requirements must be determined, and time allotments must be established for each stage of the process.

Routing, which was introduced in the previous chapter as a part of process selection, involves determining the best path and sequence of operations for attaining a desired level of output with a given mix of equipment and personnel. Routing attempts to make optimum use of the existing equipment and personnel through careful assignment of these resources. An organization may be required to analyze its routing system frequently or infrequently depending on the variety of products being produced or services being offered.

Activity scheduling

Scheduling develops the precise timetable to be followed in producing the product or service. Scheduling also includes the dispatching of work orders and the expediting of critical and late orders. Scheduling does not involve determining how long a job will take but rather involves determining when the work is to be performed. The process of scheduling is the link between system design and operations planning and control. Once the initial schedule has been established, the system is ready for operation. Of course, scheduling is a continuous activity in the life of an operating system.

A detailed scheduling system cannot be designed without knowledge of the respective operating system for which it is being designed. Scheduling for intermittent systems is very complex because of the relatively large number of individual orders or customers which must flow through the system. Numerous types of scheduling tools such as the Gantt chart, which was discussed in Chapter 8, have been developed to help the scheduler visualize and simplify the intermittent scheduling problem.

Scheduling for high-volume continuous flow systems generally involves a process of balancing the available resources to match the production rate requirements as outlined by the aggregate plan. Computer simulation has been successfully used to assist in the scheduling of continuous-flow systems by estimating the overall system impact of different scheduling decisions.

INVENTORY CONTROL

Inventories serve as a buffer between different rates of flow associated with the operating system. Inventories can generally be classified into one of three categories depending on their respective location within the operating system: (1) raw material; (2) in-process, or (3) finished goods. Raw material inventories serve as a buffer between purchasing and production. In-process inventories are used to buffer differences in the rates of flow through the various production processes. Finished goods inventories act as a buffer between

FIGURE 20-1
Inventories as buffers between different rates of flow

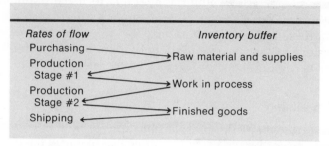

the final stage of production and shipping. Figure 20-1 illustrates these relationships.

Inventories provide added flexibility to the operating system and allow the organization to do the following:

1. Purchase, produce, and ship in economic batch sizes rather than in small lots.
2. Produce on a smooth continuous basis even though the demand for the finished product or raw material may fluctuate.
3. Prevent major problems when forecasts of demand are in error or when there are unforeseen slowdowns or stoppages in supply or production.

When making inventory decisions, management must answer three basic questions: (1) what items to carry in inventory, (2) how much

TABLE 20-1
Inventory investment of several organizations

Company	Date	Total assets	Inventories	Inventories as a percent of assets
Abbott Laboratories ...	Dec. 31, 1969	$ 345,382,000	$ 77,540,000	23
Allied Supermarkets ...	June 28, 1969	221,313,276	61,062,034	28
Eastman Kodak.........	Dec. 27, 1970	3,042,793,000	577,514,000	19
Interstate Bakeries......	Dec. 27, 1969	78,203,372	7,263,890	9
Lockheed Aircraft.......	Dec. 29, 1968	936,783,000	285,707,000	31
Merck & Co..............	Dec. 31, 1970	634,378,334	92,376,367	15
Pillsbury Mills	May 31, 1969	139,117,657	76,079,744	55
U.S. Steel	Dec. 31, 1970	3,450,149,776	923,458,156	27
John Wiley & Sons	Apr. 30, 1971	29,549,028	12,201,665	41

Source: Elwood S. Buffa, *Modern Production Management*, 4th ed. (New York: John Wiley & Sons, Inc., 1973), p. 475.

of the selected items to order and carry, and (3) when to order the items.

If it were not costly, every organization would attempt to maintain very large inventories in order to facilitate purchasing, production scheduling, and distribution. However, as illustrated in Table 20–1, inventories often represent a sizeable investment to the organization.

Potential inventory costs include such factors as insurance on the inventory, inventory or property taxes, storage costs, obsolescence costs, spoilage, and the opportunity cost of the money invested in the inventory. The relative importance of these costs depends on the specific inventory being held. For example, when dealing with women's fashions, the obsolescence costs are potentially very high. Similarly, the storage costs might be very high for dangerous chemicals. Thus, when dealing with inventory decisions, management must continually balance the costs of holding the inventory against the costs of running short of raw materials, in-process goods, or finished goods.

ABC classification system

One of the simplest and most used systems for managing inventories is the ABC system. The ABC approach is a method of managing inventories in accordance with their value. In many organizations,

FIGURE 20–2
ABC classification system

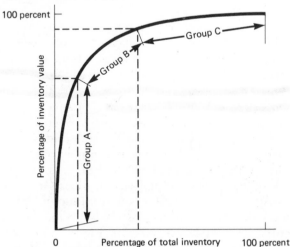

Source: James H. Greene, *Production Control Systems and Decisions* (Homewood, Ill.: Richard D. Irwin, Inc., 1965), p. 204.

a small number of products or materials, Group A, accounts for the greatest dollar value of the inventory. The next group of items, Group B, accounts for a relatively small amount of the inventory value; and Group C accounts for a very small amount of the inventory value. This concept is illustrated in Figure 20–2.

The purpose of classifying items into these groups is to establish appropriate control over each item. Generally, the items in Group A are monitored very closely, the items in Group B are monitored with some care, while the items in Group C are only checked occasionally. Items in Group C are usually not subject to the detailed paperwork of items in Groups A and B.

One potential shortcoming on the ABC method is that although the items in Group C might have very little cost value, they may be critical to the operation. It is possible for a very inexpensive bolt to be vital to the production of a costly piece of machinery. This shortcoming does not make the ABC method unuseable, but rather points out the necessity to exercise some minimum control over all items and especially those critical to the operation.

The order quantity

After management has decided what items are to be carried in inventory, the decision must be made concerning how much of each item to order. Most materials and finished products are consumed one-by-one or a few units at a time. However, because of the costs associated with ordering, shipping, and handling inventory it is usually desirable to purchase materials and products in large lots or batches.

When determining the optimum number of units to order, the ordering costs must be balanced against the cost of carrying the inventory. Ordering costs include such things as the cost of preparing the order, shipping costs, and setup costs, while carrying costs include storage costs, insurance, taxes, obsolescence, and the opportunity costs of the money invested in the inventory. The smaller the number of units ordered, the lower the carrying costs (because the average inventory held is smaller) but the larger the ordering costs (because more orders must be placed). The optimum number of units to order, referred to as the economic order quantity (EOQ), is determined by the point where ordering costs equal carrying costs or where total cost (ordering costs + carrying costs) is at a minimum. Figure 20–3 graphically shows the inverse relationship between ordering costs and carrying costs. The total cost curve in Figure 20–3 is found by vertically summing the ordering cost curve and the carrying cost curve. The lowest point on the total cost curve corresponds to the

FIGURE 20–3
Inventory costs versus order size

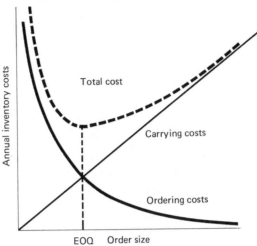

point where ordering costs equal carrying costs and determines the economic order quantity.

The greatest weakness of the economic order quantity approach is the difficulty in accurately determining the actual carrying and ordering costs. However, research has shown that the total costs associated with order sizes that are reasonably close to the economic order quantity do not differ appreciably from the minimum total cost associated with the EOQ.[1] Thus, as long as the estimated carrying and ordering costs are "in the ballpark," meaningful results can be obtained using this approach. Variations of this basic model have been developed for taking into account such things as purchase quantity and other special discounts.

Based on the relationships depicted in Figure 20–3, mathematical formulas have been developed for determining the economic order quantity. Appendix C at the end of the text discusses these formula.

Reorder point and safety stock

The operations manager needs to know not only how much to order but also when to order. There are two basic methods for determining when to order: the fixed-order quantity method and the fixed-order period method. Under the fixed-order quantity method,

---

[1] For example see John F. Magee, "Guides to Inventory Policy: I. Functions and Lot Size," *Harvard Business Review*, January–February 1956, pp. 49–60.

FIGURE 20–4
Fixed-order quantity method of reordering

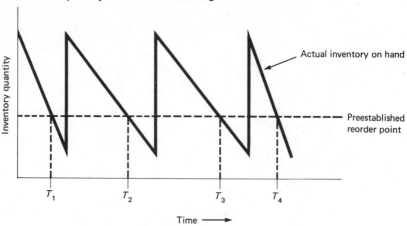

which is illustrated in Figure 20–4, orders are placed whenever the inventory reaches a certain predetermined level regardless of how long it takes to reach that level. With regard to Figure 20–4, orders would be placed at times T_1, T_2, T_3, and T_4 under the fixed-order quantity method. Thus the time between orders can vary depending on the demand. Under the fixed-order period illustrated in Figure 20–5, orders are placed for replenishment at predetermined regular time intervals regardless of how much inventory is on hand. With

FIGURE 20–5
Fixed-order period method of reordering

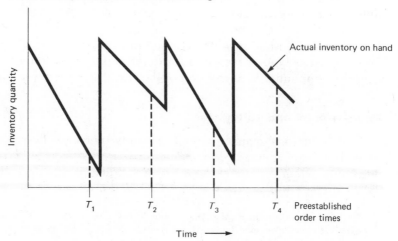

this method, the amount ordered rather than the time between orders can vary depending on the demand.

Most organizations maintain safety stocks for the purpose of accommodating unexpected changes in demand and supply and to allow for delivery time. The optimum size of the safety stock is determined by the relative costs of a stock-out of the item versus the costs of carrying the additional inventory. The cost of a stock-out of the item is very often difficult to estimate. For example, the customer may go elsewhere rather than wait for the product. If the product is available at another branch location, the stock-out cost may be simply the cost of shipping the item from one location to another.

QUALITY CONTROL

Quality is a relative term that means different things to different people. The consumer who demands quality may be talking about a completely different concept than the operations manager who demands quality. The consumer is concerned with service, reliability, performance, appearance, and so forth. The operations manager's primary concern is that the product or service specifications be achieved, whatever they may be. For the operations manager quality is determined in relation to the specifications or standards set in the design stages. Figure 20–6 lists some specific reasons for maintaining quality control.

When answering the question of what is the most desirable level of quality, management must attempt to balance the marketability of higher levels of quality versus the cost of attaining this higher quality. Figure 20–7 graphically depicts the general relationship between these factors. As shown in the graph, total revenue is a function of quality. However, consumers may not be willing to pay

FIGURE 20–6
Reasons for maintaining quality control

1. Maintain certain standards, such as with interchangeable replacement parts.
2. Meet customer specifications.
3. Meet legal requirements.
4. Find defective products which can be reworked.
5. Find problems in the production process.
6. To grade products, such as lumber or eggs.
7. To provide performance information of individual workers and departments.

FIGURE 20-7
Quality versus cost

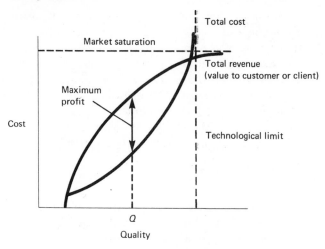

Quality

for extremely high levels of quality. For example, a housewife may desire a mixer that has three to five variable speeds and is dependable for five to ten years. However, the same housewife is probably not willing to invest substantially more money to obtain a 20-speed, lifetime guaranteed mixer. The shape of the total cost curve shows that the cost of quality generally is increasing at an increasing rate. Point Q, where profit is at a maximum, is the most desirable level of quality.

While the costs represented in Figure 20-7 are very real costs, management's task of determining the most appropriate level of quality is often based on guesses or estimates. However, once a policy decision has been made concerning the desired level of quality, the operations manager is responsible to ensure that the stated level of quality is achieved.

Quality checkpoints

If the desired level of quality is to be attained in the final product or service, several checks or inspections may be required at several different points in the operating system. Figure 20-8 shows some of the more frequent inspection points in an operating system. The first inspection point is when the raw materials are received. The quality of the raw materials must be compatible with the quality desired in the final product. The incoming materials should be checked for quality, quantity, and possible damage.

Depending on the operation to be performed, it may be desirable

FIGURE 20-8
Potential quality control checkpoints

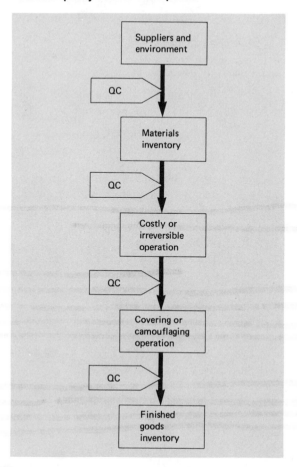

to inspect the materials again before they enter the operation. This is especially likely if the operation is costly or irreversible, such as with silverplating.

Other checkpoints may take place prior to operations which cover or camouflage defects in the process. For example, painting may temporarily camouflage a flaw which resulted from an earlier operation.

A final inspection should take place before the product or service is distributed to the customer. This provides a check on the end product or service. It should be stressed that the optimum location and number of checkpoints depend on two separate costs: (1) inspection cost and (2) the cost of passing a defective. As the number of inspection locations increase, so do the inspection costs; however, the probability of passing on a defect decreases.

In summary, quality checks might appropriately be performed at the following points in the operating system:

1. When the raw materials are received
2. Before costly or irreversible operations
3. Before operations which may cover or camouflage defects
4. Just after the product or service has been completed.[2]

Types of quality control

Figure 20–8 suggests that variations in quality can occur in the inputs to the operating system, in the transformation operations, or in the outputs. Quality control relating to the inputs or outputs of the system is referred to as product quality control. Product quality control is used when the quality is being evaluated with respect to a batch of products or services that already exists, such as incoming raw materials or finished goods. Product quality control lends itself to acceptance sampling procedures in which some portion of a batch of outgoing items (or incoming materials) is inspected in an attempt to ensure that the batch meets specifications with regard to the percentage of defective units which will be tolerated in the batch. Under acceptance sampling procedures, the decision to accept or reject an entire batch is based on a sample or group of samples.

Quality control relating to the control of a machine or an operation during the production process is called process control. Under process control, machines and/or processes are periodically checked to ensure that they are operating within certain preestablished tolerances. Adjustments are made as necessary to prevent the machines or processes from getting "out of control" and producing bad items. Process control is used to prevent the production of defectives, whereas product control is used to identify defectives after they have been produced.

Acceptance sampling

As defined in the previous section, acceptance sampling is a method of predicting the quality of a batch or large group of products from an inspection of a sample or group of samples taken from the batch. Acceptance sampling is used for one of three basic reasons:

---

[2] Richard J. Hopeman, *Production Concepts Analysis Control*, 2d ed. (Columbus, Ohio: Charles E. Merrill Publishing Company, 1971), p. 481.

(1) the possible losses or costs of passing defective items are not great relative to the cost of inspection (it would not be wise to inspect every match produced by a match factory); (2) inspection of some items requires destruction of the product being tested (as is the case when testing flash bulbs); and (3) sampling usually produces results more rapidly than does a census.

The procedure followed in acceptance sampling is to draw a random sample of a given size from the batch or lot being examined. The sample is then tested and analyzed. If more than a certain number (determined statistically) are found defective, the entire batch is rejected as having an unacceptably large percentage of defective items. Because of the possibility of making an incorrect inference concerning the batch, acceptance sampling always involves risks. The risk that the producer is willing to take of rejecting a good batch is referred to as the producer's risk. The risk of accepting a bad batch is referred to as the consumer's risk. Obviously one would desire to minimize both the producer's risk and the consumer's risk. However, the only method of simultaneously lowering both of these risks is to increase the sample size which also increases the inspection costs. Therefore, the approach which is usually taken is to decide the maximum acceptable risk for both the producer and the consumer and to design the acceptance sampling plan around these risks.

Process control charts

A control chart is a time-based graphic display which shows whether a machine or process is producing items that meet certain preestablished specifications. If the machine or process is producing items that do not meet specifications, then the machine or process is said to be "out of control." Control charts do not attempt to show why a machine or process is out of control but only if it is out of control.

The most frequently used process control charts are called mean and range charts. Mean charts (also called X-charts) monitor the mean or average value of some characteristic (dimension, weight, and so forth) of the items produced by a machine or process. Range charts (also called R-charts) monitor the range of variability of some characteristic (dimension, weight, and so forth) of the items produced by a machine or process.

The quality control inspector, using control charts, first calculates the desired level of the characteristic being measured. The next step is to calculate statistically the upper and lower control limits which determine how much the characteristic can vary from the desired level before the machine or process is considered to be out of control.

FIGURE 20–9
Mean chart

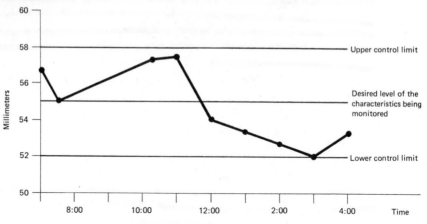

Once the control chart has been set up, the quality control inspector periodically takes a small sample from the machine or process outputs. Depending on the type of chart being used, the mean or range of the sample is plotted on the control chart. By plotting the results of each sample on the control chart it is easy to identify quickly any abnormal trends in quality. A sample mean chart is shown in Figure 20–9.

A mean or range chart used by itself can easily lead to false conclusions. For example, the upper and lower control limits for a machined part might be 0.1000 mm and 0.0800 mm respectively. A sample of four parts of 0.1200, 0.1100, 0.0700, and 0.0600 would yield an acceptable mean of 0.0900, and yet every element of the sample is out of tolerance. For this reason, when monitoring variables, it is usually desirable to use mean and range charts simultaneously to ensure that a machine or process is under control.

SUMMARY

If an operating system is to be effective, its day-to-day operation must be properly planned and controlled. The products or services must be scheduled through the system, the system processes must be monitored, quality must be maintained, inventories must be managed, and all of this must be accomplished within cost constraints.

The purpose of production control is to maintain a smooth, constant flow of work from start to finish so that the product or service will be completed in the desired time at the lowest possible cost. Aggregate output planning, resource allocation, and activity scheduling are all part of production control. Aggregate output planning is a process of determining work force requirements, production rates, and inventory levels over a specified time period (usually 12 months or less) for the entire operating system.

Inventories can generally be classified as raw materials inventories, in-process inventories, and finished goods inventories. Raw materials inventories serve as a buffer between purchasing and production. In-process inventories are used to buffer differences in the rates of flow through the various production processes. Finished goods inventories act as a buffer between the final stage of production and shipping.

When making inventory decisions, management must answer three basic questions: (1) what items to carry in inventory; (2) how much of the selected items to order and carry; and (3) when to order the items.

The ABC classification system is a simple method for managing inventories in accordance with their value.

The economic order quantity is one method for determining the optimum order size by finding the lot size that minimizes the total ordering and carrying costs of the inventory. The fixed-order quantity and the fixed-order period are the two most common methods for determining the reorder point.

Quality is defined for the operations manager by the product or service specifications. When determining the most appropriate level of quality, management must balance the marketability of higher quality against the cost of attaining the higher quality. Generally a minimum level of quality is necessary before the product or service can be sold. There is usually also a point of quality beyond which consumers are not willing to pay.

Quality checks might be appropriately performed at several points in the operating system. These points include when the raw materials are received, before costly or irreversible operations are performed, before operations which may cover or camouflage defects, and after the product or service has been completed.

Quality control relating to existing products or services including raw materials is referred to as product quality control. Quality control relating to the control of a machine or an operation during the production process is called process control.

REVIEW QUESTIONS

1. What is production control?

2. Define aggregate output planning.

3. What is the difference between resource allocation and activity scheduling?

4. What are inventories?

5. How does the ABC classification system work?

6. What costs affect the economic order quantity?

7. What is the purpose of carrying safety stock?

8. Define quality.

9. List five possible reasons for quality control.

10. At what points in an operating system might quality checks be appropriately performed?

11. What is a process control chart?

DISCUSSION QUESTIONS

1. Discuss the production control problems that arise when demand is continually changing.

2. Discuss the following statement: "A large part of most recessions can be explained by changes in inventory levels."

3. Since the cost of a stock-out of an inventory item is usually very difficult to estimate, how can the safety stock level be determined with any accuracy?

4. Since quality is a relative concept, how does a manager ever know if the quality level is optimum?

SELECTED READINGS

Buffa, E. S. "Aggregate Planning for Production," *Business Horizons* (Fall, 1967).

Buffa, E. S., and W. H. Taubert. *Production-Inventory Systems: Planning and Control.* rev. ed. Homewood, Ill.: Richard D. Irwin, Inc., 1972.

Greene, James H. *Production and Inventory Control: Systems and Decisions.* rev. ed. Homewood, Ill.: Richard D. Irwin, Inc., 1974.

Johnson, R. A., William T. Newell, and Roger C. Vergin. *Operations Management: A Systems Concept.* Boston, Mass.: Houghton Mifflin Company, 1972.

Starr, Martin K., and David W. Miller. *Inventory Control: Theory and Practice.* Englewood Cliffs, N.J.: Prentice-Hall, Inc., 1962.

Case 20–1

Production problems

The Braddock Company of Sea Shore City fabricates stamped metal parts used in the production of wheelbarrows. Braddock fabricates two basic styles of wheelbarrow trays: one is for a deep four-cubic-foot construction model and the other is for a shallow two-cubic-foot homeowner's model. Braddock's process is simple: raw metal sheets are picked up from inventory (presently Braddock maintains about seven days of the large metal sheets for the construction model and about ten days of the smaller sheets for the home owner model) and fed into a large machine which bends and shapes the metal into the desired tray. The trays are then inspected and packaged ten to a box for shipping.

In the past few days, Braddock has been experiencing quality problems with both tray styles. Undesirable creases have been forming in the corners following the stamping operation. However, the problem is more pronounced with the construction model tray and appeared almost three full days before it did on the homeowner's model.

Several incidents have occurred at Braddock during the past week that Hal McCarthy, the operations manager, thinks may have a bearing on the problem. Shorty McCune, a machine operator and labor activist, was accused of drinking on the job and thus released a few days before the problem began. Since his release, Shorty has been seen in and around the plant talking to several other employees. About two weeks ago Braddock also began receiving their raw metal from a new supplier because of an attractive price break.

Presently the only inspection performed by the company is the postfabrication inspection.

1. What do you think is causing Braddock's problem?
2. Why is the problem more pronounced on the construction model than on the homeowner model?
3. How can Braddock eliminate its problem?

Case 20–2

The purchasing department

The buyers for a large airline company were having a general discussion with the manager of purchasing in his office Friday afternoon.

Inspection was a topic that created a considerable amount of discussion. Apparently several parts had recently been rejected six months or more after being received. Such a rejection delay was costing the company a considerable amount of money since most of the items were beyond the standard 90-day warranty period. The current purchasing procedures state that the using department is responsible for the inspection of all parts including stock and nonstock items. The company employs an inspector who is supposedly responsible for inspecting all aircraft parts in accordance with FAA regulations. However, the inspector has not been able to check those items purchased as nonaircraft parts because he is constantly overloaded. Furthermore, many of the aircraft parts are not being properly inspected because of insufficient facilities and equipment.

One recent example of the type of problem being encountered was the acceptance of a batch of plastic forks that broke readily when in use. The vendor had shipped over a hundred cases of the forks of the wrong type. Unfortunately all the purchase order specified was "forks." Another example was the acceptance of several cases of plastic cups with the wrong logo. The cups were subsequently put into use for in-flight service and had to be used since no other cups were available. A final example was the discovery that several expensive radar tubes in stock were found to be defective and with expired warranty. These tubes had to be reordered at almost $900 a unit.

It was readily apparent that the inspection function was inadequate and unable to cope with the volume of material being received. Purchasing would have to establish some guidelines as to what material should or should not be inspected after being processed by the material checker. Some of the buyers felt that the material checker (who is not the inspector) should have more responsibility than simply checking quantity and comparing the packing sheet against purchase orders. Some believed that the checker could and should have caught the obvious errors in the logo on the plastic cups. Furthermore, if the inspector had sampled the forks they would have been rejected immediately. As for the radar tubes, they should have been forwarded by the inspector to the Avionics Shop for bench check and then placed in stock. Some buyers felt that the inspector should be responsible for inspection of all material received regardless of its function or usage. It was pointed out, however, that several landing gears had been received from the overhaul/repair vendor and tagged by the inspector as being acceptable. These gears later turned out to be defective and unuseable and had to be sent back for repair. This brought up considerable discussion concerning the inspector's qualifications, testing capacity, workload, and his responsibility for determining if the unit should be shop checked.

Much of the remaining discussion centered around what purchasing should recommend for the inspection of material. One proposal was that everything received be funneled through the inspection department. Another proposal was that all material be run through inspection except as noted on the purchase order. The question was also raised that if purchasing required all material to be inspected, would this demand additional inspection personnel and who would be responsible for inspection specifications? Furthermore, who should determine what items should be shop checked?

The meeting was finally adjourned until the following Friday.

1.   What do you think of the current system of inspection?
2.   Do you think the inspector is incompetent?
3.   What would you suggest at the meeting next Friday?

1) I think it is fine if someone would take the responsibility to check the items.

2) Yes it is his job to check the items & he isn't doing it.

3) Have more personal & check every item or have just some & check the rather important items like laundry gear & trash & forget about cluper & razor.

section six

Contemporary management

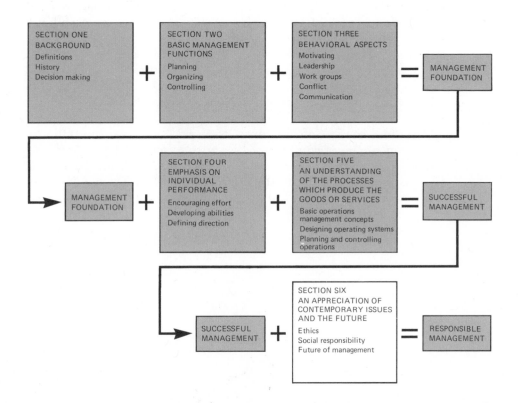

21 Ethics and social responsibility
22 Forward into the future

The first five sections of this text concentrated on providing the foundation and ingredients necessary for developing a successful manager.

All of the major segments of a manager's day-to-day job were covered. The purpose of this final section is to develop an appreciation for contemporary issues and potential future trends and, thus, develop not only successful managers but also responsible managers.

As a result of the numerous scandals that have occurred in government and in large corporations, increasing attention has been focused on the ethics and social responsibilities of managers. Thus managers' activities are being closely scrutinized in many cases. Not unrelated to ethics and social responsibility is the concern of managers for the future. Will organizational life take on drastic changes in the not-too-distant future or will the future be merely an extrapolation of the past? Today's and tomorrow's managers must have an awareness of these issues if they are to be successful and responsible.

Chapter 21 discusses the topics of ethics and social responsibility. An argument is developed that today's organizations need and should develop a code of ethics. Several arguments are also presented both for and against organizational actions concerning social responsibility.

The final chapter of this text, Chapter 22, explores the future of management and organizational life. Several potential developments which would affect management in the future are discussed. The chapter is concluded with the suggestion that tomorrow's manager will be more public-oriented than in the past.

Objectives

1. *To define the concept of ethics as related to organizations.*
2. *To outline some different approaches for dealing with ethics in organizations.*
3. *To discuss the concept of social responsibility.*
4. *To present and analyze arguments for and against social responsibility in organizations.*

GLOSSARY OF TERMS

Ethics Standards or principles of conduct to govern the behavior of an individual or a group of individuals.

Gamesmanship An approach to business ethics which argues that the ethics of businesses are gamelike and are different from the Judaeo-Christian ethic.

Judaeo-Christian ethic Generally considered to be the basis of Western ethical codes and has as its primary goal love—including love of God and neighbor.

Social responsibility Management decisions and actions taken for reasons at least partially beyond the organization's direct economic or technical interest.

21

Ethics and social responsibility

"Business ethics," the father explained to his son, "is something you couldn't do without. Take today for instance. A man comes in and pays me a hundred dollar bill to clear up his account. After he leaves, I find two bills stuck together. He has paid me two hundred instead of one. Now, son, here comes the question of ethics. Should I tell my partner or shouldn't I?"*

EXAMPLES concerning conflicts of interest, government scandals, stock manipulation by members of corporate boards, and kickback payments have plagued organizations for years. Such conduct causes one to question the code of ethics of many managers and of organizations in general. Presently no formal code of ethics exists for managers or ogranizations. As the introductory selection above implies, ethics means different things to different people.

WHAT ARE ETHICS?

Ethics are standards or principles of conduct used to govern the behavior of an individual or a group of individuals. Ethics are generally concerned with day-to-day behavior and with questions relating to what is right or wrong or with moral duties. Ethics can be developed by an individual, a group of individuals, or by society. Laws can be viewed as ethics since they are concerned with principles of conduct.

Organizational ethics are generally more concerned with the behavior of individuals or groups of individuals that is not covered by

---

* From the book, *Executive's Treasury of Humor for Every Occasion* by William R. Gerler. © 1965 by Parker Publishing Co., Inc. Published by Parker Publishing Co., Inc., West Nyack, New York.

the law. Withholding facts, stealing ideas, and padding expense accounts are issues that raise questions about ethical standards.

WHY IS A CODE OF ETHICS NEEDED?

Because of the adverse publicity that many organizations have received, society is demanding a code of ethics for organizations. Many people believe that if organizations do not voluntarily develop a code of ethics, the issue will be forced by public opinion or even government regulation.

Robert L. Heilbroner has summarized several proposals that would aid in forcing a code of ethics on organizations and individuals in organizations. These are summarized in Figure 21-1.

A second reason for developing a code of ethics is to reduce the

FIGURE 21-1
Proposals for legislating a code of ethics

Federal incorporation laws to avoid the present welter of differing state requirements and to put the corporation (or at any rate, the large corporation) directly under federal accountability.

Greatly enlarged disclosure requirements, forcing corporations to divulge facts and figures with regard to antipollution expenditures, racial distribution of employees, and so forth.

Public representatives on boards of directors, chosen to represent various constituencies such as suppliers, customers, workers, or simply the public at large.

Stiffer penalties for violation of laws that protect the consumer or the environment, with penalties that include the suspension of responsible executives.

The required appointment of corporate officials charged with responsibility for assuring the compliance of their companies with existing legislation.

Cumulative voting of shares so that small shareowners, who now can cast no more than one vote for or against each director, may concentrate all their voting power for or against one director.

Full availability of corporate income tax returns for public inspection.

Imposition of involuntary "social bankruptcy" for corporations that have failed consistently to abide by existing legislation.

Protection of the rights of corporate employees against corporate retaliation for public testimony with regard to acts of the corporation.

Source: From *In the Name of Profit* edited by Robert L. Heilbroner. Copyright © 1972 by Doubleday and Company, Inc. Reprinted by permission of Doubleday and Company, Inc., pp. 257–58.

FIGURE 21-2
Subordinate goals relevant to organizational life

1. *Survival and physical well-being (productivity).* Each individual should have access to the conditions necessary for health, safety, comfort, and reasonable longevity.
2. *Fellowship.* Each individual should have a variety of satisfying human relationships.
3. *Dignity and humility.* Each individual should have the opportunity to earn a position in society of dignity and self-respect.
4. *Enlightenment.* The individual should have opportunity to learn about the world in which he lives. He should be able to satisfy his intellectual curiosity and to acquire the skills and knowledge for intelligent citizenship, efficient work, and informed living.
5. *Aesthetic enjoyment.* The individual should have the opportunity to appreciate aesthetic values in art, nature, and ritual, and through personal relations. Many aesthetic values are attainable through both production and consumption.
6. *Creativity.* The individual should be able to express his personality through creative activities. He should be able to identify himself with the results of his own activity, and to take pride in his achievements, intellectual, aesthetic, political, or other.
7. *New experience.* An important goal of life is suggested by the words variability, spontaneity, whimsy, novelty, excitement, fun, sport, holiday, striving against odds, solving problems, innovation, invention, etc. Each individual should have opportunity for new experience.
8. *Security.* Each individual should have assurance that the objective conditions necessary for attainment of the above goals will be reasonably accessible to him.
9. *Freedom.* Freedom is the opportunity to pursue one's goals without restraint.
10. *Justice.* The Christian law of love does not imply neglect to the self. The individual is to be as concerned about others as he is about himself—neither more nor less.
11. *Personality.* The preceding goals were stated in terms of the kinds of life experiences we wish people to have. These goals can be translated into the kinds of persons we wish them to be. Goals can then be regarded as qualities of human personality; accordingly, a desirable personality would be defined as one that is favorably conditioned toward the various goals.

Source: Chart made up of data of 11 goals from pp. 50–60 of "Findings of the Study" by Howard R. Bowen in *Christian Values and Economic Life* by John C. Bennett, Howard R. Bowen, William Adams Brown, Jr., and G. Bromley Oxnam. Copyright 1954 by the Federal Council of the Churches of Christ in America. Reprinted by permission of Harper & Row, Publishers, Inc.

organizational pressures to compromise personal ethics for the sake of organizational goals. One recent study indicated that managers feel under pressure to compromise personal standards to achieve company goals.[1] In this study Archie B. Carroll found that 50 percent of

[1] Archie B. Carroll, "Managerial Ethics: A Post-Watergate View," *Business Horizons*, April 1975, p. 77.

top-level managers, 65 percent of middle-level managers, and 84 percent of lower-level managers feel this pressure.

A third reason for developing a code of ethics is to provide a general standard for measuring performance concerning ethical questions.

JUDAEO-CHRISTIAN ETHIC

The Judaeo-Christian ethic is generally considered to be the basis of Western ethical codes and thus might be the basis for an organizational code of ethics. A study committee of the Federal Council of Churches has attempted to define the salient features of the Judaeo-Christian ethic. The primary goal of the Judaeo-Christian ethic is love—including love of God and neighbor. The committee also outlined several subordinate goals of the Judaeo-Christian ethic that are relevant to organizational life. These subordinate goals are summarized in Figure 21–2.

Robert T. Golembiewski has refined the Judaeo-Christian ethic into five basic values relevant to organizational life. The numbers in parentheses refer to the items in Figure 21–2 to which the respective basic value relates.

1. Work must be psychologically acceptable to the individual; that is, its performance cannot generally threaten the individual (1, 3, 8, 10, and 11).
2. Work must allow man to develop his faculties (4, 5, 6, and 7).
3. The work task must allow the individual considerable room for self-determination (3 and 9).
4. The worker must have the possibility of controlling, in a meaningful way, the environment within which the task is to be performed (2, 6, and 9).
5. The organization should not be the sole and final arbiter of behavior; both the organization and the individual must be subject to an external moral order (5, 9, and 10).[2]

Golembiewski has also offered specific suggestions concerning organization structure and managerial techniques that are consistent with the Judaeo-Christian ethic. These are summarized in Figure 21–3.

Most of the suggestions offered by Golembiewski are concerned with the application of the Judaeo-Christian ethic to the design of jobs and the job environment. They are not concerned with the ethics of individual managers or the ethics between the organization and its stockholders, customers, or other organizations.

---

[2] Robert T. Golembiewski, *Men, Management, and Morality* (New York: McGraw-Hill Book Co., 1965), p. 65.

FIGURE 21–3
Organizational structure and managerial techniques consistent with Judaeo-Christian ethic

1. Work must be psychologically acceptable, nonthreatening..........

   1. Congruence of personality and job requirements.
      a. Proper selection to match individual with the job.
      b. Compatibility of personalities of members.
      c. Self-choice of members.

2. Work must allow man to develop faculties.....................................

   2. Organizing around "work cycles" versus "work units"; job rotation, job enlargement for supervisors and operators.

3. The task must allow the individual room for self-determination ....

   3. Managing dependence-interdependence-independence.
      a. Wide span of control.
      b. Supportive supervision.
      c. Motivating by growth vs. deficiency.

4. The worker must influence the broad environment within which he works ....

   4. "Participation": group decision making, Scanlon plan, multiple management.
      a. Monitoring a discrete flow of work versus a process.
      b. Organizing around small administrative units at low levels.
      c. High supervisory power.

5. The formal organization must not be the sole and final arbiter of behavior.....................................

   5. Decentralization versus centralization.
      a. Monitoring a product versus a function.
      b. Organizing around small administrative units at high levels.

Source: Robert T. Golembiewski, *Men, Management, and Morality* (New York: McGraw-Hill Book Co., 1965), p. 73.

GAMESMANSHIP IN BUSINESS ETHICS

Another approach to business ethics is offered by Albert Z. Carr.[3] Carr argues that the ethics of business are game ethics which are

---

[3] Albert Z. Carr, "Is Business Bluffing Ethical?" *Harvard Business Review*, January–February 1968, pp. 143–53.

different from the Judaeo-Christian ethic. For instance, is it considered unethical to bluff in a game of poker? Obviously bluffing in a game of poker does not reflect on the morality of the player. It is merely a strategy of playing the game.

Carr's approach to business ethics is summarized as follows:

> Poker's own branch of ethics is different from the ethical ideals of civilized human relationships. The game calls for distrust of the other fellow. It ignores the claim of friendship. Cunning deception and concealment of one's strength and intentions, not kindness and openheartedness, are vital in poker. No one thinks any the worse of poker on that account. And no one should think any the worse of the game of business because its standards of right and wrong differ from the prevailing traditions of morality in our society.[4]

Carr further asserts that as long as an organization does not violate the rules of the game as set by law, then profit should be the guiding goal of organizational strategy. However, Carr also states that businessmen should not take advantage of the situation to the point that employees, competitors, customers, government, or the public at large become hostile.

BUSINESS ETHICS—IS THERE ONE CORRECT ANSWER?

Few ethical questions in organizations can be easily classified as right or wrong. It is the "gray" or unclear questions that cause problems. Considerable pressures "to go along" are often applied by superiors. The consequences of not going along and the desire to get ahead frequently cause managers to agree with the decision regardless of the ethics involved. The problem lies in the fact that many managers make decisions without thinking in terms of the ethics involved. In the past relatively little time has been devoted to business or organizational ethics. Schools of business train managers in accounting, finance, management, policy, and strategy, but little time is devoted to ethics.

Robert W. Austin has offered four basic guidelines that seem especially appropriate for managers faced with ethical decisions:

> The professional manager affirms that he will place the interest of his company before his own private interests.
>
> He will place his duty to society above his duty to his company and above his private interest.
>
> He has a duty to reveal the facts in any situation where his private interests are involved with those of his company, or where the interests of his company are involved with those of society.

---

[4] Ibid., p. 145.

He must subscribe wholeheartedly to the belief that when business managers follow this code of conduct, the profit motive is the best incentive of all for the development of a dynamic economy.[5]

SOCIAL RESPONSIBILITY

While ethics are concerned with the day-to-day behavior standards of individuals and organizations, social responsibility is concerned with how individuals and organizations deal with current social issues.

A recent poll presented a cross-section of American households with a list of social concerns. The participants were asked to select the concerns to which they thought managers and business organizations should provide special leadership. Some of the results are shown in Table 21–1.

TABLE 21–1
Expectations of American households

Concern	Percent responding affirmatively that managers and organizations should provide special leadership
Eliminate depressions	88
Rebuild cities	85
Wipe out poverty	83
Find cures for diseases	76
Control crime	73
Cut government red tape	57

Source: Lloyd L. Byars and Michael H. Mescon, *The Other Side of Profit* (Philadelphia: W. B. Saunders Company, 1975), p. 4.

At least two conclusions can be drawn from this poll. First, public expectations about the responsibilities of managers and organizations are enormous, and second, a widely accepted definition of social responsibility for business organizations is sorely needed.

Defining social responsibility

As reflected in Table 21–4, the general public has a rather broad and all-encompassing definition of the social responsibility of business organizations. Generally social responsibility is used to refer to areas ranging from the quality and safety of an organization's product

---

[5] "A Positive Code of Ethics," *Business Week*, June 17, 1961.

to cures for current social problems. In short, social responsibility has come to denote participation in a multitude of issues and problems. Presently no universal definition exists for the term *social responsibility*. One representative definition of social responsibility is that it is the "obligation of businessmen to pursue those policies, to make those decisions, or to follow those lines of action which are desirable in terms of objectives and values of society."[6] Unfortunately this definition is not operational since the assumption that the business executive will know "those lines of action which are desirable in terms of objectives and values of society" is not realistic.

For the purposes of the following discussion, social responsibility will be defined as "management decisions and actions taken for reasons at least partially beyond the organization's direct economic or technical interest."[7]

Social responsibility — A historical perspective

The idea that business has a responsibility other than producing goods and services is not new. Henry L. Gantt in 1919 stated his belief that the community would attempt to take over business if the business system neglected its social responsibilities.[8] Another early management writer who discussed social responsibility was Oliver Sheldon. Writing in 1923, Sheldon emphasized the ethics of organizational responsibility. His basic philosophy can be summarized as follows:

> It is important, therefore, early in our consideration of management in industry, to insist that however scientific management may become, and however much the full development of its powers may depend upon the use of the scientific method; its primary responsibility is social and communal.[9]

However, the concern which these men showed for social responsibility was rare during this early period.

Changes began to occur in the late 1930s and early 1940s. Shorter work weeks and safer working conditions are examples of some of the first changes. Many of these early "social responsibility" changes were precipitated by labor unions. In effect, labor unions pressured

---

[6] Howard R. Bowen, *Social Responsibility of the Businessman* (New York: Harper & Row, Publishers, 1953), p. 6.

[7] Keith Davis, "Can Business Afford to Ignore Social Responsibilities?" *California Management Review*, Spring 1960, p. 70.

[8] Henry L. Gantt, *Organizing for Work* (New York: Harcourt Brace Jovanovich, Inc., 1919), p. 15.

[9] Oliver Sheldon, *The Philosophy of Management* (New York: Pitman Publishing Corp., 1966), p. xv. (Originally published in London in 1923 by Sir Isaac Pitman & Sons.)

FIGURE 21–4
Arguments for and against social responsibility

Major Arguments for Social Responsibility
1. It is in the best interest of the business to promote and improve the communities where it does business.
2. Social actions can be profitable.
3. It is the ethical thing to do.
4. It improves the public image of the firm.
5. It increases the viability of the business system. Business exists because it gives society benefits. Society can amend or take away its charter. This is the "iron law of responsibility."
6. It is necessary to avoid government regulation.
7. Sociocultural norms require it.
8. Laws cannot be passed for all circumstances. Thus business must assume responsibility to maintain an orderly legal society.
9. It is in the stockholder's best interest. It will improve the price of stock in the long run because the stock market will view the company as less risky and open to public attack and therefore award it a higher price-earnings ratio.
10. Society should give business a chance to solve social problems that government has failed to solve.
11. Business, by some groups, is considered to be the institution with the financial and human resources to solve social problems.
12. Prevention of problems is better than cures — so let business solve problems before they become too great.

Major Arguments Against Social Responsibility
1. It might be illegal.
2. Business plus government equals monolith.
3. Social actions cannot be measured.
4. It violates profit maximization.
5. Cost of social responsibility is too great and would increase prices too much.
6. Business lacks social skills to solve societal problems.
7. It would dilute business's primary purposes.
8. It would weaken U.S. balance of payments because price of goods will have to go up to pay for social programs.
9. Business already has too much power. Such involvement would make business too powerful.
10. Business lacks accountability to the public. Thus the public would have no control over its social involvement.
11. Such business involvement lacks broad public support.

Source: Adapted from Joseph R. Mansen, "The Social Attitudes of Management," in Joseph W. McGuire (ed.), *Contemporary Management* (Englewood Cliffs, N.J.: Prentice-Hall, Inc., 1974), p. 616.

organizations to consider factors other than just the profitability of the firm.

In 1948, the theme of the annual Harvard Business School Alumni Association meeting was Business Responsibility. In 1958, the American Management Association surveyed 700 companies concerning

their "managerial creed or statement of basic objectives."[10] Nearly
every company expressed the belief that they had a responsibility to
society. The 1950s and 1960s saw an increasing number of organizations and managers expressing concern with the social responsibilities
of organizations. However, socially responsible programs were actually implemented by very few organizations until the late 1960s. Minority hiring, environmental programs, and loans and technical assistance to minority-owned businesses are all examples of programs that
have been recently undertaken by many organizations.

All managers do not agree that organizations have a social responsibility. A summary of the major arguments for and against social responsibility is given in Figure 21–4. The following sections of this
chapter will deal with some of the major arguments both for and
against social responsibility.[11]

ARGUMENTS FOR SOCIAL RESPONSIBILITY

It is in the best interest of the business

The future of business organizations depends on maintaining a
good relationship with the society in which it operates. If organizations fail to take actions in the area of social responsibility, then society will take action against business organizations. Boycotting the
products of an organization, picketing not only the organization but
also customers of the organization, and even violence against the organization are examples of actions that can be taken. An extension of
this argument is that if public pressure becomes too strong, then government will force the organization to assume the responsibility.

Social actions can be profitable

The Committee for Economic Development (CED) reported on
two profit-seeking ventures.

> Two New York City corporations have established a profit-making
> venture, Construction for Progress, which is building about $6 million
> worth of low-rent apartment units in ghetto areas as turn-key projects.
> So far, construction has cost about 15 percent less than it would have
> under governmental sponsorship, has been completed in one third the
> time, and the first building has been sold to the New York City Housing
> Authority at a reasonable profit.

---

[10] Stewart Thompson, *Management Creeds and Philosophies; Top Management
Guides in Our Changing Economy* (New York: American Management Association,
1958), Research Study no. 32.

[11] Much of the material in the following sections is adopted from G. Richey Elwell,
"Key Issues in the Debate over the Social Responsibility of Business," *The Manager's
Key*, vol. 47, no. 2 (December 1972), pp. 7–19.

On a larger scale, 30 leading companies in the Greater Hartford (Connecticut) region have established The Greater Hartford Corporation to plan and direct development of the 750 square-mile metropolitan area. As a profit-making operating organization, a development corporation is raising $30 million for the acquisition of land to produce a new community out of a North Hartford ghetto area as the first stage in a $3 billion regional development plan.[12]

In 1968, the government was willing to pay approximately $3,500 per individual to any company willing to train an individual considered to be unemployable.[13] Rent supplements have been guaranteed to landlords when a low-income family is required to pay only 25 percent of their income toward rent. In a more indirect manner, donations to higher education, hiring disadvantaged individuals, urban renewal projects, and participation in conservation programs aid in the long-term profitability of all organizations.

Being socially responsible is the ethical thing to do

Since business in an integral part of society, many individuals argue that being socially responsible is a moral responsibility of organizations. The proponents of this argument feel that it is a moral responsibility of organizations to provide safe products, clean up streams, and conserve our material resources. However, as has been pointed out in the discussion on ethics, interpreting society's values is difficult. Evidence shows, however, that business decisions generally reflect the ethical system by which a society lives.[14] Thus, if the public at large feels that social responsibility is the ethical thing to do, then it can be expected that businessmen and organizations will feel the same way.

ARGUMENTS AGAINST SOCIAL RESPONSIBILITY

It might be illegal

Milton Friedman has argued that the only responsibility of business is to maximize profits for shareholders.[15] This argument assumes that managers are agents of the stockholders and that the diversion of

---

[12] Committee for Economic Development (CED), "Social Responsibilities of Business Corporations," a statement on national policy by the Research and Policy Committee (Washington, D.C.: June 1971), p. 43.

[13] U.S. Department of Labor, November 1968.

[14] Glenn Gilman, "The Ethical Dimension in American Management," *California Management Review*, vol. 3 (Fall 1969), p. 49.

[15] Milton Friedman, "Does Business Have a Social Responsibility?" *The Magazine of Bank Administration*, April 1971, p. 14.

funds to activities that do not contribute to profits may be illegal. This viewpoint was held by most managers and was supported by the courts until recent times. For instance, in 1919, a Michigan court declared that business was to be operated primarily for the profit of stockholders and forced the company to declare a dividend, which it had not done for many years.[16]

However, this argument has been considerably weakened in recent years. In 1935, an amendment to the Internal Revenue Code allowed corporations to deduct up to 5 percent of net profits for social purposes. Furthermore, in 1953, the New Jersey Supreme Court upheld the right of the A. P. Smith Company to give funds to Princeton University against the desires of some stockholders. The court stated that "it was not just a right but a duty of corporations to support higher education in the interest of the long-range well-being of their stockholders because the company could not hope to operate effectively in a society which is not functioning well."[17]

Business plus government equals monolith

The proponents of this argument feel that business should make profits and government should spend tax money to attack social problems. They argue that socially motivated business activities sublimate and compromise the profit motive. Theodore Leavitt feels that if business begins to assume more and more social responsibility, then there could ultimately be very little functional difference between business and government.[18] Without this functional difference, society would be dominated by one unopposed and unstoppable monolith.

Social actions cannot be measured

Milton Friedman has asked, "If businessmen do have a social responsibility other than making maximum profits for stockholders, how do they know what it is? Can they decide how great a burden they are justified in placing on themselves or their stockholders to serve that social interest?"[19] Also, who should decide what is good for society? Proponents of this argument feel that management cannot

---

[16] George A. Steiner, *Business and Society* (New York: Random House, 1971), p. 154.

[17] CED, "Social Responsibilities," p. 27.

[18] Theodore Levitt, "The Dangers of Social Responsibility," *Harvard Business Review*, vol. 36 (September–October 1958), pp. 41–50.

[19] "A Changing Balance of Power: New Partnership of Government and Business," *Business Week*, July 17, 1965, p. 90.

accurately measure the benefits of social action and that it is fruitless to continue spending money without measuring the return on the investment.

Traditionally the financial audit has been used to measure the profit performance of organizations. The need for measuring an organization's social responsibility has led to the idea of a social audit. Presently, however, the term *social audit* is vaguely defined.

Numerous ideas have been proposed in measuring an organization's social performance. Howard R. Bowen has suggested that firms "subject themselves to periodic examination by independent outside experts who would evaluate the performance of the business from the social point of view."[20] Some organizations have attempted to measure the quality of social responsiveness of its operations by attempting to quantify social variables in cost-benefit terms.[21]

ACTIONS NECESSARY TO EFFECT SOCIAL RESPONSIBILITY

The biggest obstacle to organizations assuming more social responsibility is the pressure exerted by owners and managers for steady increases in earnings per share on a quarterly basis.[22] Concern about immediate profit maximization makes it rather difficult to invest in areas that cannot be accurately measured and also have returns which are long-run in nature. Furthermore, pressure for short-term earnings has an impact on corporate social behavior because most companies are geared to short-term profit objectives. Budgets, objectives, and performance evaluations are often based on short-run considerations. Management may express a willingness to sacrifice some short-term profit to achieve social objectives. However, managers who sacrifice profit in their own departments and seek to justify it on the basis of corporate social goals may find that their superiors are unsympathetic.

Organizations should also carefully examine their cherished values — short-run profits and others — to ensure that these concepts are in tune with the values held by society. This should be a continuous process because the values held by society are ever-changing.

Organizations should reevaluate their long-range planning and decision-making processes to ensure that they fully understand the

---

[20] Bowen, *Social Responsibility of the Businessman*, pp. 3–13.

[21] Frederick Andrews, "Puzzled Businessmen Ponder New Methods of Measuring Success," *Wall Street Journal*, 9 December 1971, p. 1.

[22] Much of the material for this section and the following section is drawn from Lloyd L. Byars and Michael H. Mescon, *The Other Side of Profit* (Philadelphia: W. B. Saunders Co., 1975), pp. 3–13.

potential social consequences. Plant location decisions are no longer merely economic matters. Environmental consequences and impact on employment opportunities for the disadvantaged are examples of other factors that may be considered.

Organizations should seek to help not only governmental agencies but also voluntary agencies in their social efforts. This should include technical and managerial assistance as well as monetary support. Technological knowledge, organizational skills, and managerial competence can all be applied to solving social problems.

Finally, organizations should give attention to the ways in which they can help in solving social problems through the operation of their own business. Many of the social problems that exist stem from the economic deprivation of a fairly large segment of our society. Attacking this problem could be the most significant social undertaking of organizations.

EXAMPLES OF SOCIALLY RESPONSIBLE ORGANIZATIONS

Many organizations have undertaken programs attacking some of our social problems. These have ranged from certain investments to profit-seeking ventures. Table 21–2 summarizes some of the investments which have social ramifications made by the life insurance industry.

Motorola, Incorporated, has participated in a program called the Industrial Skill Center (ISC). The Industrial Skill Center resulted from the Chicago Board of Education's efforts to provide alternatives to the traditional high school. It was designed to transform high school dropouts into productive citizens through occupational edu-

TABLE 21–2

Urban investment program of the life insurance business (status as of April 1, 1973)

Housing		
Mortgages and real estate......................................	$1,321,167,000	
Securities..	24,816,000	
total housing		$1,345,983,000
Job creating and service facilities		
Medical and social services....................................	419,316,700	
Commercial and industrial	270,354,000	
Minority financial institutions	7,295,000	
Total job-creating and service facilities		696,965,700
Grand total...		$2,042,948,700

Source: Lloyd L. Byars and Michael H. Mescon, *The Other Side of Profit* (Philadelphia: W. B. Saunders Company, 1975), p. 48.

TABLE 21–3
Types of social responsibility activities

Activity	Percent Practicing
Contribution to education	86
Ecology	78
Minority hiring	78
Minority training	68
Contributions to the arts	68
Hard-core hiring	58
Hard-core training	55
Civil rights	53
Urban renewal	53
Consumer complaints	46
Understandable accounting statements	42
Truth-in-advertising	42
Product defects	36
Guarantees and warranties	32
Consumer-oriented label changes	24

cation. Motorola's section of the ISC has taught students basic electronics and how to test automobile parts for possible defects. The students at the Center not only provide a service to the company by analyzing and repairing radio parts but also provide a source of trained labor for the electronics industry.

Table 21–3 outlines the results of a study that surveyed the socially responsible actions of 96 companies randomly selected from the 1971 Forbes "Roster of the Country's Biggest Corporations."[23]

SUMMARY

Ethics are standards or principles of conduct used to govern the behavior of an individual or a group of individuals. Ethics are generally concerned with questions relating to what is right or wrong or with moral duties.

A code of ethics is needed within organizations because society is demanding it and because it would provide direction to the organization and to the employees of the organization.

The Judaeo-Christian ethic is generally considered to be the basis of Western ethical codes and thus might be the basis for a code of ethics for organizations. Another approach to business ethics is the gamesmanship approach which compares business ethics to the

---

[23] Henry Eilbirt and I. Robert Parket, "The Current Status of Corporate Social Responsibility," *Business Horizons*, August 1973, p. 9.

strategy of playing a game. Few ethical questions in business can be clearly classified as right or wrong. However, basic guidelines do exist for managers facing ethical decisions.

The term social responsibility has come to denote a multitude of issues and problems and is thus vaguely defined. The basic ideas of social responsibility are not accepted by all organizations, and many arguments exist both for and against participation by business organizations. However, many organizations have participated in programs attempting to solve social problems.

REVIEW QUESTIONS

1. What are ethics? Give some reasons why a code of ethics is needed in organizations.

2. Describe the Judaeo-Christian ethic.

3. Discuss gamesmanship in business ethics.

4. What is social responsibility?

5. Outline three major arguments for social responsibility.

6. Outline three major arguments against social responsibility.

7. What is the major obstacle to organizations being more socially responsible?

DISCUSSION QUESTIONS

1. Do you feel that organizations and managers should be evaluated with regard to social responsibility?

2. Are most managers ethical? Discuss.

3. "Profits and not social responsibility must be the primary concern of managers." Discuss.

4. Why are numerous unethical practices, such as "padding the expense account," accepted by many managers in today's organizational world?

SELECTED READINGS

Baumhart, Raymond, S. J. *Ethics in Business.* New York: Holt, Rinehart and Winston, Inc. 1968.

Davis, Keith. "Can Business Afford to Ignore Social Responsibilities?" *California Management Review,* vol. 2, no. 3 (Spring 1960), pp. 70–76.

Elwell, G. Richey. "Key Issues in the Debate Over the Social Responsibility of Business," *The Manager's Key,* vol. 47, no. 2 (December 1972), pp. 7–19.

Golembiewski, Robert T. *Men, Management, and Morality.* New York: McGraw-Hill Book Co., 1965.

Heilbroner, Robert L. et al. *In the Name of Profit.* Garden City, N.Y.: Doubleday and Company, Inc., 1972.

Henderson, Hazel. "Should Business Tackle Society's Problems?" *Harvard Business Review*, vol. 46, no. 4 (July–August 1968), pp. 77–85.

Levitt, Theodore. "The Dangers of Social Responsibility," *Harvard Business Review*, vol. 36 (September–October 1958), pp. 41–50.

Luthans, Fred, and Richard M. Hodgetts. *Social Issues in Business.* New York: The Macmillan Company, 1972.

Case 21–1

The property book officer

Lt. Max Williams had just been assigned the responsibility of keeping the property book for the 500th Engineer Company. The property book indicates all of the inventory that the military unit is supposed to have on hand. Lt. Williams decided to take an actual count of the inventory and discovered shortages totaling more than $128,000. He immediately notified the company commander, Captain Crane. That same day, Lt. Williams was called to Captain Crane's office. At that time, Lt. Williams discovered that the outgoing property book officer and the batallion commander were also attending the meeting. It was explained to Lt. Williams that the shortages had actually existed for several years and under several property book officers. Furthermore, it was explained that everyone in the military service realized that property books did not reflect the true picture and that it had been customary to cover the property book officer who was leaving.

1. What would you do in this situation? Why?
2. If Lt. Williams does not go along, what are the consequences?

Case 21–2

Padding the expense account?

Principals:

Rick Bell—Residence Accounts Manager in Midland for United Electric Company. Rick is 25 years old, is considered to have good potential as a manager, and was promoted to his present job one month ago.

Stan Holloway — District Manager for United Electric in Midland. He is 33 years old and has been in his present job $2\frac{1}{2}$ years. His district, Midland, has strong political influence in the Company, as the current president of United Electric was raised in Midland. Stan is Rick's boss.

Chester "Chet" House — Division Manager for United. He is 61 years old and is located at company headquarters about 30 miles from Midland. He is Stan's boss and is also a close personal friend of the president of United.

At 7:45 A.M. on the 28th of March, Rick Bell was preparing to leave Stan Holloway's office after chatting with him for a few minutes about the week's activities.

Rick: Oh, I almost forgot. As soon as I have my monthly expense voucher typed I'll send it to you for signature so it can be forwarded to disbursing.

Stan: I'm glad you mentioned that. I had meant to talk to you about your voucher this month. I have about $100 worth of items I want you to include on your voucher. This month my voucher is really loaded and I hate to submit an extremely high amount in light of the emphasis being placed on personal expense control. Since I have signature authority on your voucher nobody will look at it and when you get your check back you can give me the extra amount to cover my additional expenses. Here is an itemized list of expenses and dates incurred for inclusion.

Also, don't forget that Chet House is coming by today and we are to go to lunch with him.

Rick Bell leaves Stan's office with the itemized list in his hand. During the morning, Rick gives much thought to Stan's request. At about 10 A.M., Stan calls Rick on the intercom and informs him that he (Stan) won't be able to go to lunch with them (Rick and Chet) that day because the local congressman is making an unscheduled stop in Midland to confer with some selected business leaders on some local issues that will be dominant in the upcoming fall election. He asks Rick to take Chet out to lunch and give him his regrets and to tell Chet that he (Stan) will see them after lunch around 2 P.M. When Chet arrives he and Rick leave for lunch and during the meal, the following conversation ensues:

Rick: Mr. House, What would you do if you were ever approached to include expenses on your expense voucher that were not yours?

Chet: Well son, that's a hard thing to theorize on. I guess the best approach would be to look at the consequences for different courses of action. If you did it and got caught in the yearly audit (a slim but possible chance), you could be reprimanded or even fired if the violation were flagrant enough. Of course, if you didn't get caught, you would be home free unless you were repeatedly asked to do it. And if you refuse to do it and the person asking you happens to be your boss, funny things sometimes begin to happen. People get labeled as being uncooperative and nobody wants to be thought of as being uncooperative.

So I guess that every man at some time has to make a decision that determines his survival among the fittest. This situation could be one of them.

Rick and Chet finished their meal in relative silence and went back to the office where they met Stan for their conference. After the conference, Rick went back to his office and gave some thought to the events of the day. That evening after work Rick went back to Stan's office with the results of his decision.

1. What would you have done if you were Rick?
2. Do you agree with Mr. House's response to Rick?

Objectives

1. To emphasize the importance of current trends for future managers.
2. To project some changes that are likely to occur in management and organizations.

GLOSSARY OF TERMS

Administrator An individual who performs all of the management functions but whose primary emphasis is on organizing and motivating.

Future shock A term coined by Alvin Toffler to describe the stress and disorientation that results from a tremendous amount of change in a short period of time.

New morality A term used to describe a movement toward uninhibited freedom of expression and freedom in decision making.

Public-oriented manager Manages under a philosophy which emphasizes societal goals and thus seeks participation, prefers leisure and a place in the community, and generally seeks to satisfy the higher order needs of Maslow's need hierarchy.

22

Forward into the future

In dealing with the future, at least for the purposes at hand, it is more important to be imaginative and insightful than to be 100 percent "right." Theories do not have to be "right" to be enormously useful. Even error has its uses. The maps of the world drawn by the medieval cartographers were so hopelessly inaccurate, so filled with factual error, that they elicit condescending smiles today when almost the entire surface of the earth has been charted. Yet the great explorers could never have discovered the New World without them. Nor could the better, more accurate maps of today been drawn until men, working with the limited evidence available to them, set down on paper their bold conceptions of worlds they had never seen.

Alvin Toffler[*]

PREDICTIONS about the future generally arouse the interest of most people. Traditionally, references to the future cause most managers to think about growth in profits, growth in the number of employees, and other statistics which project the performance of their particular organization. As profit and staffing forecasts increase, managers interpret this as growth and expansion of the present organization with continued application of current concepts of management. Assuming that the future will be like the past and failing to consider the impact of opposing trends or potential discontinuities can be a dangerous pitfall for managers. The purpose of this chapter is to explore some of the trends that will influence management in the future and also to make some projections concerning future organizational life.

---

[*] *Future Shock*, New York: Random House, 1970, p. 5.

FUTURE SHOCK

Rapid changes are currently occurring in technology, family life, and other areas that influence individuals and organizations. The following example illustrates the rapid rate of change in transportation.

> It has been pointed out, for example, that in 6000 B.C. the fastest transportation available to man over long distances was the camel caravan, averaging eight mph. It was not until about 1600 B.C., when the chariot was invented, that the maximum speed was raised to roughly 20 mph.
>
> So impressive was this invention, so difficult was it to exceed this speed limit, that nearly 3,500 years later, when the first mail coach began operating in England in 1784, it averaged a mere ten mph. The first stem locomotive, introduced in 1825, could muster a top speed of only 13 mph, and the great sailing ships of the time labored along at less than half that speed. It was probably not until the 1800s that man, with the help of a more advanced steam locomotive, managed to reach a speed of 100 mph. It took the human race millions of years to attain that record.
>
> It took only 58 years, however, to quadruple the limit so that by 1938 airborne man was cracking the 400-mph line. It took a mere 20-year flick of time to double the limit again. And by the 1960s rocket planes approached speeds of 4,000 mph, and men in space capsules were circling the earth at 18,000 mph.[1]

Exponential rates of change, such as expressed in the above quotation, affect humans not only physically but also psychologically. In 1965, Alvin Toffler coined the term *future shock* to describe the stress and disorientation that result from too much change in too short a time.[2] Organizations and managers must learn to understand and cope with this type of stress.

SCARCE RESOURCES

Another environmental condition that seems likely to exist and intensify for many years is the scarcity of resources. In the past, organizations and managers have operated on the assumption that there was an unlimited supply of natural resources. The energy crises and other material shortages have proved this assumption to be invalid.

Furthermore, the management philosophy of most organizations has been based on growth. Growth in profits, number of employees,

---

[1] Alvin Toffler, *Future Shock* (New York: Random House, 1970), p. 24.
[2] Ibid., p. 2.

and value of assets has traditionally been high on the list of objectives for most organizations. However, recent reports conclude that growth in terms of numbers and larger size cannot continue forever.[3] In fact, one author has pointed out that if the economy continues to grow at a five-percent annual rate, by the end of another century it would become 500 times greater or 50,000 percent larger than its present size.[4]

The scarcity of resources has led many forecasters to predict that managers and organizations of the future must change their basic philosophy. The new philosophy must be concerned with "quality of life" as opposed to "quantity of life." This forecast is probably true at least to the extent that managers of the future must be much more aware of the utilization of scarce resources than they have been in the past.

MANAGEMENT AND THE NEW MORALITY

The so-called new morality of modern society has been accompanied by a challenge to the traditional foundations for managerial decision making.[5] One cannot seriously question the methods for making decisions without first questioning the authority for making the decisions.[6]

History of authority

Until recent years, little concern was expressed regarding the source of a manager's authority. In 1916, Henri Fayol, the French management pioneer, spoke of managerial authority as being derived from office.[7] Elmore Peterson and E. Grosvenor Plowman described authority in the United States as originating with the will of the people and flowing down through the Constitution, the corporate

---

[3] M. Mesarovic and E. Pestel, *Mankind at the Turning Point: The Second Report to the Club of Rome* (New York: E. P. Dutton & Company, 1974). See also Donella H. Meadows, Dennis L. Meadows, Jorgen Randers, and William W. Behrens III, *Limits to Growth* (New York: Universe Books, 1972).

[4] John Mee, "Debut of the Public-Oriented Executive," *The Business Quarterly*, Autumn 1975, p. 26.

[5] Robert M. Fulmer and Charles Wellborn, "The New Morality and the New Managers," *Business Horizons*, vol. 10 (Winter 1967), p. 98.

[6] Much of the following material is adapted from Robert M. Fulmer and Leslie W. Rue, "Competence: The Cohesive of Future Organizations," *Personnel Journal*, vol. 52, no. 4 (April 1973), pp. 264–73.

[7] Henri Fayol, *General and Industrial Management* (London: Sir Isaac Pitman and Sons, Ltd., 1949), p. 21.

laws, and so on down the line.[8] Ralph Davis described authority as being derived from the right of private property.[9] All of these views have contributed to what has become known as the formal or classical theory of authority.

The formal theory of authority was first seriously questioned as early as 1938 by Chester Barnard. Barnard suggested that authority exists by virtue of subordinates granting authority to their superiors by their willingness to accept orders or directions.[10] Barnard further stated that the subordinates' acceptance of authority is subject to the following requirements: that they understand the order, that they believe it is consistent with the organization's purpose, that they feel it is compatible with their own interests, and that they are mentally and physically able to comply with it. This concept was labeled the *acceptance theory* (the acceptance theory was briefly discussed in Chapter 6).

Although there is no universal agreement on a theory of authority, there has been a shift away from absolute adherence to the classical approach.

Major impacts on authority

Merely observing that changes have occurred regarding the source of authority does not provide a basis for predictions about the future. To make predictions, an understanding of why these changes have occurred must exist. The shifts can partially be explained by applying Maslow's hierarchy of needs, which was discussed in Chapter 9.

From the days of Frederick W. Taylor in the early 20th century through the Great Depression, formal authority was at its height. The boss or manager was never questioned and rarely disobeyed. "Times were hard," and workers could not afford to lose their jobs. Welfare programs were nonexistent, and the unemployment rate ran as high as 25 percent.

Looking at Maslow's hierarchy of needs, one can see that the great majority of workers until World War II were primarily concerned with physical needs. Putting bread on the table and clothing on their backs were the primary concerns of these workers. How can a human being who is predominantly occupied with the physical needs question the superior who has control over the survival of that person's family?

---

[8] Elmore Peterson and E. Grosvenor Plowman, *Business Organization and Management*, 4th ed. (Homewood, Ill.: Richard D. Irwin, Inc., 1958), pp. 84–85.

[9] Ralph C. Davis, *The Fundamentals of Top Management* (New York: Harper and Brothers, 1951), p. 285.

[10] Chester I. Barnard, *The Functions of the Executive* (Cambridge, Mass.: Harvard University Press, 1938), p. 167.

FIGURE 22–1
Maslow's hierarchy of needs and corresponding periods of dominance

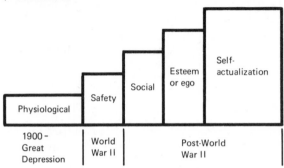

Source: Abraham Maslow, "A Theory of Human Motivation," *Psychology Review*, vol. 50 (July 1943), pp. 370–96.

The period from the Great Depression through World War II saw the economy recover and unemployment fall. As a result, the physical needs of the majority were fulfilled. However, the war kept the general level of need satisfaction at the "safety" level. The general public felt that World War II threatened the safety of the entire country and its inhabitants. How can individuals who genuinely see the safety of their homes and country threatened question their superiors?

With the close of World War II, the continued growth of the economy and the increased level of education helped to push a great many workers higher up Maslow's hierarchy. More workers became concerned with social, esteem, and self-actualization needs and more began to raise questions about traditional institutions. In this light, the questioning of authority should come as no surprise. It was only after the majority of the people had moved out of the lower levels of need satisfaction that the "new morality" concept appeared.

New morality or old immorality?

The phrase "new morality" usually conjures up images of free love, drugs, and protest groups. The term has been used to describe widely divergent viewpoints. The main thrust of the new morality is toward uninhibited freedom of expression and freedom in decision making. In other words, individuals should be free to make decisions without being bound by previous conventions.

The challenge to the traditional foundations for decision making has also raised questions concerning the authority of management.

Specific and unchanging rules can no longer be assumed to be valid in managing organizations. Instead the new moralists reason that each situation is unique. Each specific situation must be interpreted in the light of historical experience, general ethical principles, established moral norms, and the peculiar circumstances which provide uniqueness to the situation. Legalistic approaches to authority are no longer accepted as the way things must be.[11]

Who has the authority?

It seems clear that increased education, changing moral prospectives, greater affluence, and higher order needs orientation all suggest the likelihood of decreasing dependence on the power of formal authority in organizations. On the other hand, a continued trend toward greater freedom from formal authority ultimately could lead to anarchy.[12]

However, there are important countervailing influences. First, there is the impact of deep cultural preferences for order. Second, the increasing rapidity of change on all fronts calls for some system of authority to cope with the change. Finally, the computer has also had an impact on authority. Before the computer began to make significant contributions to management's information technology, decentralized decision making was practiced by a large number of firms. The existence of the computer offers the capability, but not necessarily the rationale, for recentralization.

Regardless of the other implications of computerization, this innovation has definitely increased the span of control and the competence of the top management team. Thus it is now possible for executives in home offices to be constantly aware of performance in distant operations. The computer gives them the ability to participate in the planning process and to monitor progress made toward the realization of these plans.

There is no question that many employees have resisted and will continue to resist arbitrary imposition of formal authority. But has this been opposition to authority per se or has it been opposition to invalid authority which was seen as invalid because it lacked the validity created by competence? "Because I say so" will become increasingly less acceptable as an answer to the eternal question

---

[11] This section is adapted from Fulmer and Wellborn, "The New Morality," p. 98. For additional information and references concerning the "new morality" see Charles Wellborn ed., *Challenge to Morality* (Tallahassee: Florida State University Press, 1962).

[12] Joseph Fletcher, *Situation Ethics* (Philadelphia: The Westminister Press, 1966), p. 22.

"Why?" Authority has been historically viewed as the cement that holds organizations together. Tomorrow's management must clearly utilize a better grade of cement if they are to maintain order and progress. In the future, managers who have reached their level of incompetence can expect even greater resistance to their plans while competent, well-tempered executives will find technical and moral justification for their proposals.

Actually this changing concept of competence has already begun to appear in many organizations. In companies utilizing a form of matrix organization, extensive, multimillion dollar market strategy proposals are developed by young managers.[13] While these proposals may be approved by three or four successive levels of management, competent proposals or those perceived as competent because of the reputation for competence enjoyed by the proposal's author are routinely approved.

In these firms, top management must rely on the competence of their subordinates because there is simply not enough time to adequately investigate all aspects of all recommendations. In engineering-based, technically oriented firms, top management is further restricted because they cannot expect to match or even to understand the technical competence of highly specialized subordinates. Thus the general acceptance of the individual, rather than the authority of his or her position, may be the real source of practical power.

ADMINISTRATION OR MANAGEMENT?

The term *administration* is frequently used interchangeably with *management*. Today, however, the terms seem to be taking on new implications. The administrator is more often pictured as performing well-structured routinized functions. On the other hand, the manager is pictured as performing the more general functions of planning and controlling.

The increasing divergence of the terms administration and management can be attributed to the increased rate of technical and social change. This increased rate of change has forced management to place greater emphasis on the future through the planning function. The expanded size of companies has caused increased concern for control. More sophisticated planning and control have both been made possible through the computer. As a result of these factors, top management has increasingly taken on the planning and controlling functions and pushed the administrative function further down the line.

---

[13] See Chapter 6 for a discussion of matrix organization.

While both the manager and the administrator perform all of the management functions, the emerging emphasis in the administrator's job is on organizing and motivating, while the emerging emphasis of the manager's job is on planning and controlling.

CENTRALIZATION OR DECENTRALIZATION?

Many of the arguments and predictions concerning organizations in the future deal with the issue of centralization versus decentralization. Furthermore, these arguments are often largely colored by the author's perceived impact of automation and the computer on the future. Harold J. Leavitt and Thomas L. Whisler forecast a move toward recentralization in the large firms of the future. They predict:

> . . . that large industrial organizations will recentralize, that top managers will take on an even larger proportion of the innovating, planning, and other "creative" functions than they have now.[14]

Other authors assess the impact of automation and computers from an opposing viewpoint. John Dearden states:

> I seriously doubt that the increasing use of computers and related information technology will affect top management's ability to control divisional operations, and in particular that it will bring about a trend to recentralization.[15]

One possible explanation of these divergent views is that the functions of top management are becoming more centralized while the administrative functions are becoming more decentralized. The end result is an organizational structure with "centralized decentralization." This type of structure is also consistent with the mood of the new morality in that the decentralized administration would foster flexibility and reduce the amount of undesirable structure. There should be little objection to competent, centralized control and planning as long as the administrative functions are handled on a decentralized, personal basis.

THE ROLE OF MIDDLE MANAGEMENT

Numerous predictions regarding the changing nature of middle management have been made by knowledgeable management

---

[14] Harold J. Leavitt and Thomas L. Whisler, "Management in the 1980's," *Harvard Business Review*, vol. 36 (November–December 1958), p. 41. In 1970, Whisler published two books: *The Impact of Computers on Organizations* (Praeger Publishers, New York); and *Information Technology and Organizational Change* (Wadsworth Publishing Co., Inc., Belmont, Calif.) in which he updated his 1958 predictions. His revised predictions are similar but based on a much longer time frame.

[15] John Dearden, "Computers: No Impact on Divisional Control," *Harvard Business Review*, vol. 37 (January–February 1967), p. 99.

authors. They all predict changes of some magnitude or form in the job content of middle managers.

Leavitt and Whisler predict the roles of all management levels will change substantially and particularly the role of middle management.

> A radical reorganization of middle-management levels should occur, with certain classes of middle-management jobs moving downward in status and compensation (because they will require less·autonomy and skill), while other classes move upward into the top-management group.[16]

Herbert Simon forecasts a decline in the relative number of middle management positions but concludes that the relative number of overall management positions will remain unchanged.

> We might even conclude that management and other professional activities, taken collectively, may constitute about the same part of the total spectrum of occupations a generation hence as they do now. But there is reason to believe that the kinds of activities that now characterize middle management will be more completely automated than others and hence will come to have a smaller part in the whole management position.[17]

There seems to be general agreement that the job content of middle management will change. The disagreement comes in deciding what to call middle management. Will the downgraded, routinized management functions still be called "middle management" or will a new title be developed? How about the middle-management jobs which gain status because of improved, computer-assisted competence? Do these become top-management jobs even if there are the same number of positions above them in the organization? In other words, the managers who are between the supervisory and top executive levels in the firms of the future will still be in the middle, although the nature of their work may be significantly altered.

FUTURE ORGANIZATIONAL STRUCTURES

Will the conventional pyramid predominate or will a new structure evolve in the future? Writers making predictions on this subject are predominantly influenced by one of two factors, automation and the computer, or the behavioral sciences.

Logically, following from their predicted demise of middle-

---

[16] Leavitt and Whisler, "Management in the 1980's," p. 41.

[17] Herbert A. Simon, "The Corporation: Will It Be Managed by Machines?" in Melvin Anshen and George Leland Black, eds., *Management and Corporation 1985* (New York: McGraw-Hill Book Co., 1960), p. 50.

management's role, Leavitt and Whisler envision the future organization chart as a football balanced on the point of a bell.

> Within the football (the top staff organization) problems of coordination, individual autonomy, group decision making, and so on should arise more intensely than ever. We expect they will be dealt with quite independently of the bell portion of the company, with distinctly different methods of remuneration, control, and communication.[18]

Richard D. Farmer has described modern, highly advanced firms as approaching an egglike organizational structure.[19] He has also predicted that in highly advanced firms the workers at the bottom will be automated out, thus shifting the structural weight to the middle area. Farmer sees this trend continuing until the structural weight eventually shifts to top levels of management. At this point, Farmer predicts that the future firm will resemble an inverted pyramid.

To date, neither the computer nor social pressure has caused the changes predicted in the late fifties and early sixties. Just as no other great technological discovery or social movement has completely revolutionized the American system of organization, it now appears that neither the computer nor the new morality will achieve that goal. Change will come as a result of these inputs, but as in the past it will not occur overnight. Contrary to some past predictions, the lower-level jobs are not likely to be automated out—not merely because it may be unfeasible but also because it is not consistent with the new morality. Under the new morality the social status of a position is less important as emphasis is directed to higher order needs.

CORPORATE DEMOCRACY

As evidenced earlier in this chapter, the new morality is producing a trend toward corporate democracy. In 1971, the editors of the *Harvard Business Review* published the results of a survey of 3,453 of its subscribers and several student groups. The results of part of that study are summarized below:

1. Approximately one sixth to one half of the respondents were willing to allow activist elements in the company, depending on the issue. The editors felt that this percentage was likely to increase as more young managers move up the hierarchy.

2. About one third of the respondents were willing to let employees vote on certain policy issues. The percentage increased to one half if the vote was limited to managerial employees.

---

[18] Leavitt and Whisler, "Management in the 1980's," p. 43.

[19] Richard D. Farmer, *Management in the Future* (Belmont, Calif.: Wadsworth Publishing Company, Inc., 1967), p. 80.

3. Most respondents felt that the board of directors should consider the feelings of key employee groups in selecting a new chief executive.

4. More than 60 percent of the respondents felt that the interests of the owners must be balanced with the interests of the employees, customers, and the public.[20]

The editors also investigated the following questions:

1. How arbitrary can a boss be with an employee in the name of corporate efficiency and necessity?

2. At what point does the actions that a manager can legally take become impractical?

3. When an employee has a grievance, what types of corrective procedures should he or she have?[21]

A summary of some of the findings in response to these questions is presented below:

1. Firing a manager without giving an opportunity for self-defense was condemned by almost all of the respondents.

2. Employees who are about to be fired are entitled to know the charges made against them.

3. If an order violates accepted ethical standards, then an employee is entitled to violate the order.

4. Unlimited authority to arbitrarily transfer an employee is no longer considered to be a management right.[22]

In fact, the trend toward more democracy and less emphasis on the traditional concepts of authority led Mack Hanan to propose a corporate bill of rights.[23] A modified version of that bill of rights is shown in Figure 22–2.

Managers and organizations of the future will face increasing demands for more democracy. Systems of organizing and methods of management will be required to adapt to these changes. This trend is also in agreement with the concept of the new morality which was discussed earlier.

THE PUBLIC-ORIENTED EXECUTIVE

In the past, organizations have been managed by managers using an Economic Man philosophy. Economic Man philosophy is based

---

[20] David W. Ewing, "Who Wants Corporate Democracy?" *Harvard Business Review,* September–October 1971, p. 13.

[21] David W. Ewing, "Who Wants Employee Rights?" *Harvard Business Review,* November–December 1971, pp. 22–23.

[22] Ewing, "Employee Rights," p. 23.

[23] Mack Hanan, "Make Way for the New Organization Man," *Harvard Business Review,* July–August 1971, pp. 128–38.

FIGURE 22–2
Corporate bill of rights

Article 1:	Management will not limit the expression of personal beliefs of any employee either within or without the organization.
Article 2:	Management will not make unreasonable searches and seizures of employee's offices, papers, and effects.
Article 3:	An employee is entitled to know the nature and cause of any accusations made against him or her.
Article 4:	In all disputes, the employee has the right to a speedy, and if mutually agreed on, public hearing; to be confronted by the accusers; to have witnesses in the employee's favor; and to have assistance in his or her defense.
Article 5:	No employee can be terminated without due process of deliberation.

on providing goods and services on an economic basis, acquiring property, wealth, and income, and accepting a life style of hard work, thrift, and obedience to organizational authority.

John Mee has predicted a trend toward what he calls a "public-oriented" executive.[24] Based on an emerging philosophy which emphasizes societal goals, the public-oriented manager will seek participation, prefer leisure and a place in the community, and generally seek to satisfy the higher order needs of Maslow's need hierarchy.

The emergence of the public-oriented executive will have a significant impact on organizations. Management will be viewed more as a resource to achieve results rather than a system of authority. Socially oriented values and priorities will be melted with the economic values and priorities of present managers. The public-oriented executive will be challenged to use less resources and capital while better utilizing human resources and talents. The public-oriented executive concept may be viewed as an extension of the new morality concept.

MANAGEMENT EDUCATION

The future of American society as we know it today depends to a large extent on the skills and abilities of its managers. Traditional

---

[24] John Mee, "Debut of the Public-Oriented Executive," *The Business Quarterly,* Autumn 1975, pp. 22–29.

management education has taught courses dealing with policy formulation, decision making, labor relations, leadership, communication, planning, organizing, motivating, controlling, production, finance, accounting, and others. Managers of the future will still need these skills in order to manage effectively.

However, the management education needs of the public-oriented executive will expand to include subjects such as merging social objectives with economic objectives, managing in an economy with less growth than in prior years, learning to work with government agencies assessing the economic and social impact of technology advances, understanding of values and ethics, and negotiating and consulting with employees.[25]

Thus, in addition to having the skills necessary to manage the economic aspects of the firm, managers of the future will be required to have a broader based education. The public-oriented manager will be educated not only to look at economics but also the overall impact that managers and organizations have on society in general.

SUMMARY

Authority is slowly shifting from the classical approach toward the acceptance theory. Rather than continuing indefinitely, this evolution will lead to superior-subordinate relationships becoming increasingly dependent on the competence of both parties. The merging of the formal and acceptance theories of authority will result in a new form of authority which recognizes the rights of the governed while exacting responsibility from them.

The computer is basically neutral concerning the focus of authority. It can aid in moving toward greater centralization or greater decentralization depending on management's desires. It does, however, give both top and middle managers assistance in performing their jobs.

The organization of the future will have centralized top-management functions (planning and controlling) and decentralized administrative functions (organizing and motivating).

Some of the functions performed by today's middle managers will be routinized while others will become more demanding. The result will be a redefinition of middle management. The role of middle management will not be eliminated. Middle management will assume more and more administrative authority and ultimately will have greater responsibility for planning decentralized operations. Today's top managers already spend large amounts of time in dealing with the

---

[25] Ibid., p. 29.

demands of diverse societal institutions. The predicted role of middle managers will free top executives to do an even better job of these external expectations.

The changing role of middle management, the computer, and the new morality will cause a gradual erosion of the original pyramid, but this erosion will be slow. In other words, the dominance of the traditional organizational pyramid is likely to endure throughout this century and well into the next.

Corporate democracy will continue to increase. Increasing corporate democracy and numerous other factors will lead to the emergence of a public-oriented executive. In addition to economic priorities, the public-oriented executive will manage in accordance with socially oriented values and priorities. Management will be viewed more as a resource than as a system of authority.

Management education will continue to emphasize the skills necessary to manage the economic aspects of business but also will emphasize the impact of management on society.

Finally, the past continues to serve as a prologue to the future. But just as it has been necessary to "study the past or be doomed to repeat it," it is essential that the manager consider the future or be doomed to destroy it. The future—even more than the past—belongs to those who are prepared for it. Competence will be the key to effective management of the future.

REVIEW QUESTIONS

1. What is the new morality?

2. Describe the impact of the new morality on authority.

3. What is the difference between administration and management?

4. Describe some projections for changes in the following areas:
   a. Centralization versus decentralization.
   b. The role of middle management.
   c. Organization structure.
   d. Corporate democracy.

5. What is the public-oriented manager?

6. Describe some areas of study that will be essential for managers of the future.

DISCUSSION QUESTIONS

1. "Young people cannot be managed the same way as people who went through the Great Depression of 1929." Discuss.

2. "Organization structures have always been shaped like a pyramid and will continue as such for 100 years." Discuss.

3. What do you predict will be the shape of organizations in 1990?

4. Discuss what subject areas that you feel will benefit you most in your college education.

SELECTED READINGS

Farmer, Richard D. *Management in the Future*. Belmont, Calif.: Wadsworth Publishing Company, Inc., 1967.

Fulmer, Robert M. "The Management of Tomorrow," *Business Horizons* (August 1972), pp. 5–13.

Fulmer, Robert M., and Leslie W. Rue. "Competence: The Cohesive of Future Organizations," *Personnel Journal*. (April 1973), pp. 264–73.

Hanan, M. "Make Way for the New Organization Man," *Harvard Business Review* (July–August 1972), pp. 128–38.

Meadows, Donella H., Dennis L. Meadows, Jorgen Randers, and William W. Behrens, III. *Limits to Growth*. New York: Universe Books, 1972.

Mee, J. F. "The Manager of the Future," *Business Horizons* (August 1972), pp. 5–13.

Mesarovic, M., and E. Pestel. *Mankind at the Turning Point: The Second Report to the Club of Rome*. New York: E. P. Dutton and Company, 1974.

Nanus, B., and R. E. Coffey. "Future-Oriented Business Education," *California Management Review* (Summer 1973), pp. 28–34.

Toffler, Alvin. *Future Shock*. New York: Random House, 1970.

Case 22–1

Bribes and payoffs abroad

A study published this year by *The Wall Street Journal* gave a cross-section of opinion about bribes and payoffs abroad. The survey was conducted by the Conference Board, a nonprofit business research organization based in New York and included data from 93 executives. Approximately 52 percent of the responding executives felt that U.S. ethical standards should be followed in foreign countries regardless of its impact on sales. Approximately 48 percent felt that the ethical standards of the country in which the company is operating should be followed.

Furthermore, only 25 percent of the respondents had written

policies concerning unusual payments abroad. Seventy-five percent said their company depended on "unwritten" policies.

1. What future trends do you think will influence this situation?
2. How do the concepts of new morality and corporate democracy affect this situation?
3. How do you feel companies should operate in foreign countries?

Case 22–2

Democracy at station WXYZ

Every year, Station WXYZ chooses 15 women employees as hostesses for the Star Junket, which consists of a series of cocktail parties and dinners honoring the network stars for the upcoming season. Hostessing is highly sought by the employees because it represents the equivalent of a week's vacation with free drinks, food, and a chance to hobnob with the stars. Fringe benefits such as this are especially important in the broadcasting industry since salaries are relatively low. The procedure for choosing the women is as follows. A list is circulated at the station and those interested sign up. The general manager then chooses the 15 from the list. This year Ms. Jones was among those chosen as hostesses.

Through the grapevine it became known that although approximately 30 of the company employees signed up, the general manager told his secretary's daughter that she could be a hostess. The daughter is not employed by the company, but she did help out last year when a flu epidemic hit and several of the hostesses were ill at the last minute. When several girls mentioned this to Ms. Jones, she decided to start a petition on behalf of those employees who were rejected. Ms. Jones is a natural leader and a good organizer. Within an hour she obtained about 50 signatures on the petition which stated that the employees believed that the general manager was unfair in selecting an outsider to serve as hostess. Some of those who signed it were men; some were women; some were chosen as hostesses; and some were not. Ms. Jones went into the general manager's office only to find that he was temporarily out of town. She then presented the petition to John Stand, the manager in charge of her department.

John Stand was busy and told Ms. Jones he would get back to her. Later the general manager called Mr. Stand in relation to another matter, and Mr. Stand mentioned the petition. The general manager became irate and said he would handle it upon his return the next day.

When the general manager returned, he called Mr. Stand and

Ms. Jones into his office for a closed door session. The following conversation ensued:

General Manager: John, I want you to know that I consider Ms. Jones' action as a serious affront to my authority, and I blame you for not supervising her activities more closely.

Mr. Stand: Sir, you know we had that power failure problem and by the time I got it straightened out, this petition incident had already happened. I won't let anything like this happen again.

General Manager: Ms. Jones, I want you to know that this action may hinder your future advancement considerably. I have serious doubts concerning your value as an employee here.

Ms. Jones (who is quite surprised at the general manager's reaction) But, sir, I was following the democratic process. I thought you would want to know how your people felt.

General Manager: Ms. Jones, I have always let it be known that my door is open. My staff can discuss their problems with me at any time. However, this organization is not a democracy. I am ultimately responsible for decision making and I bear the consequences of my decisions.

Ms. Jones: It would be hard for 50 people to get in to see you so we felt the petition would be more effective. We never meant to challenge your authority.

General Manager: Nevertheless, it was a serious offense for you to organize my employees in defiance of my decision and to do it on company time, especially since you never came to talk to me first and you were already chosen as a hostess.

The conference continued, but the general manager remained outraged. He replaced Ms. Jones with another hostess and remained visibly cool to her in the weeks that followed. Shortly thereafter, when Ms. Jones' annual increase was due, it was not approved.

1. Was the manager within his rights to choose an outsider as hostess?
2. Can an organization be effectively run in the democratic manner?
3. What other ways could Ms. Jones have handled the situation if she wanted to protest?
4. What trends might effect future actions of the general manager?

appendixes

A. Break-even analysis

THE PURPOSE of this part of the appendix is to illustrate the methodology and application of break-even analysis. A break-even chart is a total revenue chart superimposed upon a total cost chart. Total costs are generally broken down into fixed costs and variable costs.

FIXED COSTS

As stated in Chapter 8, fixed costs are those that do not vary with output or sales in the short run. The rental costs associated with a warehouse that has been leased do not go down if the warehouse is only half occupied. Insurance costs on facilities do not normally vary according to the use of the facilities. Administrative salaries generally do not vary with the level of business activity.

In the long run, fixed costs may go up or down. For instance, the purchase of an additional warehouse or piece of capital equipment would cause fixed costs to go up. In the short run, fixed costs must be paid regardless of what is produced (or not produced).

VARIABLE COSTS

Variable costs are those costs that vary with the level of business activity as measured by sales or output. In a manufacturing situation, the cost of raw materials and direct labor costs depend on output. In the short run, total costs can be reduced only by reducing variable costs.

DETERMINATION OF THE BREAK-EVEN POINT

The break-even point (BEP) is defined as the level of output or sales at which profit is equal to zero. This is also the same point at which total revenue equals total cost.

APPLICATION OF BREAK-EVEN ANALYSIS

Although break-even analysis does not provide the manager with a total understanding of the cost and revenue components, it can assist him or her in making decisions. Break-even analysis can aid the manager in evaluating different strategies relating to level of output. Break-even analysis can also be used as a control device to signal when and how far costs are getting out of control or when and by how much revenues are lagging.

Most specific applications of break-even analysis are related to sales and distribution problems.

EXAMPLE OF BREAK-EVEN ANALYSIS

Suppose the following data have been estimated by the ABC Company for producing a proposed new product, the Blub.

Rent	$1,000 per month
Manager's salary	$1,100 per month
Price of blub	$1.50
Direct labor required	6 minutes per Blub
Wage rate	$2.00 per hour
Materials cost	$1.00 per Blub

Assume that the labor costs are variable and that no expenses, other than outlined above, exist. The marketing department of ABC has estimated that a minimum of 8,000 Blubs can be sold per month. Should ABC put the Blub into production?

$$\text{Profit} = \text{Total revenue } (TR) - \text{Total costs } (TC) \qquad (A-1)$$

Total revenue = (Price per blub) (Number of blubs sold)

$$TR = (\$1.50)(X) \qquad (A-2)$$

where X = number of blubs sold.

$$\text{Total cost} = \text{Variable cost} + \text{Fixed cost} \qquad (A-3)$$

Variable cost = Total materials cost + Total direct labor cost

$$\text{Variable cost} = \$1.00(X) + \left(\frac{6 \text{ min/blub}}{60 \text{ min/hr}}\right)(\$2/\text{hr})(X) \qquad (A-4)$$

where X = number of blubs sold.

$$\text{Fixed cost} = \text{Rent} + \text{Manager's salary}$$

$$\text{Fixed Cost} = \$1,000 + \$1,100 \tag{A-5}$$

Substituting Equations A-4 and A-5 into Equation A-3, yields

$$\text{Total cost} = \$1.00X + \left(\frac{6 \text{ min/blub}}{60 \text{ min/hr}}\right)(\$2/\text{hr})(X) + \$1,000 + \$1,100$$

$$= \$1.00X + \$0.20X + \$2,100 \tag{A-6}$$

Substituting Equations A-2 and A-6 into Equation A-1 and setting this equation equal to zero to find the break-even point, yields

$$\text{Profit} = \$1.50X - (\$1.00X + \$0.20X + \$2,100) = 0$$

$$X = 7,000 \text{ blubs per month (break-even point)}$$

Thus, ABC should put the blub into production since forecasted sales of the product are at least 8,000 per month.

BREAK-EVEN PROBLEMS

1. A small but growing company produced a product which sells for $4 per unit. The costs incurred by the company are as follows:

    Manager's salary......................... $1,000 per month
    Rent on building and equip.......... $1,400 per month
    Materials cost .... $2.60 per unit
    Salesman's commission.............. 10% of sales revenue
    Labor cost:

	Total Cost	Capacity
1 worker	$400 per month	1,500 units per month
2 workers	$800 per month	3,500 units per month

    Production workers are not sent home if they run out of work, and no overtime labor is used. Sketch a break-even chart for this firm and indicate the monthly production volume at which the firm will break even.

2. The Que Company prints personal checks and is located in New York. The company has two options for serving its Washington customers. These options are outlined below:

    Option 1. — Maintain a sales and customer service office in Washington. Under this arrangement a clerk in the Washington office would receive orders through the mail and telephone them to the

New York plant where the order would be produced and shipped directly to the customer. The following costs have been estimated for this arrangement.

Rent for office space .... $200 per month
Salary for office person .... $480 per month
Furniture and equipment (i.e., typewriter) rental .... $200 per month
Telephone expense (WATS line)............................. $200 per month
Production cost per order in New York plant.............. $1.50 per order
Capacity of this method.. 2,000 orders per month
Price per order.. $2.25 per order

Option 2.—Open a small plant in Washington. Under this arrangement the following costs have been estimated.

Rent on plant space................... $600 per month
Manager's salary....................... $800 per month
Materials cost............................ $0.40 per order
Depreciation on equipment......... $200 per month
Labor cost:

  1 office clerk........................... $400 per month
  1 typesetter/pressman .... $500 per month
  1 binding worker..................... $450 per month
Capacity of this method .... 3,000 orders per month
Price per order .... $2.25 per order

Using break-even analysis, determine what option Que should use throughout the growth of the Washington business and when to change from one method to the next.

B. Network analysis

INTRODUCTION

THIS PART of the appendix is designed to illustrate the basic methodology and computation used in identifying the critical path of a project. It contains some general definitions and guidelines relating to network analysis as well as a discussion of the Critical Path Method (CPM) and the Program Evaluation and Review Technique (PERT).

DEFINITIONS

The following basic definitions and symbols are commonly accepted and used in network analysis.

 Activity. – An activity is any portion of a project which consumes time and has an identifiable beginning and end. Activities are represented in a network by arrows.

 Event. – An event or node is a point in time corresponding to the start or completion of an activity. An event can be thought of as the instant in time when the last activity leading into that node is completed. Events are represented in networks by circles.

 Dummy. – A dummy activity consumes no time or resources and is used to represent activity dependencies that cannot easily be shown otherwise. Dummies are represented in a network by broken arrows.

501

Slack. — The amount of time by which the actual completion time of an activity can exceed its earliest possible completion time without causing the overall project to exceed its latest allowable completion time.

NETWORK RULES

An understanding of the following basic rules of network analysis is necessary.

1. Before an activity can begin, all activities or paths leading to the starting event of that activity must be completed.
2. Arrows imply logical sequencing only, and neither the length of the arrow or its "compass" direction have any meaning.
3. Most networks will have only one initial event and one terminal event.

TYPES OF ACTIVITY DEPENDENCIES

When sequencing events, several types of dependencies between and among the activities must be considered:

1. Natural Dependencies. These occur when one activity simply cannot take place until another is completed. For example, the roof cannot be put on a house until the frame has been erected.
2. Resource Dependencies. These occur when different activities require the use of the same resource and therefore cannot take place simultaneously. For example, if two activities require the use of the same machine, then they cannot take place simultaneously.
3. Policy Dependencies. These occur as the result of an organization policy. For example, it may be a construction company's policy not to begin building until all materials are on site.

ESTIMATING ACTIVITY TIMES

The following statements provide useful guidelines which should be followed when estimating activity times.

1. Estimate activity durations using working days not man-days.
2. Do not build in safety factors for major contingencies such as fires, floods, strikes, and so forth.
3. Assume normal levels of resources for each activity unless contradictory information exists.

4. Build in considerations for weather, machine down-time, and other common contingencies on an activity-by-activity basis, depending upon the nature of each activity.
5. Account for weekends and holidays in the case of unusual activities such as the drying of paint.

CRITICAL PATH METHOD (CPM)

As discussed in Chapter 8, CPM is best employed when the project activity durations are relatively well-defined.

Basic scheduling computations

The basic scheduling computations involve first a forward pass followed by a backward pass through the network. The forward pass computation yields the earliest possible finish time (EPF) for each activity as well as the earliest possible occurrence time (EP) for each event. The backward pass, which cannot be computed until the forward pass has been completed, gives the latest allowable start time (LAS) for each activity as well as the latest allowable occurrence time (LA) for each event.

After both the forward and backward pass have been completed, the slack can be computed for each activity. The critical path is then determined along the path or paths having the least amount of slack.

The following notation is suggested for use in performing network computations.

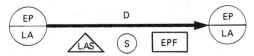

D = Estimated duration of activity.
S = Total slack of activity.
EP = Earliest possible event time.
LA = Latest allowable event time.
EPF = Earliest possible finish time for activity.
LAS = Latest allowable start time for activity.

Forward pass rules

The following statements outline the specific rules that are necessary for performing the forward pass computations.

1. The initial project event is assigned an earliest possible event time; usually this is zero.
2. All activities are assumed to begin as soon as all of their predecessor events are completed.

3. The earliest possible finish time (EPF) of an activity is merely the sum of the earliest possible event time (EP) for the event at the start of the activity (tail of the arrow) and the estimated activity duration.
4. The earliest possible event time (EP) is equal to the maximum earliest possible finish time (EPF) of all activities, including dummies, contributing to the respective event.

Example of forward pass

Figure B–2 shows the results of the forward pass computations based on the data and network provided in Figure B–1.

FIGURE B–1

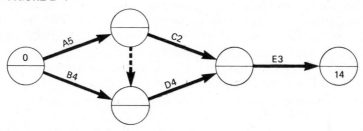

FIGURE B–2

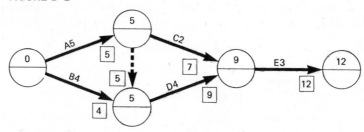

Backward pass rules

The following statements outline the specific rules that are necessary for performing the backward pass computations.

1. The latest allowable event time for the project terminal event is equal to its earliest possible event time (EP) as computed by the forward pass unless an arbitrary completion time has been stipulated by management.
2. The latest allowable start time (LAS) for a given activity is equal to the latest allowable event time (LA) for the event at the end of the activity (head of the arrow) minus the activity duration.

3. The latest allowable event time (LA) for a given event is equal to the minimum latest allowable start time (LAS) for all activities, including dummies, that immediately follow (lead from) the respective event.

Example of backward pass

Figure B–3 shows the results of the backward pass computations using the data and network provided in Figures B–1 and B–2. In this example management has stipulated that the project must be completed in 14 days.

FIGURE B–3

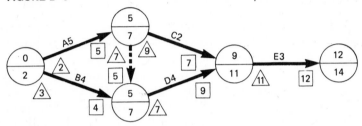

Slack computations

The total slack for a given activity is equal to the latest allowable event time (LA) for the event at the finish of the activity (head of the arrow) minus the earliest possible finish time (EPF) of the respective activity.

Determination of critical path

The critical path(s) falls along those activities (from the initial event of the project to the terminal event of the project) which have the smallest slack value. It should be noted that the slack will be the same for all activities on the critical path. This aspect of the total slack is somewhat misleading in that if one activity on the critical path is delayed then the slack time of all the following activities on that same path is reduced by the amount of the delay. Thus there is not as much slack as might first appear.

Example of determining slack and critical path

Figure B–4 presents the results of the slack computations based on the data and network given in Figure B–3. The heavy lines represent the critical path.

FIGURE B-4

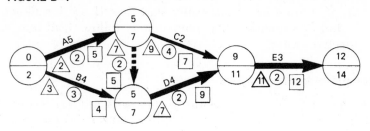

PROGRAM EVALUATION AND REVIEW TECHNIQUE (PERT)

PERT recognizes that the duration for most activities cannot be stated in advance with total certainty. The PERT procedure attempts to account for this limitation by allowing the networker to state an optimistic, a pessimistic, and a most likely duration for each activity. Using these time estimates, the expected time and the variance of each respective project activity can be calculated. After this analysis has been completed for each activity, an expected completion time and associated variance can be calculated for the entire project. With this information, it is possible to make statements concerning the probability of completing the project within a given amount of time.

PERT time estimates

The following statements define the time estimates used by PERT.

Optimistic time (a). The length of time required if exceptionally good luck is encountered during the performance of the activity. Normally the optimistic time is expected to be equaled or bettered only 5 out of every 100 times the activity takes place.

Pessimistic time (b). The length of time required if exceptionally bad luck is encountered during the performance of the activity. Normally the pessimistic time is expected to be equaled or bettered 95 out of every 100 times the activity takes place.

Most likely time (m). The time required for the activity if normal conditions are encountered. If the activity were repeated a large number of times, the most likely time would be the most frequently occurring time.

The expected time (t_e) for a given activity time is calculated using the following formula which is basically a weighted average of the three estimates:

$$t_e = \frac{a + 4m + b}{6} \tag{B-1}$$

The expected time is equivalent to that time estimate which has a 50–50 chance of being completed and is equal to the most likely time only if the optimistic (a) and pessimistic (b) times are equidistant from the most likely time (m). The activity variance (σ^2) is computed according to the following formula:

$$\sigma^2 = \left(\frac{b - a}{3.2}\right)^2 \tag{B-2}$$

By using the expected times (t_e) as the activity durations, the same computational procedures and rules used in CPM are used in PERT for performing the forward and backward passes and for determining the critical path.

Example PERT time calculations

Assume the following three time estimates have been obtained for a given activity:

Optimistic time (a)   = 5 weeks
Most likely time (m) = 7 weeks
Pessimistic time (b) = 10 weeks

Substituting into equations B–1 and B–2, we get

$$\text{Expected time } (t_e) = \frac{5 + 4(7) + 10}{6}$$

$$t_e = 7.17$$

$$\text{Variance } (\sigma^2) = \left(\frac{10 - 5}{3.2}\right)^2$$

$$= 2.44$$

Thus the expected time is slightly greater than the most likely time estimate. The variance is 2.44 weeks, which means that if the activity were repeated a large number of times, in 67 percent of the cases the activity should take between 5.61 and 8.73 weeks ($7.17 \pm$ one standard deviation or $7.17 \pm \sqrt{2.44}$).

The variance of the entire project can be calculated by summing the variances of each activity along the critical path. Probability statements can then be made concerning the entire project.

CPM/PERT PROBLEMS

1. Given the following information construct an appropriate network.

Activity	Immediate Prerequisite
A	—
B	—
C	A,F
D	B
E	C,D
F	—

2. Based upon the following narrative description of a project, draw a CPM logic network that accurately shows the natural dependencies among the activities involved.

   The Sheffield Manufacturing Company is considering the introduction of a new product. The first step in this project will be to design the new product. Once the product is designed, a prototype can be built and engineers can design the process by which the product will be produced on a continuous basis. When the prototype is completed, it will be tested. Upon completing the process design, an analysis will be made of the production cost per unit for the new product. When the prototype testing and the production cost analysis are both finished, the results will be submitted to an executive committee which will make the final go-ahead decision on the product introduction and establish the price to be charged. Assuming that the committee's decision is positive, several steps can be taken immediately. The marketing department will begin designing sales literature. The production department will obtain the equipment to be used in the manufacture of the new product, hire the additional personnel needed to man the process, and obtain an initial stock of raw materials. After sales literature has been designed, it will be printed. The new equipment obtained for the production process will have to be modified slightly. The production personnel will be trained as soon as the equipment modifications are complete, all necessary personnel have been hired, and the initial stock of materials has been obtained. When the printing of the sales literature is completed and the production personnel have been trained, the sales literature will be distributed to the salespersons and the product introduction will be considered complete.

3. Perform all forward, backward, and slack computations for the following network and indicate the location(s) of the critical path(s).

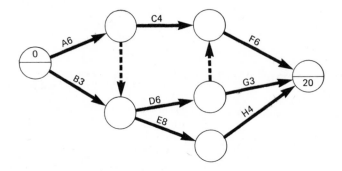

4. Using the network given in Problem 3 above, calculate the earliest expected completion time for the project based on the following PERT time estimates.

Activity	Optimistic (a)	Most Likely (m)	Pessimistic (b)
A	4	6	8
B	1	3	4
C	3	4	6
D	4	6	8
E	7	8	10
F	4	6	7
G	2	3	4
H	3	4	5

C. Economic order quantity (EOQ)

INTRODUCTION

THE PURPOSE of this part of the appendix is to discuss the methodology and computations used for determining the economic order quantity.

DETERMINING THE ECONOMIC ORDER QUANTITY (EOQ)

As discussed in Chapter 20, the optimum number of units to order (the economic order quantity or EOQ) is determined by two inversely related costs: (1) carrying costs and (2) ordering costs. The lower the number of orders processed the lower the ordering costs. However, fewer orders mean larger sizes for each order, which results in higher carrying costs. Figure 20–3 in the text graphically depicts the relationship between carrying costs and ordering costs.

The basic idea of the EOQ is to find the order size that minimizes total inventory costs incurred during the period. Total inventory costs associated with a given period are composed of the total carrying cost, total ordering cost, and the actual purchase cost of the inventory. Mathematically, total costs can be expressed as follows:

$$\text{Total costs} = \text{Total carrying cost} + \text{Total ordering cost} + \text{Actual purchase cost of the inventory} \qquad \text{(C–1)}$$

The total carrying cost is determined by multiplying the average inventory on hand during the period by the carrying cost per unit of inventory. Normally the average inventory on hand is approximated by dividing the order quantity (Q) by 2. This assumes a linear usage rate of the items in inventory.

510

$$\text{Total carrying cost} = \text{(Average inventory during} \qquad \text{(C–2)}$$
$$\text{period)(Carrying cost per item)}$$
$$= (Q/2)(C)$$

where

$$Q = \text{Order quantity}$$
$$C = \text{Carrying cost per unit}$$

The total ordering cost is equal to the number of orders placed during the period times the cost associated with placing each order. The number of orders placed is equal to the total demand for the period (D) divided by the order quantity.

$$\text{Total ordering cost} = \text{(Number of orders placed during the} \qquad \text{(C–3)}$$
$$\text{period)(Cost of placing an order)}$$

$$= \left(\frac{D}{Q}\right)(P)$$

where

$$D = \text{Period demand}$$
$$P = \text{Order cost per order.}$$

The actual purchase cost of the inventory (the total dollars invested in the inventory) is equal to the demand during the period multiplied by the unit cost.

$$\text{Actual purchase cost of inventory} = \text{(Demand during the} \qquad \text{(C–4)}$$
$$\text{period)(Unit cost)}$$
$$= (D)(U)$$

where

$$U = \text{Unit cost.}$$

Substituting Equations C–2, C–3, and C–4 into Equation C–1, we get

$$\text{Total costs} = \left(\frac{Q}{2}\right)(C) + \left(\frac{D}{Q}\right)(P) + (DU) \qquad \text{(C–5)}$$

The minimum total costs can then be found by taking the first derivative of Equation C–5 with respect to Q, setting the result equal to zero, and solving for Q.

$$\frac{d(\text{Total costs})}{dQ} = \frac{C}{2} - \frac{DP}{Q^2} + 0 = 0 \qquad \text{(C–6)}$$

$$Q = \sqrt{\frac{2DP}{C}} \qquad \text{(C–7)}$$

Thus the order quantity (Q) is equivalent to the economic order quantity (EOQ) and can readily be found using Equation C–7. Slight variations of Equation C–7 are available for accommodating special situations such as quantity discounts.

EXAMPLE EOQ PROBLEM

Suppose the following data have been collected by the AAA Company on a major inventory item:

Annual Demand: 5,000 units per year
Ordering Costs: $25 per order
Carrying Costs: $0.50 per unit per year

Determine the economic order cost.
Substituting in Equation C–7, we get

$$Q = \sqrt{\frac{(2)(5,000)(25)}{0.50}} \qquad \text{(C–8)}$$
$$Q = 707.11$$

Therefore, the AAA Company should order approximately 707 units at a time.

EOQ PROBLEMS

1. The following data have been collected for an item in inventory:

Annual sales: 10,000 units per year
Ordering costs: $32 per order
Item cost: $4 per unit
Inventory holding costs: $0.25 per unit per year

  a. Determine the economic order quantity.
  b. Determine the annual cost for holding and reordering inventory.
  c. If the ordering cost had been erroneously listed at $64 rather than $32, what would the resulting order quantity have been? How much would this increase the total annual inventory carrying and order costs?

2. The Beta Company purchases widgets from an external supplier. A total of 5,000 widgets are used each year by Beta. Beta figures that it costs $20 in fixed charges for sending purchase orders, receiving goods, and paying bills for each order. Through the years, Beta has found that the carrying costs for most inventory items

can be closely approximated by using a figure of five percent of the cost of the item. The basic cost to Beta of a widget is $2.

a. Determine the economic order quantity.
b. Suppose the fixed cost for sending purchase orders, receiving goods, and paying bills for each order had been erroneously calculated and was actually $40. What effect would this have on the economic order quantity?

indexes

Name index

517

Subject index

This book has been set in 10 point and 9 point Caledonia, leaded 2 points. Section numbers are set in 24 point Helvetica Bold; chapter numbers are set in 54 point Weiss Series II. Section titles and chapter titles are set in 20 point and 18 point Helvetica respectively. The size of the type page is 27 x 45$^1/_2$ picas.